CHAINS OF LOVE AND BEAUTY

Chains of Love and Beauty

THE DIARY OF MICHAEL FIELD

Carolyn Dever

PRINCETON UNIVERSITY PRESS
PRINCETON & OXFORD

Published by Princeton University Press
41 William Street, Princeton, New Jersey 08540
99 Banbury Road, Oxford OX2 6JX

press.princeton.edu

First paperback printing, 2025
Paper ISBN 9780691264776

The Library of Congress has cataloged the cloth edition as follows:
Names: Dever, Carolyn, author.
Title: Chains of love and beauty : the diary of Michael Field / Carolyn Dever, Princeton University Press.
Description: Princeton : Princeton University Press, [2022] | Includes bibliographical references and index.
Identifiers: LCCN 2021033791 (print) | LCCN 2021033792 (ebook) | ISBN 9780691203447 (hardback) | ISBN 9780691234977 (ebook)
Subjects: LCSH: Field, Michael—Criticism and interpretation. | Field, Michael. Works and days. | Bradley, Katharine Harris, 1846–1914. | Cooper, Edith Emma, 1862–1913.
Classification: LCC PR4699.F5 Z59 2022 (print) | LCC PR4699.F5 (ebook) | DDC 828/.809—dc23
LC record available at https://lccn.loc.gov/2021033791
LC ebook record available at https://lccn.loc.gov/2021033792

British Library Cataloging-in-Publication Data is available

Editorial: Anne Savarese and James Collier
Production Editorial: Ellen Foos
Jacket/Cover Design: Layla Mac Rory
Production: Erin Suydam
Publicity: Alyssa Sanford and Charlotte Coyne
Copyeditor: Cathryn Slovensky

This book has been composed in Miller

. . . The rest
Of our life must be a palimpsest—
The old writing written there the best.

In the parchment hoary
Lies a golden story,
As 'mid secret feather of a dove,
As 'mid moonbeams shifted through a cloud:

Let us write it over,
O my lover,
For the far Time to discover,
As 'mid secret feathers of a dove,
As 'mid moonbeams shifted through a cloud!

—MICHAEL FIELD, FROM *WILD HONEY FROM VARIOUS THYME* (1908)

CONTENTS

ILLUSTRATIONS

PREFACE AND ACKNOWLEDGMENTS

MICHAEL FIELD WROTE *Works and Days* over three decades and across two centuries, one volume at a time, typically beginning each volume in January and concluding it in December. Though it took me more than twenty years to write my book about their book, my own process was far more meandering than the cyclical discipline Katharine Bradley and Edith Cooper practiced year after year. Yet both endeavors were introspective, and also profoundly social, beginning with an important walk around the Nashville Parthenon with Yopie Prins, to whom I am forever grateful for sending me off to the British Library on the trail of *Works and Days*.

Other sodalities, too, supported this process, including child-care workers and administrative and finance staff members at Vanderbilt University and Dartmouth College, all of whom created the conditions for my research and writing. Like much of the Michael Field archive, *Works and Days* remains available largely in manuscript form. Archives like this one exist because of the dedicated stewardship of executors, conservationists, and special collections librarians. I have relied on the expertise of dozens of such librarians, including those at the British Library, the Weston Special Collections Library at the Bodleian Library at Oxford, Villa I Tatti, the Houghton Library at Harvard University, the Mark Samuels Lasner Collection at the University of Delaware, and the Rauner Special Collections Library at Dartmouth College. Marvin J. Taylor, director of the Fales Library and Special Collections at New York University, has taught me so much over the years about queer archives. Anne Savarese, James Collier, Ellen Foos, Cathryn Slovensky, Steven Moore, and their colleagues at Princeton University Press have been remarkable partners in bringing this book into being. Leonie Sturge-Moore shares the role of literary executor of the Michael Field estate with her sister, Charmian O'Neil. Ms. Sturge-Moore has been a valued source of encouragement, and I thank both executors, as well as the British Library and the Bodleian Library, for their permission to cite unpublished Michael Field manuscripts.

My colleagues at Vanderbilt University were instrumental in shaping this work; thanks especially to Diana Bellonby, Jay Clayton, Sarah Kersh, Janis May, Richard McCarty, Elizabeth Meadows, Rachel Teukolsky, and Melissa Wocher. At Dartmouth College, I thank Aden Evans, Alysia Garrison, Kate Gibbel, Bruch Lehmann, Andrew McCann, Peter Orner, Don

Pease, Jeff Sharlet, and especially Colleen Glenney Boggs and Christie Harner for their generous help and support. Within the world of Michael Field scholarship, my heartfelt thanks to Jill Ehnenn, Dustin Friedman, Catherine Maxwell, (eagle-eyed) Alex Murray, Sarah Parker, Fred Roden, Margaret Stetz, Marion Thain, Kate Thomas, Ana Parejo Vadillo, and Martha Vicinus. Thank you, Emma Donoghue, Elizabeth Freeman, Regenia Gagnier, Marjorie Garber, Amy Kahrmann Huseby, Diana Kardia, Ann Kraybill, Devoney Looser, Teresa Mangum, Sharon Marcus, Melanie Micir, Renata Kobetts Miller, Beth Phillips-Whitehair, Simon Reader, Catherine Robson, Talia Schaffer, Rebecca Walkowitz, Stephanie White, and Carolyn Williams for all your support, including the moral kind.

This work started in Nashville, Tennessee, and ended in Hanover, New Hampshire, but unfolded largely in the UK. At a very sensitive stage in this long journey, Charlotte Bacon coaxed a book from an amorphous mass of thoughts. She did so gently most of the time, and always kindly and with good humor. George Justice helped me to understand the connections between leadership and scholarship. Heather Freeman, Frances Pool-Crane, and Jessica Weil were splendid research assistants and true partners in the work. Marion Thain, Peter Logan, Hazel-Dawn Dumpert, and John Bell have been great stewards in moving the *Works and Days* digital archive to Dartmouth, and I am grateful for their collaboration. I would not have anticipated finishing a manuscript in a pandemic, but with extensive support from colleagues in the Dartmouth College Library, including Wendel Cox, Shawn Martin, Ken Peterson, Jay Satterfield, Dave Sturges, Morgan Swan, and especially Jon Whitney, we pulled it off. Finally, my heartfelt thanks to Mark Samuels Lasner and the special collections staff for their help sourcing images in the Mark Samuels Lasner Collection of Victorian art and literature at the University of Delaware.

To Charlotte Bacon, Kimberly Christopher, Mona Frederick, Colleen Glenney Boggs, Gregg Horowitz, Ellen Levy, Andrea Macdonald, and Susanne Mehrer: thank you, dearest friends. To my cousins Liz Bersell, Kathleen Braden, Katie Crawford, Julie Jorgensen, Stacey Rodenkirk Ryan, and Gail Ryan, my niece Amber Lewis, and my sister-in-law Valérie Kindt: I wrote this book for all of you to read. No pressure. But I really did.

And last, and most, and always, thank you to my guys, Paul Young, Noah Dever Young, and Carter. This is for you, with all my love.

EDITORIAL METHOD, KEY FIGURES, AND FAMILIAR NAMES

EDITORIAL METHOD INCLUDES the following practices:

- *Manuscript information.* The British Library Western Manuscripts collection holds "The 'Michael Field' Journals (1868–1914)," comprising twenty-nine volumes from 1868–1914, Add MS 46776–46804. These twenty-nine volumes are available in digital form at michaelfielddiary.dartmouth.edu; creation of that site has been led by Marion Thain in cooperation with a community of scholars, with the more recent support of faculty, students, and staff at Dartmouth College. The Bodleian Library at Oxford University holds Katharine Bradley's single-volume diary from 1867–68, MS. Eng. Misc. e. 336, as well as other personal and literary papers and letters from Michael Field.
- *Pagination.* After the first citations from *Works and Days* and Bradley's 1867–68 diary, I cite quotations parenthetically by volume year, page number indicating recto or verso, and author's initials.
- *Textual transcription*: Working from the manuscript of *Works and Days*, I transcribe quotations as closely as possible, including indicating strikeouts (~~strikeouts~~) on words the authors deleted, carets (^ ^) on words they inserted, and "[illeg.]" after words that I cannot decipher. Michael Field make frequent use of "+," which I silently change to "and." I note with brackets ellipses that I have added to quotations, and I let Michael Field's ellipses stand as written.
- *Naming and numbers.* In the discussion that follows, I refer to Katharine Bradley as "Bradley" and to Edith Cooper as "Cooper"; occasionally I use the familiar names Bradley and Cooper used for each other and for friends, as listed below. I refer to the corporate personality of Michael Field as "Michael Field." Where distinctions of speaker(s) or actor(s) are unclear to me, I make a judgment about usage in the context of the discussion. When referring to Michael Field, I make similar contextual judgments about plural and singular pronouns and possessives.

Key Figures

Katharine Harris Bradley (1846–1914)

> Michael Field

Edith Emma Cooper (1862–1913)

Amy Katharine Cooper Ryan (1863–1910): Younger sister of Edith Cooper, niece of Katharine Bradley; married James Ryan in 1899, converted to Catholicism, died in Dublin.

James Robert Cooper (1818–97): Father of Edith Cooper, brother-in-law of Katharine Bradley.

Emma Harris Bradley Cooper (1818–89): Mother of Edith Cooper, older sister of Katharine Bradley.

Bernhard Berenson (1865–1959): Lithuanian American art historian and art dealer.

Mary Costelloe Berenson (1864–1945): American Quaker, art historian, and dealer in art and antiquities.

Havelock Ellis (1859–1939): Physician, reformer in the science of human sexuality, author of the first medical textbook about homosexuality.

Louie Ellis (n.d.): Close friend to Michael Field and collaborator in the creation of their dresses; sister to Havelock Ellis.

Charles de Sousy Ricketts (1866–1931): British artist, illustrator, book designer, publisher; partner of Charles Shannon.

Charles Haslewood Shannon (1863–1937): British portraitist; partner of Charles Ricketts.

Thomas Sturge Moore (1870–1944): Poet and woodcutter; literary executor for Michael Field.

John Gray (1866–1934): Poet; Dominican priest; partner of Marc-André Raffalovich.

Familiar Names

For Katharine Bradley: Michael, Sim; together with Edith Cooper, Michael Field; together with Edith Cooper, the Poets (to Ricketts and Shannon).

For Edith Cooper: Field; Henry, Hennie, Heinrich; Pussie, P; together with Katharine Bradley, Michael Field; together with Katharine Bradley, the Poets (to Ricketts and Shannon).

For Amy Cooper Ryan: Little Pickie, Little One.
For Emma Cooper: Sissie, the Mother, the Beloved Mother-One.
For James Cooper: The Father.
For Robert Browning: The Old Gentleman, the Old.
For Bernhard Berenson: The Doctrine, the Fawn.
For Charles Ricketts and Charles Shannon: The Artists.
For Thomas Sturge Moore: Tommy.

CHAINS OF LOVE AND BEAUTY

INTRODUCTION

"Axial in the Spin of Life"

"Axial."

THIS IS A story about two women who had a great deal to say, in a world that was not yet ready to hear them. It is a story about two women who were in love with an idea about life lived so artfully that it became an act of artistry itself, and who worked to translate that vision into something bold and lasting for the world. Yet it is also a story about entangled family ties, ones the two women cherished deeply but that threatened to smother their artistic vision and their most intimate selves.

So, they fought. Their pen was their sword: together, the two women published eight volumes of poetry and twenty-seven plays. Together, for nearly three decades, they kept a diary, where, across twenty-nine volumes and 9,500 handwritten pages, they wove entangled narratives of desire, art, sex, and death; of loves requited and unrequited, of loneliness and joy; of family, celebrities, and deities; of books and bills, carpets, dresses and hats, rings, forks, sugar tongs, plates, trains, wallpapers, mirrors, bookcases and caskets, soup, eggs, and tobacco; of poetry and more poetry, and paintings, and beautiful flowers; and, of course, always, dogs.

One diary, two women. Day by day, year by year, between 1888 and 1914, Katharine Bradley and Edith Cooper spun a narrative of events great and small, public and private, aimed at once outward and inward. Bradley and Cooper called the diary *Works and Days*, and they referred to it within the narrative itself as the "White Book," reflecting the tall, cream-colored foolscap notebooks they used to write most of this book (fig. 1). Bradley and Cooper intended the text for posthumous publication and secured arrangements for conveying its manuscript to executors and archives, and thus to readers in a future they would never know. What did they imagine those future readers would make of their narrative? What did they hope to convey to us about the two complex voices they figured? *Works and Days* is a diary that breaks almost every formal convention known to diaries, including presumptions of privacy and singularity in the writing process: that is, the convention of a diary as the vehicle for one person alone to record events and reflections about everyday life. Framed instead by two voices, *Works and Days* stages an extended dialogue internal to a pair of writers and lovers engaging sensitive questions of beauty, desire, and fame. While the diary is certainly full of the stuff of everyday life, it is equally introspective, delving deep into the private thoughts and conflicts of each of the two narrators. For that matter, it is intraspective as well, focused on what happens between the text's two voices when they find each other on the page. The two narrative voices fragment across time, uncannily sensitive to the historical past, intensely anxious about what the future will bring and where they might stand within it. Strung tight between yesterday and tomorrow, Bradley and Cooper write a present pregnant with urgency, from which they feel displaced, unseen, and often out of step. "So every hour is under ideal claim," wrote Cooper in 1907. "[W]hat is simple, what is axial in the spin of life I am training to set my hours to."[1]

How, Cooper wonders, might she put each hour to use on behalf of life's axial principles? As an accounting of works and of days, *Works and Days* presents a reckoning of the two, inviting its readers to contemplate the role of time in doing; in the case of Cooper, doing the work of poetry. The question of time is not incidental to Bradley and Cooper as writers of the English fin de siècle as the nineteenth century, and with it the big themes of change and progress that conceptualize the "Victorian," careened toward the twentieth century and the mystery and promise of modernity. Bradley and Cooper lived and died and wrote their way across the line that linked the nineteenth century and the twentieth, that divided Victorian literature from modernism. Central to my work here is the claim that the massive, multiplot narrative of *Works and Days* negotiates forms of transit between centuries: the channel from past to future routed through a present that seems to the writers as strange as the writers themselves seem to the people around them, relative to the forms and conventions that shape women's identities, sexualities, voices, and stories in the fin de siècle.[2]

Works and Days is the subject of this book, and its formal experiments in presenting the lives of its central subjects the focus. I track the narrative Bradley and Cooper built to carry all their stuff and ideas along as they traveled from the familiar Victorian world toward an unknowable

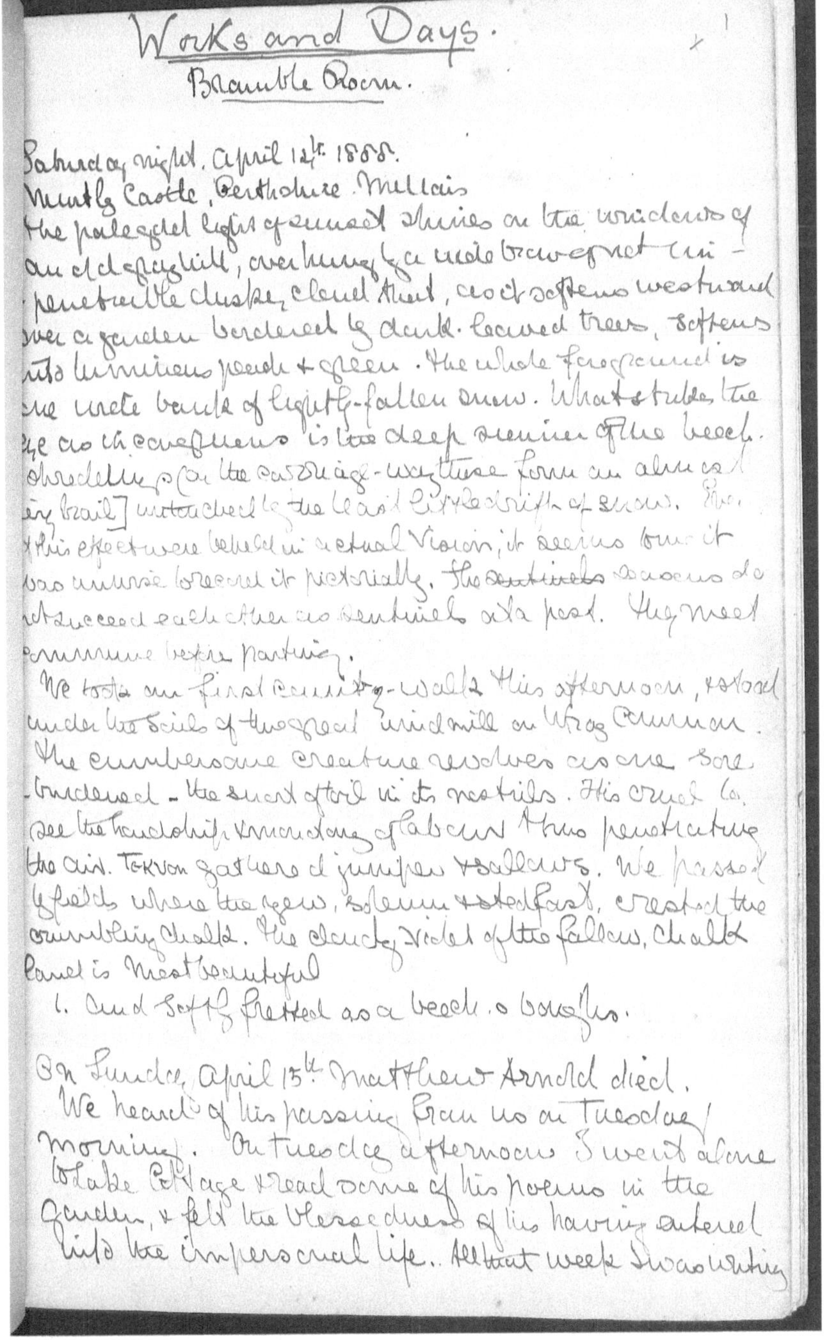

Works and Days. 1

Bramble Room.

Saturday night. April 14th 1888.
Huntly Castle, Perthshire. Millais
The pale gold light of sunset shines on the windows of an old grey hill, overhung by a wide brow of yet un-penetrable dusky cloud that, as it softens westward over a garden bordered by dark-leaved trees, softens into luminous peach & green. The whole foreground is one white bank of lightly-fallen snow. What strikes the eye as incongruous is the deep crimson of the beech shrubberies (on the east side - why these form an almost [illegible]] untouched by the least little drift of snow. [illegible] this effect were beheld in actual vision; it seems to me it was unwise to record it pictorially. The seasons do not succeed each other as sentinels at a post. They meet & commune before parting.
We took our first country-walk this afternoon, & stood under the sails of the great windmill on Wrag Common. The cumbersome creature revolves as one sore-burdened - the snort of toil in its nostrils. It is cruel to see the hardship & murdering of labour thus penetrating the air. To Kron gathered juniper & sallows. We passed by fields where the yews, solemn & steadfast, crested the crumbling chalk. The cloudy violet of the fallow, chalk land is most beautiful
1. And softly fretted as a beech's boughs.

On Sunday, April 15th Matthew Arnold died.
We heard of his passing from us on Tuesday morning. On Tuesday afternoon I went alone to Lake Cottage & read some of his poems in the garden, & felt the blessedness of his having entered into the impersonal life.. All that week I was writing

FIGURE 1. Katharine Bradley titles the *Works and Days* project in red ink on the first page of the first volume she kept with Edith Cooper (1888, 1r, KB). © The British Library Board, ADD MS 46777: Vol. 2 (Apr. 1888–Dec. 1889), 1r.

future, from the past that they cherished into a new century that left them by turns apprehensive and ambitious. In the chapters that follow, I link *Works and Days* to another unwieldy, prosy Victorian literary form: the novel. Of the many ways to approach a text such as *Works and Days*, I have chosen to dive deep into six of its volumes—1888, 1892, 1897, 1899, and 1906–7—in order to show Bradley and Cooper at work, shaping the narrative through distinctively novelistic strategies. I have asked *Works and Days* questions, and sought its answers, through methods more typically addressed to Victorian novels, and particularly those written by women such as Bradley and Cooper, who wonder about the standing of ordinary female lives measured against the sweep of history. In the conclusion to *Middlemarch* (1871–72), George Eliot's narrator has the last word about the novel's protagonist, Dorothea: "[T]he effect of her being on those around her was incalculably diffusive: for the growing good of the world is partly dependent on unhistoric acts; and that things are not so ill with you and me as they might have been, is half owing to the number who lived faithfully a hidden life, and rest in unvisited tombs."[3] In *Works and Days*, Bradley and Cooper signal their dissatisfaction with the "hidden life" and "unhistorical acts" to which intelligent women such as Dorothea are consigned. They issue an invitation to us on behalf of a more audacious story: they aspire to heroism, to romance, and, not least, to historical significance.

More than a century after their deaths, Bradley and Cooper have entered the literary canon, but not yet for the magnificent literary achievement *Works and Days* represents, nor for the vivid stories we find on its pages. Bradley and Cooper made their mark in the 1890s as a distinguished poet called Michael Field, author of those published volumes of poetry and verse drama. That "Michael Field" was the pseudonym of two women writers was an open secret after the early, heady days of his career, thanks to an indiscretion on the part of Robert Browning (fig. 2).[4] Yet to this day, Michael Field's remarkable diary remains largely unpublished. It is widely acknowledged to represent an original literary achievement in its own right, but the diary is still primarily known to the community of scholars who have made their way to the Manuscripts Reading Room of the British Library following a new surge of interest in Michael Field that bracketed the centenary of his deaths in 1913 and 1914, respectively.

Two women writers, twenty-nine volumes, a single narrative. Considered as a landmark literary work, *Works and Days* reads like the great unknown novel of the nineteenth century—or better, the living record of the transition from a Victorian worldview to a modernist one, from

FIGURE 2. A photographic portrait of Michael Field, likely taken in Birmingham in the early 1890s. Mark Samuels Lasner Collection, University of Delaware Library, Museums, and Press.

George Eliot to Virginia Woolf.[5] Viewed as a coherent narrative, *Works and Days* challenges our understanding of women's voices, their passions and their worldly ambitions, and the formidable challenges they navigate as they engage with a rapidly changing world. Behind the curtain that the literary character "Michael Field" provided them, Bradley and Cooper were aunt and niece. They were also an intimate couple through the 1880s and beyond, until Cooper's death in 1913 and Bradley's a few months later in 1914, both from cancer. "Katharine became to Edith everything one woman can be to another: mother, aunt, sister, friend and, eventually, lover," writes Marion Thain in the first full-length study of Michael Field.[6]

In *Works and Days*, Bradley and Cooper write a narrative for Michael Field across several decades of desire matched with frustration. Keen appreciation for their poetry yields to negative literary reviews, and ultimately to public indifference to their published work. Cooper's passion for her own personal Rochester, the art critic Bernhard Berenson,[7] gives way to humiliation in the wake of his cruelty, and ultimately to his attentions elsewhere. Beloved parents and pets die. Friends drift away. Michael Field become increasingly idiosyncratic and increasingly isolated.

Versions of these and many more expansive narratives find life in *Works and Days*.[8] Exposing the pretense that a diary is a private domestic document, Bradley and Cooper left posthumous instructions to Thomas Sturge Moore, executor of their estate, to deposit the diary—which they describe as an "unpublished manuscript"—in the British Museum.[9] Following the instructions in Bradley's will, Sturge Moore published a volume of excerpts from *Works and Days* in 1933, a book that shaped perceptions of Michael Field as onlookers rather than contributors to late-Victorian literary culture. "With all their conventionality," Sturge Moore writes in the editor's preface, Michael Field "are simplicity itself, as open as children."[10]

I disagree. Read on its own merits, *Works and Days* emerges not as the wistful tale of sidelined femininity found in Sturge Moore's framing but as a strong, purposeful intervention into the art world Bradley and Cooper observed so perceptively. Michael Field knew what they were doing when they wrote this book; indeed, they frequently drafted their diary entries elsewhere before writing fair copies in the notebooks themselves. The "craftedness" of the text shows even in its orderly physical appearance.

Angela Leighton characterizes *Works and Days* as full of "gossipy energy and wit." Thain describes the text as a "well-written and carefully-crafted literary work."[11] Following their cue, I present *Works and Days* here as a monumental experimental work of late-Victorian and early-modernist British writing: in both formal and thematic terms, *Works and Days* is strong, complex, and literary. Far from the unassuming diary of two spinster "wannabe" poets trapped on the edge of the literary mainstream, Michael Field's massive prose narrative is a time machine engineered to challenge our ideas about women and voice, about family, love, sex, and art in the Victorian fin de siècle. I do believe that Sturge Moore was right to note the writers' "conventionality." Unlike Sturge Moore, however, I believe that Bradley and Cooper used conventions—social and literary, spatial and temporal—as forms that gave them cover to explore topics and modes of expression that were exceptionally difficult, especially for literary women.[12]

"Enwombs."

> *My gift from Michael is* Placidia*—the satinwood chest that enwombs* Works and Days.[13]
>
> —EDITH COOPER, *WORKS AND DAYS*, 1904

Well known now as a poet and a verse dramatist, Michael Field are not writers often associated with prose. Yet, "The simple answer to the question 'What did Michael Field write?' is—everything," write Thain and Vadillo.[14] As gifted, energetic Victorian women who had access to education and to an income sufficient to secure them time and private space, Michael Field produced an enormous amount of writing of all sorts. They were doubtless proudest of their published poetry, whether lyric or dramatic. As close and thoughtful followers of the aesthetic movement, for Michael Field poetry was the highest of the literary arts; they quite deliberately styled their shared identity with the signature "poet." The association with aestheticism provided Bradley and Cooper resources for formal experimentation; as Talia Schaffer has argued, aestheticism offered women writers empowering tools: "[I]ts elaborate language allowed them to write the pretty visual descriptions that critics liked, yet it was also avant-garde enough to permit a new range of daring topics. Aestheticism let women articulate their complex feelings about women's changing roles, and thus it tended to attract precisely those writers whose gender ideas were in flux."[15] Michael Field understood formal and linguistic experimentation as one way of achieving such a combination of literary appeal and innovation, of putting new forms (and old language) to work refashioning familiar stories. In an 1892 letter, Bernhard Berenson wrote to Michael Field: "The reasons for not writing Elizabethan verse nowadays are manifold. To begin with, Christ who had a fine palate in wine tells us not to put new wine into old bottles. I need scarcely tell you, that you directly were foreseen in that command, the new wine being the new spirit, and the old bottles being the Elizabethan rhymes, vocabulary and turns of phrase." Alex Murray and Sarah Parker argue convincingly that Michael Field acted in strong response to Berenson's judgment, shifting the purpose and intention of their formal experiments: Michael Field deliberately pour their "archaic" language into bottles shaped for—and by—the contemporaneous moment. Michael Field wrote a prose play in 1892, unfortunately lost to us now, titled *Old Wine in New Bottles* (1892, 135r, KB; emphasis in original; see fig. 6).[16] From here forward, form's the thing for Michael Field, their vehicle to link the past and the present to the future.

Michael Field's legacy of "new bottles" is vast. Within Michael Field's prose archive alone, *Works and Days* itself dominates if we measure by mass alone. Beyond the scope of the diary, thousands of Michael Field's letters—some fraction of what they produced in life—remain on deposit at the Bodleian Library, the British Library, Villa I Tatti, the Houghton Library, the University of Delaware, and elsewhere.[17] In about 1882, Cooper rewrote the conclusion to Hawthorne's *House of the Seven Gables*.[18] A number of Michael Field's short stories survive, cataloged as undated manuscripts among their "miscellaneous papers" in the Bodleian. Bradley and Cooper grouped two batches of those stories formally as collections.[19] As all of this suggests, Michael Field are prolific writers of narrative prose, as well as important and increasingly canonized poets.

Edith Cooper (1862–1913) was born and raised in a household that included her mother's sister, her aunt, Katharine Bradley (1846–1914). The fifteen-year age difference between niece and aunt belied the intense closeness that developed between the girl and the woman as Cooper entered her adolescence.[20] By the time Cooper was in her twenties, the women had invested their primary affective devotion in each other: they were committed within an intense emotional and physical dyad that they described explicitly as a marriage. Indeed, Michael Field were even "closer married" than their fellow poets, Robert and Elizabeth Barrett Browning, by their own reckoning: "those two poets, man and wife, wrote alone; each wrote, but did not bless or quicken one another at their work; we are closer married."[21] Theirs was no ordinary marriage but a partnership that "quickened" with the figure of Michael Field.

> *And then we buy flowers—and the man looks as if he were entertaining angels that would stay or at least return—four bunches of fresias, four of anemones, and a love-knot of Neapolitan violets—We have to* ~~return~~ *^travel^ part of the way home third-class—and ^to^ know the separate existence of each penny in our purses.*
>
> —EDITH COOPER, *WORKS AND DAYS*, 1899

The name "Michael Field" serves as a new bottle for several serious complexities of gender and voice. Take, for example, a male nom de plume that seems more challenging somehow than those of the Georges, Sand and Eliot, and other transgendering women writers of the time. Michael Field's pen name introduces the familiar gendered pronoun challenge: he or she? But "Michael Field" also goes the transauthorial tradition one better, introducing what Holly Laird calls new "pronomial problems" of singular and plural: Is Michael Field a he? A they? Two shes? Which is less odious, a singular proper name and plural verbs and pronouns: Michael Field are women writers? Or the plural "Michael Fields" with matching collars and cuffs: the Michael Fields write Sapphic poetry?[22] To approach "Michael Field" as one's critical subject is to grapple with his/her/their foundational unspeakability, the essential (and I do mean essential) challenge Michael Field pose to language and meaning. Should Michael Field's reader take the straight and narrow approach of making an inherently imperfect choice and sticking to it? Or capitulate, as I have, to the more playful practice of mixing Michael Field's pronouns and numbers as the moment seems to warrant?[23]

More serious still than pronomial trickery is the devilish ideological trap Bradley and Cooper set for feminist thinkers a century hence. When we default to "he," are we participating in the erasure of talented women writers? If we consider Field not as male but as a proxy for two women's voices, are we erasing those women's strategic appropriation of male social authority in poetry and beyond? To talk about "Michael Field" at all is to find oneself mired in imperfect, offsetting choices about language and gender, with the recognition that linguistic imprecision—and the brutal ineffability of gender itself—is the point. Even in name only, Michael Field were writers in a fruitfully adverse relationship with the very medium of their artistic practice. Michael Field were also writers who fielded constant criticism that their language did not sound right; that it was archaic or Elizabethan or somehow ill fit to the moment. "You have a tendency to use 'art' words, or shall we say 'slow' words, when the quick common words would be better, more nimble and more intense."[24] This uneasiness—relative to language, relative to conventions literary and social, relative to gendered authorship—is central to the most challenging aspects of Michael Field's work, and to the great artistic experiment they left to us in *Works and Days*.[25]

The diary takes up the complexity of voice differently than literary texts published by Bradley and Cooper as Michael Field. Throughout *Works and Days*, Michael Field looms large. He is everywhere, a figure of and for professional authorship. He is also a token of mutual affection between Bradley, who boasted "Michael" among her many nicknames, and Cooper, often known as "Field," among her many nicknames.[26] As a signifier of the women's union, the equation Michael + Field equals the coverture of their "closer married" voice, their married name, with a typical Michael Field twist; as Laird writes, "The pseudonym of Michael Field clearly enabled them to play a game with sexual as well as literary and gender identities. Like Eve's fig leaf, it became a sign that pointed to even as it concealed their transgressions." Virginia Blain describes the Michael

Field signature as a "security screen," protecting private dynamics and contestations behind it. For Ruth Vanita, "The male pseudonym was . . . not just a ruse to forestall male [critical] bias. It was also . . . part of the erotic charge between the two women. They continued to write under this name long after their identity was well-known and used it in private interaction too."[27]

In contrast to the public and published figure of Michael Field, poet, however, the voices—plural—of Bradley and Cooper are entirely distinct from one another in *Works and Days*.[28] As long as we read *Works and Days* from or in reference to its manuscript, Michael Fields' very different handwriting makes it entirely clear which of the narrators is "speaking" at any given moment. In their published work, their authorial voices stand as one, and male. In *Works and Days*, they are emphatically two: two voices and two bodies, figured in and by two hands. They are two writers sharing notebooks (and a bed, a life, etc.), rather than one male author standing in for two women writers, that is, two female poets writing about aesthetic subjectivity in a male voice.[29] Two very different people, not one, encountering each other as much in tension as in unity. If the published work of Michael Field is where the poets experiment with the marriage of voices, *Works and Days* instead displays their differences and invites a distinctive approach to understanding the incorporation of those differences under the figure of Michael Field. Blain states the case directly: "They lived together, worked together, wrote together, holidayed together, slept together, were converted together, and almost died together, in what seems a perfect orgy of togetherness; yet they were never simply one person. In fact, they were two quite different people, with quite different poetic talents and impulses."[30]

And then there is the question of sexuality. As a mostly committed, emotionally codependent, usually bed-sharing couple, Michael Field has long been claimed by feminist, lesbian, and queer critics eager to trace the epistemologies of same-sex desire that survived closets and other masquerades. Bradley and Cooper absolutely belong in this rich, important line of critical inquiry; indeed, Laird takes this suggestion further, writing: "Field in fact anticipates the feminist, historicizing scholar, the scholar who seeks representation of women and gender in the fracturing mirror of past texts in order to put the fragments together in her own documents."[31]

Less often pondered, however, is the incestuous nature of Michael Field's lesbian coupledom: two women, aunt and niece; in Thain's formulation, all that two women can be to each other.[32] This is as important as, if not more important than, Michael Field's same-sex marriage to the challenges they faced socially and psychologically, and to the challenges they present as powerful writers. My point has nothing to do with moral judgment about an erotic arrangement. It has to do, rather, with the structural enclosure of both Bradley and Cooper in an endogamous or centripetal marriage plot, depending on whether we borrow a metaphor from anthropology or physics.[33] This is a marriage plot that stays in the domestic sphere of girlhood, and that does not, that will not, that cannot betray a girlhood family by choosing something or someone else. It is orbital to the family of origin, and it is the source of ambivalence—rich passion and poetic inspiration crossed with frustration—expressed by Michael and especially by Field in *Works and Days*: "I am reading Gustave Flaubert's *Correspondance* [*sic*]. He is so like me, he excites by similarity—as two flints make a spark. He gives a sense of space to imagination—language takes deep breaths of air" (1893, EC). "Sameness" was the axle of devotion for Michael Field, almost to the very end. It provides a vocabulary for the narrative of Michael and Field: as women, as lovers, as members of the same family, as one author. Sameness is also the frame that Cooper uses to test the world for affective alternatives. When she falls deeply in love with Bernhard Berenson, for example, Cooper consistently cites Berenson's familiarity—indeed, the twinship of his soul and hers—to define the exceptionalism of her unrequited love. In 1895, she writes, "A kind of recognition of the dearness of identity—that is such a terrible power of attraction in Bernhard" (1895, 54v, EC). In 1901, "the most wonderful day in my life. That exclamation from him and me of *the same, the same*" (1901, 89r, EC; emphasis in original).[34]

Arguing that post-Victorian readers understand endogamous or incestuous plots differently than Victorians did, Mary Jean Corbett makes a case for the importance of "historiciz[ing] and re-theoriz[ing] the intersecting elements of the family-sex-marriage triad, making space within it for alternatives to the dominant story of the exogamous heterosexual plot, the triumph of companionate marriage, and the installation of the nuclear family as a hegemonic institution."[35] *Works and Days* benefits from Corbett's historical project. For in the narrative of Michael and Field, the poets put into play a series of very different affective allegiances that create a marriage plot that both cites and departs from the conventions of the form. For example, as it is expressed in literary conventions of heterosexual marriage, Victorian womanhood is founded on a form of disloyalty, which Ruth Perry describes as the "reassign[ment] of family loyalty from . . . consanguineal kin to a new conjugal family."[36] Michael Field, in contrast, stand firm in his/her/their loyalty to the nuclear family, however ambivalent. In 1901 on Midsummer's Day, as she reflects on the anniversary of her father's death four years earlier, Cooper strikes the analogy of her own father and Oedipus:

> [Michael] has read to me the call of Aedipus at Colonnus—how he heard the Zeus of the Shades and spoke to his heavily-tasked children ~~that~~ ^the^ most magnificent ~~word~~ ^justification^ an old man cd have spoken—that one little word, *Love—his Love*—attoned for all they had had to bear in tending him. What sureness in the quality of what he gave—he, white-headed and pleasurable no more. *We have experienced ~~that~~ ^such^ love; its loss has cast us afar from the race of men, for none ~~they~~* ^of them^ *could ~~never~~ ever have that kind of love in their hearts or in their eyes for us, while we live.* (1901, 79v, EC; emphasis mine)

Cooper has experienced the love of her father as second to none: it can be matched by no other love a mortal might offer. The place of love in her life, as in her narrative arc, is thus retrospective, focused on the family of origin; it cannot be prospective. There is no possibility of a new or different or future love for her, for Michael Field.

That Michael Field understand exogamous marriage as a betrayal of existing bonds emerges explicitly when their friend (and later literary executor) Thomas Sturge Moore shares news he believes will "horrify" Michael Field: that he is engaged to marry his cousin, Marie Appia. Cooper writes: "It is a shock . . . and for Ricketts! It breaks up the little celebate [*sic*] company—we lose a friend for no man who is married can be a friend; the old wine is not for new bottles" (1903, 91v, EC). Clearly the "little celebate company" led by Ricketts has provided a stand-in for another (ostensibly, but not actually) celibate company, the nuclear family, equally betrayed by Tommy's infidelity in the name of heterosexual marriage. Reaching for their familiar aphorism of wine and bottles, Michael Field refuse—for now—flexibility in response to Tommy's betrayal of his queer family of origin.

Michael Field are not ignorant about the implications of their choice: they have opted out of exogamous social and erotic circulation. By opting out, they have foregone a set of transactional conventions available to Victorian women by means of that circulation.[37] Though Bradley and Cooper have made a bonded commitment to each other, that bond remains within the family of origin rather than breaking through its walls to form a new, separate family. In *Works and Days*, Michael Field write about the feedback loop of the family of origin, of a story that begins and ends with that first loyalty, instead of marking its progress through departure. The sustenance of erotic coupledom within that first family is at the heart of Michael Field's conception of poetic and artistic achievement. But it is also at the heart of what they experience as a deeply gendered sense of stasis and frustration.

> *Yesterday I was holding the ^whole^ Times in front of the fire in Michael's bedroom: there was a bright stab at it inside, and the whole mass was flame between my hands. The moment was perilous [. . .] With shovel and tongs and most deliberate movements at last I got the flashing heap on the top of the fire and breathed ^again.^ I even trembled for half an hour after. How near one is to death among common movement. Time, there is no need we should recognize this, Death should be out of sight behind a blood-red curtain, that life may dance and be healthy: but only a gray veil is between us and we always see the menace that should be thickly hidden—therefore we halt or falter ^trip^ in our steps measure and are languid.*
>
> —EDITH COOPER, *WORKS AND DAYS*, 1899

Works and Days is a handwritten text featuring not one but two versions of Victorian women's handwriting. The feeling of immanent connection to Bradley and Cooper is inescapable when holding each notebook, reading casual notes and drafts of poems, coming across saved flowers, clippings, postcards, or photos, and reading thousands of entries in the two women's scratchy hands.[38] A contemporary reader cannot help but notice that Cooper and Bradley were not only the authors of this text, but also, given that each presumably read everything the other wrote, they were the text's first reader(s) as well. Here we see Bradley and Cooper navigating the dynamic of two-in-one, or one-in-two, in yet another way. Conventionally, a diary entry might be presumed private to its author. Is the text of *Works and Days* best read as a private dialogue between Michael and Field, between Bradley and Cooper? But—what about me? How do I fit in here? Am I, as the reader of *Works and Days*, an intruder, an interloper? A transgressor into the spaces and pages of the most intimate of relationships? Or a participant in the dialogue, in this marriage of two minds and hands?

A visit to Germany in 1891 shifted Cooper's perspective on the erotic possibilities of triangulation. Michael Field undertook their European adventure as preparation for their book *Sight and Song*, the volume that attempts to realize in poetry "what the lines and colours of certain chosen pictures sing in themselves"; Bernhard Berenson directed these early efforts in connoisseurship.[39] While Michael Field were in Dresden, Cooper became terribly ill with scarlet fever. She was hospitalized and, while separated from Bradley, received care from "Schwester," or "Sister," a nurse who developed a passionate attachment to Cooper. In a signal of the discombobulation between Michael Field, Cooper later transcribed in the notebook Bradley's contemporaneous impressions: Bradley looks on as "Sister kisses [Cooper] with a kiss that plunged down among the wraps" (1891, 105v, EC). And again, Cooper records Bradley's impression: "Pussie wakes from its 'lye' and rings for Schwester, who comes straight to grasp and kiss. She is like one who has been in a desert, who finds an oasis and simply throws himself down and drinks. The wrinkles of the worn peasant flesh ~~were~~ ^are^ felt by P against her cheek—the kisses are almost too rapid to have an aim; her eyes, over-ful of love, ~~could not~~ ^cannot^ bear to meet [~~illeg.~~] her beloved's—she buries her sight in deep anguish against P's face" (1891, 108r, EC).

Note that Cooper has intervened in the diary entry above: as she does frequently throughout this period, she takes a pencil to the page and changes past-tense verbs to present. Here again the diary itself mediates between Michael and Field; on this occasion, Cooper's editorial intervention enhances the felt immediacy of the episode. When Cooper speaks for herself of her own experience, she describes what she calls Schwester's "assault" in rather remote, abstracted terms:

> While my Love is, by chance, *fort*, sister assaults me with a gt. love in bed—kissing me on the lips and breast, gathering my limbs in her arms as if veritably I were a child under its Nurse's or Mother's handling. She would embrace "die ganze Edith." In this love there is the fearful passion of mere severance—and the still more fearful passion of unsatisfied senses in a strong nature. Last of all she lay looking into my eyes—"die hello Augen"—as if to learn how long they could be true. (1891, 113v, EC; emphasis in original)[40]

Speaking in her own voice as she speaks in Bradley's, Cooper seamlessly translates Schwester's assault further into the idiom of family: from sister to mother to passionate lover reflects a flexibility familiar within the Bradley-Cooper household.

In the real time of her hospitalization, Cooper was delirious, yet nonetheless narrated her remarkable fever dreams in the pages of the notebook after the fact. And where was Bradley in all of this? Sidelined, to be sure. Frustrated. And yes, jealous to be banished to the remote end of the hypotenuse, the away side of the *fort-da* game. Cooper reports, parenthetically interrupting her transcription of Bradley's perspective: "(My love was a little jealous, standing tearful that Nurse should have forestalled her on my lips. . . . but I know whose kisses were vernal—not received for what had been, but for what would be. Still the motherliness in the wonderful passion of Nurse's gave me delight)" (1891, 105v, EC). The Dresden episode awakened in Cooper a new sense of her autonomous power to command and repel motherly/sisterly passion. With this awakening came a new dynamic in the relationship of Michael and Field: while Bradley oriented herself toward Cooper, Cooper oriented herself outward toward other social and erotic possibilities. The crisis also produced a new (gender) identity for Cooper; as Bradley writes at year's end: "Illness has made [Cooper] sweeter, younger, more a child. Heinrich has been born" (1891, 161v, KB). Cooper retains the nickname "Henry" or "Heinrich" from the moment her hair was shorn in the Dresden hospital until the end of her life. Along with her new name, Cooper transformed from a woman of twenty-nine to a new role, a beautiful young boy who aged over the decades no more than Dorian Gray. As Martha Vicinus argues, in fin de siècle lesbian culture, and in Michael Field's work in particular, young boys wielded a formidable erotic power, a "protean nature [that] displayed a double desire—to love a boy and be a boy."[41] Like Freud's little grandson in *Beyond the Pleasure Principle* (1920), Heinrich masters the dynamics of *fort* and *da* to resolve ambivalence and gain sexual agency relative to mothers, fathers, and others; for Michael Field as for Freud, Eros and Thanatos are never far apart.[42]

As the example of Schwester demonstrates, Michael Field expressed their commitment as a couple, to herself and to each other, through a series of long-term experiments with triangulation. A number of "thirds" commanded their attention over the years. Prominent among them were Bradley's sister/Cooper's mother, known as "the Beloved Mother-One"; Robert Browning, known as "the Old" or "the Old Gentleman"; Bernhard Berenson, known as "the Doctrine"; and their beloved dog, known as Whym Chow, memorialized in a fuzzy russet volume of elegiac poems as the "Flame of Love."[43] We might even think of poetry itself, and *Works and Days* itself, as spaces that bring Cooper and Bradley together to establish perspective on their twoness. And, of course, hidden in plain sight is Michael Field himself/herself/herselves/themselves, the third name that is one speaking for two. Each of these triangles refers back to the drama contained in the Cooper family of origin, and all of them play to the audience of the Father: seeking attention, approval, validation, education, and love from an elusive, intensely powerful, paternal figure.[44]

I walk round the great weedy garden of nasturtiums, and leave Chow in the garden, the rabbit in his hole. I come in: I look forth—Chow and the rabbit are one—Chow pecks, the rabbit rolls, and Chow pecks again. I run forth, I shriek, and chase. He locks and closes again, and again—Finally Edith extracts and exalts the rabbit apparently lifeless. [. . .]

Slowly my boiled blood cools; we set set the rabbit up under shelter of shavings [. . .] But the Chow! The incident has made a man of him. I shall never forget the air with which he dashed in, and drank water, like a young hero who flings aside his casque and refreshes himself.

—KATHARINE BRADLEY, *WORKS AND DAYS*, 1902

Rudyard Kipling's rabbit died on Monday—slain by Michael Field's Chow. He was but a white lump by our flaming little Minister Whym—but I am sorry death came so leisurely.

—EDITH COOPER, *WORKS AND DAYS*, 1902

"Marriage is an eternal triangle," writes Claude Lévi-Strauss, "not just in vaudeville sketches, but at all times, and in all places, and by definition."[45] Michael Field triangulate through us as well: in Michael Field math, I or you play an important, even perhaps a constitutive, role. Far from serving an intrusive function, the reader of *Works and Days* is the audience that commands the tension of witnessing, that in turn affirms the coupledom of Michael Field. They need to be seen to be believed, and under those terms they invite us in. Reading Michael Field's 1892 poem about Giorgione's *The Sleeping Venus*, Hillary Fraser writes, "The body of Venus, who has fallen asleep after pleasuring herself, is appreciatively described by the poet-lovers. 'No one watches her,' they write. And yet of course *they* watch her, and through them so do *we*."[46] Just as Fraser watches Michael Field watch Venus, I watch Michael Field drafting their readers into the conspiracy of triangulation and desire, implicating "me" or "us" in their ways of looking, wanting, and being. The text models the same pattern of emotional, erotic consolidation that Bradley and Cooper seek in the relationships they explore in its pages. We, as their readers, are as much part of the action as the Beloved Mother-One, the Old, the Doctrine, and the dog.

As each of those visitors to the Michael Field dyad doubtless experienced, Cooper and Bradley were challenging individuals. The passages above describe the poets' celebration of Whym Chow's bloody slaying of Rudyard Kipling's pet rabbit during an afternoon visit in 1902. In 1901, Charles Ricketts wrote in his diary, "To the Michaels. The older one spread about her at times a stifling exhalation of sentimentality, cant and nagging femininity. One is astonished how the younger one has kept her wits and a great measure of perception and delicate response."[47] Writing about Michael Field in 1936, Logan Pearsall Smith tells a story of the poets' visit to the home of his sister, Mary Costelloe Berenson. There, Bradley and Cooper admired a picture by Charles Condor: "Michael Field, finding that the forms and movements . . . expressed in a way they felt unique the inspiration of their life, decided that it belonged to them; and when they left the cottage they took it with them and hung it in their Richmond home. They perpetrated this appropriation in pious obedience to that law of possession, which, inscribed in Heaven, if not on earth, decrees that objects of beauty belong to those who love them most."[48] Later in life, Smith regretted his callow insistence that the poets return his picture, that "I had not proved myself a more obsequious courtier of these bewitched Princesses, these inspired, autocratic, incredible old maids."[49]

True to its authors, the diary, too, is challenging. The texts' physicality is equal parts forbidding and enticing, which seems just right for Michael Field. Reading them in manuscript form is by turns thrilling, boring, and impossible; indeed, sometimes all three at once. It can be impossible to decipher a word or phrase. I find Cooper's handwriting—and to be honest, her insights—far more accessible than Bradley's. (I have been known to step out for fortifying coffee before diving into a section of Bradley's pages.) The writers were neither systematic nor predictable in their organization of individual entries nor of the books as a whole. Some volumes are dominated by one narrator's voice, others by a more-or-less equitable division between the two. Some volumes include pages upon pages of thoughts about paintings and sculptures;[50] others delve into deepest private emotions, wants, or needs. Some are funny. Some, inscrutable.[51]

The book is formidable in its format: thirty or more (depending on how we count) tall, thick, bound notebooks filled with page upon page of handwritten reflection. It is thrilling to feel the weight and texture of the paper on which Bradley and Cooper wrote, to see marginal comments or corrections in very light pencil—Cooper might have been in love with Berenson, but it took her a very long time to spell his name as he did—and to notice handwriting grow messy in cases of distress or grief, to come across tearstains on pages describing deaths. A feeling of closeness to the hands and bodies of Bradley and Cooper is inescapable when handling their manuscripts. Reading their words in their own handwriting on their own pages makes the reading process intimate and personal; there is nothing abstract about language nor poetic figuration here. To read *Works and Days* is to be fully implicated in a physical relationship with the writers who are using *Works and Days* to fathom, among other things, their physical relationship; as Simon Reader writes, "reading materials in or close to the hands of these canonical figures involves getting close to their bodies and how they carried them."[52] Yet as enthralling as this text is, in both its media and its content, it is also enervating. At times, it requires contortionate physical acts relative to the page to read without provoking the ire of the Manuscripts Room's watchful librarians. I fully believe that the reader of *Works and Days* has a great deal in common with those who encountered its challenging authors in life.

Temporality is also uniquely complex here, given the diary form of *Works and Days*. Cooper and Bradley usually, though not always, write as they go.[53] Those occasions when they write retrospectively are fairly contemporary to events described, such as when they save up entries about trips or events until their return.[54] Yet the historical reader has some information that the authors lack. For example, when I read the 1889 volume from beginning to end, I was fully aware that the Beloved Mother-One would die on August 20, an event dreaded by, but not unexpected to, our poet. Unlike Michael Field, however, I knew that Robert Browning would die, too, in December; to Michael Field, this was a devastating surprise. Their reader a century on has information about certain landmark events—what happened to Oscar Wilde? What was the outcome of the Boer War, which transfixed the poets for quite some time? When did Queen Victoria die? Did Michael Field ever achieve the fame they sought?—that unfold in the work's "real time."

That reader also understands the critical legacy of Michael Field; she understands not only that Michael Field are interesting to readers today but how Michael Field are interesting. I am sure Bradley and Cooper would not have anticipated queer theory; judging from their response to the first edition of *The Yellow Book* ("We have been almost blinded by the glare of hell" [1894, 37v, EC]), they would have been quite horrified by it. Yet Michael Field are important to queer theory, and queer theory is important to them. What would they think of my own efforts to read *Works and Days* in the context of fiction, in order to illuminate something important about the voices and lives of Victorian women? "What if the archive refuses our entreaties for transhistorical communication?" asks Melanie Micir. "What if our would-be subjects turn their backs on us? What if they refuse our touch?"[55] I believe I know Michael Field well enough (at least in my own imagination) to be sure that they would be interested in, and certainly pleased by, the attention I am giving them here. But ultimately, I believe that they would discover me to be missing the point, they would take umbrage over . . . something, and they would move along, because that is what they did with stunning consistency throughout their lives.

The text of *Works and Days* is widely variable in its structure and form, with the exception of an important artifice involving the calendar. Just as the almanac form serves Djuna Barnes in the *Ladies Almanack* (1928), Michael Field's diary mode hangs Michael Field's formal and narrative experiment on the reliable scaffold of the year.[56] As a diary, *Works and Days* is governed by the concept of the one-year cycle: usually, though not universally, Cooper and Bradley open a book on January 1 and close a book on December 31. Typically, they use New Year's Eve entries to reflect back on the year gone by and New Year's Day entries to document their hopes and aspirations for the year to come. Entries for December 31 and January 1 appear in different volumes of the work, and they differ dramatically in tone. Their emotional heat tends to differ as well, with December in the more elegiac mode and the next morning's entry more concerned with beginning the world. In 1902, for example, Cooper expresses the oppressive nature of the year's potential: "The ritual of New Year's Day is the reception of dividends, the burning of rubbish, a raw state of mind, a body lax with vigil—a sense of fetters clanking round a womb with child—the iron of temporal circumstance noisy even ~~around~~ ^above^ the foetus of a year. I hate the day—It is abominable" (1902, 4v, EC). Though only a single night's sleep over the new year divides the tropes of retrospect and prospect, the poets labor to differentiate them as sharply as possible: "How we loved one another then [. . .]—the year before we entered the Catholic Church. Out with thy tablets, truth: we have never loved each other since, as then—" (1914, 7r-7v, KB).

The poets' conversion to Catholicism in 1907 caused them to reflect on the mode of temporality the diary has offered them over the years. On January 1, 1908, for example, Cooper describes the women as newly "free from temporal control" because "one's supernatural year has begun a month earlier than New Year's Day"—even as she marks that freedom by hewing to the tradition of opening the Year Book with anticipation of the worldly year to come (1908, 1r, EC). Much later in the same volume, Cooper writes, "I have left my White Year Book for the Divine Office—my Time has been learning to work in chains" (1908, 195r, EC). Cooper is newly conscious of the claims of the Divine Office to organize Michael Field's time differently: "Now the Office is become sweet as the winning of Daily Bread, and we feel superannuated, like retired bread-winners, if we have been so industrious as to leave nothing to do after breakfast. With the Office one leads the inner life of the Church, even of the Holy Mass itself" (1908, 195v, EC). Yet the "White Year Book" remains the container for this new "inner life of the Church" that Cooper attempts to embrace. Regardless of variations in their mode of temporality, the diary is remarkably persistent as the tool Michael Field use to give voice and form to their shared reality.

Bradley and Cooper develop a certain cadence to each year's volume, framed between January 1 and December 31. In any given year, including 1908's Divine Office, they typically mark the seasons, and especially the advent of spring. Michael Field are attentive to birthdays and to the wedding anniversaries of close family members such as Cooper's parents and Bradley's parents. Conspicuous within each year is the intensive attention to death anniversaries, with rituals that include altars of flowers, portraits, and artifacts dedicated to the lost loved one—especially Emma Bradley Cooper, who was Cooper's mother and Bradley's sister: "the Beloved Mother-One." Many years Michael Field make note of specific Christmas presents exchanged and silly games played on Christmas Eve with the servants. One year, they underscore with some sadness that such activities are no more than a pretense.

> *If, ten years ago, I cd have seen my lovely old rooms, my glowing bits of satin-wood, my darting and lustrous river, my long-bodied hound, and cd have known I had all these things, with the complete fellowship day and night of my Beloved, a joy almost too terrible in bliss would have been over me—and now it is within, ^it is^ of my heart, it is my very life. And My gratitude is commensurate with my joy. And next Census—will it find us by our River? I believe it will find us together and that is enough to satisfy all hope.*
>
> —EDITH COOPER, *WORKS AND DAYS*, 1901

Bradley and Cooper make efforts to be forward-looking, or prospective, in the pages of this text. But both psychologically and formally, they fight a tendency toward retrospection: psychologically as Victorian women attuned to the immanence of loss; formally because a diary tends to operate most vividly as a recording device for what has happened lately. Cooper and Bradley were tethered to the current events around them: they marked significant public deaths, including those of their dear friend Browning, Tennyson, and Queen Victoria. They followed the career and trials of Oscar Wilde, and Wilde's imprisonment and death. They looked on with envy and some bemusement at the prominence of other women writers such as Olive Schreiner and Vernon Lee. As the 1890s went along and the turn of the century loomed large, Bradley and Cooper became more explicitly thoughtful about the end of the nineteenth century—and hopeful about their own relationship to "modernity" in the twentieth.[57] "[W]e trust to unite two centuries in our work," Cooper protests to Charles Ricketts when he expressed his intention to remain firmly rooted in the nineteenth century, at a dinner just before the new year 1901 (1901, 5r, EC). The poets proudly filled out their 1901 census form from their own home at 1 Paragon, Richmond. They listed Cooper as head of the household (1901, 45v, KB and 49v, EC). On August 25, 1914, a few months after Cooper's death and days before her own, Bradley wrote: "Europe is seething in blood. On August 5th England de-clared war" (1914, 34r, KB).

Yet, *Works and Days* is not a record of the events and concerns of daily life. To be sure, daily life intrudes, sometimes spectacularly. I went to the journals first in search of quotidian details of housekeeping, finance, transport, planning, and so on—details, in other words, of how a queer couple managed the particulars of the everyday—but did not find much of this at all. Michael Field record some gossip but not a great deal. Rather, the work is psychological and introspective: Who are these women against the great backdrop of poetry in particular and art more broadly? What are the transcendent qualities to which they aspire? How do these aspirations relate to the reality checks of everyday life—including checks to Michael Field's artistic and romantic dreams? And to Cooper's? And Bradley's?

"Derogate."

What games we have by our bed-room fire at night!
We lie in our bed, read proofs and poems, and stick roses in our ears.

—KATHARINE BRADLEY, *WORKS AND DAYS*, 1897

Henry James once described Victorian novels as "large loose baggy monsters," a description I take seriously to consider what was afforded Michael Field by the vast scope of *Works and Days*.[58] Baggy monsters provided writers such as Charles Dickens and George Eliot with a certain formal capacity—comprising, literally, an enormous swath of cognitive and textual space—to work through complex representational questions.[59] Yet, as internally diverse as vast Victorian multiplot novels are, they remain unified formally by important literary conventions: expectations of narrative voice, of time and space, of authorship. At the most literal level of their materiality, Victorian novels are unified by conventions of publication: a binding or bindings in the case of single- or triple-deckers; authorial signature and mode in the case of serial publications.

"The nineteenth-century novel was one of the most important cultural sites for representing and shaping desire, affect, and ideas about gender and the family," Sharon Marcus writes in her pathbreaking book about women's relationships with women in Victorian England.[60] As one such relationship narrative, *Works and Days* provides Bradley and Cooper with the capacity, realized across thousands of pages over cycle after cycle of years, to work through their exploration of gender, love, and art, of the challenges women face when they attempt to claim voice or sexual agency or both, and of how elusive the plot of one's own life can seem. *Works and Days* shares many material and formal conventions with Victorian novels. It is massive. It is complex, or, if you will, baggy, albeit in an aesthetic cognitive wrapping. Its volumes appear serially and clad in uniform bindings. The text's two narrators glide seamlessly between modes of objective observation and those of subjective psychological conflict. *Works and Days* observes internal codes of seriality; each part tracks the familiar narrative arc of beginning-middle-end. The text marks narrative benchmarks of female identity, including love, lust, loss, ambition, authorship, marriage, domesticity, and motherhood—and also puzzles over its uneasy relationship to such powerful concepts. It observes larger, overarching codes of narrative unity: the narrators' voices are stable, even as the narrators themselves change dramatically over time, independently and in relation to each other. Figures of time and space remain formally constant throughout the text, though variable and wildly complex in their particulars.[61]

To think about *Works and Days* as something like a novel opens up new ways of thinking about how literary forms such as novels afford their readers templates for organizing their perceptions of the world, and making meaning of the patterns they recognize. The experiment also yields a new perspective on Michael Field as an author concerned to participate in this work of "representing and shaping desire, affect, and ideas about gender and the family," in Marcus's terms. We also gain a new way of understanding Michael Field as an important figure in the transition from Victorian to modernist literary fiction,[62] even as I note that as a proud and serious poet, they would not thank me for this description. In his own contemplation of the transition from Victorian to modernist narrative forms, Joseph Allen Boone thinks about E. M. Forster's claim that we read novels in order to experience "[the] secret life each of us lives privately." He continues: "This interest in the privately lived 'secret life'—what Woolf calls 'the privacy of the soul'—is of course a hallmark of the modernist turn to modes of interior representation, . . . [of] those novelistic experiments that have attempted to evoke the flux of consciousness and the erotics of mental activity in new or altered narrative forms."[63] Through a deft combination of citation and departure—marking Victorian narrative expectations and adapting them from within—*Works and Days* offers "altered narrative forms" in abundance. Because it is a diary, the text flaunts its claims to privacy, secrecy, and intimacies both emotional and bodily. Yet as a shared diary that voices two versions of privacy, it flouts those claims. In turn, as the shared diary of a female couple, it teases of an eroticism here signaled in the interplay of voices; love speaks its name openly in these pages, even as the diary form marks that candor under the seal of the secret. As the shared diary of female lovers practicing male authorial subjectivity, *Works and Days* exports conventions of male authorship—along with related expectations of privacy, sexuality, intimacy, gender fluidity, voice, form, and even irony—in the name of something else. All of this, but especially that mercurial "something else," represents the great narrative experiment of *Works and Days*.

> *We cannot possess what we experience.*
>
> —KATHARINE BRADLEY, *WORKS AND DAYS*, 1888–89

Written continuously by Michael Field from about 1888 until Michael followed Field in death from cancer in 1914, *Works and Days* falls chronologically between Elizabeth Barrett Browning's *Aurora Leigh* (1856), an autobiographical novel written in the form of an epic poem, and Gertrude Stein's *Autobiography of Alice B. Toklas* (1933), an autobiography written by its subject's lesbian spouse.[64] Throughout *Works and Days*, Bradley and Cooper conduct experiments with form, voice, and identity that share qualities with both Barrett Browning and Stein. Early in her career Bradley even went so far as to draw a clear line back from herself to Elizabeth Barrett Browning, choosing as her first pre–Michael Field nom de plume "Arran Leigh."[65] Michael Field always orient toward "the modern," and in *Works and Days* they model formal practices that will emerge clearly, and canonically, very soon after their deaths: in the Cubists' (as well as Sappho's) exploration of the relationship between fragment and whole; in the prominence of the cut or splice in the films of Georges Méliès; in Ezra Pound's *Cantos*, which similarly challenges concepts of linearity and plot; and in Djuna Barnes's *Ladies Almanack*, which uses an archaic calendrical form to negotiate female homoerotic networks.

Michael Field frame their particular experiment by rattling the central organizing structure of Victorian narrative: the question of family itself, beginning with the matter of one another: aunt and niece, committed lovers, a writer. Though they maintained a primary loyalty to each other,

Bradley and Cooper wrote their narrative avatars in *Works and Days* as complex protagonists whose lives featured experimentation with alternative allegiances, new possibilities, and different outcomes that felt as deep and painful as compelling.[66] I argue here that Michael Field's marriage narrative works in two important ways to situate *Works and Days*. First, their "marriage plot" adds a compelling model to our sample of Victorian narratives. Second, by commingling marriage and authorship as literally as they do, Michael Field redeploy the codes of temporality—and specifically, of futurity—that heterosexual marriage narratives so often secure.

Like fairy tales, Victorian novels often focused on coming-of-age myths. In the case of female protagonists, childish innocence gives way to curiosity, to a test that results in courtship and, ultimately: "Reader, I married him." Elizabeth Freeman writes, "Literary critics have long described the wedding in terms of aesthetic, social, and psychic closure. In theories of comedy, of which the 'courtship plot' is paradigmatic, narrative itself moves inexorably forward toward a wedding, which situates the characters in their proper social relation to one another and quashes any unstable subplots that the narrative has generated along the way."[67] The marriage plot charts a girl's transfer from childhood to adulthood, from her family of origin to her family of destiny. The transition from one family to another counts as narrative for girls and women in Victorian fiction. Novels that end in marriage suggest a few things about female identity: that marriage is the crowning achievement of a woman's life; that marriage ends the part of a woman's life that is interesting enough for a story.

Talia Shaffer makes an important case for ambivalence at the heart of Victorian marriage plots: in contrast to a linear building toward heterosexual consummation, Shaffer reframes Victorian marriage narratives as a competition between two drives, the romantic and the familial. The first facilitates the development of a modern female subject, "a liberal, autonomous, essential, rights-bearing citizen, with unique individuality and deep psychology." The second, rooted more in rational esteem than in passion, enables "the history of alternative female subjectivity, the motion of selfhood as relational, affective, and networked, governed by feelings and duties instead of rights and reasons." Victorian novels, Shaffer argues, consistently stage and negotiate the rivalry between romantic and familiar desires:

> Romantic suitors—those smolderingly charismatic men, their antecedents unknown, their intentions murky—include Wickham, Willoughby, Frank Churchill, Henry Crawford, Rochester, M. Paul

> Emanuel, Sir Francis Levison, Stephen Guest, Ladislaw, Grandcourt, and Gilbert Osmond. Opposing them are the familiar suitors, those unthreatening and trusted men who offer safe haven: Knightley, Edward Ferrars, Colonel Brandon, Edmund Bertram, St. John, Dr. Graham Bretton, Philip Wakem, Archibald Carlyle, Casaubon, Daniel Deronda, and Ralph Touchett.[68]

The familiar marriage advances a sense of self in relation, mapped against the panorama of the social world and the *longue durée*, as opposed to the short, sharp shock of desire. "Familiar marriage spoke from tradition," writes Shaffer, "while romantic marriage expressed modernity. Familiar marriage promised settled, stable residence, romantic marriage embraced mobility, relocation. . . . Working through the choice between these models, or struggling to adjust, compromise, or alter them, was a way of figuring out how one should be in the world."[69] From their secure perch in the familiar, Michael Field experiment with dynamics of rivalry; indeed, this is a desire constitutive to *Works and Days*.

Works and Days challenges Linda Peterson's observation that late-Victorian women's writing collaborations tended to break down in the context of marriage: "[I]t was not simply marriage that ended the collaborative effort of these women artists but, significantly, a disagreement about women's work."[70] In the peculiar case of Michael Field, collaborative authorship *was* the sign of marriage, its artistic and worldly validation. More specifically, their collaborative authorship of the text *Works and Days* afforded Bradley and Cooper the opportunity to emplot narratives of marriage and authorship as one, entwined, inextricable. In the mid-Victorian period, Marcus argues, "marriage was legitimated by activities other than sex": "Women who established longterm relationships with other women . . . saw themselves, and were seen by others, as placid embodiments of the middle-class ideal of marriage: a bond defined by sex that also had the power to sanctify sex."[71] Bradley and Cooper observed such tropes of romance closely. They partook of those tropes to interpret their own "closer married" relationship not as a social scandal but, as Marcus shows, as the epitome of a stable ideal.

Michael Field's structural entrapment involved not their same-sex marriage but the resolutely familial nature of their incestuous union. Michael Field's marriage was far more an original state than a destination; they found it right in the girlhood home, and they were held tightly within a familiar space that they valued and resented, in equal parts. Field's bond provides an important inflection to the gendered archetypes that sit awkwardly on the horizons of their own experience. They offer a counterpoint to the master narrative of Victorian femininity by situating both the origins and the outcomes of their marriage differently.[72]

After reading an interview with Dr. Alfred Russel Wallace on the topic of "Women and Natural Selection" in December 1893, Cooper spent a sleepless night. In his interview, Wallace vests women with the agency behind natural selection, and the power to ensure that the human species is on a trajectory toward evolutionary improvement. The instrument of a woman's power is marriage, sought and created outside the family of origin. Education brings the power of choice to women; educated women hold all hope for eugenic "progress" in their soft, slender hands. "In order to cleanse society of the unfit," Wallace writes, "we must give to woman the power of selection in marriage, and the means by which this most important and desirable end can be attained will be brought about by giving her such training and education as shall render her economically independent."[73]

Educated women such as Bradley and Cooper can be economically independent, as their own case demonstrates. In turn, economically independent women can afford to be selective when it comes to their marriages. Bradley and Cooper were most concerned with this point, and one can certainly argue that they were selective indeed. What kept Cooper up all night, however, is something else: her contemplation of the social power that Wallace would attribute to her as an educated, economically independent woman. There is no evolution, nor devolution, without reproduction. Cooper is educated. She is economically independent. She has selected a marriage partner carefully. But that marriage will yield forth poetry, not children. So how does Cooper fit into this framework? What power does she have? What can she do with her responsibility for the future of the species? "I thought I am not a dramatist unless I can evolve a plot," she wrote. "I said to my brain *evolve*!" (1893, 95r, EC; emphasis in original).

Cooper understands the relationship between evolution and plot as one of progress, of amelioration. In a discussion of gender and evolutionary discourses in the fin de siècle, Rita Felski writes: "Darwin's theory of natural selection, which might appear to indicate the random and purposeless nature of human activity, was frequently refashioned to convey a view of history as purposeful and goal-directed, offering a secularized vision of a Christian redemption narrative."[74] Cooper, however, feels inhibited from participation in the evolutionary trajectory of redemption, and thus from the possibility of greater artistic achievement as a dramatist and as a poet. In evolutionary theory, development occurs when the species is made hybrid through exogamy: the necessary combination of different genetic strains to produce a new genetic specimen that shares qualities with, but differs essentially from, its progenitors. Like marriage plots themselves, the species requires the formation of new families through the departure from—the abandonment of, even the betrayal of—the family of origin. Living at the very heart of domestic ideology is a disloyalty in the transition from girl to woman: a girl must betray first love in favor of new love in order to fulfill the destiny of her gendered role.

Michael Field have a different perspective on sexuality and evolution, one that places pleasure at the heart of progress. In 1895, Cooper reports on an opinion held by both Bradley and Berenson: "The best children are those conceived in hot passion . . . illegitimate often and often becoming artists and men of genius. The idea of seeking the healthy mate is not a civilized One. [. . .] Imagine the lovers of Browning visualizing a ^healthy^ child as the end for which they live! If we bother Nature at her work of natural selection we injure her work that in her infinite benignity she does for us—leaving us free to love" (1895, v. 1, 67v–68r, EC). In this view, domestic quietude is the rate-limiting factor in progress. In other words, hot poetry has nothing to do with the production of healthy infants; and "hot passion" is the true engine of social progress.

In her 1922 biography of Michael Field, Mary Sturgeon reads the poets' outwardly placid existence as a lack of experience that shows up in their writing: "It may be that this seclusion from life will be felt in Michael Field's poetry as a limitation; that the final conviction imposed upon the mind by the authority of experience is wanting; and that the work lacks a certain dry wisdom of which difficult living is a necessary condition."[75] Yet Bradley and Cooper both work hard to try to "evolve a plot" by intervening in the world, by seeking friendship, fame, and worldly respect; simply by seeking. In *Works and Days*, the narrative of seeking, in and by "hot passion," is experience itself. The narrators fight against stasis, against the built-in quietude of affluent daughterly existence. Michael Field write the open struggle to balance loyalty and plot, to respect the anchor of the family of origin while also drinking of the excitement of modernity, mobility, and the new. Viewed over the long narrative arc of this text, Bradley and Cooper repeatedly encounter outside forces—third terms—that would offer them the chance to expand or even terminate their private relationship of two. This happens over and over again; it is the central structural feature of *Works and Days*. Not coincidentally, it is also the central structural feature of many British nineteenth-century novels. Those novels find narrative resolution in the plot of exogamy: the substitution of a new domestic sphere for an old one, and with that substitution the promise of a procreative future. The pulse from three to two to three to two tracks the creation of new families from families of origin, and it provides a mechanism for the transgenerational evolution of the species.[76]

In light of the episodic cadence of *Works and Days*, what does it mean, then, to read *Works and Days* as a unified literary work? The text is organized in one-year, loosely autobiographical chunks. Cooper and Bradley channel its narrative through plot devices familiar to us from Victorian fiction. They borrow from an important, and accessible, literary tool, using long-form, complex narratives to explore women's inner lives against the background of social constraints and expectations. Novels provided Victorian writers with powerful tools for making meaning in the context of tectonic shifts in the social order. A certain kind of novel—specifically, the massive, multiplot novel familiar from the mid-Victorian period and associated with certain forms of realism—affords Michael Field space to negotiate the unusual domestic narrative at the heart of their experience. Bradley and Cooper were unconventional in many ways, but not so very unconventional that they bypassed the most powerful literary codes available to women such as they were, attempting to make their way in the world.

Perhaps it makes no sense to talk about Michael Field (or Cooper and Bradley) in relation to the Victorian novel. They do not write novels, and in fact as a poet, they felt vaguely sorry for acquaintances such as George Meredith, whose serious poetry writing was interfered with by his occasional novel, in Michael Fields' view anyway. As a faithful reader of *Works and Days*, I can testify that Bradley and Cooper did not report reading many novels, and those few that they did read they selected from European ranks—Flaubert, Tolstoy, Turgenev, Huysmans—rather than English. They had a subscription to Mudie's Lending Library, and they knew the work of the Brontës, Dickens, and Eliot well enough to mention them in passing. They disliked the fiction of Thomas Hardy. I would love to know what they thought about Henry James, and what he thought about them. But compared to their intense engagement with poetry, painting, sculpture, and aesthetic philosophy, the novel was not particularly on their radar.[77]

Of course it was not on their radar: novels were not art in the eyes of this aesthetic poet, for whom art was the pinnacle of all striving and poetry the pinnacle of its realization. But *Works and Days* is the product not of Michael Field but of Bradley and Cooper, together as individuals. And as a document of works and a document of days, this text orients itself toward the material world in a dramatically different way from the worlds created in Michael Field's poetry. *Works and Days* gives its authors a repository for all those elements of the here and now that do not belong in their published poetry and plays. It is not aesthetic. Although it is not generally descriptive of the writers' everyday lives, nor attentive to quotidian details, the text is prosaic, in all senses of the term. Robert Browning was disturbed to hear that his "dear, Greek women" were writing prose, not poetry. Bradley reports, "When he heard we were writing prose, he said—*'take care you do not derogate'*" (1888, 13r, KB; emphasis in original). But derogate they did. The diary is the closest thing to "realism" that Michael Field ever produced. Insofar as it was not easy for Michael Field as female aesthetes to leave the world out of their writing altogether, it is important to read the diary in dialogue with the poetry—but as an important work in its own right, not as a glossary for the poems and verse dramas.

Works and Days presents a double narrative, emplotting female marriage on one hand and rejecting on the other follow-on conventions of time, space, and futurity, including reproductive futurity. In refusing the transactional power of heterosexual narrative, Michael Field refuse the narratives of temporality that predicate future stability on female reproduction: the metonymic relationship between babies, and futures, the orientation that ultimately gives selective, educated women social power. Note that to Wallace, women's transformative power inheres not in women themselves but in their capacity to ameliorate the species through their offspring, the serial progress of generations marching forward like the serial numbers of a Victorian novel.

Michael Field have full confidence in their transformative powers as women, but the nature of their plot has nothing at all to do with reproduction. Theirs is akin to what Lee Edelman has described as "*Sinth*omosexuality . . . —denying the appeal of fantasy, refusing the promise of futurity that mends each tear, however mean, in reality's dress with threads of meaning (attached as they are to the eye-catching lure we might see as the sequins of sequence, which dazzle our vision by producing the constant illusion of *con*sequence)—offers us fantasy turned inside out."[78] In *Works and Days*, Michael Field do indeed present a logic of future consequence, but theirs differs entirely from the reproductive futurity that endows heterosexual marriage plots with their stabilizing force. In Dustin Friedman's powerful formulation, their literary practice offered late-Victorian queer writers such as Michael Field a space for their otherness, a marriage realized in and as poetry: art, Friedman writes, is "a realm where queers can resist a hostile social world by developing an autonomous sense of self, one that is inspired by their sexual difference and grounded in the ability to resist dominant power relations."[79] Together, Edelman and Friedman suggest the importance of looking hard at the "Michael Field" union not as a naive simulacrum of marriage but as a vehicle that afforded the writers truly radical social, psychological, and temporal perspectives.

"For Victorians," Marcus argues, "marriage meant the union of sexual and spiritual impulses, the reconciliation of sexuality with propriety. Marriage was a socially acceptable exhibition of sexual intimacy because it was predicated on fidelity and thus advertised not only the sexuality of the spouses but also their acceptance of restraints and limits. For this reason, female marriage was not associated with a savage state of sexual license but instead was readily integrated into even the most restrictive ideas of social order."[80] To that point, *Works and Days* presents the story of two women, intimate family members, married to each other but always, from within their dyad, peering outward at the external world in search of something and someone else. Female marriage in Michael Field's case signaled fidelity's ambivalent heart: a public claim to the virtuous constraints of marriage—while the marriage itself is a blind, enabling the women to keep an eye out for more worldly alternatives. Those alternatives—of something and someone else, of qualities of mobility and modernity, of sensation and worldliness, of romance and family—represented for Michael Field the tantalizing prospect of "plot."

> *I have just signed the Census-Paper, as Father signed it ten years ago. I can see his silver hair outspread over the blue document—I can hear our laughter and discussion, and the sudden anguish of silence when he wrote himself down as a widower.*
>
> *And now, [. . .] I write myself as head of a house, and [. . .] entertain as guest or lodger the choicest of my sex—the Beloved One, Single and F.—even as I am. We, dramatic writers, living on our own means, with our two servants, both single—what a quaint household! [. . .]*
>
> *And as I write the Thames runs by [illeg.] cloudy and energetic with the South Wind—the River that binds our days together with its influence of light and tide.*
>
> —EDITH COOPER, *WORKS AND DAYS*, 1901

"For me the noise of Time is not sad," writes Roland Barthes synesthetically. "I love bells, clocks, watches—and I recall that at first photographic implements were related to techniques of cabinetmaking and the machinery of precision: cameras, in short, were clocks for seeing, and perhaps in me someone very old still hears in the photographic mechanism the living sound of the wood."[81] Recalling us to Placidia, the cabinet that "enwombs" this text *Works and Days*, Barthes writes of the ontological work performed by time and its constitutive technologies. For Michael Field, too, those technologies concern the original cabinet of curiosities, the female body that enwombs family and text, that promises pleasures, that may or may not point to a future.

Barthes's theory of the *punctum* in *Camera Lucida* is illuminating for Michael Field as well: reading photographs as I am reading *Works and Days*, Barthes meditates on his response to the punctum, "sting, speck, cut, little hole—and also a cast of the dice. A photograph's *punctum* is that accident which pricks me (but also bruises me, is poignant to me)."[82] The punctum is for Barthes the detail that snags the eye or grips the heart—that conjures immanence and melancholy, that makes a dead photo live and sing. Studying a photograph of Queen Victoria ("Queen Victoria, entirely unesthetic," reads the caption attributed to Virginia Woolf), Barthes writes:

> Here is Queen Victoria photographed in 1863 by George W. Wilson; she is on horseback, her skirt suitably draping the entire animal . . . but beside her, attracting my eyes, a kilted groom holds the horse's bridle: this is the *punctum*; for even if I do not know just what the social status of this Scotsman may be (servant? equerry?), I can see his function clearly: to supervise the horse's behavior: what if the horse suddenly began to rear? What would happen to the queen's skirt, *i.e.*, to *her majesty*? The *punctum* fantastically "brings out" the Victorian nature (what else can one call it?) of the photograph, it endows this photograph with a blind field.[83]

Here the punctum pulls back the curtain, or the skirt, on the disciplinary organization of Victoria's queenliness. That queenliness requires acknowledgment of *her majesty*—that is, the equation of Victoria's hegemonic status and the naked body that would be revealed for all to see if her horse should rear. The punctum exposes as uniquely Victorian the story that the photograph attempts to conceal: "it endows this photograph with a blind field."

The experimental edge in Michael Field's *Works and Days* involves just such a blind field: dislocations and accidents of time, space, and cognition that introduce counternarratives and suggest what is hiding in plain view. What, then, is the blind field of *Works and Days*?

Even as they spurned female conventions of futurity (babies), Michael Field thought carefully about their place in a future world. This had to do with literary reputation, and on that concern, Robert Browning was certain that they would find their audience—though the women would have to "*wait fifty years*" (1888, 5r, KB; emphasis in original). Browning, it seems, was right, even if he was off by a factor of two.

Browning perceived Michael Field, his "dear, Greek women," as both premature and belated: born too soon to find their audience; born too late to realize their authentically antique selves.[84] Browning may have been the first to perceive Michael Field's odd relationship to chronological time. But he was not the last. To list a few examples from the early reception of Michael Field:

- In 1893, Thomas Wentworth Higginson suggested that if the poet laureate were named "on the ground of pure strength of genius, and what may be called the Elizabethan quality, it would doubtless go to a woman. Or it would go, more awkwardly, to two women—that unnamed aunt and niece who jointly hide themselves under the masculine title of Michael Field."[85]
- In the mid-1890s, Lionel Johnson wrote, "In their virtues, and in their vices, they are Elizabethan: the virtues are many, the vices are few."[86]
- In 1922, the poets' biographer Mary Sturgeon followed suit: "The weeks of Michael's passing witnessed the passing of the age to which she belonged, for they were those in which the Great War began. It is clear that Michael Field, in the noble unity of her life and work, represented something that was finest in the dying era; and yet she was, in certain respects, aloof from that Victorian Age, and in advance of it. It is profoundly moving to see how, even in extremity, her genius remained true to itself."[87]
- And in 1936, Logan Pearsall Smith echoed Browning's early prediction: "Those who read the works of Michael Field are not many, but I believe that, as time goes on, they may grow in number."[88]

Michael Field's earliest critics were attuned to the poets' temporal asynchrony. And although *Works and Days* is a text formally predicated on cyclical, repetitive patterns of diurnal experience, Bradley and Cooper use the predictability of the diary form as cover for their larger experiment with time and with space, as well as with categories such as self and matter, which they make metaphysical.

For the two Greek women, this observation might suggest an odd temporal coordination with life in the fin de siècle. Freeman, via Wolfgang Schivelbusch, reminds us:

> [D]uring the latter half of the nineteenth century through the period before World War II, new technologies such as the railroad, photography, the cinema, and air travel made time seem suddenly pliable, such that the ordinary rhythms of things sped up or slowed down, events could be made to run backward, or a juxtaposition of disparate moments could

> invoke change over time. A multiplicity of possible times, and interventions in the systematized time of capitalism, opened up during the latter part of the long nineteenth century, emblematized by the wanderings and flaneurship that comprised life for the denizens of urbanized spaces.[89]

Works and Days abundantly rewards reading through the filter of technological change: trains, Tubes, and buses, as Vadillo has written, automobiles, photographs, telegrams, telephones, the dread prospect of a Channel tunnel, and a suggestion of "motor-buses in the sky" gradually gain purchase on Michael Field's pastoral existence. But notwithstanding the relentlessly cyclical nature of the diary form—1892, 1893, 1894, and the volumes that followed—technological advancement is neither linear nor predictable for Michael Field.

The steady march of cyclical time serves a disciplinary purpose that Michael Field manage to elude. Freeman writes that temporal socialization uses time "to organize individual human bodies toward maximum productivity. And I mean that people are bound to one another, engrouped, made to feel coherently collective, through particular orchestrations of time."[90] Freeman's theory suggests important new ways of understanding Michael Field's persistent feeling of disjointedness, of standing outside, away from, apart from their historical moment. Bradley and Cooper have a finely honed sense of their relationship to the past, and the women—and their critics—harbor confidence that they will claim their place in the future (and clearly, they were quite correct). The "now," however? The "here"? This is less clear for them. Freeman continues, "Chronobiopolitics harnesses not only sequence but also cycle, the dialectical companion to sequence, for the idea of time as cyclical stabilizes its forward movement, promising renewal rather than rupture."[91]

The serial narrative *Works and Days*, which Michael Field wrote between 1888 and 1914, speaks to the serial narrative that their near-contemporary, and queer-contemporary, Proust published between 1913 and 1927, *À la recherche du temps perdu*. For Michael Field as for Proust, reproductive futurity is a primarily literary proposition. Writing about Proust, Martin Hägglund explains: "Marcel's chronolibidinal insight is that nothing can be experienced or desired as paradise without the sense that it can be lost. Far from devaluing temporal life, the dimension of loss is precisely what makes it emerge as valuable. Following this logic, the valuation of a past experience may be enhanced when it is infused with the pathos of being lost, just as the value of a current experience may be enhanced by the sense that it will be lost." Like Marcel, Michael Field were exquisitely attuned to the immanence of loss within presence, and the immanence of presence in what is lost. Theirs is indeed a Victorian story, every bit as much as Wilson's photograph of queen/skirts/horse/reins/servant is. Hägglund continues: "[T]he theory of chronolibido reads the ambivalence of desire as a response to the investment in the undecidable fate of survival: in temporal finitude as the source of both the desirable and the undesirable. The reason desire is ambivalent is ultimately *not* because we are driven toward the absolute but because we are invested in survival—an investment that gives rise to acknowledgment *and* denial, compassion *and* aggression, vital change *and* deadening repetition."[92]

Michael Field organize desire, in all its ambivalence, on behalf of a future they are certain they will realize. The relentlessly cyclical and sequenced nature of *Works and Days* gives the appearance of chronobiopolitics at work: queen, horse, servant. But then, punctum. Michael Field are not harnessed to the biopolitics that govern identity for Victorian women, and especially for Victoria, woman. Michael Field's investment in futurity is decidedly queer, linking to the enclosure of a generative female body for different purposes altogether, relating to a future expressed in a different mode. In the chapters ahead, I will show that in the hands of Michael Field, *Works and Days* presents a formal technology for the refusal of temporality, and with it for the refusal of mourning, for the preservation of all life and love in the metaphysical amber of feeling, deep and immanent, powerful, embodied, sumptuous, and beautiful. Theirs is a metaphysics not of what was and not of what is; it is an illumination of what will be. In the words of José Esteban Muñoz, writing about a queer claim to the future in the present, "Such illumination will provide us with access to a world that should be, that could be, and that will be."[93] Perhaps it is not too much to hope for a happy ending.

"Dust."

> *Lord Tennyson's Funeral. [. . .] It is lovely autumn when we come out. And so closes the Victorian epoch—~~It is~~ ^an epoch^ already yesterday: it is for us, England's living, and yet unspent poets, to make all things new. We are for the morning—the nineteenth century thinks it has no poets—nothing to lose. Verily it has nothing: for we are not of it—we shake the dust of our feet from it, and pass on into the 20th century.*
>
> —KATHARINE BRADLEY, *WORKS AND DAYS*, 1892

As Michael Field dust themselves off departing Tennyson's funeral, they look forward to the new century ahead, as "England's living, and yet unspent poets," ready "to make all things new." As much as Ezra Pound's claim to "making it new" stands as a slogan for modernism, Pound himself was a writer immersed in both Western and Asian antiquity. Just as for Michael Field, Pound's claim to the "new" partakes not of the "now" but of the "then" of history.[94] Each of the chapters that follow will examine the poets' project of "making it new" within a volume, or close group of volumes, of *Works and Days*. I treat the text's volumes as large chapters that contribute to the whole; viewed another way, I treat these individual volumes as encapsulated experiments on their own terms, every bit as disruptive and disjointed relative to the serial whole as they are continuous. Across these situational experiments, I track the complex politics of time, space, and cognition, and argue that Michael Field create—and realize—a strategy for futurity from new materials.

I first focus on Michael Field's narrative of the year 1889, which was noteworthy for Bradley and Cooper for several reasons. The year saw two key deaths for Michael Field, those of Cooper's mother and of their mentor Robert Browning. It was also the year of the triumphant publication of their book *Long Ago*, which was well regarded critically and put "Michael Field" on the map as a new poet with something to say. I have argued elsewhere that the dead mother plot enabled Victorian writers to canonize an ideal of femininity: motherhood in absentia, sealed off by death, erecting a bodiless ideal divorced from the needs, wants, and failings of women. The death of the mother is the incitement to narrative for Bradley and Cooper, just as it is for many Victorian writers: they fill the space vacated by Emma Cooper with authorship. That triumph was short-lived, however, and Browning's surprise death at the year's end seemed to seal Michael Field's achievement in a sarcophagus of disappointment. For Bradley and Cooper, authorship and motherhood are bound for all time in a knot of passionate love, devastation, and public shame.

The year 1892 represented a moment of resurgence in Michael Field's worldly ambitions. It was the year in which Cooper's passion for Bernhard Berenson rose to heights of intensity before crashing in a slow, unfolding series of humiliations that haunted her until her dying day. On October 27, 1893, Bradley and Cooper succeeded in staging a production of their play *A Question of Memory* at the Independent Theatre in London. This period witnesses the escalation of their ambition for worldly recognition and engagement, opening possibilities that seemed so newly accessible: possibilities of exogamous love and the chance to participate in a theatrical life brought ever closer to them by Ibsen.

However unfortunately, the patterns established in 1889 held true several years later. The swelling forth of excitement gave way to humiliation, such as Cooper experienced in the dead silence of the morning after

Michael Field's play completed its one-day run at the Independent Theatre: "Not a flower had any one sent us yesterday," she wrote that morning. "[N]ot a flower was given to us. No word, no letter, no visit, only the execrations of the Press!" Cooper's diary entry that morning begins: "It seems more natural to be dead than alive" (1893, 86v, EC). The public humiliation of this episode only amplifies the authorial struggles of these two women writers attempting to navigate an inhospitable world that feels entirely alien to them. Even when they think they are catching on, they come up disappointed. Attending their own play as Michael Field, two women wearing their finest, they felt at once exposed and ignored. Michael Field have tested the world, and in their shock and pain, they recoil.

In 1897, Edith Cooper's father disappeared off the face of the earth. The family patriarch, head of a household that included his sister-in-law, Katharine Bradley, and his daughters Edith and Amy Cooper, James Cooper departed for Zermatt, Switzerland, on holiday with his younger daughter, leaving the female couple of the family at home alone. And on Midsummer's Day, James Cooper was no more. First suspicions of murder gave way to the belief that he had suffered an accident, and to the painful acceptance of his certain death. In *Works and Days*, Bradley and Cooper describe their trip in haste to Switzerland, the pain of uncertainty and unknowing that went on for months until James Cooper's body was discovered the following October. Bradley and Cooper also describe their marriage ceremony, celebrated privately, the two women alone exchanging rings in a meadow close to where they imagined (incorrectly) James Cooper might have fallen. They marked the moment and the location in *Works and Days* with a clipping of clover, now dried but entirely intact between the notebook's pages (see fig. 8).

Michael and Field use the death of the patriarch to reverse the cycle of love and loss that had been their more common experience. In 1897, though devastated, they filled the gap left by the dead father with a Phoenix-like consolidation of their shared identity: Michael + Field, closer married. They pledged themselves to each other on the site of the father's death. Materially and psychologically, the plot of paternal death enabled a new plot: that of domesticity.

Michael Field decided very early in 1899 that the time had come for them to claim a home of their own. Resources left to them by James Cooper offered a limited but meaningful financial flexibility, just as the engagement of Amy Cooper to James Ryan of Dublin intervened to create new options for our poet. In 1899, Cooper and Bradley engaged fully with the materiality of domestic life. Domestic ideologies were extremely powerful in their time, to be sure. They were familiar to Michael and Field, as they would be to any bourgeois Victorian women, even or perhaps especially those of the "spinster" variety. The difference for Michael Field in 1899 was the need first to "found" a home, which they did through the good offices of their friends, the artists Charles Ricketts and Charles Shannon ("the Artists" to Michael Field's "the Poets," in the nomenclature of their close friendship), and then to make a home.

That home at 1 Paragon, Richmond, on the outskirts of London, was Michael Field's self-declared married home. Their homemaking required meticulous curation, including decisions about construction, paint, carpets, drapes, desks, settees, and, of course, satinwood furniture. In their 1899 narrative, Michael Field replaced the erotics of writing with an erotics of consumption; base materiality helped them anchor a married identity that gave them hope for the future. As December hurtled toward January, however, Cooper and Bradley express ambivalence: worry about leaving their deceased loved ones behind in the nineteenth century; excitement about their intention to embrace futurity. As Berenson told them repeatedly, to be modern is to be "contemporaneous": "The little boil in my nostril is broken, and I walk un-vexed through the palace of my brain. We have not made a friend this year. [. . .] We are too quarrelsome, and this we must set ourselves to overcome in 94" (1893, 105r, KB).

How did it turn out? The most challenging element of biographies, autobiographies, journals, and diaries for me as a reader is the ending: the hope into which they're born must—*must*—give way to the sadness of conclusion.[95] "There is a paradox about biographies," writes Terry Eagleton in a review of two biographies of Thomas Hardy. "We read them to savor the shape and texture of an individual life, yet few literary forms could be more predictable. Everyone has to be born, and almost everyone has to be educated, oppressed by parents, plagued by siblings, and launched into the world; they then enter upon social and sexual relationships of their own, produce children, and finally expire. The structure of biography is biology."[96] Notwithstanding the formal experiments of *Works and Days*, the trope of (auto)biographical conclusion is one form that Michael Field did not or could not or perhaps simply would not break; nor did they repurpose it. However, they traveled to their ending in a characteristically interesting way, planting seeds for renewal even in death.

The last great Victorian plot that Bradley and Cooper tackled in *Works and Days* was the plot of motherhood. The complexity of this plot for these writers is not captured in a year but rather in a decade or more. In fact, motherhood was Michael Field's twentieth-century plot. Their beloved dog, Whym Chow, came to them in January 1898 as a gift from family friends. The poets named the dog in honor of the explorer Edward Whymper, who had been instrumental in the discovery of James Cooper's body in Zermatt, and helpful to the family in the aftermath of Cooper's death. Freud, writing in Austria at exactly this time, would doubtless find it apt that Michael and Field gained their canine "child" from a savior figure who intervened in the fresh gap left by the lost father. And Whym Chow himself? Stroppy, demanding, and occasionally violent—to the detriment of Rudyard Kipling's pet rabbit, violently killed by Chow during the poets' visit to the Kipling family in 1902.

Just as Freud adored his series of Chows as if they were his children, Michael Field adored their "Whymmie," their "Chuckles."[97] He was the ultimate third term that made their dyad a triangle, and that turned 1 Paragon, Richmond from a house into a home. After Chow's death in 1906, the family plot was over, and in exchange, Michael Field entered a new triangle: that of the Father, Son, and Holy Ghost in their conversion to Catholicism in 1907. Cooper died in 1913 and Bradley a few months later, in 1914, when she was dressing to attend morning Mass. When Bradley followed Cooper into Catholicism, they exchanged the marriage bed for the confessional. Vicinus writes: "Bradley and Cooper held onto a belief in their unity of blood (as aunt and niece) and art (as Michael Field). But conversion destroyed their union as a single poet. Although it gave them shared delights in the Church's rituals and commands, the ensuing years did not bring them 'new confidence in each other as poets.'"[98] This was a period of worldly obscurity for Michael Field, with very little contact with friends of the past century. As the excitement of furnishing 1 Paragon in 1899 suggests so vividly, Michael Field craved engagement and choice. They took great pleasure in aesthetic adornment, not in ascetic discipline.

Michael Field's retreat in grief and desolation marks a very sad ending—not to be confused with the provocatively recursive mode of conclusion of *Works and Days*. As Paul Ricoeur writes, "By reading the end into the beginning and the beginning into the end, we learn to read time backward, as the recapitulation of the initial conditions of a course of action in its terminal consequences. In this way, the plot does not merely establish human action 'in' time, it also establishes it in memory."[99] In their adaptation of the diary as their narrative mode, Bradley and Cooper have always represented a psychological desire for plot as the index of forward progress. Yet throughout *Works and Days* they have inhabited a concept of plot that they organized recursively by enfolding pastness and loss into the immediacy of "now." In *Works and Days*, Michael Field teach us what Ricoeur recognizes too: qualities such as temporal nowness, spatial hereness, and even (and perhaps hardest for Michael Field) material thingness are pseudonymous fronts, fake unities, and psychological fictions. Here is Ricoeur again, reading Heidegger: "when we speak of becoming, either in the field of nature or of history, we imply an indefinite extension of duration both backward and forward."[100]

Thus, a coda. Cooper and Bradley left wills. Bradley, as the last to die, used her will to write and unwrite Michael Field's conclusion. The will all but systematically reverses the homemaking narrative of 1899: it scatters the books, papers, and furnishings of 1 Paragon in a fashion reminiscent of their assemblage when the newly married couple took residence: the marriage plot unwound, the film run backward. The world might have been inhospitable to Bradley, Cooper, and Michael Field, but the worldly world is haunted still by their stuff: the very pages of *Works and Days* in the British Library; various gifts from Charles Ricketts in the Ashmolean Museum; other pieces in private households and now who can imagine where? But somewhere. "We cannot always choose the things that will be preserved," writes Abigail Joseph, "just as we cannot always choose the objects of our desire."[101] Michael Field's material legacy remains enmeshed with their brightest literary aspirations; in the words of Deborah Cohen: "Since I can remember, I have wondered about the stories that material things can tell us about the people who bought, sold, prized, and despised them. That way of putting the question is perhaps itself a late Victorian artefact—the legacy of an era in which the boundaries between a person's inner self and her belongings came to seem surprisingly indistinct."[102]

Bradley's will once again pulls the closet door closed and locks Michael Field firmly inside. It describes Cooper as Bradley's niece—formal, public nomenclature elsewhere seen only in the earliest and latest volumes of the diary, during times of significant stress and transition that demanded a metalanguage. Further, throughout both wills, Cooper and Bradley refer to themselves as "spinsters": a reflection of their legal status but alien to the discourse of the fiercely, even compulsively, partnered nature of their intimate lives.[103] Just as the material disaggregation of their household goods unwrites Michael Field's plot of domesticity, the legal language of their last wills and testaments unwrites the marriage plot they lived and often suffered for all the days of their lives. That their last wills conventionalize this most unconventional author seems entirely wrong. It tells us something important about the knowingness that Michael Field brought to the creation of their private world in *Works and Days*.

But—Michael Field are too canny to remain caught in this trap. It all comes back to *Works and Days* itself. At the center of Bradley's will is a series of directions to ensure that this text, this story, this making of women's art and life together, will survive—will somehow make its way to us. Death can take away the satinwood and mirrors that Michael and Field so painstakingly assembled for their married home. Legal language can put conventional dress on their passionately unconventional, lifelong love. Yet the manuscript known as *Works and Days* has traveled across time to loosen the bonds of lived experience for Michael Field, and to reintroduce their voices to yet another century.

There was always something heroic about Michael Field's commitment to speaking from beyond the grave. To participate in the recovery of their voices promises, too, a sense of purpose and union, a share in the romance of their project. Micir offers a helpful reality check to such narcissism in the archivally based scholar: "At its most romantic, this is a vision of the researcher as a kind of hero who swoops in to make sense of the forgotten or otherwise illegible wreckage of the past. It is a vision of the archive that allows us, as scholars, to make sense of nonsense, to build a cohesive story out of forgotten fragments, and to rescue marginalized historical narratives from their obscure and often damaged archives."[104] The would-be heroic researcher—the Whym Chow of special collections, flinging aside his casque—is a mythic creature, skirts concealing a mountain of dependencies, everything from child care to research funding to British Library soup and coffee to the scholarly community to the labor of archivists and librarians in curating, cataloging, and maintaining fragile archival materials. The last punctum? It is, of course, the one in the eye of the reader, its surprise the belief that you have found a window, only to discover a mirror after all.

In 1899, Ricketts wrote to Cooper with advice for decorating Michael Field's home at 1 Paragon: "Here the mirrors should be allowed to *talk*: provide them with subjects of conversation, carnations, roses, anemones, woodbine, rings on hands, fruit in a basket or on a silver dish—Chinese embroideries" (1899, 35v, letter from Ricketts transcribed by EC; emphasis in original). Perhaps after all, the point is to join the conversation, and to listen very hard to what the mirror has to say.

CHAPTER ONE

"A Rebellious Hand"

1867–68 AND 1888–89

[T]he pain and the joy—like weft and woof.

—EDITH COOPER, MAY 31, 1889

WHERE TO BEGIN? How to begin?

For a diary, questions of beginning differ dramatically from those of conclusion. Even in the case of *Works and Days*, this most experimental of narratives concludes with the death of first one author and then the other. The voices silenced, the text ends.

Beginnings are a different story altogether. When we regard the diary as a literary work—not an extempore record of daily life but as a thoughtful experiment expressed in relation to other literary works—the problems of where, when, and how to begin are questions of form. Yet, for an author for whom conventions of time and space seem infinitely elastic, the conditions that incite narrative for Michael Field are clear.

In this chapter, I argue that the grand experiment of *Works and Days* begins not once but twice, and that the situation prompting each of these commencements is at once close to identical to and deeply enmeshed in Victorian novelistic forms. This situation involves three critical elements: reclaiming loss as strength and absence as presence, the power gained from fetishistic objects, and the worldly force, transcendent over time and space, that Michael Field claim for themselves, and for Edith Cooper in particular.

For good reasons, scholars typically credit Michael Fields' 1888–89 notebook as the first formal volume of *Works and Days*. At the same time, though, we regularly acknowledge the existence of an anomalous 1868 volume, written by twenty-two-year-old Katharine Bradley solo, partly in French. The 1868 book documents Bradley's visit to Paris, where she met—very briefly—and flirted with the sculptor and stained-glass artist Alfred Gérente, brother of a friend. Bradley rapidly conceived an infatuation for Gérente, and hoped it was reciprocated. Before her hope could fizzle, or could be realized or dashed, Gérente died, plunging Bradley into full-on mourning for lost love, and inciting her vow—honored in the breach—never to love again. For years in her later life, Bradley observed the solemn anniversary of Gérente's death. Though the 1868 diary differs dramatically from *Works and Days* in most elements, including its format and authorship, the British Library has cataloged this volume along with the rest of the diary: it is tagged as volume 1 of the run of twenty-nine of Michael Field's *Works and Days* in the modern manuscripts collection.[1]

It seems entirely apposite to *Works and Days* that it begins with/in a historical misfire. I suggest that it also begins with a historical misfiling—which is to say that the diary's *first* first volume ended up with the Michael Field materials cataloged at the Bodleian Library rather than those deposited at the British Museum.[2] The Bodleian collection includes a green softcover book of the same size and type as the volume 1 book in the British Library. Dated 1867 and running into 1868, the Bodleian diary, also written by Katharine Bradley alone, inaugurates many of the formative tropes we will see much later in *Works and Days*. Indeed, it does so far more conspicuously than the 1868 book in the British Library, which technically comprises volume 1 of *Works and Days*. I would go so far as to say that reading the 1867 diary first snaps the subsequent twenty-nine volumes to grid. Further, I believe that had the 1867 diary remained alongside the other twenty-nine *Works and Days* volumes, the unified nature of the text, and its standing as a bold, direct, and novelistic literary work, would have been clear much sooner. Once again, we encounter Michael Field disjointed in time and place.

Bradley's 1867 diary narrates the entire arc of her experience from her "first deep sorrow"—learning of her mother's fatal illness—to her mother's death. On the book's final page, "rough hands" bear forth the coffin carrying the mother's corpse. "The funeral was recorded on the last page of Katherine's [*sic*] diary," writes Emma Donoghue. "Was this a coincidence, or was she already expert at shaping the narrative of her life?"[3] This is indeed a narrative carefully shaped by Bradley, and keenly attuned to the conventions of beginning that characterized novelistic narratives of the 1850s and 1860s. Bradley, having cast herself as the young woman left behind, newly orphaned, remains determined to believe that "we were not parting with what we loved": "We came home very quickly, back to the old threshold, and now we have to see what Newton will be without *Grandma!*"[4] (94r; emphasis in original).

The 1867 text ends with a beginning. "Now we have to see": Bradley equates the precipice of new life experience with her fresh womanhood, framing maternal death as the predicate to the life narrative that will follow. Even as she grieves, Bradley sorts through the forms of womanhood that will now make themselves available to her. She pursues three tropes that will chime through the diary's later volumes with similar implications: the temporal and spatial abundance that makes absence presence; the sealing of bonds with material objects, and especially rings; and the conjuring power of Edith Cooper, here a "little grandchild" (4r) or a "chick" (48r), a five-year-old girl who sparkles with prescience, and later a grown woman who in turn summons her own mother's spirit forth from her body and into her arms. The infrastructure that will later sustain "Michael Field" depends on all three of these mythmaking gestures.

On October 26, 1867, Bradley celebrated her twenty-first birthday. Paired with her mother's decline, Bradley's birthday provided an occasion to focus on prospects for her own womanhood. She writes, "Next Sunday I am 21 but not a woman, even after this gt sorrow. I feel a girl through yet, with unconquerable hope and power of re-bound and an elasticity that is amazing to myself" (11r). On the birthday itself, Bradley enumerates the fourteen gifts she received, including "13. A pincushion from Edith" (12r). The most significant of those gifts she lists first: "1. A broach [*sic*] of emeralds and pearls, and emerald ring, from my own dear Mother" (12r).

Bradley frames her mother's presence as absence, as a "gt sorrow." Her representational and emotional strategy marks the transition from girlhood—rebound, elasticity—to womanhood through loss. Coming to her mother's side on her birthday morning, for instance, Bradley writes: "When I went to kiss my Darling, she said, 'I hope *you* have many, many happy birthdays.' But it was very sad to hear the way in which she emphasized the you, as if the future birthdays must be spent alone, and how can they be happy without her" (13v; emphasis in original). The dying woman has the prospective power to launch her daughter's understanding of the form and meaning of her womanly life. "My sorrow has come with my womanhood," Bradley writes. "I look back to the sunny childhood, and untroubled girlhood God has given to me, and feel that I can trust my future womanhood to him" (14r).

And what is that womanhood to be? Bradley offers a self-critique, naming her "ruling sin" of selfishness, and pointing to the educational benefits of her "great sorrow," "which has, thank God[,] taught me to forget myself for one I love. . . . I must also seek to realize that the things that are not seen are eternal; . . . I must learn to be a delightsome and pleasant presence to those around me like a sweet smelling rose, or a goodly fruit" (16v–17r).

The prospect of disciplining herself to resemble a "goodly fruit" signals Bradley's alienation from the same narrative conventions of femininity to which she aspires. These are conventions that Bradley clearly knows well; a source that she cites directly, for example, is the Christmas number of *All the Year Round*, which Sissie Cooper read to the gathered Bradley-Cooper family on the evening of December 9, 1867 (31v). The text of the 1867 Christmas *All the Year Round* was a story by Charles Dickens and Wilkie Collins titled *No Thoroughfare*, which the two authors released as both a novel and a play that month. As it so often does in the work of Dickens and Collins, the novel features interlocked questions of identity and childhood abandonment, all stemming from confusion around one or more dead, missing, and/or abandoning mothers. On the novel's opening page, the narrator focuses on the odd array of clocks keeping "London Time," more or less, on church steeples all across the town:

> What is this clock lower than most of the rest, and nearer to the ear, that lags so far behind tonight as to strike into the vibration alone? This is the clock of the Hospital for Foundling Children. Time was, when the Foundlings were received without question in a cradle at the gate. Time is, when inquiries are made respecting them, and they are taken as by favour from the mothers who relinquish all natural knowledge of them and claim to them evermore.[5]

Among all the clocks in London, one, near to the ear, keeps time poorly and thus sings solo. In the ticktock of "Time was" and "Time is," Dickens and Collins present maternal abandonment, through their abandoned children's lost stories, as a problem of both time and "natural knowledge." Even as time moves forward, the recovery of those lost stories is the motive force of narrative.

Mothers in the novels of both Dickens and Collins wield a formidable shaping power over their children, mirrored in the diary in Bradley's verging-on hagiographic representation of her own mother. As often as not, mothers in Dickens and Collins express their shaping power through child abandonment: when they die or otherwise depart the narrative, they cause boundary problems that provoke the narrative of Bildung and its resolution. The trope was universal enough to attract parody from Oscar

Wilde, a notably sharp-eyed reader of Dickens: recall Lady Bracknell's riposte, "I merely desire information. Until yesterday, I had no idea that there were any families or persons whose origin was a Terminus."[6] The normative condition of personhood in Victorian novels involves maternal loss, and the Cooper family, facing the maternal deathbed, gathers around the hearth for a story about maternal abandonment and its consequences. Bradley's diary functions mise en abyme, as the frame narrative around *Household Words*, with the mother receding ever infinitely from the center of the nested narratives, and the protagonist emerging into the foreground in direct proportion to that loss. Bradley, fresh with young womanhood, emerges as protagonist of her story. When *Works and Days* begins more formally in 1888, it adds a new layer to this pattern, beginning in yet another narrative of maternal loss, and framing the 1867 diary in turn; Michael Field is the protagonist of that story.

Victorian novels offer Bradley abundant examples for imagining her nascent womanhood through the loss of her mother; put differently, her mother's death incites her initiation as a grown subject. Hers is a womanhood that involves some ambivalence about social expectations. Bradley "cannot bear the children [her nieces Edith and Amy] about always" (19v) because she needs time and space to think, yet she also mourns the loss of certain ceremonies of womanhood: choosing a wedding dress and house linen, for example, as her sister and mother had done together. Or, "if ever I know the joys of human love; she will not be there to bless the love. I shall never bring my baby to her—there will be no grandmama for my little ones. And if I am to live all alone always—how shall I bear it—I have seen [illeg.] women bear life pretty cheerfully when they have had kindly loving mothers; but if they have been left all desolate—" (17v–18r). The question broken off here at "desolate," in fact, suggests another path for Bradley, one different from "bear[ing] life pretty cheerfully." Perhaps the release from maternal rituals offers Bradley a new freedom, unanticipated before this point?

From the first, that prospect has to do with freedom from the threat of a certain kind of marriage. "Who can fill up the void in the heart of a desolate mother," Bradley writes. "Who can be a sacred parent to an orphan child" (40r). Bradley shapes her mother as a soulmate, and her imminent loss as a form of widowhood for the daughter left behind. "I shall not be first with any one on earth now. Sis will have her husband and the children before me, and with her I was the one great thought. She lived to me" (80r). Only rather grudgingly does Bradley grant a distinction between filial and matrimonial love: "[T]here are so few people with fleshy hearts together. . . . So rare do these meet, that the disappointed soul, having tried and failed, must still try again, seeking rest and finding none. So the endless misalliances and miseries that desolate married life" (40r–40v). Courtships are typically disastrous for a woman who finds she must "mould her whole nature" to her husband's. Bradley knows that if she had been in love when very young, she, too, would have "married blindly with no fore-thought but in [illeg.] love" (40v).

What social and erotic possibilities might be left for an intelligent young woman for whom the aspiration to life as a "goodly fruit" holds few charms? "O it is so sweet to have her with us," Bradley writes shortly before Christmas. "Can we think of what the earth would be without the sunlight, or the night without the stars, the trees without their foliage, and the rose without thorns, the bird without its song, the waters without their flow; what anything wd. be without fragrance music and lustre" (32r). I suggest that the refrain "without" becomes an axle of identity for Bradley here, and well into the future—that loss, which precipitates the looming presence of absence, becomes a conditioning aspect of womanhood for her. Indeed, Bradley presents melancholy as a general condition of female subjectivity. For example, on the day after Emma Harris's birthday, Bradley frames her own melancholy through the vehicle of her mother's: "It is sad to see her look out on the sunshine so longingly. It must have been terrible for her to look back yesterday, on her early motherhood, when she was so young and fair, and had a child so beautiful, when my father used to come and look at them both, till the tears came into his eyes. Now her husband has gone and she is stricken: and the terror of it is more than it is well for us to think of" (47v). Time itself is the vehicle for maternal melancholy.

The challenge, then, is to make melancholia powerful, to reclaim absence on behalf of presence. Here and elsewhere, Bradley meets that challenge through the relentless reclaiming of the dead as undead, just as Bram Stoker did in *Dracula*, his contemporaneous novel also composed in and as a sequence of diaries. The gifts awaiting Bradley on her twenty-first birthday morning thus become fetishes ready to transport her directly to the moment and the person, present tense. Her mother gave her the emerald brooch and ring: "She put the ring on my finger. I said to her 'Do you know what the emerald means, and why it was chosen. She said no. I said, It means 'Faithfulness': and she replied that it was emblematic on both sides" (13v). Even in the midst of moving the family from one home to another, Bradley recognizes that her mother's "touch is enough to make anything sacred to us; a withered rose-leaf even: the garments that she stitches, the books she reads, the trees she loves are all precious"

(5v–6r). So too the knitting-wools and doll decorations: "Sissie spoke at tea-time of her carafe—the first thing she bought for housekeeping and Mama laughed when she brought it home. I thought of how she had been with Sissie, throughout her engagement, aiding her in all the sewing for the new house, and being ever by her side, when she was choosing her wedding dresses and house linen" (17v). And the new dresses, which even in their loveliness signal the penumbra of grief: "[W]e have just been trying on our new dresses—the two loveliest we have ever had. My delicate fawn with the blue trimming is beautiful . . . our Darling beamed at us with her warm Mother eyes. If I cannot wear my dress *for her*, I will lay it reverently aside in a drawer, and should I ever be married I will wear it on my wedding day" (71v; emphasis in original).

Similarly, the mother's corpse, the locks of hair gathered for mourning jewelry, the flowers that bedeck her corpse in her coffin, and even the coffin itself, with its brass plate that triumphantly heralds the same text as the marble tablet Jane Eyre erected for Helen Burns forty years before—"Resurgam"—all reroute affect for Bradley from the material to a much more powerful realm, the psychological.[7] Quotidian household items shine with powerful associations that create immanence out of loss: "Resurgam." To what future, then, might Bradley aspire as a newly motherless child? And as a newly motherless woman fully empowered by her loss to chart a new course? Standing at her mother's deathbed, Bradley cried that she was "motherless," causing her sister Sissie to enfold her in her arms and promise to be her mother in deed if not in word from this day forward. Yet "motherless" has the force of psychic power for Bradley: "I had no fear—I was able to say my heart is not troubled, nor afraid. A deep peace washed on my heart. I felt that that coffin lid did not shut away from me my mother. *She was not there*" (89v; emphasis in original).

As early as this first diary, we find Bradley taking herself seriously as a poet, though one of an unusual stripe: "I think the difference between me and a true poet is this: a true poet gives out his poetry, it is of him, as much as the fragrance is of the flower; I *suck* a bit of sweetness here and there, and make honey of it, bee-fashion" (53r; emphasis in original). Unlike her reflections here on heterosexual marriage and motherhood, this statement sounds strikingly like the Bradley we will meet in the 1890s—and the Bradley of *Wild Honey from Various Thyme* (1908), the poet for whom metaphors of sweetness have more to do with Christina Rossetti ("She clipp'd a precious golden lock, / She dropp'd a tear more rare than pearl, / Then suck'd their fruit globes fair or red: / Sweeter than honey from the rock") than with Matthew Arnold (culture, beauty, intelligence).[8]

This early diary of 1868 deftly establishes the conditions necessary to conjure Michael Field two decades hence. Little Edith Cooper is everywhere in this book, already standing apart from her younger sister Amy—poor Amy, already ordinary—with her precocity. "Edith told me the other day she loved everyone in the world. I verily believe the child has no unkind or disagreeable feeling connected with any living soul" (26r). "Edith is quiet and reverent," in contrast to Amy, the livelier and more mischievous of the two, the Dora to Edith's Agnes.[9] The girls' dying grandmother "heard the children's voices last night and had them called up. She was pleased to look on Amy, but the sight of Edith seemed to bring back all her old tone and look and manner" (78v). Immediately following her mother's death, Bradley emphasizes the power of her own selection in the realignment of the family chessboard: "I went to the poor little children, and found them in the garden with white blurred faces. I knew how she would have grieved to see them so; and I folded her precious grandchildren close to my heart. Poor Amy, I think, felt sadly neglected, and when I reminded Edith that Grandma had been pleased to hear her sing, she said, 'And I sang too.' I promised Edie to be . . . what Grandma had been to her, and always to love her dearly. And Amy said, 'And you will love me dearly too?'" (84v–85r).

Even as early as 1868, we find Bradley observing conventions of femininity warily, and understanding them well enough to manipulate them. The answer to the question of the social and erotic—and artistic—possibilities that lay ahead for the newly motherless Bradley stands right before her, a quiet girl of five. Bradley turns her newly motherless status inside out—her mother is not gone; she is right here, and far more present than she would be if she were, well, present—in order to fashion a new social identity out of the woolens, rings, pincushions, orts, and fragments that signal domestic order, even as they mean something much more vast and emotional to the living.

Bradley continues to keep a diary after her mother's death; the next volume, 1868–69, which the British Library counts as the first of *Works and Days*, picks up continuously from its companion in the Bodleian. The volume following that one—volume 2 in the British Library—comes a full twenty years later, beginning in April 1888 and concluding in December 1889.[10] The volume that begins in April 1888 formally initiates the text we will know as *Works and Days*, which takes up its annual cadence on January 1, 1890. In the British Library's volume 2, the origin is once again a terminus: among the deaths of Matthew Arnold and Robert Browning, it tracks the decline and death of "Sissie" Cooper. Sissie was Emma Bradley Cooper, Edith Cooper's mother and Katharine Bradley's sister. In 1867,

Sissie read the classic missing-mother story by Collins and Dickens, *No Thoroughfare*, to the gathered family during Christmas. She held Bradley at their dead mother's bedside, and she pledged to be a mother to Bradley for all time. The narrative arc of 1888–89 is identical to the arc of 1867–68: in each of its two beginnings, *Works and Days* begins not with but in the death of the mother.

On May 31, 1888, on the back of page 6 of Katharine Bradley's diary, we encounter Edith Cooper's hand for the first time: she describes a conventional landscape, using the bottom third of an otherwise blank page. Shortly afterward, on the back of page 8, we encounter Cooper again. This time, she writes in response to an entry that Bradley has written on the facing page 9. Cooper begins: "*This has waked my muse. She is with me" (1888–89, 8v, EC). Here is our first instance of Cooper as Bradley's reader, and vice versa. And of narrative dialogue—even flirtation—resulting from the practice of reciprocal reading, the muse as an awakened female presence. On June 13, on the diary's page 9, Cooper writes her first full entry, an account of the poets' visit to an exhibition at the Burlington Art Club. From here, the diary proceeds almost as if the poets were using it as a workbook: it features multiple drafts of poems in both hands, lines crossed out and written over. In contrast, Cooper claims the January 1, 1889, entry, beginning the new year in her own voice, though deep in an ongoing book. What had begun as Bradley's diary proceeds in workbook mode for drafts and occasional set pieces written by both women.

Only—*only*—with the "Beloved Mother-One's" announcement of her imminent death do the two poets begin to write this diary in the model that they will pursue until their own deaths, featuring thoughtful narrative explorations of their respective and conjoined psychological landscapes. For the first time, and also again, the death of the mother instigates the grand experiment of *Works and Days*. Like Victorian novelists before them, Michael Field fill the space vacated by a mother or mother figure with private and professional narratives that depend on maternal absence for their realization. In the truly experimental twist of this unique text, the mother creates the space to hold the distinctive intimacies of the Michael Field "voice": speaking quite literally, at the level of page and pen, her death initiates Michael Field in narrative.[11] The subsequent death of Robert Browning—figured by turns as father and as lover—seals this moment's shape for them, and also seals the text's narrative form and the narrators' dual voices, entwined yet distinctive.

Michael Fields' formal concerns are also thematic concerns. Michael Field are always true to form: the mechanics—and the challenges—of starting and stopping, beginning and ending, identities joined and individual, preoccupy them throughout this volume. If, for example, the death of the mother is a device used in novels throughout the period to catapult Victorian children into the fray of maturity and marriage, Michael Fields' version of this experience launches two already-coupled adult women toward a new version of their identity that feels less like launching than like a deepening of the status quo. This is a status quo that they love, and that holds them hostage. If the circadian rhythm of their diary typically awakens on January 1 and sleeps on December 31, then 1889 gets a running start in April 1888, commences formally in medias res, and realizes the starting trope of maternal death, not at the volume's beginning but a full seventeen months into what is typically a twelve-month narrative cycle, in August 1889. There are more narrative interpellations to come.

Their grief created the conditions for Michael Field to frame their artistic ambition and its meaning. Maternal loss provided Michael Field a vocabulary for understanding the meaning of their authorship—and specifically the meaning of their voices as women writers. In this volume of *Works and Days*, Bradley and Cooper negotiate new psychological, social, and literary ways of being. Read as a trope rather than as a biographical fact, the dead mother frames Michael Fields' negotiation in familiar terms: it creates the mythologized backdrop of a maternal ideal, a force of female stability in death that liberates Bradley and Cooper to explore other modes of female identity in life.

Their explorations disrupt the codes of Victorian femininity as soon as they invoke them. Yes, the death of the mother is critically important for their emergent identities, both independently as Cooper and Bradley and as the "male" writer Michael Field. But these women are twenty-seven and forty-two years old, respectively, and in clear contrast to their counterparts in countless near-contemporary dead-mother plots, they can hardly be said to be beginning the world. Indeed, 1889 is for Bradley and Cooper about contemplating maturity rather than youth.

Related, it is also a year to contemplate the death of the poet—in the here and now, male poets such as Matthew Arnold and Robert Browning, and one day also a "male" poet, Michael Field. Michael Field come hard up against the deaths of beloved figures who wield formidable artistic and social power over them. The poets refuse their losses by claiming the omnipresence in life of their beloved dead, their immanence evoked in poetry and in flowers, and in the brimming over of feeling that the women constitute together.[12] Poetic knowledge transcends the empirical in a world where feeling and specifically passionate love outlive death itself.

On the first page of *Works and Days*, volume 2, Bradley writes: "On Sunday, April 15th [1888,] Matthew Arnold died. We heard of his passing from us on Tuesday morning. On Tuesday afternoon I went alone to Lake Cottage and read some of his poems in the garden, and felt the blessedness of his having entered into the impersonal life" (1888–89, 1r, KB). Shortly after, Bradley quotes from a letter she had sent to Robert Browning: "Still it is getting lonely singing in England now that the voices of Rossetti and Matthew Arnold are hushed and we beg that you will stay with us and help us through the harsh draughty bit of century remaining to us" (1888–89, 3r, KB).

Alas, that was not to be. As Arnold's death begins the volume, Browning's ends it. This time, in Cooper's handwriting, peeking out from under a newspaper clipping reporting from Rome on the state of Browning's poor health:

> *December 12.*
>
> Louie [Ellis] has just sent us this news of our Poet's illness. Sim is gone through the dark with letters and a telegram. Is this year going to bereave us again—yet again, O God? . . . He said of our Song-book, "Try me!" Shall we never hear the caressing voice give judgment and praise? It will half-kill our poetry, and make all the deep parts of our love memorial, wh: means that the value of life strikes the ground and is over (at least as the young estimate it). His kiss comes to my lips again, as I think of him—that seal of his comprehension of one's womanhood—flawless in stamp, tender with knowledge—warm, warm as all action is that is divine and reverent. (1888–89, 119v, EC)

In death, Arnold and Browning flank this volume like bookends, the passing of Arnold gaining meaning for the bereaved poet in communion with Browning. The death of Browning strikes Cooper doubly, both as a poet and as a woman. To "make all the deep parts of our love memorial" suggests the exchange of something vibrant and fierce—"deep"—for a cold tombstone. It is over. Warm lips that kiss. Browning's comprehension of Cooper's womanhood. Tenderness, warmth, and depth. Those feelings, and their poetry: gone, at least in the eyes of the young.

It is hard to look past the erotic language Cooper used to describe her bereavement. Indeed, Browning was always an erotic figure for Cooper, if less so for Bradley: "the Old" was one of the third terms they used to animate their own coupledom through triangulation. The women craved—and in Browning found, for a time—male approval of their standing as a poet and as Michael Field.[13] Browning is as much a surrogate father as he is a surrogate lover.

But there is a twist here as well. In their vision of "Browning," Michael Field conjures himself/herselves as the third term that makes Robert Browning's marriage to Elizabeth Barrett a triangle as well. Anticipating news of Browning's death, Cooper recognizes in his passing the triumph of the married bond:

> *Prospice!* He is no longer nearing the place—he is there—It makes me stiff—till I think of the beyond and her breast, that soul of his soul. She was a woman, a poet. His coming will be all gain to her—to him!—can I wish that he should die, as I did for my Darling's blessedness? Perhaps there is a remote strength in me that could say *yes*—but it is very far away among the hills. He is so great I am tearless as I write of him—the moment I slip back into myself my tears burn. (1888–89, 119v–121r, EC; emphasis in original)

Cooper frames Browning's death in his own words. In the aftermath of his wife's death, Browning embraced the prospect of death, and recast loss as reunion, in the 1864 poem "Prospice": "Then a light, then thy breast, / O thou soul of my soul! I shall clasp thee again, / And with God be the rest." The married afterlife of the Brownings has Robert roosting at the bosom of his beloved, body to body, soul to soul, poet to poet. Elizabeth Barrett Browning was the apex of desire for Browning. She was a woman, a poet, while Michael Field was . . . a women? A man? "How do I love thee? Let me count the ways."

Elizabeth Barrett Browning was a figure of fascination and ambivalence for Cooper and Bradley, both as a woman and as a poet. In March 1889, nine months before Browning's death, Bradley was gossiping about him with her friend, the feminist intellectual Anna Swanwick.[14] Bradley reports that

> [Browning] spoke to Miss Swanwick of the sonnets from the Portugese [*sic*]. It seems to me, if I had written such sonnets, they w[oul]d have burnt through my desk, she said. But the poets had been wedded two years before Elizabeth Barrett placed them in her husband's hands. Then, had he consulted his own feelings, he would have kept them sacred from the light; but he remembered he was the guardian of his wife's genius, and bade her publish them. Choosing this sublime old maid for this deep confidence of his nuptial life is a sign of the Old Gentleman's fine faculty for selection—the fool, or insensitive person never looks where he is talking. (1888–89, 59r–59v, KB)

I am not sure Browning would have been pleased to imagine the "sublime old maid" retailing in the intimate implications of his marriage bed—nor to imagine the erotic details of EBB's sonnets burning through Miss Swanwick's desk in their heat and passion. Yet Michael Field are entirely prepared to understand the intimacy of nuptial poems; in 1889, for example, Michael Field published the Sapphic marriage poem, "Oh, not the honey, nor the bee!":

Honey nor bee! The tingling quest
Must that too be denied?
Deep in thy bosom I would rest,
O golden blossom wide!
O poppy wreath, O violet-crown,
I fling your fiery circlets down;
The joys o'er which bees murmur deep
Your Sappho's senses may not steep. (ll. 9–16)

Michael Field are clearly writers well practiced in poetic intimacy; they figure eroticism not as utilitarian but as a function of pleasure. Browning also figured poetic enmeshment in marriage and, like Browning, Michael Field were prepared to manage the politics of publication. Notwithstanding Browning's reported impulse to protect his heart and bedroom, he evidently realized that the better part of chivalry is regard for genius. So, publish EBB did.

As desirable as Browning was to the poets, he was also an ambivalent figure to them. Cooper speaks of him in erotic terms, but the painful awareness that his death will "half-kill" Michael Field's poetry is real. This is both psychological and practical. On the side of psychology, Michael Field sought powerful inspiration from many sources: from one another, from art, from flowers and rich scents. "The Old Gentleman" was one of those sources; again, Cooper: "He is so great—I am tearless as I write of him—the moment I slip back into myself my tears burn." Browning transports her somewhere beyond fear, beyond even her weeping, burning body, beyond the hot sonnets scorching a hole in the desk. But there is no prospect of real intimacy with Browning; he remains a somewhat remote figure, kind but as yet new and unproven to Michael Field.

And the practical. Browning was Michael Field's supporter and proponent. Yet he also exposed the secret behind the pseudonym and quite potentially caused Michael Field serious professional damage. Just as he placed poetic genius ahead of his own marital privacy, Browning pulled back the curtain that hid not a talented young man but a pair of bourgeois "spinsters." As Emma Donoghue reports, Cooper let him in on the secret when she responded to a query from Browning about the identity of "Michael Field": "My Aunt and I work together after the fashion of Beaumont and Fletcher. . . . She has lived with me, taught me, encouraged me and joined me to her poetic life. . . . This happy union of two in work and aspiration is sheltered and expressed by 'Michael Field.' Please regard him as the author."[15] Uniquely equipped with this information, Browning broke the confidence, revealing both the fact of Cooper and Bradley's collaboration and the authors' gender. On Wednesday, May 9, 1888, Bradley reports Michael Field's attendance at Browning's home, full of flowers:

> Mr Browning came in greeting us as his "two dear, Greek women." He opened . . . a faunt of kisses. Ardently then and afterwards he spoke of the Sapphics, expressing especial interest in *Tiresias* wh. he had once himself thought of treating. When I remarked I wished he had treated it—he said "No: it ought to be treated by a woman.["] He said to Edith he liked the 2nd series of poems even better than the first, and prophesied they would make their mark. But he refuses to write a preface. We must remember we are Michael Field. Again he said: *wait fifty years*. (1888–89, 4r–5r, KB; emphasis in original)

Browning exposed Cooper and Bradley to public scrutiny, refused to write a preface to their new book, and foretold a long, cold half century before Michael Field would find his public. To Browning, Michael Field were doubly displaced in time, ancient Greeks arriving anachronistically in the fin de siècle, half a century premature.

Then Browning died. For Michael Field, there was expediency to Browning's death: it was much easier for the poets to project positive feelings, desires, and attributions into the void left by Browning's absence than it would have been to deal with their ambivalence about Browning alive. On the eve of his funeral at Westminster Abbey, Bradley writes, "We possess a relation with the dead, a vital, influencing relation. The morrow of the death of a great friend one rises impoverished one feels and dwindled in the eye of the world; *in oneself it is as if a great fortune had come to one*. How much more than bequest is this acquisition. One cannot open one's being to such riches—'Such knowledge is high, one cannot attain it'" (1888–89, 124v, KB; emphasis in original). In his postmortem persona, "the Old" was Michael Field's for life: "I love him as I love my Mother," wrote Cooper (1888–89, 121v, EC).

By this point in late December 1889, Cooper's mother had been dead for several months. So yes, indeed, she loves Browning just as she loves her mother: each death marks the transubstantiation of a powerful figure into an ideal. The Old and the Beloved Mother-One die to become tropes, figures that Bradley and Cooper use to stabilize their perspectives and identities, both personally and artistically. Their deaths were psychologically functional, if only to the narrative progress of *Works and Days* at this early moment in the text's establishment.

Though Emma "Sissie" Bradley Cooper died on August 20, 1889, when the 1889 volume of *Works and Days* was an epic seventeen months along, her passing was anticipated from an early point. In perfect alignment with the introspective mode that Michael Field would pursue in *Works and Days* for decades to come, death is a fact of the immediate present. Yet Sissie's death is one of the few episodes in *Works and Days* where the perspectives of Michael and Field diverge as a matter of structural difference. Though they both refer to Sissie as "the Beloved Mother-One," she was mother only to Edith Cooper. She was Katharine Bradley's sister. The distinction is important in several ways. They attempt to find identical meaning in Sissie's passing, but Bradley and Cooper have different viewpoints. Recall that Sissie is the only person who formally bears both poets' surnames: Bradley, Cooper. In this and in other ways, she belongs to both Katharine and Edith, but differently. Her passing consolidates aspects of the poets' relationship, even as it changes things forever; Vadillo views the Beloved Mother-One as the omphalos of Michael Field, the mark of maternal presence and absence.[16]

Bradley introduces the topic of Sissie's imminent death obliquely, as "it," on May 20, 1889, parallel to her own mother's death sentence in 1867. "We were alone," she wrote in 1889, "—we spoke of it. She feels with every morning's light she is ready to go. When she spoke of the earthly side of it and of burial—I begged her to think of providence and the joy she was going to—and she said she did—'of God, and Christ—and my father, and the Dawsons.' We were *very* close. I have been walking twice in the straight top walk—and I shall never forget the kind, almost Motherly look" (1888–89, 67r, KB; emphasis in original). "We were alone—we spoke of it." The unnamable, unthinkable looming immanence of death in life. Bradley reports her sister's material concerns, "the earthly side of it and of burial," and also her own eagerness to shift the conversation to the immaterial or perhaps the postmaterial, to a joyous and sociable afterlife crowded with long-lost friends and family, and also deities. Note that the dying woman wants to focus on the clay: the material disposition of the body, "soaked and tossed by the pitiless sea" of cancer (1888–89, 40r, EC). But her sister hurries the conversation to the spiritual, reframing the afterlife as a bourgeois drawing room. Bradley tells this as a story of intimacy valued and sealed by "the kind, almost Motherly look" from older sister to younger.

On the heels of the introduction of Emma's deathbed narrative come two developments, one for Michael Field together and the other for Katharine Bradley alone. May 1889 witnessed the arrival of Michael Fields' new book, *Long Ago*: "*God be praised for this accomplishing*," wrote Bradley to mark the moment, in red ink (1888–89, 68r, KB; emphasis in original). The development for Katharine, at her only sibling's deathbed, is a new consciousness of aging: "Mid-age." Try though Bradley must, this is a concern of the flesh. She writes:

> Our first cause of distress springs from a deterioration perceptible in all we are or effect. To one with a poignant sense of beauty the change in a flower a few hours after it has been gathered is more painful than its withering or decay. The body has outlived its ideal moment; coarser materials are being substituted for the delicately woven textures of youth. We walk denuded and impaired. Self-love, it is decreed, henceforth can have no part in our love of beauty. We lose our sense of being welcome in the world. A quality has fallen from our actions, our gestures, our speech—that splendour from the gods that made Laertes lustrous and divine in the eyes of ~~Achilles~~ ^Ulysses^ Odysseus—we are no longer young.
>
> O deep allure of youth! (1888–89, 68r–69r, KB)

Perhaps watching the decay of her sister toward death strikes a chord of identification, making Bradley aware of her body's "deterioration." The body is no longer an ideal; it comprises "coarser materials." No longer aglow with youth, the poets cannot count their own self-regard as part of their aesthetic appreciation of beauty. Michael Field at middle age are not part of the economy that would make them "welcome in the world"; they are undesirable, or so they fear, and undesired. Youth has become another melancholic chronotope for Bradley: though she still feels it, she possesses it no longer. In the midst of the narrative contemplation of beginning looms the awareness of the end, the finitude, by definition, of works and days.

Cooper's response to her mother's decline is notably different, though no less anguished. Like Bradley, she speaks of the news first obliquely: "Mother came to be nursed in our bedroom after quiet, terrible talk with me alone" (1888–89, 67v, EC). If Emma's illness transfixes Bradley on the material body, it displaces Cooper to the body's spiritual ascent. Later in May, for example, Cooper reads to her mother and notes, again in words that stand all but alone on the page: "She lay beatified, her snow-hair round her as white as the hair in Revelation—holy, and spiritual" (1888–89, 72v, EC). For Cooper, the experience of her mother's deathbed is transcendent in its "holy, and spiritual" qualities. Alone one evening, Edith said to Sissie: "'It is beautiful to me to think that some of the life you gave me is gone out into the world.' After a long pause she breathed—'And is giving joy'—Then after a longer pause 'Let the stream run pure . . . Your highest and best.' 'It shall: God and you helping me'" (1888–89, 73r, EC).

While Bradley feels belated and bereft in this period, Cooper grows aspirational. She foresees in her mother a power akin to God's, to help her to achieve her "highest and best." Cooper imagines a worldly future for herself, whereas Bradley does not. Yet, "She has been a part of all the loveliness of the world we have loved," Cooper wrote on May 30, leaving tearstains on the page of *Works and Days*. And the very next day, Michael Field received letters from "our beloved 'Old' and 'Sarianna' about our sorrow and *Long Ago* (ah, they are bound together . . . the pain and the joy—like weft and woof)" (1888–89, 74r, EC). Here Browning and his sister and companion, Sarianna, struck twin chimes of sympathy and praise, again juxtaposing for Michael Field personal strife and worldly acclaim. Pain and joy. Weft and woof.

Shortly afterward, Sissie's decline seemed to accelerate. On June 1, Cooper reported that her mother had a "terrible heart-attack at three in the dawn." The family gathered round:

> Through the open window the cuckoo's roving voice wandered to us—far away we heard the coo of a wood-pigeon; the world looked beautiful through the flicker of aspens; the day was under promise to come on the enlighted horizon; within all was grave and quiet. Slowly over the face of our Beloved came a darkening, like the twilight on mountains, recluse, august, passionless . . . —[t]he head lowered with the descent of the shadows—the eyes were half-put to rest. Of a sudden the pulse leapt again, and she was given back to Life. She still thought the end was near, and one by one she blessed us, speaking the *God bless you* with a kind of pressure in the voice. A cock crew its lusty signal to daylight; there was a stir of workmen's feet—she said "Man goeth forth to his labour"—it seemed like the quiet comment of a Spirit from the midst of the Rest that Remaineth. (1888–89, 74r–74v, EC; emphasis in original)

Nature asserts her powers in this scene, window open to birdsong, the horizon brightening in contrast with the gravity of the deathbed. As dawn broke, Emma Bradley Cooper darkened "like the twilight on mountains," becoming as one with the natural world.

Then—"Of a sudden the pulse leapt again, and she was given back to Life." Birdsong gives way to the crow of the rooster, and workmen's boots break the spell. The world intrudes. Sissie's voice "seemed like the quiet comment of a Spirit from the midst of the Rest that Remaineth." The dead speak. *Resurgam.*

Sissie was not dead. "This was an ideal death-bed," Cooper wrote after the fact, "—simple and noble. God seemed to be working like an artist—with the divine choiceness of consummation: The issue was a cruel irony—" (1888–89, 74v, EC).

"The issue was a cruel irony." Even in grief, Cooper recognizes the misfire of an ideal death scene, pathetic fallacy and all. On the next page of *Works and Days*, Cooper pressed a flower blossom that remains there to this day, with a quotation from John 14, "Let not your heart be troubled" (1888–89, 75r, EC). Below the blossom, Cooper recalls reading to her mother the "Death Carol of Walt Whitman," and the dying woman's reply: "That is scripture too."[17]

Yet I am reminded of Oscar Wilde's devastating puncturing of sentimentality in Dickens: "One must have a heart of stone to read the death of little Nell without laughing."[18] Like Wilde, Cooper knows a deathbed scene when she sees one that ticks all the boxes. And but for the "cruel irony" that it failed to produce a corpse, she found a great one here, the pathos of nature and events aligned almost—but not quite—precisely. Again, we find Bradley and Cooper exquisitely attuned to the nuances of Victorian narrative, particularly as they involved women and the possibilities that may or may not exist for women's lives. Michael and Field find a way to fuse pain and joy, weft and woof, to create prospective artistic energy from the death of the mother.[19] The strategy emerges opportunistically, not only from the story they tell but from the techniques they use to tell that story; not only the *what* but the *how*.

Twelve days after the near miss narrated above, Cooper reports that Michael Field has received a letter from George Meredith containing praise for their new volume of poems, *Long Ago*, praise that has given the poets "intense pleasure."[20] "This morning," she continued, "when we read it to mother, her face went tremulous and her eyes ^were^ larger and pale with the joy. She said 'Is not that something for a mother and sister to hear!' and added 'It must be read to me every day ~~[illeg.]~~ ^while^ I live.' When I said 'now you must go to sleep' she broke into laughter with the sound of tears in it" (1888–89, 77v, EC). From Sissie's perspective, the poets' professional acclaim helps her to frame and spin the unconventional bond between her daughter and her sister. She bestows her maternal and sororal blessing on that bond, providing Michael Field a way to exist within a family that will soon realign absent her softening, mediating influence. In her dying, the Beloved Mother-One erects poetry as a shield to protect and validate her sister and her daughter, as a couple and as a poet, against paternal judgment.

From this point forward, the poets' daily talks and readings with the invalid "mother and sister" include tantalizing bits of news about their work in progress—the verse drama *Carloman*, in particular—and word of *Long Ago* as it makes its way in the world. Their work, and even more importantly their standing as a poet, emerge as a feature of the death narrative. Michael Field replace mortality with realized poetic ambition. On June 20, Bradley wrote, "A divine day! Word came in the morning of the last six copies of *Long Ago* being bought . . . Amy broke the news [to her dying mother]." Bradley continues:

> When we went up there was that warmth in her eyes more perilous than tears . . . She said a little later, with faltering voice—"I call this my Indian summer." And she has bent towards me quite close with divine whisperings from time to time till my heart is filled with honeyed sorrow[.] . . . And the blanched face lies still as a tomb, on which the sunlight is playing. She has parted from us, and returns: we grow together: the threads of our lives re-mingle—how can we part? (1888–89, 80r, KB)

Sissie Cooper brims with joy at the news of Michael Field's professional triumph, her "Indian summer" consecrating the moment with a warmth that gives way to a tomb-like pallor. She comes and she goes, and "We grow together—two threads of our lives re-mingle—how can we part?" We have seen Bradley and Cooper consciously become one in Michael Field. We have seen them attach themselves as a pair to a third figure such as Robert Browning for the purpose of adding plot to their lives. The "we" in Bradley's entry here is ambiguous, and effective at that: we have Bradley, Cooper, and Bradley Cooper mingling and re-mingling. Preparing to part and refusing to part at the same time.

Michael Field must also account for Amy, Cooper's younger sister who brought the news of *Long Ago* to the invalid; this episode represents maternal loss for Amy too. From a narrative perspective, Amy is a hair in the soup of *Works and Days*. So pitifully aware of her also-ran standing as far back as her aunt's 1867–68 diary, Amy also serves as an awkward reminder of the incestuous nature of Michael Field's marriage: she is Bradley's other, less-beloved niece. In yet another sign of the narrative's formal and psychological fragmentation, Amy is put to the task of writing some of the diary entries during the time of Emma Cooper's protracted decline. Very shortly following Bradley's mournful statement that "We grow together: two threads of our lives re-mingle," Amy's hand—mercifully legible—appears on the pages of *Works and Days*: "One morning early in June *she* heard the cuckoo. He sang it seemed all night long, but she had not heard him till then—I softly stole to the book-case to read to her, 'Oh, blithe new-comer.' Another morning about the same time I read the prayers from the 'Visitation of the sick,' quite early, about four o'clock" (1888–89, 81r, Amy Katharine Cooper; emphasis in original).

Is the "I" in this entry Amy herself? Or Amy reporting on, or even taking dictation from, her aunt or her sister? If Amy herself, this is a stunning moment of conventionality for *Works and Days*, taking it from incestuous lesbian poet marriage plot to an ordinary family document of a loved one's final days. On the other hand, if Amy is operating here as secretary or amanuensis, we face questions about the stability of the "I" offered by her hand, and even about the interchangeability of sisters, nieces.

Amy's emergence highlights the various modes of interpellation that effectively undo the death of the mother in *Works and Days*, making this transformative event so elusive that it looms both everywhere and nowhere. Michael Field further interject themselves into chronotopic disarray. In their July visits to the Brownings, they are transported from the seclusion of the countryside into the thick of literary action: "Suddenly from being shut away in our dull bit of Surrey we felt ourselves removed to the white central point of London life—to the mid-edge of the intensest passion there" (1888–89, 86r, KB). Home is inhospitable for Michael Field under the circumstances; they complain to Robert and Sarianna Browning about the working conditions in their claustrophobic home in darkest Surrey. Cooper reports: "Sim spoke of our tiny house and its turmoils of common sounds—how we thought of him in his great still study. [Browning] said ^answers^ solemnly that he had never been able to say he could have done better if he had had the opportunity—throughout life he has been blessed with good conditions for work" (1888–89, 93v, EC).

Around the edges of their bereavement, Cooper and Bradley long for more: more privacy, more quiet, more space to work, more excitement in the give-and-take of literary London. At the same time, the narrative flow of *Works and Days* staggers, breaking down like Clarissa's Mad Papers. In an entry dated before her mother's death, Cooper backdates again, reporting, "I gave these words in the letter I sent to Mr Browning the morn after her death" (1888–89, 94v, EC). On the diary's page 94r, Bradley starts a sentence that breaks off, interrupted by a narrative in Cooper's hand,

and takes up again two times over with a narrative not about death but about writing poems for/to Browning. Someone has pressed a trio of dried husks, fawn colored with brown speckles, between the pages.

As Sissie Cooper transitions toward her death for a second time, she transubstantiates once again, not into nature but into art. Her daughter Edith writes on August 19:

> The great Sculptor Death has been firming the lids and brow and nostrils—he takes each ~~[illeg.]~~ beauty of form and solemnizes it in his great art. The eyes will never open full again—the ~~[illeg.]~~ ^patient^ necessity of being closed forever is beginning to press on them. The noble brows bend so dark with another darkness under them—the hollowed gloom that ~~[illeg.]~~ repeats their lovely curves—the forehead is peerless and sacred—~~it is~~ not thought but ^its^ sollution ~~that~~ lies between temple and temple. (1888–89, 97r, EC)

Elizabeth Meadows argues: "Cooper's narrative makes a process of dying into a process of aesthetic production, in which the final product, the corpse, is a perfect aesthetic form."[21] For Michael Field, the great Sculptor is the most formidable actor of all. The poets prepare for Mother's last living appearance in *Works and Days*. The diary recycles key passages from a letter Cooper wrote close to contemporaneously to Browning:

> We got her out of her chair on to the Ilkley Couch . . . by the side of the bed.[22] Sim and I sat by her wiping the dear lips and giving her drops of nourishment. Once I bent over her and said "The *dear* Mother-One." Out of the obliterate weakness on the beloved face came a smile as if I had launched the deep joy of her being—once again I said *Mother*, and again came the smile, the unutterable acceptance of the sweet word in the midst of all of the strangeness of herself. I just caught a *God bless you*, the last benediction she spoke. . . .
>
> She wanted my hand. I pressed the loved fingers fearlessly that the passion of my love might be with her a long way ~~into the~~ ^on the^ ~~[d-illeg.]~~ ^[illeg.]^ ^tract^ of unconsciousness. When Father said *my Queen* she looked at him with the most confidingly radiant smile. And once when he asked one of us ~~[in]~~ ^after^ his old ~~way~~ habit "What . . ." (1888–89, 97r–97v, EC; emphasis in original)

The page retains traces of spilled tears, whether from the moment of writing itself or from rereadings in years to come, or both. It breaks off in the middle of James Cooper's question: "What," which was completed several pages along in the diary (". . . was that!"), following Emma's death.

But that death is not reported in the diary. It was reported in a letter to Browning, a letter later transcribed into the diary in a little space on the page in the middle of James Cooper's sentence: between his "What" and his "was that!" This is how Edith Cooper represented the moment of death to Browning:

> August 20. ^Written on Tuesday Morning in a letter to "The Old"^ The beloved Mother died at four o'clock in the dayspring. She recognized us with looks of travelling love till one o'clock. Her beautiful eyes grew large enough to receive death, but love rose up in them instantly and surmounted their great doom. Those looks will live in me like a Second Birth. After she became un-conscious I went apart to read the grand half-chapter of *Corinthians*, and when I reached the words "For this corruptible must put on incorruption, and this mortal must put on immortality" I cried out "O Mother, Mother, come to me, leave that body, and come!" She died on the instant—and kissed me in her arms—a glorious spirit. I felt her round me and at my lips in an embrace that was like Pentecostal flame—it made me stronger than death. "O thou soul of my soul, I shall meet thee again—and with God be the rest." (1888–89, 98r, EC)

Cooper presents her mother's death as her own second birth. But she was not in the room at the moment of passing; she was nearby, reading her Bible. Cooper reports the death as a conjuring. At the prompt "this mortal must put on immortality," Cooper summoned her mother, who promptly shuffled the mortal coil and materialized in Edith's arms in the next room—kissed her, died, and sealed her daughter in a state stronger than death. Paraphrasing Browning's "Prospice," "O the soul of my soul, I shall meet thee again," Cooper casts herself as the spouse bereaved, anticipating a triumphant reunion with the beloved after death. She might have borrowed this figure from her aunt's expostulation twenty years earlier: "I shall not be first with any one on earth now."

The agency here is Cooper's. Just as she did at her grandmother's deathbed in 1868, she works in otherworldly ways, summoning her mother's soul from her body, through the walls, into her own arms, and away. Cooper continues:

> Our bond is so deep it seems to be back into my first Creation. For a few hours after she was free I was firm and glad, (and able to bring poor father down stairs, and light the deathly ashes of the grate into a mocking life.) Now I am weak with anguish at missing ~~her face~~ her dear

> long-tended body, her humorous, determined little ways, her inciting face—so calm and watchful. O the great moonlight eyes! Defects of course she had—(my darling!)—but not weaknesses. I could find no sparkle of vanity on her womanhood, no jealousy, no love of mere details. She rejoiced in the vaults of sky, their larks, in the high-tide sea, and in the least thing that had the universal touch of beauty on it. Oh, I can see her in everything, in each book, each picture: I see her, and then all grows dark in tears. (1888–89, 98r–98v, EC)

The language of Cooper's grief emerges in distinctive ways. Sissie Cooper now enjoys a freedom that Edith Cooper does not, trapped along with Bradley, family, and servants in a tiny house with its "turmoils of common sounds." Her mother's spirit now soars through walls and doors. And the universe in which Sissie once rejoiced is now tremulous with her presence throughout. Anticipating the texture of the maternal postmortem in *To the Lighthouse*—"Empty it was not, but full to the brim. She seemed to be standing up to the lips in some substance, to move and float and sink in it, yes, for these waters were unfathomably deep."—Cooper's world now shimmers with the plenitude of her mother's ubiquitous presence.[23] That their bond was so deep "it seems to be back into my first Creation" seems like a self-evident statement from the biological daughter of the dead mother. Cooper's remark refers to a truth that is more cellular to her than ovarian to Sissie: she came from within her mother, and she takes her mother back within herself in turn.[24]

As we might have come to expect, Bradley and Cooper narrate the deathbed story yet again, this time following the completion of James Cooper's "What" with his "was that!" pages later. Yet again, it is Edith's story to tell within the broken narrative of *Works and Days*. She does so in terms that differ from the version presented to Browning.

> I went into the blue room. I only came back once and then she lay like one of Blake's figures, the head far back on the pillows, the mouth widely opened to the night and air, the breath like a child's, and the eyelids impermeable sculpture. I did not stay; I felt it blasphemy for my imagination to ^take^ an overwhelming impress of her mortal end, when she wished me so to remember me her living—"You must think of me as I was." So I read Corinthians xv where we read it last together on Easter Day and called her to me from the hindering body. Then she came—just as I turned to the New City of Revelation where there shall "be no more death, neither sorrow nor crying, neither shall there be any more pain: for the former things are passed away"—I felt her press me

> against the heart of her being and fold me in the immortality we have fed in each other. I threw myself down by the blue bed and thanked God for "the Newly Born"—my darling, my ~~[illeg.]~~ ^darling.^ . . . We went down with a single candle into the comfortless dining-room. I lighted the fire. It was so cold by the grate, but she had kissed me in her immortal life. Mrs Walters came and the offices of death were quietly and lovingly done. I slipped out, cloaked to please *her*, into the dawn and the rain. I went to the laurel hedge, ~~and~~ ^there,^ broke a dual bough off of the heavy weeping drops of the rain splashed from the green leaves over me. I brought it in to Sim that she who has conquered Death and is a Victor ^might^ lies with it on her breast as the Mother and Sister of poets should. Then began the details of mourning, and my force departed. (1888–89, 99r–99v, EC; emphasis in original)

Whereas Cooper presents herself to Browning as the powerful conjurer of her mother's spirit into the next world—"this mortal must put on immortality"—she presents herself more privately as one taking consolation from the prospect of the New City, absent death, tears, pain. She is more fragile in private, feeling her way toward hope. And as she does that, she also claims a new identity for her mother, and for herself. Cooper brings in a laurel branch from the rainy garden, "that she who has conquered Death as a Victor might wear it on her breast as the Mother and Sister of poets should." It was not Cooper alone who was braced and ennobled by her mother's goodness. Her mother went triumphant into death as "the Mother and Sister of poets should"—poets plural. In death, Emma Bradley Cooper was distinguished as no mere mother and sister but as the mother and sister of poets. Just as the narrative of her deathbed was consumed by poetry, the sacrifice of Emma Cooper begat poets.

In writing the psychopathology of the blended Bradley and Cooper family, this is an important subtlety. The mortals Katharine Bradley and Edith Cooper need maternal benediction to assert standing in the "tiny house" as something other than daughter figures. Michael Field are rather prominent in the literary world at this exact moment in time, so there is a truth—and with that truth, a dignity—in the family embrace of the poets' worldly, literary prominence. There is also a fig leaf quality to it, in the sense that Michael Field are conspicuous category breakers: aunt and niece, lovers, a couple, a male poet. Michael Field claim the poet's laurel in and through the death of the mother, transcending their limited, daughterly roles, and erasing the many obvious ways they did not hew to feminine conventions. In her coffin, Sissie wore the crown of laurel that befits the Mother and Sister of poets, claiming the power of poetry through death. The death of the Mother affords shifts in both directions, private and domestic, public and worldly, for Michael Field's identity as women.

Sissie went to her grave festooned in fetish objects of great personal and poetic significance. In addition to the laurel branch, Sissie's corpse bore letters from the two poets: "On the envelope she had written in pencil: Put this over my still heart that it may never grow *cold*" (1888–89, 100r, EC; emphasis in original). In her letter, Cooper wrote: "How I bless God that I was born, that you were my Mother, and that you are still living to exalt and ennoble your child: you have always been in the home an ideal: that ideal you have never betrayed; our confidence in your nobleness has made our love for you a very holy thing. [. . .] Oh, darling, you are mother and friend in one—the two most beautiful bonds are twisted together between us" (1888–89, 100r, EC). Whereas Cooper invokes Victorian domestic ideals and then breaks boundaries as she often does ("you are mother and friend in one"), Bradley writes much more conventionally as a sister, to her sister: "My heart today is full of deepest gratitude to 'the Old Couple' [James and Emma Cooper] [. . .] for the home they have made and kept for their motherless sister, and the two fair babes they have given her" (1888–89, 100v, EC transcription of KB letter).

Here we get a glimpse of the historical circumstances that made this family's home, and acknowledgment that Bradley was taken in as an adjunct to a nuclear family that included a couple and their two children. For Cooper, her mother has been "in the home our ideal"; Bradley is a visitor to that home, and in fact a presence that rearranged both the relationships and the power dynamics among its players. And now, absent the Beloved Mother-One, Bradley and Cooper face discomfort in the home that she had made, in which their unusual bond could be accommodated by the authority of her blessing.

Michael Field express love and loss through the matter of poetry. Bradley and Cooper crammed the Beloved's casket with poems. Also with flowers, pictures, and in a characteristically quotidian touch, a matchbox painted by Amy. Cooper writes:

> Our solemn white mother lies in her coffin, softly, with her love-letters and our letters on her heart, the laurel on her breast, her right hand on her beautiful white copy of *Brutus Ultor* (the most beloved play) and on the original M.S. Copy of the Fawn Scene I gave her—the left hand holds a cream sparcely-flushed [*sic*] rose, a deep red one such as she loved, and a silver-pink one with a spray of rue and the little

> poem "From thy Amy Bird" and the fingers close round the little green match-box with a trail of pimpernel on it, painted by Amy in the happy Sidmouth days, a bit of work Mother was always looking at with joy in its artistic life. (1888–89, 102r, EC)

Yet this is just the beginning of the pyre.

Recalling Bradley's list of twenty-first birthday presents in 1867, Cooper continues with the heading "The relics laid on her holy, fondled Coffin" on Friday evening, August 23. The relics so named include:

- All five of Michael Field's published books to date (Amy's copies), in the order of their publication.
- The letter of condolence from Browning to Michael Field sent at The Mother's death.
- A miniature portrait of Amy, and prints from her artwork.
- A(nother) copy of *Long Ago*, and Cooper's personal copy of Michael Field's play *Queen Mary*.
- The bough of laurel.
- Blake's figure of the Creator dividing darkness with a compass of light.
- A poem Cooper wrote to accompany the gift of the Blake image.
- A photograph of Michelangelo's Adam.
- Edelweiss from Cousin Harriet.
- A cherished stand hand carved by James Cooper.
- Rosa Cooper's little bunch of mignonette, kept "livingly" [*sic*] in water in the little sea-weed glass vase.
- Portraits of grandfather and grandma.
- Several manuscripts of Michael Field's plays, in various stages of progress.
- Katharine Bradley's Bible.
- And a little oak table carrying a massive "pyramid of living flowers and leaves," offering "such a breathing, hopeful autumn above her!" (1888–89, 102r–102v, EC)

That was the coffin. There was also an altar set up on the mantel nearby; let the details of that display go unnamed in these pages. Clearly, grieving expresses itself in this family in objects, particularly paper and flowers. Cooper and Bradley cover the dead mother's body and coffin with their writing, an association of coffin and text again reminiscent of Richardson's *Clarissa*. The poetry and plays of Michael Field take up an enormous amount of space in and around the dead mother's corpse, legitimizing

Michael Field's work within the domestic sphere: the maternal corpse validates it, and them. The assertion of "Michael Field" at this point claims space for him within this family: a man, perhaps, to rival James Cooper; a male figure with worldly agency and authority that the bereaved widower lacks. He was a force to be reckoned with. The assertion of Michael Field also serves to express a truth about the female figures that comprise him: this is who they are, and—two in one—this is who they will remain.

Musing on the funeral preparations and the early stages of mourning, Cooper writes, "The dear Mother-One told us she would be closer to us after death than in her earthly days—she has fulfilled her promise, and she rules her home and our hearts so fully that we have scarcely felt what mourners call 'a void'" (1888–89, 103v, EC). Indeed, it should be said that it would be difficult to make space for any such "void" in the family home, if only because it is so entirely stuffed with relics.

The heart is another matter. Katharine Bradley wrote to Browning describing the plans for her sister's burial. Bradley, along with James and Amy Cooper, will follow the "sweet white relic" to the grave. Cooper, at her mother's request, will spend the hour alone at home, in Bradley's "little blue bedroom." Though the coffin and its accessories will find a new home in Gatton Churchyard, Bradley describes the Mother-One herself as a new, and newly permanent, component of Michael Field. She writes: "We will work for her—her hand closes over the first copy of the Faun Scene and *Brutus Ultor* (her favorite play). Henceforth she will be with us not as our reader only, but intimated in the shaping of our work. Ah, how good to have one's dear ones not outside one any more—but with and of one's art and life!" (1888–89, 106r, EC transcription of KB letter).

Bradley and Cooper frame the death of the mother as even more than an introjection; Sissie is absorbed uniquely into the singular persona Michael Field. As Meadows writes, "Cooper and Bradley represent death as an accession to poetic authority and freedom, converting the melancholic introjection of the lost love object into poetic productivity."[25] In turn, "Michael Field" offers the poets a flexible concept for understanding identity, for affording social and artistic mobility, and for expressing the intense emotional connection they feel toward each other: they are not two; they are one. The language of the mother-child relationship is not incidental here: psychoanalysts have long considered the compromised boundaries of mother and infant formative, and also ambivalent precisely because they are compromised.[26] Bradley and Cooper, maternal aunt and niece, focus attention on the boundaries that at once connect them and divide them. The language—and the psychology—of domestic love provides the reasoning that makes of Michael Field "poets and lovers ever more." Again: "How good to have one's dear ones not outside one any more." Though in Victorian novels, maternal death or desertion launches the child outward from the familiar toward manifest destiny, Michael Field wrap the journey of romance tightly in the mother's embrace. "To mourn," writes Hägglund of Virginia Woolf, "is to learn to accept the loss of the past and to form new attachments in its place."[27] Michael Field refuse mourning, opting instead to carry forward a deep and dogged loyalty to first attachments: a melancholy that preserves loss within the real, and that also binds the poets inexorably to a past they cannot escape.

There was a lull in the autumn of 1889 between the deaths of Emma Cooper and Robert Browning. Little knowing the sadness they would experience again at year's end, Cooper and Bradley took a holiday in Scotland, where they found themselves walking once again at night, on a beach. Cooper writes on Thursday, October 24:

> Last night on the shore I and my Beloved One walked together—she is as close as God when I am worthy of her Companionship. We listened to the continual, pouring voice of the sea. Tawny light was in the sky, wreathed storm and clouds that "dove-like sat brooding." The sand was streamy with the advance of the tide, and over the reflective channels we saw the little [~~old~~] ^ancient^ city making an horizon of towers, one by one the lighthouses sparkled and the stars rose. It is beautiful to know as one looks at the human lamps on the waters that they are kindled by *love*, by man's sympathy for man; it makes one feel that the stars are not lighted otherwise. As I thought this the near and far—yea, the very far—became indivisible: she and I grew all the closer. (1888–89, 113r, EC; emphasis in original)

Edith walks with the Beloved One. The mother who has died? Or the aunt, her mother's sister, who is/is not like her mother? The scene is quiet, its serenity marked by brooding storm clouds. Here, in sympathy, basking in the light of the home, which is the light of the stars, the speaker and the Beloved One "became indivisible." Woolf, writing forty years later, reached for a similar conceit to express the collision of scales, the magnificent and the quotidian, at such a moment of heightened emotional intensity: "And as happens sometimes when the weather is very fine, the cliffs looked as if they were conscious of the ships, and the ships looked as if they were conscious of the cliffs, as if they signaled to each other some message of their own. For sometimes quite close to the shore, the Lighthouse looked this morning in the haze an enormous distance away."[28]

When Cooper is "worthy of her [beloved's] Companionship," the seal is as close as the one with God. It is, for Michael Field, both the beginning and the end, or so they hope. And though this story has the feel of a coda to it, we know too well that it is no mere postmortem on grief and mourning; it sits just in advance of new grief and mourning. The streaming sand, the horizon of towers, the variegated lights of homes, lighthouses, and stars reveal quiet activity observed even in the equipoise of "she and I." As much as they crave equipoise, the two voices, the two hands, of *Works and Days* also crave activity, and activity they will find.

In Porchester Terrace, London, on Sunday afternoon, May 26, 1889, the week she learned of her sister's imminent death, Bradley paid a visit to a palm reader. Upon inspection of Bradley's hand, the palm reader reported that the poet has "a rather rebellious hand," but that she "will do any large thing well. You see your end, and make straight for it," the palm reader continued, adding, "you have no power over detail. You have an entire lack of fortitude" (1888–89, KB, 64r). "You have an art-hand . . . much dramatic—latent, and could probably [illeg.] speak in public, if trained" (1888–89, 65r, KB).

If Michael Field's characteristic as an experimental diarist involves chronic atemporality, the palm reader is quickly attuned to the fact that past, present, and future do not line up for the client before her. Witnessing Bradley's consternation at the prediction of bad tidings ahead, the palm reader quickly changes her story, doubtless aware of her client's reaction to news of looming distress and disaster. Bradley reports: "[B]ut when she heard my age—some ten years older than her estimate of my hand—she appeared quite cheered and said—'Oh then that is all passed, and you will have a smooth time'" (1888–89, 65r, KB). The palm reader does not exactly offer Bradley a story brimming with encouragement. Bradley was said to have "[p]lenty of imagination, and a rather passionate heart—but very little of the other (sensual) kind of love. My great want she seemed to think was a sustaining, steady, cherfulness [*sic*]. Great and probably successful ambition . . . and much worry over work, and self-distrust. Altogether my life evidently gave her the impression of much inward distress, apprehension, and agitation—of nerves and health, with tendency to [a] weak heart" (1888–89, 65r–66r, KB).

The positive dimensions of Bradley's profile, such as imagination, ambition, and a passionate heart, come wrapped under cover of worry, distress, apprehension, agitation, and—in her heart, the organ previously described as "rather passionate"—weakness. Bradley was also written off as lacking in sensual love. That must have stung for the author of the "tingling quest" of the honeybee. Whatever tale her palm tells, the poet who writes so about the tingling depths of sweet lust knows something about sensual love and the passionate heart, though not perhaps in terms immediately evident to a Bayswater palm reader in 1889.

Sissie Cooper went to the grave clasping two Michael Field manuscripts in her hands. Two years married, Elizabeth Barrett Browning put the manuscripts of her love sonnets in the hands of her husband Robert. *Works and Days* comes to us today as a manuscript, the handwriting of its two authors connecting us as by a hot wire to the women's living bodies. In this unusually odd volume of *Works and Days*, a third hand intrudes—Amy, the sister and other niece? And the handiwork of the diary's pages is interrupted by the tears of the poets themselves.

Like *Works and Days*, the palm reader that Bradley visited this year looks backward and attempts to look forward. Like the formal breaks in this volume of *Works and Days*, the palm reader realizes a characteristically broken temporality as she first warns Bradley of bad times to come, then backtracks, notes Bradley's "true" age, and says never mind, your hard times are in the past. The palm reader interprets Bradley's hand as surprisingly youthful, or so the poet would have us believe. And she characterizes Bradley's hand in two specific ways: as a "rebellious hand" and as an "art hand."

It is tempting to force an equation of "rebellious hand" and "art hand." Michael Field are certainly an unconventional artist, albeit one writing in highly conventionalized ways, and an unconventional man too; the pronouns break down, as we know. In the end, just as in the beginning, I think the noun—hand—is far more important than any uncomfortable adjectives that might be asked to modify it. In *Works and Days*, Bradley and Cooper present themselves as writers, and as women, and as lovers. Their hands were their mode of agency—writing voluminously, caring for the bodies of the sick, touching one another, and taking the other's hand as they seek a life as one.

CHAPTER TWO

"The Hot Hands of the Modern"

1892–93

It was deep April and the morn
Shakespeare was born;
The world was on us, pressing sore:
My Love and I took hands and swore
  Against the world to be
  Poets and lovers ever more;
To laugh and dream on Lethe's shore,
To sing to Charon in his boat,
Heartening the timid souls afloat
Of judgment never to take heed,
But to these fast-locked souls to speed
Who never from Apollo fled,
Who spent no hour among the dead.
  Continually
  With them I dwell,
Indifferent to heaven or hell.

—KATHARINE BRADLEY, *WORKS AND DAYS*, APRIL 23, 1892

Men are worse than dead when women's feelings are in question.

—EDITH COOPER, *WORKS AND DAYS*, MAY 1892

ON SATURDAY, APRIL 23, 1892, Edith Cooper saw Katharine Bradley off on the train to Dover, writing that "We swear ~~in the~~, with the bright world round us, that we will remain Poets and lovers whatever may happen that ^to^ hinders or deflects our lives" (1892, 77v, EC). Bradley developed the poets' shared thought, and she later wrote the poem above during the morning's train journey.[1] Cooper transcribed the text into *Works and Days*. In classic Michael Field fashion, Bradley's words are brought to us here by Cooper's hand. The poem, canonized among Michael Field's lyric best, expresses the embattled stance of two, hand in hand against the world: "My Love and I took hands and swore / Against the world to be / Poets and lovers ever more." The poem embraces spring and the birth of Shakespeare, before descending to the underworld and the afterlife where the poets and lovers counsel the dead against fearing judgment. Dwelling still in the world of the living, the poem's speaker is yet indifferent to heaven or hell, "poets and lovers evermore."

Michael Field have embraced the mutual permeability of life and afterlife on other occasions as well. Since her death in 1889, for example, the Beloved Mother-One has dwelled within the poet, an engine of their voice as much as their love. Michael Field fuel the intensity of their shared passion from a sense of immanence that keeps the departed close, represented in memorial altars laden with flowers and photographs, and experienced in the private passions of the poets themselves.

In 1892, however, Michael Field face an existential threat to their existence as poets and lovers evermore. During this year, we witness Cooper falling in love with the art critic Bernhard Berenson, who repelled her passion through a series of grindingly humiliating rejections—of Cooper herself, of Bradley, and of Michael Field.[2] In this volume of *Works and Days*, the two narrators negotiate the entanglements of art and desire brought into focus by the Berenson crisis. Recalling Barthes's punctum, as embodied in Queen Victoria's skirts, 1892 finds Michael Field writing about clothing, and about the nakedness it covers. Michael Field write about marriage and sex, about bodies and about corpses, about the clothing that covers nakedness, and about the naked bodies that fill out clothing from the inside, as old wine fills new bottles.

On her thirtieth birthday, January 12, 1892, Cooper feels the depths of the triangle she shares with her two Beloveds. One of those is living—Bradley—and one is dead: Emma Bradley Cooper, "the Beloved Mother-One," dead for more than two years. Cooper writes: "[A]fter tea my Love and I have a great love and talk of the past and of the Beloved Mother-One—of how we miss the greatness of her nature, the dramatic impulse she gave to our work—of how I brought the best of beauty, in literature in earth to her, as a consecrated minister to her nobleness. Life is so much less worth living since she left us" (1892, 12v, EC). The Beloved Mother-One remains the force that binds the poets she left behind, more powerful perhaps in death than in life.

Yet, for the first time, Cooper's valediction takes a turn: "And this is Field—his Confession." Along with the familiar heaping praise, Cooper admits to her mother's clay feet: the Beloved Mother-One "did not understand my need of freedom, she bound and overawed me where I wanted to be free and personal. Such an influence is a crime against me . . . I suffered torments, struggles such as the hermits of the wilderness knew, under my Beloved's construction. She understands an artist's inspiration—she could not understand an artist's temperament" (1892, 13r, EC). Cooper's lover is more understanding:

> What a divine blessing it is to me to have my Love, who checks no self-expression, who brings beauty to my eyes, and gladness to my life, who loves me and whom I love with strenuous force, that is half-hidden by our caresses and humorous names, and utter familiarity! Alfred de Musset felt his heart at 30, to see if it still beat—mine sings out its love to her more loudly than ever—it loves art more devotedly, and the South where pictures fill every white town; it loves language with deeper awe and unweariable service. . . . alas it loves Man much less, and lads and causes not at all. (1892, 13r, EC; emphasis in original)[3]

As she begins her fourth decade, Cooper doubles down on her passions: her lover, who like Browning "checks no self-expression" in a poet, and who loves her with a "strenuous force" that goes much deeper than ordinary displays of affection and camaraderie might suggest. And her art: paintings of the Italian Renaissance, and poetry that shares an aspect of the beauty captured in good paintings. Not on the list? "Man." And lads and causes. Though the gendering of "Man" and "lads" would seem to suggest a statement of sexual selection on Cooper's part, her emphasis on the capital "M" in "Man" suggests that she is thinking conceptually rather than specifically. Events of the year ahead will bear out her marked interest in *a* man, if not in "Man."

Cooper walks a quieter path that bypasses even "causes" such as suffrage, which she had cared about deeply in the past: "I should never fight for any freedom that to gain ^wh^: would perturb my art. I have only so much energy—if the god demands it—the cause of womanhood must go hang" (1892, 99v, EC). Cooper has selected "strenuous force" over causes and laddishness over even feminism. On Sunday, February 14, she expresses the intensely private nature of her desires: "My ~~[illeg.]~~ Love is away [. . .]—I am away from my own identity. I want and want . . . my own

Love, and nothing else" (1892, 46r, EC). Here again we see the centripetal force of Michael Field: the objects—art, love, Bradley, Cooper—move along a fixed course, always pulled inward toward one another. It is no coincidence that Cooper counterposes "the cause of womanhood" with the cause of "art." Psomiades writes about how Michael Field see and write about the *Mona Lisa*: "What Michael Field give us . . . is the femme fatale without the femme. Femininity appears to them wholly a matter of form, and while the language of artificiality implies that somewhere, a natural femininity lies, oppressed by this falsity, nevertheless at this particular moment, the pure formality of femininity becomes visible."[4] Art admits Cooper to a domain of presence—"strenuous force"—that surpasses the hollow forms of feminine convention.

Just as Bradley and Cooper experienced the twinned deaths of the Mother and Browning in relation to the publication of their book *Long Ago*, this moment of "want and want" occurs in the final stages of publication of their next book of poetry, *Sight and Song*. The new book is an exercise in the "translation" of paintings into poetry, and an exploration of the shared vocabulary of beauty and feeling that the two art forms evoke. Cooper explains Michael Field's objective in *Sight and Song*: "To render what the lines and colours of certain beloved pictures sing *in themselves* or would express, not so much what they are to us as poets, but rather what poetry they objectively incarnate" (1892, 30r, EC; emphasis in original).[5]

The mission to evoke the incarnate poetry of the visual arts represents a significant aesthetic burden for a slender volume of poetry. Indeed, the production of the physical book itself challenged the combined high standards of beauty and of practicality; as Mary Sturgeon observed, the poets "desired their children to be lovely in body as well as in spirit."[6] The book proved too bulky for the unmounted parchment cover its authors had hoped for, and they were left at a very late hour with no cover design at all: "Suddenly our little book is disappointed of its clothes and we do not know how to cover its nakedness. Olive-Cloth is suggested" (1892, 62v, EC). After considering various options, Michael Field celebrate *Sight and Song*'s physical manifestation. The book arrived at their home in the late spring, "charming in its simple cover, the lettering perfect. Alas, the red-orange device inside, belonging to an earlier scheme, is out of place—a blot. There is terrible famine for our Mother-One in our hearts. Men are worse than dead when women's feelings are in question. Father is a sepulcher—spite of his kind attempt to be a sympathizer. My Love and I clasp—knowing there would be little worth living for if either were alone in the world" (1892, 89r, EC). Holding each other as they hold their new book for the first time, Michael Field invoke, and suffer from, a terrible famine for "our Mother-One." "Father" is no help. They are consolable only in each other's arms.[7]

They worry about how the book will be received. Cooper continues: "O flowers of the apple, what is the doom of *Sight and Song*, how will it live—what is the perfect witness of all-judging Jove concerning its method, its achievement, its influence? And what will that Faun, that Bernhard think of it! But the time begins in wh: we shall know, God willing" (1892, 89v, EC). How will this infant live? Born of the female trinity of Michael Field and Mother, its most important audience is "that Faun, that Bernhard." Berenson, the expert on the paintings Michael Field are translating into poetry, is the book's father. Not coincidentally, he has arrested Cooper's passionate attentions, and at this moment he holds existential power over Michael Field.

In 1892, Michael Field were invited by Mary Costelloe to join her for a stay in her brother's *appartement* in Paris during the summer months. The subsequent journey to Paris and cohabitation with Mary Costelloe will offer a surprise, acutely painful to Cooper, as the poets encounter and begin to understand the depth of Costelloe's relationship with Berenson. In 1892, Costelloe was separated from her American husband, father of her children, who died in 1899. She married Berenson in 1900, and she is credited as the Svengali of much of his writing, as well as the formative influence of the social circle that came together at their home outside Florence, Villa I Tatti.[8]

Michael Field first negotiate their fascination with bodies, with the clothing that covers them, and with the activities their inhabitants undertake, through a focus on weddings. The first, that of the early sexologist Havelock Ellis to the lesbian feminist Edith Lees,[9] came to them in a chat with Ellis's sister Louie. Cooper reports that when Havelock and Louie Ellis arrived at the Registrar's office,

> The bride was waiting [. . .], shook her umbrella (!!). The party was shut in a waiting room for ¼ of an hour. H was not nervous and talked . . . there must have been something fearsomely unnatural in that easy talk. Then the civil marriage took place, the sun shining full on the couple through the Registrar's eastern window. H looked handsome in the light—he was calm; his umbrella-shaking bride pale and disquieted! Bride, Bridegroom and Sister walked home arm in arm. Soon after the Bride departed to her rooms in town, travelling by herself in the Underground. She gave an At Home that afternoon to wh:

her husband came. They parted and only met again next day when they started for Paris. The Bride was married in an ulster. This is a true account of the modern Sacrament of matrimony. It is revolting. "Free love, free field" is sacreder. (1892, 58v, EC)

"This is a true account of the modern Sacrament of matrimony." The imagined spectacle is "revolting" to Cooper and Bradley, even as the image of bride, bridegroom, and sister walking home after the marriage ceremony evokes (un)conventionalities similar to Michael Fields' own coupling. I can imagine that Michael Field were repelled by the aspect of chumminess, rather than gravitas, that seems to characterize the story: calm, chatty bridegroom, bride in an ulster riding home on the Tube and hosting a gathering at her own home that afternoon.[10] Nowhere is passion suggested; indeed, Louie, as translated by Cooper, seems to emphasize the coupled unity of the brother and sister, and the distinct separateness of the bride. Is the "strenuous force" of emotion present here? If not, what motivates the marriage in the first place? Why bother? "Free love, free field"—what the poets share partakes of the sacred.

"This is a true account of the modern Sacrament of matrimony." "Off to the wedding!" Cooper writes in April 1892, as the poets travel to Birmingham for a nuptial event in their extended family. "We storm the attic stairs, the attic," Cooper reports, "—but we pause, so deathly is that sight that meets us—the dress laid out as if it were a corpse. Had I been the bride I should have wept over and dreamt of that whiteness. Sim flies blanched with augury" (1892, EC, 76r). No mere ulster, the Victorian bridal gown lays on the bed, a virgin corpse, ghost of a virgin sacrifice. Cooper is disgusted by the whiteness of the empty dress; its agony blanches Bradley's face.

The next morning, Cooper continues. I will quote the scene in its entirety:

Wednesday—The Wedding Day.

Cold, raw: The morning a mere slough of waiting; boys at every turn, in unnatural lavender trousers, and at wrestle with half-fitted white gloves; the girls and mother harassed with details, the Bridge and East-wind. Arnold's ironic, historical exposition of the Marriage-service (brilliantly witty) is a little human relief from the stultifying strangeness.

At last the pleasure of dressing, the arrival of the flowers. Sim carries a great bunch of delicate roses and I advance bearing a lilac-bush.

A sight of the Bride, glancing at herself with cynical hatred from under the veil, which a young ~~shop-woman~~ ^dressmaker's assistant^ arranges: a Bride and not beautiful!

> Her simple ivory dress becomes her form, proportioned so slenderly. The Bridesmaids wear white dresses trimmed with a buttercup-sprinkled white silk and rustic hats over wh: hang butter cups. They carry yellow posies.
>
> We drive to Church with Francis, who follows us up the nave—"to waft us on as a god." So curious to be with him on a marriage-day!
>
> The Bride delays, the music irritates by repetition. At last she comes, scattering wide April smiles, finally giving her Bridegroom a starry look, a real gift, I never saw her look so illuminated.
>
> The seven brothers are pale opposite to me, the sisters make their posies quiver behind the Bride—she stands like a willing victim, but a victim to the first Great Illusion! I feel as if I am assisting at some rite of an old world. The Illusion is strong as the Earth, but the worship paid to it must have new forms or new freedom if it is to be living as the power it celebrates.
>
> Then comes all the defamation of love by cake, champagne, stupid hopes, emphasis of the new condition—Ugh! But the cake is excellent—the honey-moon is indeed honey laid up by cunning cooks.
>
> The Bride bids a cool and gracious goodbye in her ruddy cloak and red-black hat. A storm of rice rattles over her. Shoes fly meteorically. There is no reason ^after this^ why we should be gathered together. We go to our beds and ^last of all^ crown our fatigue with a family dinner to wh: 18 sit down. The evening is sad, gusty—an envious sense hangs about that the feast is gone elsewhere. The Bride and her ^Bride^groom are not popular. (1892, 76–77, EC)

Cooper did not find much to care for in the New Woman version of the marriage ceremony celebrated by Ellis and Lees. But this more traditional version is worse, perhaps because it demanded participation on behalf of Sim of the roses and Henry, bearing a lilac bush. The bride stands victim to the "first Great Illusion," and love is defamed by cake and champagne, "stupid hopes," and the emptiness of the powerful condition itself.

The family ceremony offers a pretense of emotional authenticity on the part of the bride, who runs through a repertoire of affective possibilities: she looks disgusted with her own slender form, beams with "illumination" at her bridegroom, and departs "cool and gracious" as her loved ones pelt her with rice and shoe meteors. "The Bride and Bridegroom are not popular," Cooper wrote, seeming to identify something lacking or hollow in the forms and rituals of marital convention. The wedding dress is a corpse. "Shoes fly meteorically."

"What would it mean to celebrate, instead, 'Free love, free field'?" asks Yopie Prins.[11] Only several days later came April 23, the day Bradley wrote: "My love and I took hands and swore / Against the world to be / Poets and lovers ever more." "Closer married" than the Brownings, Michael Field are clearly wondering about the social forms that might or might not be available to them, "Poets and lovers ever more." Is the empty wedding dress an object of desire?

"A marriage is the aim of English and American literature," Berenson reminded Cooper several weeks before this marriage ceremony (1892, 59v, EC). Yet, if marriage is a hollow form, what is the future of English and American literature? If Free Field are "closer married" but not formally married, what literary forms exist to express the meaning of their lives, their life, their "strenuous force"?[12] And at a moment when Berenson, the third party to the Michael Field relationship, is testing Cooper's affective loyalty intensely, can she remain "poets and lovers ever more" with Bradley while also coupling with the person she later describes as her "twin-soul" but not her "lover-soul" (1893, 67r, EC)?

The literary and artistic forms of the past fail to hold as the world pitches toward modernity; the social forms that inhabit those literary and artistic forms suffer accordingly. Cooper explains, after a concert in London: "How strange the tone of these old instruments—what far-off, tinkling youthfulness! They cannot express the subtilty [*sic*] nor volume of our modern emotion—the meaning, the experience, the acuteness in what we feel. They have a sunny, *gala* thinness, or a quaintness sorrow that scarcely swells into passion. Men must have been half-crickets when this music satisfied them" (1892, 49v–53r, EC; emphasis in original). The instruments of old express emotional insufficiency that fails to approximate "the meaning, the experience, the acuteness in what we feel." The "modern" for Cooper here is precisely the sort of ephemeral intensity of primal passion that she finds lacking in the two marriage ceremonies she describes during these early months of 1892. The question of the "modern" is clearly on the poets' minds in spring 1892; in March, Bradley reports incidentally that Cooper "brought me a perfect piece of modern prose—matter for warm tears" (1892, 56v, KB).

"I continue to sleep with my Love, I continue darkling to be happy," writes Cooper in late April (1892, 78v, EC). This ominous note immediately precedes a strange set of narratives around an 1891 painting titled *Idyll*, by Maurice Greiffenhagen (fig. 3). Among several odd qualities of this description is the fact that Cooper's writing is interrupted by a blank strip of paper across the page, about two inches from the bottom: part of this page was torn away, and the blank likely inserted by conservation librarians, to ensure the stability of the page that remains. Taken in this full context, the page reads—or doesn't, as the case may be—like this:

> A young shepherd takes to his lips and his breast a yielding girl. She is huddled up to him—the blessedness of receiving, of being passive under love is softly moulding^s^ the look of her face. Her
>
> [BLANK]
>
> arms fall straight to the left, her bosom is pressed toward her throat by the lover's arms, her head nestles against his insatiable mouth. There is summer in her eyes and on her mouth while her cheek is kissed. The dark shepherd-boy, in hat and violet-shadowed goat-skin, takes a simple possession of her that is ardour at its purest heat. (1892, 78v–79r, EC)

We will almost certainly never know what the missing text here said nor showed—nor, just as interestingly, why and by whom it was torn away and concealed from private and/or public readership. Peculiarly, Cooper's narrative description of the Greiffenhagen painting seems to proceed continuously before and after the break, making it no break at all. Except that it is. The blank page inserts an interruption in an intensely passionate and embodied scene, "ardour at its purest heat," if mediated for the modern viewer by its ancient and pastoral setting. Notwithstanding that mediation, Cooper continues:

> There is an amazing ^astonishing^ truthfulness in the picture—its subject is old as the meadows, its treatment modern, modern—life in every sweep of the brush. It is instantaneously passionate. The figures are seen as if by someone standing upright also as they. It is one of those works of art that "reveal what woman in her self must feel." The diverse sexual frankness of enjoyment in giving (or rather taking) and receiving is clear [. . .]—also the woman's more cloudless delight in her part that even the man's in his. Rossetti's conventional poppies are lustreless and of the past beside this Impressionist dance of poppies. (1892, 79r, EC)

Michael Field understand the potential power in a remote theme, or as Bradley has described it, pouring "*Old wine in new bottles*" (1892, 135r, KB; emphasis in original). In the *Idyll*, the theme is pastoral but the bottle of its form is contemporary—contemporary, it seems, because it discovers

FIGURE 3. Michael Field admired this painting by Maurice Greiffenhagen, *Idyll* (1891), as an example of "ardour at its purest heat." Courtesy National Museums of Liverpool, Walker Art Gallery.

the truth in female feeling, and "the diverse sexual frankness of enjoyment" in the woman's full participation in giving and taking. The painting is "modern, modern" because of this passion, and because it represents life in every sweep of the brush.

Life. Michael Field know urgent and strenuous force of love. They know sexual frankness and enjoyment, and they also know it when they see it. The anxiety that remains concerns life itself. Is there a place in this modern world for Michael Field? In March, Bradley wrote:

> In the afternoon I simply give way as an ill-built house—I fall in. With horror I recognize that outside of our art we are not living at all. We do not walk with any of the great souls of the past; we live under the blessing neither of the living or the dead. We are not thinking: we cannot act. And we care for fewer things day by day. We believe less, we hope less, and—God forgive us!—I fear we love less. We do not hunger less: we are hungry, and mowed up with husks. We *must* study: the mind must labour with its hands daily, or perish." (1892, 71r, KB; emphasis in original)

Bradley fears that Michael Field are an empty, withered husk, like the empty husks pressed into the pages of *Works and Days* during the Beloved Mother-One's death. She fears that they are not living. They are not modern. They do not walk with the great souls of the past. They do not care and cannot act. They are a house falling in on itself. And yet they hunger all the same: "We do not hunger less." Study and labor alone are left to them as the only instruments for addressing hunger and the needs of the body: "We are hungry."

For Michael Field, everything that could go wrong in Paris did go wrong. Michael Field were cross when they crossed the Channel; Cooper wrote, "A day of blight!" (1892, 106r, EC). George Moore had published an article on "sex in art" that reconsigned all women writers to second-class status. Michael Field took this personally, as one more sign that they were out of step in this modern world. Cooper fumed that Moore "would stamp M.F. as an artist with the stamp of inviolable inferiority—A clever article, frank, almost convincing in its downrightness for the moment—with a power of blackening ~~one's~~ ^the^ sky ^for us^ as the devil's wings do in *St. Antonie*. G.M. writes as that devil argued" (1892, 106r, EC). Feeling powerless and hopeless toward the prospect that their work will be judged fairly, Cooper writes: "Any how we are dark, we are irritated—we hate London" (1892, 106v, EC).[13]

Arriving in Paris, Michael Field present themselves at Mary Costelloe's door, and jump from the proverbial frying pan into the fire. "Mary meeting us in a plum-coloured dress, a dubious look in the eyes set in so frank a face, the honey masses of her hair: then the sudden entrance into the little salon—the small torturous form of Bernhard, his excited eyes, the shock of finding him different from my memory of him" (1892, 107r, EC). What had first seemed a straightforward invitation to visit Mary in Paris turns out to have been nothing of the kind, as Mary's initial apprehension signals. Finding Berenson quite at home in the flat is among the first surprises. Cooper finds Berenson shocking—different from what she remembers, uglier but more fascinating. She makes a note to herself at the bottom of the page regarding Mary's plum-colored dress: "*B hates this dress, and implores her to change it—of course in the end she does."

Michael Field are lodged in the box-room: "It looks impossible at first sight—so small a bed, such dingy wash-stand, few chairs and Mary's boxes. We have a sense we are beginning a life in which the impossible easily becomes possible" (1892, 107v, EC). To her great irritation, Berenson persists in paying Cooper compliments about her appearance. Yet the very next morning, June 21, "Mary, in a tawny dressing-gown, with streaming hair above it and naked feet below, comes to prepare our cold bath. We open our bedroom-door: Bernhard twists round to us—he is there—and bids us good morning. Mary is in a white gown—she looks very positive, clear, and level. Seeing her and seeing him, I have a speechless weight on my whole nature—the beginning of 'peine forte et dure'" (1892, 108r, EC). The cues of intimacy are discomfiting to Cooper: Mary in various stages of dress and undress, her participation in Michael Fields' bath, Berenson there first thing in the morning, most unexpectedly. *Peine forte et dure*: strong, hard punishment.

Mary is a married woman, though married to nobody sharing the Paris *appartement* in July 1892. Mother of two children, she is separated from her husband, Frank Costelloe. Berenson is not entirely cohabitating with Mary Costelloe, but he is certainly a fixture of the household and partner to her in daily life: "How curious our arrival at Rue de la Grande Charmière—up the narrow stairs, a ring, and Bernhard as door-keeper!" (1892, 110r, EC). Prior to this point, Cooper and Bradley did not seem fully apprised, nor much at all aware, of the closeness between Costelloe and Berenson; Berenson's presence at breakfast each morning is certainly surprising. Rather gently and elliptically, Costelloe clarifies her circumstances to Cooper: "He goes—we unpack. Mary shows me the studio under our vine-tree where a painter lives with his mistress—a *grisette*. We seem to live in the air of a French novel; there is a great strangeness in us—an awe that is not sacred. Then she speaks to us of life, of the dissolution of family-bonds, of the divorce she hopes to get, by residence in America. With her soft voice . . . Oh, it is like the delicious sweep of the scythe, mowing down what is ripe for destruction!" (1892, 108v, EC).[14]

Berenson has earlier instructed Cooper that if marriage is the aim of English and American novels, its violation is the aim of the French (1892, 59v, EC). Cooper is shocked to wake up and find herself in a French novel: Bernhard at breakfast, Mary seeking to dissolve her marriage, to become a divorcée, to change her family absolutely and permanently. In the studio just below, a painter and his young mistress. Sexual possibilities abound on Rue de la Grand Charmière.[15]

Michael Field confront conflicting romantic and social conventions in Paris. The blend of formal and informal social structures highlights the ambivalence of their attachment to traditional roles and known arrangements. Not only did Cooper realize that Berenson and Costelloe were a couple; the couple, at Berenson's instigation, systematically excluded and even ostracized their visitors. There is no provocative Michael Field math to be had here: no complicated, energetic triangle of "Michael Field," Berenson, and Costelloe. No jealous love triangle of Bradley, Cooper, and Berenson. The configuration of two pairs of lovers, with no commingling, makes no sense to Michael Field: "They say they are going to the Louvre—we will go too. There is scarcely a welcome to us in the way they start off together. We are like two 'souls forbid' on the top of the Odéon 'bus—our friends address us seldom. It is curious—why did they not say they were engaged if they are?" (1892, 111v, EC). Once in the galleries, Michael Field stand off to themselves and watch the opposite party across the way, welcoming a stray friend to make three, chatting and laughing among themselves while standing before pictures Cooper longs to understand. When Cooper approaches to join the group, Berenson "turns sharp on us—he amazes us with the injunction 'Don't follow me!' Our wrathful astonishment must have checked him, for he tarries to say to me 'I hope you don't mind—but I can never explain pictures to several people *with any pleasure to myself*'" (emphasis in original). Berenson has made it clear to Cooper that her participation in the group's conversation actually deprives him of the pleasure of the experience. "From that moment," Cooper writes, "my life can be expressed in two words—infatuation and wounds" (1892, 112r, EC).[16]

Berenson is systematically insulting, especially to Bradley. He shames her French, suggesting that she would benefit from the practice of ordering her own meals in restaurants. He insults Bradley's clothing—and Cooper's too. He insults Bradley's appearance. From Costelloe, Michael Field learn that Berenson's circumstances are reduced; he has recently lost a patron whose annual grant had subsidized much of his activity, leaving him "needy and beset with a grasping hunger for cash." Michael Field feel trapped, unable to depart and unwilling to stay under these terms: "We are in a tragic coil, as it is" (1892, 114v, EC). Cooper concludes: "[I]ndependent action is our only shield; we agree that we will walk together, plan our separate plans, have no expectancy in our manner—but this wisdom comes from the bitterness of our hearts, is sour and unripened. We feel there is much that we cannot grasp in the circumstances we encounter: the magnetic trouble Bern^h^ard and I awake ~~in each other~~ in each is an incalculable element: and we cannot trust the Sapphic frenzy that ~~drags~~ ^forces^ us, in spite of ourselves, to follow him" (1892, 115r, EC). Cooper feels torn between elemental forces: one, the magnetic force of the mutual attraction she and Berenson share; the other, the "Sapphic frenzy" that "forces" the Greek ladies to follow Berenson around Paris even after he warns them away.

Bradley decides independently to change the nature of the relationship between Michael Field and Berenson. Cooper was shocked to overhear Bradley offering cash in exchange for Berenson's companionship and instruction in art; while resting one afternoon, Cooper overhears "Sim's frank voice questioning Mary as to the reason why Bernhard makes no time to help us, and offering *Money*! If he will ~~help us~~ give us instruction" (1892, 126r, EC; emphasis in original). Berenson takes the money, and finally begins to usher Michael Field through galleries, as they had originally hoped. The relationship that Cooper had idealized as the stuff of the soul is in fact a paid arrangement.

The poets interpret, and internalize, Berenson's voice as the authoritative take on the "modern"—a mode of life they aspire toward, but in vain.[17] They want to be part of the "modern," in life and in art, in magnetism and in Sapphic frenzy, yet this desire itself arrives coated in shame and humiliation. On their first morning in Paris, for example, Cooper writes: "Bernhard drinks his coffee, eats his roll and eggs, while he talks as naturally as he breathes of God, fate, art, and man. [. . .] [God's] one command is: *Be contemporaneous*! The people who are so make tomorrow. To be contemporaneous is to digest today's meat. The great people of all ages are those who have been contemporaneous" (1892, 108, EC; emphasis in original). The concept is abstract to Michael Field, but they associate it with intensity and energy, with the "digestion" they undertake as they study paintings intensely. While sharing some of their work with Berenson, he recognizes himself and Cooper in the text's lovers, and he exhausts and dispirits Cooper with his "modern" conversation and "ex-cruciating love-talk in disguise" (1892, 120r–120v, EC). "This goes on two hours, till hunger ends the symposium, and we go forth to Duval's. There, I nearly faint with fatigue, shame, revolt: we order Chateaubriands—Bernhard and Mary, soup, wh: quickly comes, while we are kept waiting. Bernhard, with one glance at my weary face, and a peculiar sympathy in his action, hands me his soup and gently insists on my having it. Mary looks at me, says nothing—but looks long" (1892, 120v, EC). It is difficult to digest the meat of the day when one's Chateaubriand is delayed, and one must rely on borrowed soup.

Recall Bradley: "We do not hunger less—we hunger." Their time in Paris was intensely hungry for Michael Field, hungry to the point of fainting and to the point of savagery. The poets crave intensity, immanence of force and feeling, and the objective encounter with possibilities that extend beyond hollow social conventions. They need the stabilizing element of an aesthetic experience apart from Berenson, and they find one in the one place Berenson refuses to go: the Paris Morgue. Berenson reproaches Cooper for her visit to the morgue: "It is not Greek, it is morbid and shocking. I defend myself—death is one of the facts of life, modernity reaches to all facts and includes them: classic antiquity ignored many; but the new art and literature is great enough to bear all truth" (1892, 123v, EC). At the morgue, Cooper claims modernity for herself through her willingness to embrace the full breadth of all life's facts, death included, exposing Berenson's omnivorous "contemporaneity" as a sham. Cooper aligns herself not with Berenson but with an artist such as Greiffenhagen, who uses an old form—in his case, the pastoral—to express new truths; in the case of the *Idyll*, the truths of female desire. In the case of modern art and literature, death as a fact—as the conditioning fact—of life.

What did Cooper learn at the morgue, "the mortal den in which death is confined"? On this visit, she sees three men, a "dusky, tragic old man," a "most open-faced corpse with a smooth French pleasantness on the wrinkled alabaster features," and "a boy with fierce pitiful brows and a mouth that has become triangular" (1892, 122v–123r, EC). Recalling the corpse-like wedding dress draped across the attic bed, in the Paris Morgue the corpses' clothes "lie over them—such utter 'lendings.'" Cooper finds herself struck by the smallness of death: "I have before me the shapes of men some few feet long—but where is the magnation that passing from these shapes could fill a room, fill other hearts, fill those flat clothes—where is the expressiveness that only used these features as the centre of its flight over the world?" (1892, 123r, EC). The body is small. The "magnation"—a portmanteau, perhaps, of magnetic and imagination?—is grand. Magnation fills out shapes, rooms, hearts, and flat clothes—it fills new bottles with matter, ideas, wine, and stuff.[18] Perhaps it even animates the flat shell of a wedding dress.

"[I]n so far as we live shut up in bonds," Cooper realizes, "without self-expression, mobility, freedom—we are ~~living~~ ^but^ corpses and ^are becoming every day more^ like these little models on their backs behind the bars of the morgue. Yes, this is my Sunday lesson—that *life, life* is what the living must seek with heart and soul and strength and might. The only poor escape from the fixedness of a corpse is through the psychology that traces a past in the forms—a past is always piteous—it is sorrow ~~or past~~ happiness that is over: present and future have alone to do with life—Heigh-ho, we must live, till this machine is cast from us" (1892, 123r, EC; emphasis in original). With a "heigh-ho," Cooper has allowed herself to own the Doctrine's doctrine of the "contemporaneous" on her terms, not his. Her effort is to live life for the present and future—to leave the concerns of the past, to shuck bonds, and lay claim to self-expression, mobility, and freedom. To focus on the spirit, the feeling, "the psychology."

And yet: "We do not hunger less—we hunger." Forms are important: old or new, wine still needs bottles. If bodies are forms to the spirit, Michael Field's bodies only grow hungrier with desire for the modern. Some of the shame and humiliation they undergo at Berenson's hands has to do with their bodies, and particularly their bodies in comparison with Mary Costelloe's. Berenson did not like Mary's plum-colored dress on the day of Michael Field's arrival—he criticizes the clothing of Bradley and Cooper often—but he quite likes one of the period's most famous nudes, Manet's *Olympia* (1865): in contrast to the passive corpses of the morgue, their flat clothes draped across their bodies, Olympia meets the gaze of the viewer unflinchingly. Whether you consider her nude or naked, figure and spirit are as one in Olympia (fig. 4).[19]

The contemplation of the male nude is an entirely different matter for Michael Field. During this difficult Paris journey, Bradley and Cooper see a naked, living, grown man for the first time. Entering an atelier with Costelloe, they glimpse female models in various states of dishabille. Then:

> But what is that crouching, yellow thing? The model, the first man we have seen in the state of nature at close quarters—in dear's phrase

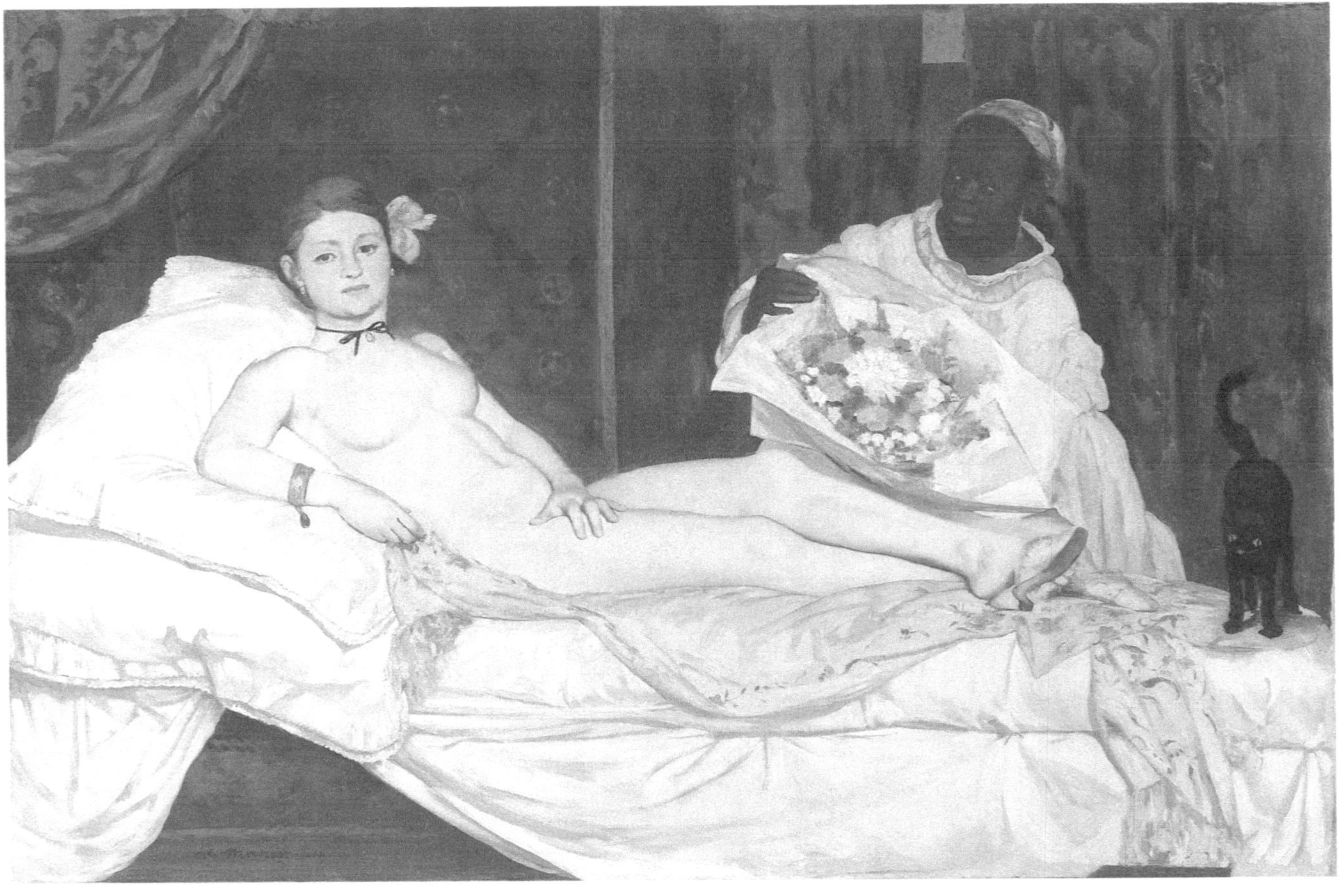

FIGURE 4. The 1865 painting *Olympia*, by Édouard Manet, was a favorite of Bernhard Berenson's, notwithstanding Berenson's hypercritical view of living women. Reproduced with the permission of the Musee d'Orsay.

> he looks "unaccommodated"—dreadfully so. Tho' the day is hot—he looks cold—he has nothing but his black hair and white loin cloth. He poses—he is startlingly like a figure from the Morgue exposed—he seems to be made, not of flesh but of *wax*, beeswax—and the black hair streaks his thighs and ~~[illeg.]~~ seat and bosom. I did not know that men were such savages, much to Mary's amusement. (1892, 129v, EC; emphasis in original)

Horrified, Michael Field immediately consign the grotesque male body to metaphor: the model is made "not of flesh but of wax, beeswax." Beeswax represents a different apian by-product than we usually see from Michael Field's bees, which more typically direct their humming and vigorous sucking on behalf of honey, not wax. But beeswax is important, too, in a more practical mode: it forms the combs that contain the honey. Michael Field repurpose their bee metaphor as a containment strategy for something not beautiful and not erotic—something streaky, savage, yellow, "unaccommodated." Aestheticism's Utilitarian sibling has a hairy bosom.[20]

"The little villain begins," writes Cooper: "'Miss Cooper, you will forgive me—I like everything about you, but your hat—these flowers in front are too dreadful. They try my nerves every time I look at them'" (1892, 121v, EC). Though proud of her hat, specially arranged with French flowers for Parisian taste, Cooper immediately busies herself with the project of reforming it: "soon the table in our bedroom is a holocaust of grass-green leaves, red velvet, bright bunches of spring-flowers, a spray of dark cherries, green velvet, red ribbon. In wantonness of Bacchic homage to the new Bacchus [. . .] we heap the Salon table with the garish spoil" (1892, 122, EC). Here is the negative image of the table next to the Beloved Mother-One's coffin, heaped with flowers in tribute to her, "the mother and sister of poets." Here Cooper describes an aesthetic holocaust that stands only for the garish, for the artificial. And for all that, Berenson barely remarks on her new hat; Cooper is infuriated, and she feels like a fool for humoring him.

Michael Field have just published a volume of poetry that seeks to express in lyric form the feelings "incarnate" to paintings. Michael Field are interested in variable modes of expression—how different artistic media produce different effects, and then in the ways those differences might encounter one another. As her visit to the morgue suggests, Cooper remains intensely interested in the human carnal form. She knows that it is not possible to embrace life purely as a matter of the spirit, absent flesh of the body. *Sight and Song*, too, was naked at first, with nothing to cover its shame, until the right cloth for it was found.

"What a deep interest attaches to them clothes from the first skin-coats to the latest gossamer," Bradley wrote in February of this year (1892, 48v, KB). The bride's ulster and the other bride's "simple ivory dress," the bridesmaids in buttercup, the book in olive, the dishabille of the shepherd and shepherdess in the *Idyll*, and the frank "skin-coat" of Manet's *Olympia*. The clothes draped on corpses in the morgue are flat because they are not inhabited by the human form. Michael Field are interested in the bodies that inhabit clothing, and in clothing as a signifier of what is hidden underneath: like the moniker Michael Field, the fig leaf that both covers and points to anatomical reality.

The evaluation of clothing is a female homosocial activity for Michael Field. When they first meet George Meredith's daughter Nesta ("plain black, long fawn jacket, black lace turned over the neck, a black hat with pure blue ribbons") they do not like her, finding her elegant but haughty and ungracious (1892, 68r, EC). The second time they meet her ("a dark serge, tailor-cut, with gold edge and brass buttons, a white blouse and sky-blue bow") they find her a nice young woman after all (1892, 82v, EC). Cooper is rather proud of her ensemble that day, perhaps because it bears a resemblance to *Sight and Song*, her nakedness dressed in olive cloth—"my new dress of black cloth faced with olive silk ^that is^ darkened by ~~[illeg.]~~ black lace; black hat with olive bow, a lilac spray, and ^black and^ lilac baby-ribbons"—and Bradley's: "her Velasquez dress and black plumed hat" (1892, 81v, EC). Worth noting for its viciousness alone is Cooper's description of the outfit of the wife of poet Richard Le Gallienne: "Mrs Le G is a boneless heap of green Liberty stuff and smocking—over her heapy aestheticism she pokes her chin. Her hair is light and frizzled—her features common—queer and yet commonly so; and her eyes seem to curve like gr blue bays, monotonous and convex" (1892, 82v, EC). Michael Field stand in judgment of Mrs. Le G.'s off-the-rack, mass-market aestheticism. "Heapy aestheticism" is clearly an insult for the ages, managing to say "tacky" and "failed art" at the same time.

Bradley and Cooper are not always kind when judging other women on their appearances; Sarah Parker has argued persuasively that for all their male identification, Michael Field were keenly interested in the dress codes that comprised aesthetic femininity, heapy or not, and that reading for their clothing helps to deconstruct gender binaries within Michael Fields' aesthetic experience.[21] As exchanges with Berenson suggest, it is a different matter altogether when men get involved in judging women's clothing, faces, and bodies. Oscar Wilde, for example, lives in a glass house and, according to Cooper, should not throw stones.

Bradley and Cooper stand in a London gallery with Mary Costelloe in the spring:

> As we are looking at this Costa Oscar comes up; he shakes hands with Mrs. C. and thereafter I put out ~~[illeg.]~~ ^my hand,^ wh: he takes (afar off) and never addresses a single word to me after. Sim bows, he returns the bow (afar off) and never addresses a word to her after. I have not often seen such rudeness—he is not of the men who can be rude offensively and yet escape. There is no charm in his elephantine body tightly stuffed into his clothes—with a gross, gorged effect—no charm in his great face and head of a unselect Bohemian cast—save the urbanity he can adopt or the intelligence without wh: he can vitalise his ponderousness. When he shows himself as a *snob* he is disgustingly repulsive. We were not well-dressed, as the day had begun with rain—we do not belong to the fashionable world—so Oscar rolls his shoulders toward us. When next I meet him in my choicest French ~~[illeg.]~~ hat I will turn my back on him, ^and that^ decisively. The artist strain in him is crossed by the vulgar-respectable. Gods and woman ~~[illeg.]~~ cannot endure such a cross. (1892, 97v–98r, EC; emphasis in original)

Though they are at other times more sympathetic to Wilde, Cooper and Bradley are scathing about him here, his "elephantine" body engorging his clothing, his visage blanker and less vital than the expressive faces Field will later encounter in the Paris Morgue. Those corpses are not grotesque, but Wilde is. Yet curiously, Michael Field feel the cut he offers them, and they infer that his snobbishness reflects a judgment on their unfashionable clothing. Their excuse: bad weather caused them to leave their chic French hats at home.

However, as we know, her French hat does Cooper no favors with Berenson; recall the "holocaust" of discarded trimmings when she attempted to gain favor through its redaction. Just as Michael Field often feel that they do not know how to be of this world, they are frequently embarrassed by their clothing choices. Returning one evening to Mary's flat in Paris, they find Mary dressed for evening: "Her 'robe' ^is^ of white silk, striped with blue and trimmed with blue—a soft old china blue. Her chest is bare—the feathers of a white fan curl round her hand; her beauty is radiant." Mary, "cool, yet smug," credits the hot weather for décolletage. Michael Field are mortified: "We go into our room, furious, impotent—for my Love has only an ugly ancient satin, grey and pink. I, thinking that in Bohemia one needed no evening attire, had put none in my box. A parti-coloured blouse of pink and rose, over a long black cloth skirt is all I can manage." They do not have the right things to wear. And Berenson is viciously condescending: "Does not Miss Cooper wear pretty colours—don't you like the fold at the waist?" (1892, 115v, EC).[22]

The hot weather makes dressing a challenge. In early July, as they prepare for an evening at the Opera, Mary suggests that the women wear blouses because of the heat. Cooper reports:

> Bernhard turns to Sim—"You will not go in yours." "Why not?" "Well, you do not want to look a guy." "Then why should I wear one?" asks Mary. ^"Yes," Sim says, "Why should Mary wear hers?"^ "O ~~[illeg.]~~ ^Mary^ can wear anything . . ." "Why should you mind Miss Bradley's dressing as she likes?"—"Oh, I am a man"—is the insulting rejoinder. I cannot remember what we say—I only recollect how Mary comes into our room and offers her feather-fan, anything—to break the brutality of the insult. (1892, 129v–130r, EC)

Cooper's verdict: Berenson "was guilty of the most intolerable offence—the humiliation of one woman by a compliment to another in the presence of both" (1892, 131r, EC). Later in the summer, Michael Field report, they had the opportunity to clap back at Berenson when Berenson found himself in need of a nightshirt when staying at Costelloe's flat. Mary did not have something to lend him, so Bradley provided a nightgown of her own: "She has one all lace and little tucks wh: is laid on his sofa-bed. The whole affair is unutterably comic." The women are "haunted in our beds with thought of the mystic bearded young face above the feminine ~~[illeg.]~~ trimmings of the night-dress" (1892, 157r, EC). Now who looks like a guy? Clearly, for Michael Field, revenge is a dish best eaten cold.

Wilde with his engorged elephantine body, the Doctrine in his nighty, and the hairy, crouching, yellow "thing" that Michael Field encounter naked. There is something monstrous, grotesque about these three living men whose bodies Michael Field confront in 1892. They are so different from the seemingly approachable male corpses in the Paris Morgue, men whose still, waxen faces suggest traits of character from which the poets can easily imagine identities, lives. Living men are far more challenging to Michael Field. Living men frustrate their comprehension.

So, the poets departed Paris. Having tasted the world, they found it unsuitable to their particular hunger. In August, Bradley writes directly to Cooper in the diary: "O Henry, Henry, my Boy, let us cleave to art—with a small a, and *grow* toward life, as toward the sun, not rend our path toward it. God bless Henry!" (1892, 134r, KB; emphasis in original). Cooper is less certain than Bradley about what it might mean to grow toward life.

Her desire for Berenson was battered by the summer's experience, but not killed. With Bradley away in Oxford, she is home alone, and writes a message that she knows Bradley will see:

> I am without my Love, in the twilight, when at the best one is sad to death. She is in Oxford—I am here a fragment. But I love my Art and will not dare to injure it—I love my own Love and could not do violence to her or myself—so let her not fear. Although ~~these~~ ^'the Doctrine's'^ wonderful eyes—~~[illeg.]~~ a Faun crossed with the traditional Christ's—pursue me, ~~with~~ ^tho, they have^ a charm that maddens, I will never go off to the hills like agave only to rent my own flesh and blood—my artistic personality. I die in the presence of the face I love—the man's.
>
> There is no fellowship, no caress, no tight winding-together of two natures, no tenderness when my Love is severed from me; and there seems to be no life in people—no life to be got anywhere—if one is withdrawn from *the Doctrine.*
>
> So I sit by my table doubly dead. (1892, 134r, EC; emphasis in original; fig. 5)

The remainder of that diary page has been torn away. Bits of Cooper's handwriting peek out above the tear that conservationists have mended with a piece of blank paper.

In all likelihood, we will never know what was lost to us when that page was torn out—nor who did the tearing. Nor why. But Bradley need not fear the loss of her lover. Cooper will do no violence to her art or to her Love. Indeed, she will protect what is her own flesh and blood, her own artistic personality: two women, one poet. She loves the man, who brings the world alive for her. The woman is her Love, their two natures tightly wound as one in tenderness. In choosing her Love, Cooper makes a choice against the world for which she longs—notwithstanding Bradley's exhortation that they will *grow* toward life.

"Cooper artfully constructed a duality of faun-like souls," Vicinus writes, "but the discovery of raw heterosexual desire dazzled her."[23] Cooper feels doubly dead, trapped in the past. And she recognizes that this is her choice. For Michael Field, there was ambivalence in progress. In August, on the eve of the Mother-One's death anniversary, they assemble the customary altar, and Bradley expresses a worry: "We who are growing so close to the modern, are we growing further away from her?" (1892, 135v, KB). Forward progress threatens to leave the past behind. If Michael Field are "contemporaneous" in the modern world, does that attenuate the bonds

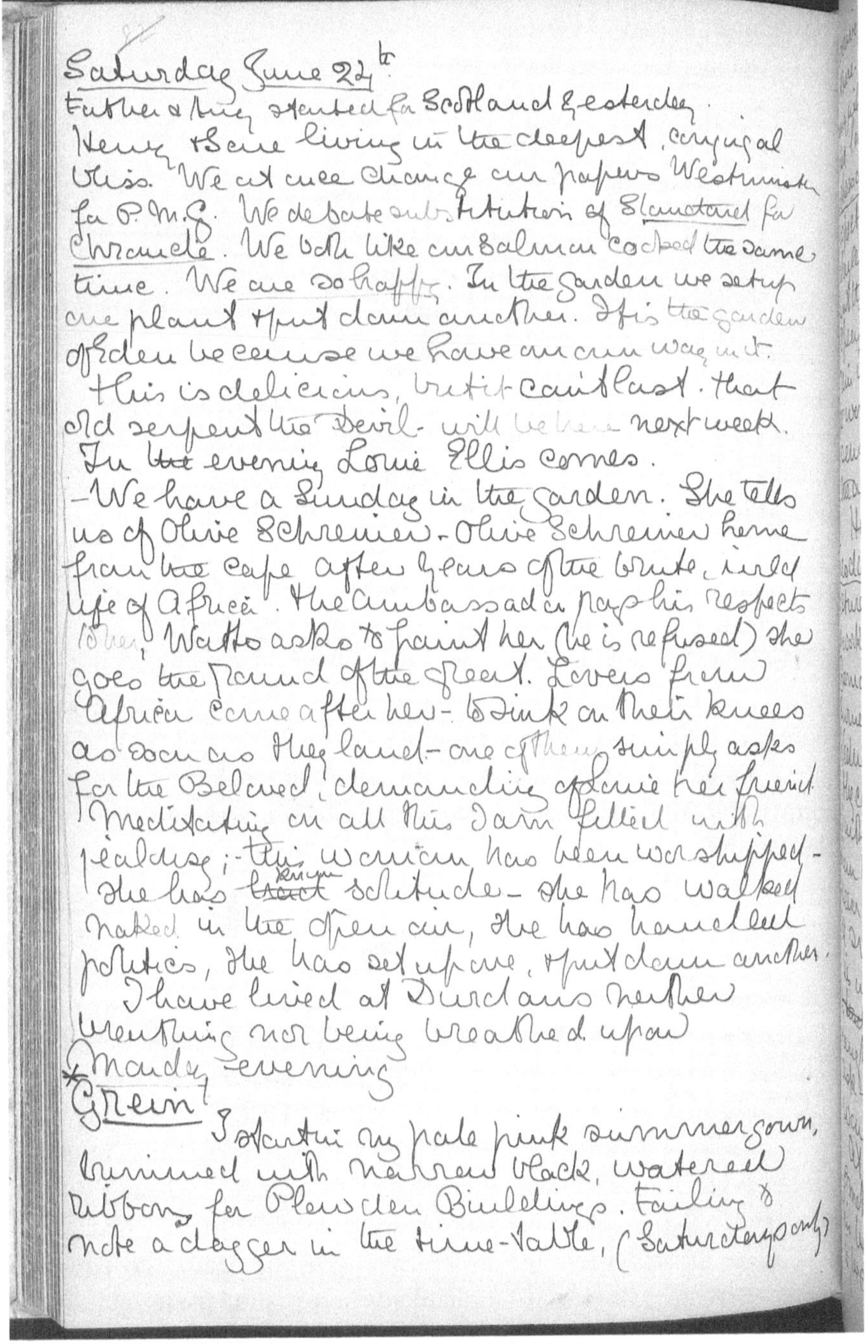
Saturday June 24th
Father & Amy started for Scotland yesterday.
Henry & I are living in the deepest, conjugal bliss. We at once change our papers Westminster for P.M.G. We debate substitution of Standard for Chronicle. We both like our salmon cooked the same time. We are so happy. In the garden we set up one plant & put down another. It is the garden of Eden because we have our own way in it. This is delicious, but it can't last. That old serpent the Devil – will be here next week.
In the ~~the~~ evening Louie Ellis comes.
– We have a Sunday in the garden. She tells us of Olive Schreiner – Olive Schreiner home from the Cape after years of the brute, wild life of Africa. The ambassador pays his respects to her, Watts asks to paint her (he is refused) she goes the round of the great. Lovers from Africa come after her – sink on their knees as soon as they land – one of them simply asks for the Beloved, demanding of Louie her friend.
Meditating on all this I am filled with jealousy; – this woman has been worshipped – she has ~~tract~~ known solitude – she has walked naked in the open air, she has handled politics, she has set up one, & put down another.
I have lived at Durdans neither wreathing nor being wreathed upon
Monday evening
*Green!
I start in my pale pink summer gown, trimmed with narrow black, watered ribbon for Plowden Buildings. Failing to note a dagger in the time-table, (Saturday only)

FIGURE 5. Katharine Bradley, feeling the constraints of her quiet life and longing for the adventures that other women writers seem to have, in 1893. © The British Library Board, ADD MS 46781: Vol. 6 (1893), 45v.

that remain so immanent for them? Is that a form of loss they are willing to tolerate?

In October 1892, Bradley and Cooper spotted a headline on a newspaper in the Tube:

Death
of
Lord Tennyson
Illustrated tragically
a penny
(1892, 139r, KB)

The laureate voice is now silent. Departing Tennyson's funeral, Bradley writes, "It is lovely autumn when we come out. And so closes the Victorian epoch.—~~It is~~ ^an epoch^ already yesterday: it is for us, England's living, and yet unspent poets to make all things new. We are for the morning—the nineteenth century thinks it has no poets—nothing to lose—verily it has nothing: for we are not of it—we shake the dust of our feet from it, and pass on into the 20th century" (1892, 140r, KB).[24]

The year 1892 was one of shame and humiliation for Bradley—for Cooper, all that, plus life-changing disappointment. They were brave in that context to count themselves among "England's living, and yet unspent poets," poised to "make things new." Michael Field shook the nineteenth-century dust from their feet and prepared to stride bravely into the twentieth century.

Coda: 1893

Still operating under the influence of Berenson, Cooper and Bradley turn their aesthetic eye to Durdans, the Cooper family home in Surrey. In spring cleaning they describe as "the battle of the [past] modern," they strip their little study of all but Italian art. It hurt; Michael Field liked their reproduction Millet and Turner images: "Our eyes no longer desire the Turners, our heads testify against them, yet the pain of parting from them is keen. Memory is a harpy—pluck her roots and she bleeds."[25] Bradley struggles to adapt to life under the rule of Berenson: "This new god's single command—*Be contemporaneous*[—]is harder to keep than all the ten old commandments" (1893, 47r–47v, KB; emphasis in original).[26]

We know that Cooper has chosen a modern path: she wants to embrace life and all its emotions, good, bad, and ugly. Yet the command to the "contemporaneous" remains elusive for Michael Field. And as for the embrace of life: What if life does not want to embrace back?

Cooper begins 1893 alone in bed: "A dark beginning. My cruel Love leaves me for early service, an unsatisfied heathen in our little bed" (1893, 3r, EC). Reading *Anna Karenina*, she finds herself astonished at the book's vibrance: "Passion, quieter love, birth, death, kinship, motherhood, the fields, the railway, the restaurant, the race-course—every phase, every circumstance of life finds its place in the pages as in life itself" (1893, 12r, EC). Unfortunately, Michael Field are not living in Tolstoy's world. They feel isolated, lonely, shunned, bewildered by the world's indifference to them. Cooper cannot help but contrast her personal circumstances with the grand scale of activity she encounters in *Anna Karenina*: "We are desperately alone in this world that shuns us. What can it be! [. . .] We are boycotted in the papers, by the men (Pater, Meredith, Hutton) to whom we have sent our book, and by even literary society. It is mysterious" (1893, 7r, EC). Later Bradley describes theirs as an "intense smothered, smouldering life" (1893, 53r, KB). The family home at Reigate seems devoid of oxygen.

The jaws of isolation have snapped shut on Cooper. She will not leave her Love. At thirty-one, she remains in her girlhood home, technically under her father's care. Cooper's restlessness is everywhere in early 1893, expressed in her reading of Tolstoy and of Poe—and her experience of Ibsen with a production of *Ghosts*, translated by William Archer, and shortly afterward, crucially, *The Master Builder*. These literary influences, and especially Ibsen, equipped Cooper anew to channel her frustrations: "Then . . . the play *The Masterbuilder* is acted in real life, and Ibsen's power of giving blood to an Allegory tested, proved in terrible earnest" (1893, 19v, EC). The result? Bradley had a terrible falling out with Cooper's father, James, over socialism. James declares that Bradley must leave the home. Cooper: "I join my hand to hers and we go out, not looking at him or speaking to him again" (1893, 19v, EC). Cooper foments a plan to establish a separate residence in London with her Love. The plan would entail her father selling the Reigate house and moving closer to London with his younger daughter, Amy. Cooper herself would then shuttle back and forth between the homes in order to remain a benign force in Amy's life; Amy, nicknamed "Little One," would celebrate her twenty-seventh birthday in 1893. Cooper fortifies herself for these difficult conversations: "I invoke the Mother-One and the Modern—enter the Dining-room, saying in calm tones that I want to have a long talk" (1893, 20v, EC).[27]

Just as Edward Barrett, father of Elizabeth, had done before him, James Cooper expressed his dread about what this poet, his daughter, was about to tell him: "You want to tell me you are going to leave me forever" (1893, EC, 20v). "Leaving forever" was, of course, the great impermissible, unspeakable, impossible deed within the families of origin of Edith Cooper and Elizabeth Barrett Browning, solved differently in the case of Michael Field than of the Brownings.[28] Yet Cooper's plan to break up the household foundered, not because of her father or her sister but because of Bradley. She reports that Bradley confessed: "[M]y Love is dreading the idea of London as a home, now it is so friendless for us. This relaxes my will. [. . .] We remember that our visit to Rome is lost, if we set up in London—we remember that we must often part, leaving each other lovesick, that my life would be distracted, that our art would be hurt by noise and fret. [. . .] We agree to go on the same—except that we have gained immense courage for the future" (1893, 21r, EC).

The suggestion of a private home for Michael Field alone holds immense appeal, even if the drain on their resources proves impracticable; the women confront an unresolvable tension between the travel, companionship, and creative freedom they enjoy while using the father's home as their base, and the independence they would enjoy with a home of their own. Still, they find ways to create a private coupling in the family home. When James and Amy Cooper departed for their holiday in Scotland, for instance, the poets remained at Durdans, "living in the deepest conjugal bliss." Bradley continues: "We at once change our papers Westminster for P.M.G. We debate substitution of *Standard* for *Chronicle*. We both like our salmon cooked the same time. *We are so happy*. In the garden we set up one plant and put down another. It is the garden of Eden because we have our own way in it. This is delicious, but it can't last" (1893, 45v, KB; emphasis in original). Their friend Louie Ellis visits the would-be honeymooners, and the women spend Sunday in the garden. Louie tells the poets of Olive Schreiner:

> Olive Schreiner home from the Cape after years of the brute, wild life of Africa. The ambassador pays his respects to her, Watts asks to paint her (he is refused) she goes the round of the great. Lovers from Africa come after her—to sink on their knees as soon as they land—one of them simply asks for the Beloved, demanding of Louie her friend. Meditating on all this I am filled with jealousy;—this woman has been worshipped, she has ~~had~~ ^known^ solitude—she has walked naked in the open air, she has handled politics, she has set up one and put down another.

I have lived at Durdans neither breathing nor being breathed upon. (1893, 45v, KB; fig. 6)

Schreiner embodies (nakedly) a version of the ideal of modernity to which Michael Field aspire. She is an artist who has also had a life of mobility and adventure. She is sought after by friends and lovers, painters, and the great. She has commanded worship, and she has enjoyed solitude. Fresh air has caressed her naked body. By comparison, Bradley feels even more smothered and constrained than she did before, but even so, she has just chosen this life—chosen to remain at Durdans, elected not to try life in London or beyond. In contrast, Cooper is far more willing to recognize that an embrace of the "modern" requires action on her part. Bradley is likelier to imagine that the modern will come to her. Ambivalence, thy name is Katharine Bradley.

Nonetheless, the modern seems to come within grasp of Michael Field in 1893. On August 4, they received word that their play, *A Question of Memory*, would be staged in October at JT Grein's Independent Theatre in London.[29] Michael Field are thrilled—they are apprehensive. They are heading to London.

Bickering to an unusual degree ("nervous quarrelsome females" [1893, 73r, KB]), Michael Field land in a London flat in the Verulam Buildings near Gray's Inn Road in advance of the production on October 27. Cooper is in her element, attending and advising on rehearsals on a daily basis: "I so love Rehearsal. It is so wonderful to see one's words growing pictures, movements, persons—to watch a play being secretly fashioned down in the Earth" (1893, 74v, EC). As thrilling as the rehearsal experience was for Cooper, Michael Field were unaccustomed to the particular collaborative nature of theater; they are startled when their vision began to give way to other approaches, and by the need to fight for what they want. Ultimately, Cooper became ill from the stress and activity; she was "the colour of uncooked pastry, my inside like an angry net of wasps. I was sent home to opium pills and quiet" (1893, 79v–80, EC). Cooper sizzles with anticipation in advance of the play's one-night run. Two nights in advance of the production, she writes, "Tomorrow I shall be wishing my Love that deepest joy of being born again in the hearts of a multitude" (1893, 84r, EC).

As Michael Field, Bradley and Cooper write a painful tension between the centripetal passion that characterizes their emotional and artistic relationship, and an aching desire to find love in the world. Hence Cooper's eagerness to congratulate Bradley on "that deepest joy of being born again in the hearts of a multitude." Cooper is eager to have a more active life that

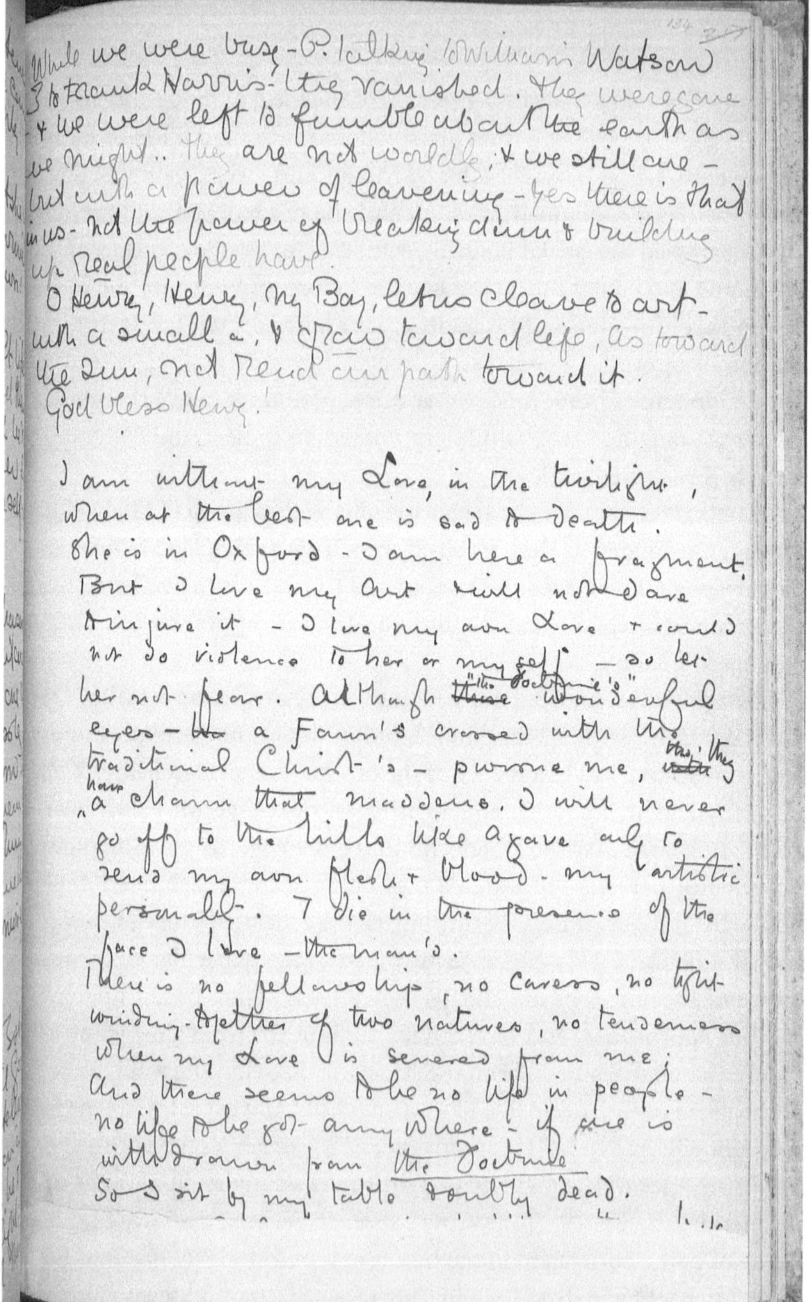

While we were busy—P. talking to William Watson & Frank Harris—they vanished. They were gone & we were left to fumble about the earth as we might.. They are not worldly; & we still are—but with a power of leavening—yes there is that in us—not the power of breaking down & building up real people have.

O Henry, Henry, my Boy, let us cleave to art—with a small a, & grow toward life, as toward the sun, not rend our path toward it.

God bless Henry!

I am without my Love, in the twilight, when at the best one is sad to death.
She is in Oxford—I am here a fragment.
But I love my Art & will not dare to injure it—I love my own Love & could not do violence to her or myself—so let her not fear. Although the Doctrine's wonderful eyes—a Faun's crossed with the traditional Christ's—pursue me, they have a charm that maddens, I will never go off to the hills like Agave only to rend my own flesh & blood—my artistic personality. I die in the presence of the face I love—the man's.
There is no fellowship, no caress, no tight winding-together of two natures, no tenderness when my Love is severed from me;
And there seems to be no life in people—no life to be got anywhere—if one is withdrawn from the Doctrine
So I sit by my table doubly dead.

FIGURE 6. "So I sit by my table doubly dead." Edith Cooper, torn between two loves in 1892. © The British Library Board, ADD MS 46780: Vol. 5 (1892), 134r.

involves multitudes, and new possibilities. As they near the end of the nineteenth century, Michael Field understand the importance of staking a place for themselves in the future; this is for them the "modern." But Bradley is particularly happy in the conjugal state of two; she demonstrates repeatedly her reluctance to introduce change. In the emotional logic of their relationship, Cooper consistently heeds a primal loyalty that keeps her as one with Bradley—but she persistently presses forward and outward to create new affective bonds. Call them what you will—Bernhard Berenson, perhaps, or a pied-à-terre in London away from her father—Cooper is always seeking something new, something more, something else. But her efforts to embrace a forward trajectory are always thwarted.

So, the morning after *A Question of Memory* was staged, Cooper wrote: "It seems more natural to be dead than alive" (1893, 86v, EC). The play was a horrendous flop. In the face of the setback, the poets play to type. Bradley is stoic and matter of fact. Cooper: "I ~~was~~ ^am^ in helpless pain like a dumb animal at first" (1893, 86v, EC). Longing for the quiet of sculpture, she takes refuge alone in the British Museum: "I long to lie ~~down~~ in one of those sarcophagi covered with hieroglyphics, and to know that the weight of ages would hold the lid down" (1893, EC, 87r). The poet who so wishes for escape now wishes for captivity, suffocation.

What went wrong?

Given their track record, I should mention that the problem was not the poets' choice of dress, of which they were quite proud: "My Love wore her black and coral dress and a lovely green velveteen opera-cloak with silver clasp and black fur edgings. Two white ~~[illeg.]~~ flowers were bunched under the collar. [Cooper] wore a dress of shimmery beryl green-white lace and, black satin sash and breast-bow, deep red leaves and a venetian-red opera cloak, with black fur edge" (1893, 89r, EC).

According to the poets' account of the painful evening, reception of the play was initially warm, but cooled rapidly as the production continued. By the end, all was lost. Cooper reports: "Act IV was lost from the beginning [. . .] toward the end the Beattys kissed, there was a laugh and a shout of *no*! [. . .]—then we ran behind the stage. The applause must have been good, for the actors seemed warm—I cannot say I heard it and not once did I catch the word *Author*" (1893, 88v, EC; emphasis in original). The day or two that followed the play were characterized by painful silence on behalf of friends and family from whom Michael Field would have hoped to hear, accompanied by vicious newspaper coverage; reviews were hard to read, "like a lot of unchained tigers" (1893, 87r, EC). "Not a flower had any one sent us yesterday, not a flower was given to us. No word, no letter, no visit, only the execrations of the press!" (1893, 86v, EC). Both Cooper and Bradley tried to rally through the pain and isolation, and Cooper attempted to be philosophical—while also interjecting a rare note of humor. She writes: "Not a soul has been near us—our rooms are full of the sound of a winter-wind, on our desk are the Daily journals . . . but though everything is against us we are strong, thank heaven and our race! We have ~~had~~ gained great experience, we have won the *friendliness* of our Caste, we have tried our forces for once, we have held an audience—*we regret nothing* [except Mrs. Creswick's acting!!]" (1893, 87v, EC; emphasis in original).

It is not only that Michael Field failed—it is how Michael Field failed.

A few days later, the truly awful part hit, showing Michael Field how very far they were from their aspiration to modernity, contemporaneity, or even, they feared, relevance. In a review in the *World*, the critic William Archer delivered, in Cooper's words, "a merciless attack on our archaic style" (1893, 90v, EC).[30] "The ladies who choose to be known as 'Michael Field' must be numbered among the many victims of the Elizabethan drama," Archer wrote, situating the poets in the "worship of a dead convention that has produced an infinite mass of still-born literature."[31]

Dismissing Michael Field as "natives of the land of Sentiment," Archer continues:

> In the first, second, and fourth acts there is scarcely a single natural sequence of thought, feeling, and expression. The dialogue is always flying off at unexpected tangents, and trying to obtain subtlety by means of incoherence. The authors have observed, quite justly, that feeling *is* incoherent—or rather, that consciousness is like a swirling stream, in which the unexpected and apparently irrelevant objects are always floating to the surface for a moment and then disappearing again, in obedience to laws which we cannot formulate. [. . .] Dialogue [. . .] is not the dialogue of life, but a world evolved from the playwright's inner consciousness.[32]

As David Moriarty writes in response to Archer, "Archer has defined the stream of consciousness style well, but he has missed the significance of this experiment in adapting it for the drama because he has been conditioned by his taste for Ibsen to expect 'the dialogue of life,' realistic dialogue, in a play with realistic setting and based on real occurrence."[33] Reading Michael Field in the light of a different conception of realism—stream of consciousness—Moriarty suggests that Archer has misdiagnosed the temporal crisis. The implication is clear. Michael Field are not too late in their idiomatic mode; they are too early.

Cooper hastened to rewrite the play's most offending scene, and she posted the new draft to Archer along with a letter, part of which she transcribed in the diary, bowing to Archer's authority. Cooper expresses Michael Field's temporal asynchrony as a crisis of contemporaneity for a poet struggling to capture the now.

> Eight years ago you said in print that our use of the Elizabethan Method was enough to make a critic weep tears of blood. We do not ask so exhausting an interest in our mistakes—we want to realise where we go wrong and how we are to start afresh. 1590 is second nature to us—we sometimes fear it is first nature, for we are even accused of speaking "Quaint Elizabethan English" in ordinary life. It is very discouraging not to know when one is antiquated or when one is contemporary. We wish at last with all the strength in us to be contemporary, to write a direct prose with natural sequences. (1893, 91r, EC)

Cooper continues her overture to this well-regarded critic, asking Archer to provide Michael Field instruction in a sort in contemporary idiomatic English: "The M.S. we send is the measure of what we have as yet learnt; we want to know how far it is the measure of what we have still to learn. Mark the M.S. without reserve and kindly return it to Mich. Field, Durdans, Reigate" (1893, 91v, EC).

Michael Field's fierce desire to join the modern world, to be "contemporaneous," extends all the way down to their idiomatic language. Indeed, just as Bradley and Cooper begged Berenson for lessons about the very paintings they enjoyed visiting regularly, here they seek lessons from a male authority in the very medium in which they work. They do not offer to pay Archer for the pleasure.

Here again is the ambivalent core to Michael Field, revealing itself in their relationship to past and present, and negotiated with male authority figures—Berenson, Archer—who find them lacking. Thinking about Michael Field's historical voice, Bradley writes a letter to Cooper, dated August 28, 1885, that begins, "Sweet Wife, the hardships of early married life are beginning":

> [D]earie, I want to say some grave words to you. Do not desert Shakespeare and the Elizabethans. Those with the sobering influence of the great Greek dramatists, whom you ought to resolve at once to study, are the only Masters for us. Every dramatic writer must be full of his

> Shakespeare, as every religious writer Must be full of his Bible. We Must give up the tricks, the externalities, the archaisms,—to copy these is imitation, but we must seek to study and touch life as he—Shakespeare studied and touched it, and our speech Must always be utterly different from ordinary speech; because ordinary speech is not transfigured by emotion, and the ordinary speech of an Age like ours is base with the exceeding Vulgarity of Materialism. God shall give our thought a body as it pleaseth him.[34]

Literary style is the body God gives to ideas, in Bradley's reckoning. The high style of poetic language is transfigured, not base, not ordinary; it endeavors not to copy Shakespeare but to learn from his dedication to "study and touch life."

That said, Michael Field were clearly capable writers of idiomatic narrative; the very diary in which Cooper records her tensions with Archer comprises about 9,500 pages of generally idiomatic narrative prose. Surely she must recognize that her very plea—to help Michael Field "to write a direct prose with natural sequences"—is expressed in direct prose, with natural sequences. Indeed, throughout *Works and Days*, Bradley and Cooper express themselves in lucid, often eloquent, prose that does not seem remotely "Elizabethan."

But when they close the diary and write for contemporaneous publication, Michael Field feel the need to clothe themselves in Elizabethan garb—and, more broadly, in mannered, highly formal, allusive, and often elusive discourses that hold their readers at arm's length, far from the embrace of the modern they so desire. Yet we have seen that at this very same time, Cooper was reading and responding intensely to Tolstoy based on the compellingly "comprehensive" quality she finds in his prose. In the mid-1890s Michael Field were intensely interested in Ibsen, too, for his success in bringing dynamics of gender and authority alive on the stage in naturalistic, accessible ways. All that Michael Field admire in Tolstoy and in Ibsen is alive in their own work—in *Works and Days*.[35] But *Works and Days* was to be a private document until the 1930s, whereas the very public *A Question of Memory* seemed sufficiently out of step with its moment that it met with unfriendly reception.

At a performance of *Measure for Measure* later that fall, Michael Field spot William Archer sitting with Oscar Wilde. Cooper writes, "The next moment our ^my^ eyes met ^his^—for what seemed like a great while, there was so much in the look, such waves of understanding, of fascinated magnatism [*sic*] passing from stall to dress-circle! It was a most modern encounter—'frightfully thrilling.' His eyes are like doors into a lethal chamber, but they certainly are capable of expressing Ibsenism in real life" (1893, 92v, EC). Shortly after this sensationalistic encounter, Archer terminated their brief correspondence, writing back to Cooper to ask her not to send him anymore of *A Question of Memory* to edit: "Archer has written—having come to the conclusion that he must beg us not to send him the rest of the play—he is too busy; and 'moreover, the very weight that you are good enough to attach to my remarks renders me unwilling to accept the responsibility of a sort of collaboration in whose value I do not myself believe.'" Archer concludes his request with a humiliating postscript: "When the play is published pray do not mention that any portion of it has been through my hands" (1893, 100r, EC).

Cooper does not regret the experience of producing *A Question of Memory*. Afterward, she says she would do it all again, even knowing it would end as it did. Stanley Addleshaw tells her that a man would not repeat the experience, and Cooper replies, "But then you see, I am a woman and to bring out a play is experience of life—just what women feel so crushingly that they need. You men get it like breathing" (1893, 91v, EC).

Indeed, Cooper is buoyant as the poets approach the year-end review in the 1893 volume of *Works and Days*. She anticipates Clarissa Dalloway, born just over thirty-two years later, in 1925, writing:

> [T]hen came a plunge into *real* life at Grays Inn and the Opera Comique. We have faced the technique of our art, we have faced (and for half an hour held) an audience; our aims have been consolidated by experience, our spirits tried by opposition. I am twice the woman I was this time last year—I am afraid just now nearly as bitter, for no friend stood by us, even to rebut false reports; and the one man who could have been of inestimable virtue to our art-life has withdrawn his aid. [. . .] I ~~[illeg.]~~ do not ~~[illeg.]~~ ^yet^ realise where *modernity* is taking me; I am moving with it as if down a stream, not using it enough ~~as a~~ ^for^ motive force like a ~~mill-wheel~~ waterfall turning a mill. But I do not get frightened—I maintain a resolute patience. [. . .]—though I am certain that we are doing an unnatural and destructive thing if we allow the claims of others to mar the freedom of self-realisation as the central need of our lives—and the condition of happiness. (1893, 104r–104v, EC; emphasis in original)

Though the water is cold, Cooper feels exhilarated by the great plunge she has taken. She recognizes that modernity is carrying her along, like it or not, toward the unknown—in this case, 1894: "I greet 'the unknown'

(1894) with a cheer!" She has not yet figured out how to use modernity to supply power for her vision, but she remains resolved to adopt the modern imperative to self-realization. Ibsen has inspired in Cooper a determination to break free of her Oedipal home life, both physically and psychologically governed by her controlling father: "*The Master-builder* and the succeeding crisis gave me a far more solid influence over father, and much more intense and therefore outer freedom" (1893, 103r, EC). First and last, "when I love my Love,—the dark things seem to drown and I see how much self-realisation there really is in my life, though not in its daily conditions" (1893, 104v, EC). She closes the year with the Catullan salute: "*Vale atque salve!*" (Hail and farewell!).

Michael was in nowhere near such an enthralled mood as 1893 drew to its close. In contrast to "*Vale atque salve!*," she offers this: "The little boil in my nostril is broken, and I walk unvexed through the palace of my brain. We have not made a friend this year. [. . .] We are too quarrelsome, and this we must set ourselves to over-come in 94" (1893, 105r, KB). Bradley brings Cooper's festive New Year's tone back to earth with a thud, imposing a reality check on Cooper's exuberance. Bradley reasserts the bodily grotesque, loneliness and isolation, and the most unflatteringly quarrelsome bits of the poets' relationship. Cooper as ever seeks the plot of the Michael Field story in the world outside, and notwithstanding the year's stunning defeat—following the humiliation of Paris in 1892—she remains oriented to the future with an open embrace. Bradley is querulous by comparison, turned inward, uncertain of the path ahead.

CHAPTER THREE

"The Infamous Cliché"

1897

IF MICHAEL FIELD were in search of worldly excitement, they found it in 1897. They root the year's narrative in the tropes of Victorian melodrama: suspected murder, a missing body, a rogue photographer, hostile and inscrutable foreigners, and a dashing hero. And romance: in this year's narrative, Michael Field exchange wedding rings, and in earnest—and in private—commence their life as a couple in the full flush of married harmony. In the year they turned fifty-one and thirty-five, respectively, Michael Field are "daughters" no longer; they are out from under the thumb of a tyrannical and angry patriarch.

The 1897 text presents a classic tension between *fabula* and *sujet*, between the worldly events that were public—indeed, tragic—and tangible, and the deep affective bedrock of those worldly events' narration. *Sujet* decisively trumps *fabula* for Michael Field in 1897. Though the events of the year are painful and, for a while, all encompassing, the text's real story is the bedrock of affective intensity that frames the headlines. As we will soon see, this is the year Michael Field write—repeatedly—about giggling in bed with one another. Theirs is narrative, Michael Field style, realized in the immanence that can only come from surpassing emotions; plot submerged, its narrative signifying a resilient private identity, however precarious it remains.[1]

First, though, the headline story of the year. Nearly two months after the fact, Cooper writes the moment of discovery, in the roundabout mode Michael Field use when narrating a painful subject. Though Cooper writes these words in the diary, she attributes them to Bradley: "A rose-morning in June—a telegram came to me, brought in, through Amy's tenderness to her sister by a Quaker friend, a neighbor—'Am afraid Father had met with an accident[.]' I went up the stairs—I heard the voice of my darling—'Master!' in cooing, gayest call, and I had to break the news" (1897, 76r, EC; fig. 7). In faintest pencil above the word "darling" is the word "Michael," casting in question which of the poets performs the call of intimacy and which breaks the bad news. Notwithstanding who is the scene's darling and who its master, the death of the father intrudes directly into a scene of intimacy introduced by playful flirtation, "in cooing, gayest call."[2]

Cooper and her lover have again enjoyed a private honeymoon while James Cooper, her father, and Amy, her sister, are on holiday. The holiday this year had as its destination the Swiss Alpine village of Zermatt, in the shadow of the Matterhorn near the Italian border. But though two Coopers departed for Zermatt, only one returned. The telegram brought news that "the sweet, old father is gone" (1897, 76r, EC). Literally gone; no euphemism. James Cooper was missing—was believed dead—was perhaps murdered. On the day of the summer solstice, he went for a walk and he never came back. "At last I feel I must write of him," says Cooper days later, calling him, "my sweet old father, so much myself. He may have been murdered (might they be flogged and hanged who wd dare do such an infamy!) or he may have fallen over a rock, straying from the path, or he may have gone of his 'own will,' in mystery and peace to his Beloved, called to her from among the snowy mountains she adored in her maiden days: he is gone, leaving us the little home he put his heart into for us" (1897, 78v, EC).[3]

As Cooper's account demonstrates, his loved ones cannot help but project speculative stories into the void of information surrounding James's disappearance. Whether by murder, accident, or the lure of his late wife's siren song, James Cooper is gone. Even the belief that he is dead, from which Michael Field take comfort, is conjecture. The family doctor, summoned to Durdans to address the poets' sleeplessness, advances a detailed theory:

> His first impression on hearing the news was that Father had an attack of apoplexy—to wh: medically he thinks his patient was a little more liable than men of his age usually are on account of his gouty tendencies. ~~They~~ ^He^ thinks our loved one may have been tempted from the track by flower or view, and then painlessly fallen among thickets or mounds, and that the search hitherto may have been too ambitious—only precipices and river searched. The relief of such a hope! (1897, 80r, EC)

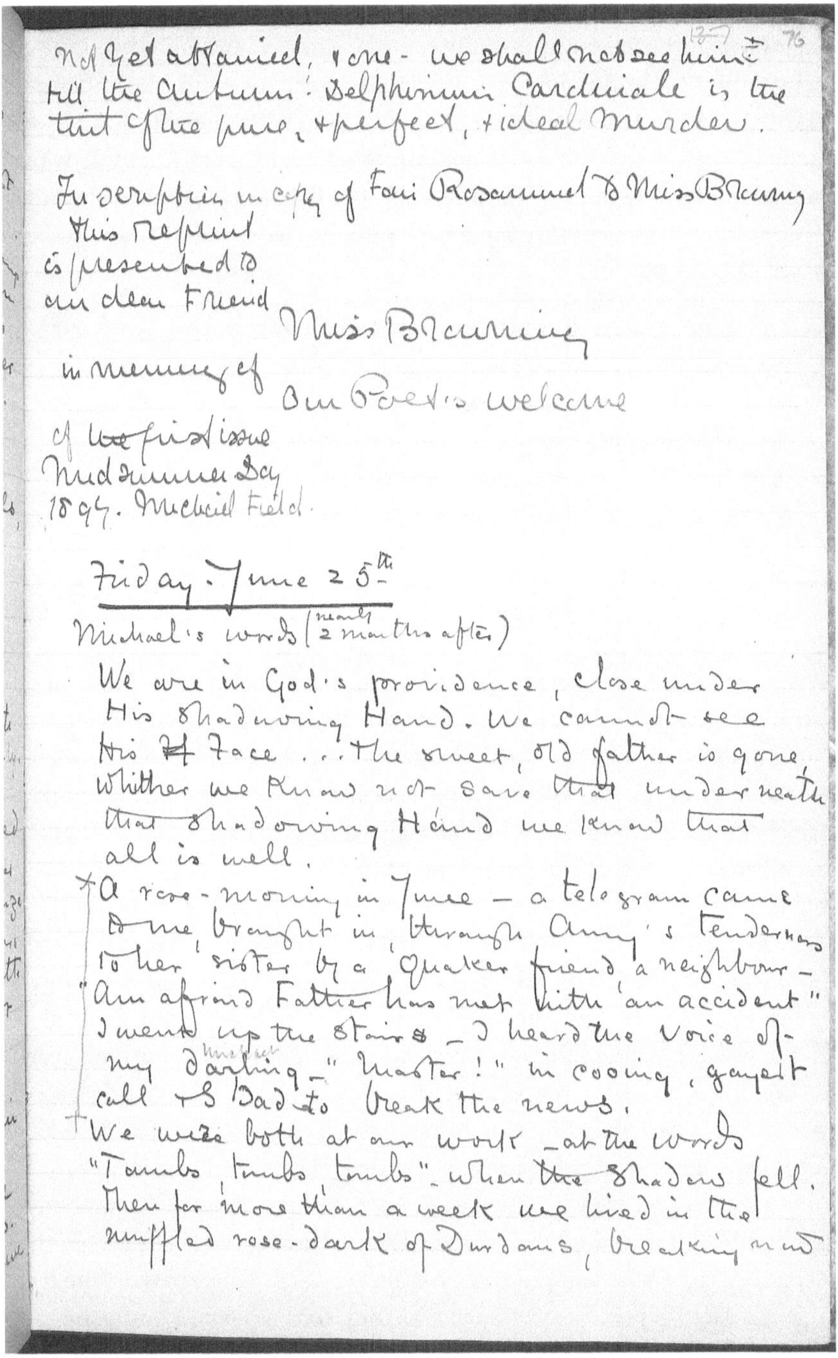
76

not yet arranged, & one - we shall not see him till the Autumn! Delphinium Cardinale is the tint of the pure, & perfect, & ideal murder.

Inscription in copy of Fair Rosamund to Miss Browning

This reprint
is presented to
our dear Friend
Miss Browning
in memory of
Our Poet's welcome
of ~~the~~ first issue
Midsummer Day
1897. Michael Field.

Friday. June 25th

Michael's words (nearly 2 months after)

We are in God's providence, close under His shadowing Hand. We cannot see His ~~H~~ Face . . . the sweet, old father is gone, whither we know not save that underneath that shadowing Hand we know that all is well.

A rose-morning in June — a telegram came to me, brought in through Amy's tenderness to her sister by a Quaker friend, a neighbour — "Am afraid Father has met with an accident" I went up the stairs — I heard the voice of my darling — "Master!" in cooing, gay-it call & I had to break the news.

We were both at our work — at the words "Tombs, tombs, tombs" — when the shadow fell. Then for more than a week we lived in the muffled rose-dark of Durdans, breaking not

FIGURE 7. "Master," probably Katharine Bradley, has to break the news that James Cooper is missing and feared dead. © The British Library Board, ADD MS 46786: Vol. 11 (1897), 76r.

One can imagine. An elderly man (James Cooper was seventy-nine in an era when the average mortality for men hovered around fifty), his eye caught by an Alpine blossom—Edelweiss, perhaps—tumbles, his final resting spot hidden in plain view. Aside from death, the speculative fictions of Cooper's death share a common element. Regardless of what happened, he is with his "Beloved" now: the Beloved Mother-One works unseen to welcome her loved one back into the fold. Bradley writes to her other niece, Amy:

> I am sure of the end. Darling, in the white dawn when I asked our blessed Mother to help us as she has through so many tragedies, my soul saw her clearly and the wings of her spirit were no more folded over us to cover us from cares, but pointed erect, so that my sight went up to them, as if they were sunbeams, and I felt somehow that she had a new treasure with her, all the humble love, the years of devotion of her bridegroom, living at her side. She has called him to her among her Alps—the snows she loved have been a second wedding. So be happy about this joy and hers. (1897, 77r, KB)

Her wings erect, the blessed angel Mother beams with the adoration of her new treasure, her old bridegroom with her now till eternity. The poets repeatedly credit the Mother with agency over the Father's death, less in the context of murder, and more in the context of a "second wedding," which casts the afterlife as a dematerialized married home. Edith Cooper also frames her father's death in the context of his marriage: "Our sweet, old father is with his Beloved—but, oh, he has left us and we weep for him. He was good and ripe in beauty of spirit. He will help us in life and always be side by side with our darling Mother in our passionate and living love" (1897, 81r, EC). Just as the dead Mother-One has a crucial role to play in the poets' ongoing life, the sweet, old father joins her to form an everlasting force of dead parental love. Though Cooper presents her deceased parents as a pair standing side by side, the implication is clear that the afterlife is the domain of maternal, and thus blessed and gentle, love.

As we so often see with Michael Field, the projection of a disembodied ideal of beatific parental love plays to their advantage: it is clear from the very beginning that James, dead, is much easier to tolerate than the live version. He has been an obstacle, a barrier, to the poets. Months before his disappearance, Bradley wrote wearily as she and Cooper departed on a brief holiday: "We have fled from Reigate, as from a land of abortions, drains and damp" (1897, 5v, KB). The father's house is equal parts beloved and oppressive. We know that it took Cooper several years after her mother's passing to temper her idealization of the Beloved. In the case of her father, however, candor emerges almost immediately. Ambivalence toward him and what he represents is right on the surface and clearly conscious to Michael Field. To begin, his sister-in-law, Bradley:

> It is so impossible to realise here in the home round wh: he has turned his whole life in love for us, thought for our future, toil for our pleasure, that he will never see the plants we have set in the beds for his eyes, the melons reared for him, the noble roses he gave us. With all his faults of mood, his tenderness, affection, simplicity, sweet paternity, chivalry, poetic temperament ~~[illeg.]~~ and beautifully gained ripeness, his trust in God and his loved ones, ~~he was~~ ^made him^ indeed dear and irreparably precious. (1897, 77r, KB)

The family home is about him but it is also about them; James Cooper was moody and grumpy, but he was also lovable. He was, indeed, "dear and irreplaceably precious."

His elder daughter Edith builds on the ambivalence. She writes:

> [He] is gone, leaving us the little home he put his heart into for us, the fiery roses, his gift, his plastic wood-carving, and the memory of his own personality—a great one, of gripping virtue, lonely, proud, violent, affectionate, tender, jealous, quaint, simple as a child's, hearty and yet dark as night when the evil spirit from God came upon him, with something of an early thrush in his few moods of joy—despondant [*sic*], complaining, piteous, excitable, reverent, loyal—his impress is on everything by the hearth and in the home, on everything he touched, on the hearts of the few he loved. With such a nature, it was impossible ^for others^ to weave him into life—the attempt was doomed failure. (1897, 78v, EC)

He is gone but the house remains, the paternal imprint everywhere; to realize the bodily metaphor by which Cooper describes the "little home," the poets are trapped in the father's heart. Cooper considers the memory of her father's personality, sketching a figure as dark and volatile as Heathcliff himself, lonely, proud, violent, affectionate, tender, jealous. Like Heathcliff, as one with nature, darkening with the night. And like his own daughter and her lover, James Cooper was an isolate from the world, his personality not readily assimilated within society.

Cooper continues, in the same passage:

> [O]ne could but twist one's own threads with his and remain unwoven into general existence. Round Michael whom he loved with passion,

> round me whom he loved with devotion, round Mother whom he loved with veneration he simply created a wilderness. There must be *his* love and a desert. He nearly killed me with nervous fear and anxiety, I dreaded the least conflict between him and Michael as the end of my home-life with him, I dreaded some violent scene, I had a sense of doom growing with the years; no man could be received by us with comfort or dignity, every friendship was blighted as it rose to growing vigor by his hatred—yet I loved him and love him—we love him, Michael and I, we twain—with an overwhelmming force. He created a desert round us and built an altar in our hearts. [. . .] Sometimes the pain and fear he brought me almost made [illeg.] me long, out of a life-impulse, for his death—but now fear is cast out, my love for him is perfect. He was to me as Oedipus to Antigone—only Sophocles can express our bond and my mourning. (1897, 78v–79r, EC; emphasis in original)

His family had no choice but to twist their threads with his and, by doing so, to remain detached from the fabric of the world at large. They are prisoners trapped in a home constituted in the name of family love. They worship at the prison keeper's altar, and in the fierce twining of love and existential fear. Before even his body was found, his own daughter confessed that she wished for her father's death. Judith Butler has described Antigone's relationship to Oedipus as chiastic: "Her act is never fully her act, and though she uses language to claim her deed, to assert a 'manly' and defiant autonomy, she can perform that act only through embodying the norms of the power she opposes."[4] Cooper's wish has come true. Oedipus is the one imprisoned now. Her fear cast off, she can claim "perfect" love for the idea of her father.

James Cooper was only recently reported missing. His family suspects, but is not certain, that he is dead. Though Michael Field would soon travel to Zermatt, they hadn't yet departed home. Only months later will the body be discovered, his death and its likely terms confirmed. And yet we already have a tale of passion and violence and oppression, a fight to the death that the scarred, frightened daughter has somehow won. Because she is no longer afraid of her father, "my love for him is perfect." Antigone, as in Butler's formulation, at once assumes and usurps the father's authority.[5]

When Edith Cooper expresses with plain clarity and perfect insight that "there must be *his* love, and a desert," she gives words to a painful reality of her life as half of Michael Field: his love, and a desert, Michael Field isolated from a modern world they so long to join, but which they cannot quite catch. Or perhaps we are witnessing here the origins of a habit particular to Michael Field, to Bradley and Cooper: the overwhelming force of family love fortifying those inside against threats from without. Call it a wilderness, call it a moat or a desert, call it a family. James Cooper has left them the house, and with it a psychological habit of centripetal emotion that leaves no bridges to the world beyond. That "No man could be received . . . with comfort or dignity" suggests that a conventional narrative of exogamous courtship and marriage was never a real possibility for Cooper or for Bradley. In the logic of this patriarch's heart and home, Michael Fields' endogamous marriage was the only option available to them.

In order to ensure that the Swiss police will continue to investigate Cooper's case, Michael Field make their way to Switzerland. "I say good-night to the Matterhorn and its one star," writes Cooper. "We sleep at least in the same land where *he* sleeps forever—that is much to us—and we are there to serve him, to do the work of sons in his honour" (1897, 85r, EC; emphasis in original). That "work of sons" is formidable, involving tense negotiations with Swiss police and bureaucrats. Cooper writes of her lover's distress as the poets work to reinterpret the experience in the characteristic Michael Field language of flowers:

> We have had a terrible night [. . .]. Michael sobs and cannot eat and wildly straightens our room—[. . .] [W]e go up to the knoll where *he* was happy the morning of that last Wednesday and sang to himself—there we read of Aedipus and his mysterious call in the foreign land to his death. The death of our beloved was Sophoclean. We wander where he picked his spray of Alpine Rose, we lie on the damp, sweet-smelling hay. [. . .] We confess on our return how we have been hoping for a dream to clear the mystery—we do not want to know *his* grave, it might take away the blessing from this land—we should like that sacred as the grove of Aedipus—but if we might know the spot he last trod before carried off into the secret shades we should be at rest. (1897, 87r–87v, EC; emphasis in original)

If Cooper casts her father as Oedipus to her Antigone, she also perceives his link to Oedipus, called to death in a foreign land. The poets hope that like Oedipus, James Cooper will rest in sacred nature; they would simply like to know where he last stood.

Oedipus and family were very much on Edith Cooper's mind in the summer of 1897, while elsewhere in Europe that summer, Sophocles's play was on the mind of Sigmund Freud. Freud spent this summer 902 km to the east of Zermatt, completing the manuscript for *Die Traumdeutung*, or the *Interpretation of Dreams*; James Strachey's introduction to the first edition of the book in English translation pinpoints "the summer and autumn of 1897"—the span, perhaps, from James Cooper's fall to his discovery, the period when he lay exposed on a rock in the deep woods—as the period when Freud developed the Oedipal theory.[6] In the dream book, Freud would use the Oedipal story to establish a number of principles that became bedrock to modern psychoanalysis, including a child's deep and unresolved ambivalence toward both the father, a figure of rivalry, and the mother, a figure of desire: "It is the fate of all of us," Freud famously wrote in the summer of 1897, "to direct our first sexual impulse towards our mother and our first hatred and our first murderous wish against our father."[7] The dynamics of the Cooper family mirror important elements of the family drama Freud wrote that summer, including the child's projection of strong, unresolved, and highly distinctive feelings toward the mother and the father: mother beneficent, father menacing. Michael Field also model the location within the family of origin of all dynamics of a person's sexuality, including both desire and rivalry, whether known or unknown to the subject. Freud put into theory what Cooper lived: the family of origin is the first and dispositive container for all sexualities. Any subsequent erotic activity is but a reflection or repetition or reenactment of what happened first at home. Cooper knows that story well; she could have written it herself. Perhaps she did.[8]

Though they were well acquainted with the psychologist and early sexologist Havelock Ellis, I have no reason to believe that Bradley and Cooper knew or even knew of Freud, particularly as early as 1897.[9] It is anachronistic to read Cooper's recurring comments about Oedipus in terms of a theory that an Austrian neurologist was hatching just that summer. But without doubt, Browning's "dear, Greek women" knew their Sophocles, and Cooper makes good use of all three plays from the Oedipal trilogy. In *Oedipus Rex*, powerful King Oedipus blinds himself in rage when he realizes he has fulfilled the prophecy that he will kill his father and marry his mother: the father is a figure of potency and impotence, the mother a figure of eros and incest. Hobbled and diminished, in *Oedipus at Colonus*, the blind king goes to die in a grove whose location is unknown to his loyal daughters. And in *Antigone*, the heroic, dutiful daughter, the product of incest between her father and his mother—the Edith figure—battles authority for the right to bury her dead.[10]

What Sophocles describes as prophecy—Oedipus will kill his father and marry his mother—Freud describes as both inevitable and necessary for the Oedipal subject to mature toward whatever awkward erotic compromises the father-killing-mother-marrying young child might evolve. Ambivalent though this process must be, Freud calls it "development." For Michael Field as well, father killing and mother marrying are both inevitable and necessary. And necessity is the mother of invention.

As they linger in Zermatt, exploring the glaciers, glades, and rapids that may or may not comprise the father's resting place, Bradley and Cooper move that plot along. Cooper explains:

> *Wednesday*. Brave, assured sunlight. While I write to the Consul, Michael goes out, and sees a ring of warm, broad gold in the depths of which a sapphire grows blue or darkens like a mountain-lake. The ring is almost a wedding-ring, yet something beyond. Here is the *cadeau*, the chain of love that will bind us together in spite of fire and scissors. I go to secure it, and then my Love insists I shall try some rings. They say nothing on my finger till at last a brilliant guarded by two ^orient^ pearls takes possession. He costs £10 . . . it is paid, and the glorious chain of love and beauty is mine to bind me to my Love. But we do not give the little rings to each other—that must be done by the Matterhorn Bridge. We are quite gay and eat little Madeleine-cakes. (1897, 96r, EC)

What better time to go wedding-ring shopping than while awaiting discovery of one's father's perhaps-murdered corpse in a country far from home? Indeed, just as Freud saw the Tiresian prophecy not as a suggestion but as a necessity, there is necessity motivating the consummation of marriage for these poets on this land. Catherine Maxwell has underscored the Sapphic nature of the sapphire for Victorian lesbians: "[I]n the late nineteenth century sapphire rings may have been given by one woman to another as a sign of 'sapphic' devotion."[11] Contemplating the rings, the weather shifts for Cooper from violent and threatening to warm and calm. Bradley's ring recasts the terrifying rapids of the Zmutt River as a dark, tranquil mountain lake. Cooper's ring features a brilliant guarded by pearls. She is safe in a "glorious chain of love and beauty" that binds her to Bradley, protected against fire, against scissors. The *cadeau* of the ring protects her.[12]

"Lyric voice is doubled by means of an eroticized textual exchange that is figured within [Michael Field's] poems as interweaving," writes Yopie Prins. She continues: "The self-doubling figure of Hymen enacts the rhetorical reversal and inversion of gender differences; and Tiresias embodies an interchangeably doubled self. This continual interchange defines the closer marriage of Bradley and Cooper, who invoke a traditional Victorian ideology of marriage even while they rework its fixed opposition of masculine and feminine."[13] "The ring is almost a wedding-ring, yet something beyond," wrote half the poet who had earlier compared their bond to that of Robert Browning and Elizabeth Barrett Browning: "closer married," something beyond, more than—better than. Cooper continues: "When at last we are near Matterhorn Bridge, we dismiss Franz, and go to our mead by the torrent where we read the Burial-service for him, but not to that spot. We sit down, our feet buried in sweet willow-herb and there plight the troth of our fresh life together—a life that springs from the deep tragedy we have shared from its brim to its hollow—we who love him, whom he loved with such peculiar passion—loving me that I loved Michael as he would have loved her" (1897, 96v, EC). The tragedy of James Cooper's accident is fecund for the poets. The burial service dispatched, the father dismissed, Michael Field are free to "plight the troth of our fresh life together." Her wish has come true, her father is dead, and Edith/Oedipus/Edithpus marries her mother, or more precisely, her mother's sister, her longtime lover and other poetic half. Adding a classic triangulating twist to the occasion, Cooper channels her sexual passion for Bradley directly from her father to his wife/her sister: "loving me that I loved Michael as he would have loved her."[14]

After uttering cries of inspiration on behalf of their literary efforts, and summoning forth from the torrent the future's inspiration, Cooper writes: "Then I pluck the willow herb in a bunch, we wash our rings in the Zmutt, and suddenly Michael, filling her hand, drinks to him. That I cannot do—I feel it is a lover's right. We walk home in unity of spirit" (1897, 96v–97r, EC). The rings are baptized, the communion of the father taken in the water of the river that may or may not contain his corpse. The subject and object of Cooper's belief that "it is a lover's right" to drink to the (presumed) dead will remain lost to history; leading candidates in this syntactic puzzle might include her own lover, namely, Bradley; her mother's lover, namely, her father; her father's lover, namely, her mother; or her father's would-be lover, namely, her mother's sister, who is also Cooper's lover. "Antigone is one for whom the symbolic positions have become incoherent," writes Butler, "confounding as she does brother and father, emerging as she does not as a mother but—as one etymology suggests—'in the place of the mother.' Her name is also construed as 'anti-generation' (*gone* [generation])."[15] To be sure, the Coopers' incestuous plots would not have come as a surprise to Freud, for whom the template of libidinal eroticism—not to be confused with socially sanctioned exogamous bonds—originates in the family of origin. Yet, as Lévi-Strauss reminds us, "Society expressly forbids only that which society brings about." The incest taboo is where culture imposes structural imperatives that transform biology into social systems; it is "at once on the threshold of culture, in culture, and in one sense . . . culture itself."[16]

And those willow herbs? They are pressed in the opening pages of this 1897 volume of *Works and Days*. In Cooper's hand, the note "Gathered by Smutt when we exchanged our rings." On the same page, a few leaves and flowers, which she has marked: "Gathered at the Knoll where he was so happy and where he sang the day before he died—Wednesday, June 23rd" (1897, 3v, EC; fig. 8). From the very beginning of this volume of the White Book, the women's "beyond" wedding stands in a relationship of equivalency to the father's death. Even before the extrafamilial reader knows what events are to come in 1897, Cooper establishes a relationship of cause and effect: he was happy; then he died; then we exchanged rings. First that. Then this.

Michael Fields' wedding recapitulates two family traditions for Katharine Bradley. The first, the practice of keeping a diary or commonplace book. The Michael Field archive in the Bodleian Library includes the commonplace book of Charles Bradley, father to Katharine, a grandfather that Edith Cooper never knew. Charles Bradley's commonplace book was a gift to the bridegroom from his fiancée, Emma Harris. The second tradition: reclaiming weddings from the law, on behalf of a model of consent, of a gift of the self from one beloved to the other. Charles Bradley's diary includes his account of his own "marriage affair," on May 4, 1834. The young Dissenter presented the marriage with some pride in his independence:

> At Lawrence St Chapel Birmingham May the 4th after the morning service was over, Four Christian Dissenters, desiring the congregation to stop took "the marriage affair into their own hands" in the following manner.
>
> Copy Before this congregation I C Bradley Jr give you Emma Harris this ring to wear as a memorial of our marriage, and this written pledge stamped with the impression of the "United Rights of Man and Woman" declaring I will be your faithful husband from this time henceforth.
>
> Signed by Charles Bradley Junior.
>
> Copy Before this congregation I Emma Harris received this ring to wear as a memorial of our marriage and give you Chas Bradley junior this written pledge stamped with the impressions of the United Rights of Man and Woman, declaring I will be your faithful wife from this time henceforward.
>
> Signed by Emma Harris.[17]

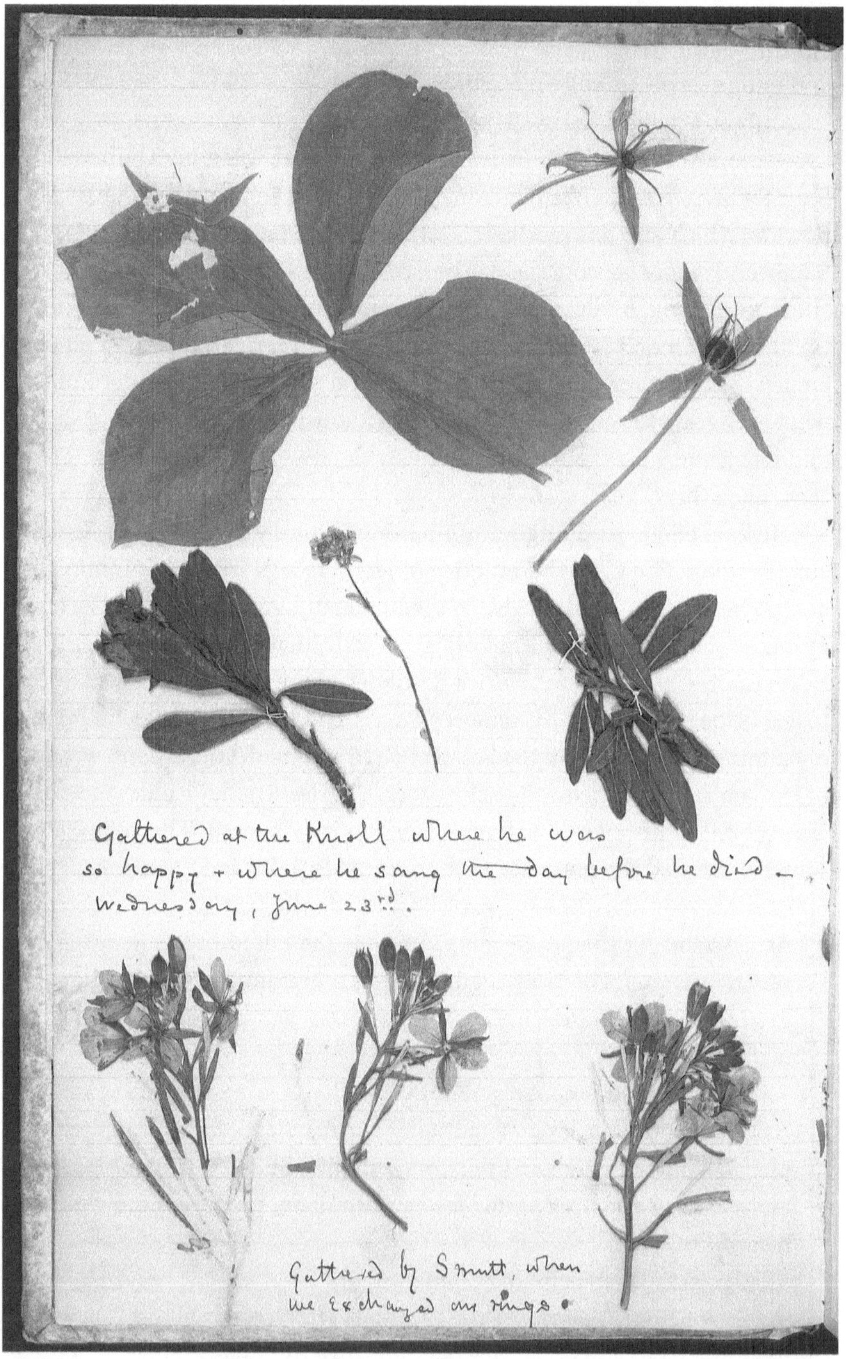
Gathered at the Knoll where he was
so happy + where he sang the day before he died –
Wednesday, June 23rd.
Gathered by Smutt, when
we exchanged our rings.

FIGURE 8. Souvenirs from the field in Zermatt where Michael Field exchanged rings. © The British Library Board, ADD MS 46786: Vol. 11 (1897), 3v.

Two generations later, what does the poets' private ceremony enable for them? Elizabeth Freeman describes marriage ceremonies as a means of "*separating* a couple from broader ties and obligations." Michael Field, already separate from broader ties and obligations, must engineer an important psychological shift enabled by their new bereavement. Freeman continues, elaborating that the words of the wedding ceremony, and in particular the utterance "I do," "was actually capable of severing the couple's relationship to any further context, for they took precedence over both the parental supervision of betrothal and secular community's raucous involvement in the nuptial ritual, and their status as the sole test of validity stood *in clear opposition to the secular authority of the father or guardian*."[18] For Bradley and Cooper, the private ceremony very clearly (and quite literally) signals their appropriation of postpaternal authority, in the chiastic relationship to the Oedipal father that Butler describes.

The implications of this appropriation will play out in their shared narrative in the years ahead. But first, and here, the exchange of rings consolidates a bond of primacy between the women. In this life, they will be daughters no more. That is clear. But where does that leave them? In contrast to the tropes of recognition, visibility, explicitness, and tangibility that typically accompany a wedding ceremony, Michael Fields' exchange of rings represents a private realignment of figures on the family chessboard: the two women move together to the household's center, holding the fact, the meaning, and the permanence of that shift between them. "Is it perhaps the unlivable desire with which [Antigone] lives, incest itself, that makes of her life a living death, that has no place within the terms that confer intelligibility on life?" asks Butler.[19]

Let me suggest that this question, the question of "the terms that confer intelligibility on life," is exactly where Michael Field seek their representational challenge at this fragile moment. Like Antigone, they find themselves in thrall to the unburied corpse of a loved one. By claiming the space—the field, if you will—of the father's disappearance for the ceremonial confirmation of their married bond, Michael Field return a challenge to the very conditions of intelligibility that would confine them. "Thus death is figured as a kind of marriage to those in [the] family who are already dead, affirming the deathlike quality of those loves for which there is no viable and livable place in culture."[20] Michael Field carry forward death's signature, embedded within the origin story of their marriage. The poets' effort to carry their dead forward into the present and the future fuses with their representational practices as a writer: the signature "Michael Field" asserts conventional social legibility in the name of a man.

That the puppet master hidden behind the curtain is two women exposes the artifice of social legibility itself.

James Cooper's corpse, uncovered like Antigone's brother Polynices, was discovered at long last by woodsmen outside Zermatt on October 25, 1893. Bradley provides the diary with the expository details of his discovery first with two newspaper clippings from the *Daily Mail*: "The body was found by two wood-cutters at a spot about an hour's walk from the east of Zermatt. It had not been touched. He lay as one asleep—his right arm under his face. His clothes were still in a good state of preservation, his jewels being all intact. His hat was discovered a few paces from him and his stick fixed in the rock" (1897, 132v).

Facing the page that includes only the two brief newspaper clippings, the poets affixed a large mourning card, trimmed in heavy black, the story told in Bradley's handwriting:

> To the beloved, abiding memory
> of James Robert Cooper
> of Durdans, Reigate, Surrey;
> (aged 79)
> who was lost on Midsummer Day, 1897,
> and found in the Wittiwald on October 25th
> of the same year, beneath the shadow of
> a rock, as if sleeping.
> "The Lord Himself is thy Keeper"
> (1897, 133r, KB)

Within days, Bradley and Cooper had returned to Zermatt to perform a variety of melancholy errands. The tone this time was far from ebullient; it was dark. The corpse's features are no more, so the poets were asked to describe his clothing for identification by the vice-consul. The coffin was kept open for that express purpose.

Michael Field perform a light version of the death rituals familiar to us from the Beloved Mother-One's passing: "He is lying near us in his coffin with palms over him and a great wreathes [*sic*] of fir and alpine-rose-leaves at his head and feet, while the candles gather in stars about him. Mother lay in no more solemn glory, that he in his mortuary chapel among his wreaths twisted by men" (1897, 134v, EC). Cooper's face had deteriorated to the extent that he was unrecognizable—"the loved features are gone"; the coffin was kept open only to allow the poets to identify the corpse from the clothing and jewelry that remained on the body. The women handed over the artifacts of home and family to M. Seiler, the manager of the spectacle, to place in the coffin. They included "the Mother's letters, her portrait, the Dresden portrait of Michael and me, Amy's little hooded portrait—when she was his 'little Pickie'; an Iona ring from Michael, and the birthday flowers, with a few roses from his garden" (1897, 135r, EC). Bradley and Cooper choose a gravesite: "A Hamlet grave-digger hobbles forward on the darkened stage of this mountain cemetary [*sic*] . . . it is weird" (1897, 135r, EC).

Perhaps predicted by their encounter with the weird grave-digger direct from *Hamlet*, Michael Field find almost everything about Zermatt alien. During their first visit, when James was missing and presumed dead, Cooper is blunt in her views: "The Zermatters look to me most repulsive—the spawn of vile conditions of life: they might all be assassins" (1897, 84v, EC). When the poets return in October to claim the body, Cooper's views are only slightly tempered. "The people are respectful but unsympathetic," Cooper writes, recalling the walk through the village following the coffin from the mortuary to the graveyard. "The people stand and gaze . . . foreign, foreign!!" (1897, 135v, 137r, EC). It is not clear to me whether Cooper is expressing her own feeling of foreignness in the villagers' stark gazes, or whether she is expressing her own disgust at the onlookers' foreignness. "The ropes that cling to the coffin as one's heart-strings to the dead ~~were~~ ^are^ not horrible to me, but instruments of blessing that give the secret earth ~~with~~ ^what^ belongs to its secrecy. There is for me happiness in the tap of the soil on the lid." At the end of the funeral service, "Michael and I come to the brink, throw in white, snow-white, chrysanthemums and roses tied with ~~locks~~ ^tresses^ of our hair—mine such a long ~~lock~~ ^tress^" (1897, 137r, EC). The poets' heart-strings are tied to the dead, and their own hair ties the funeral flowers that land on the coffin's lid. They have agency now over those ties: it is not terrible to be tied as coffin ropes to James Cooper, who has returned to the earth. The poets have agency over their hair, their signature flourish on the top of the patriarch's permanent home.

Though the secret earth now has final claim to James Cooper, the facts of his violent demise confront Michael Field for the first time. After the burial, Cooper writes:

> Michael comes to me in a harrowing passion of hysteria . . . Photographs of the rock and one of the dear body have brutally been put into her hand without a word of warning . . . Yet in her agony her one thought is to get possession of the infamous clichés (not taken by for judicial purposes, but as a bit of private speculation by a poor wretch

> ^or a Zermatt [illeg.] demon^) and dash it to pieces. Her torrent will overbear all opposition and the thing is brought and executed as if it were one of the Lord's ^Chief^ Enemies. The fragments are thrown into the Visp. The photograph of the rock we are overpersuaded for the sake of Zermatt ^not^ to prohibit in the journals, caught as we are in the hour of mortal weakness when the grave is being closed in ~~one's~~ ^our^ own ~~life~~ ^lives^ as well as in the churchyard. (1897, 137v, EC)

There is no dressing up with roses or carbuncles the photographic image of James Cooper's corpse in situ, flat on the rock where it spent four months until its discovery. His facial features decomposed on that rock. The "cliché" made infamous by Bradley is the photographic negative of the image of that scene captured by the Zermatt demon photographer. According to the *Oxford English Dictionary*, a "cliché" in idiomatic English of this period is "A stereotype, electrotype, or other plate used for printing an image." But it is also true that in 1897, the usage more familiar to us today—"A phrase or expression regarded as unoriginal or trite due to overuse"—had begun to circulate. Our Elizabethan poets have found a tellingly flexible contemporary term to describe the primal scene of the father's corpse.

Both contemporary meanings of the word "cliché" haunt Michael Field on the day of James Cooper's burial in Zermatt. Bradley was enraged by her discovery of the photographs of the accident scene, and by the enterprising speculation of the demon photographer. She sees to it that all but one of the clichés from the scene are shattered to pieces and thrown in the river. Later Michael Field regret that they were pressured into allowing one plate, a shot of the rock, to remain intact and to be published in newspapers.

In what sense is the cliché-as-unoriginal-or-trite in circulation here? If we understand Michael Field as the most conventionally unconventional of writers, we find it everywhere. These authors use the clichés of social discourse in order to disrupt them from within. To smash them if you will, and to throw their fragments into the Visp—but even as they do that, they let one or two survive. In Zermatt, Bradley and Cooper face several highly conventionalized life events: the death and burial of a father, and their own wedding, with the exchange of rings on the patch of mountain field where they imagine the Father might have trod his last. There is not much that is conventional about how James Cooper died, nor about how his daughter and his sister-in-law responded to his death. That said, the narrative frame of bereavement that they apply to all the events is highly conventionalized within their idiomatic style: coffin heaped with flowers, letters, images. "The ring was almost a wedding-ring, but something beyond." Michael Field invest rigorously in the theater of mourning, all the while wearing their new wedding rings and glaring side-eyed at the "foreign" demons among them. These are the tools Michael Field use to manage the Oedipal drama in which they find themselves. Later, Cooper reports, "That demon photographer at Zermatt demands the cliché and proofs. I write to the Vice-Consul that the cliché is smashed and scattered. I beg him to threaten the rogue with the judge's instruction. When shall I have to cease to fight for that dear father!" (1897, 145v, EC).

The cliché may be smashed and scattered, but the fight for James Cooper's honor goes on. His daughter Edith sums up her feelings:

> How close he is to me now the wide dread of months is gone, now we know something of his death. With all the sorrow he has made us bear through his faults, they were perversions of love, and the pity of them alone remains, while the greatness of his love, all the more magnificent because husbanded, is the wonder and delight of our mourning. Like me he was terribly true to three or four beloved ones—he gave them simple love, bare, absolute, tender, necessitous—by others in the world he was scarcely known, but always liked, because of his bracing voice and good, bright eyes. (1897, 140v, EC)

James Cooper made his family unhappy, but he did so as a way of showing his love. He was meager in his displays of love, "husbanding" his affections, which made that love all the more valuable. Indeed, such husbandry is "the wonder and delight" of the poets' mourning process. Mourning is not typically characterized as wondrous or delightful. The infamous cliché is smashed.

The disappearance and death of James Cooper may be the most exciting external events that ever occurred in the lives of Katharine Harris Bradley and Edith Emma Cooper. That is not to say that Michael Field enjoyed the experience; just that for two writers who crave activity, enmeshment, engagement, and "plot," this would seem to give them what they are looking for, right down to the repulsive foreigners.

I suggested earlier, though, that this conventionally sensationalistic plotline is a decoy in the 1897 volume of *Works and Days*. It is not the most interesting or unusual thing to happen in Michael Field's lives that year, or more precisely, in their life *narratives* that year. The real story of 1897 is the story of the emotional and physical intimacy, the enjoyment, the humor that connect Michael and Field together, quietly but powerfully, throughout this volume. This involves their wedding vows, to be sure, but also surpasses or underpins that singular occasion with a bedrock of deeply resonant affect. Michael Field enjoying themselves is a sight to behold, particularly in light of James Cooper's tragedy. The death of the mother had the power to warp and reshape the identities that comprise Michael Field. The death of the father, however, does not. The poets are appropriately sad about the tragedy, but it comes upon them in the due course of an existing life.

Intense intimacy frames the entire volume, even six months before James Cooper's death. The volume opens on New Year's Day, on the journal's fourth page, following the page where the leaves and flowers from Zermatt remain carefully pressed to this day (Michael Field have had to circle back and retrofit the narrative of 1897 to orient around the signature event that occurred in midsummer). Cooper writes: "1897 *New Year's Day*. All night the drain-men were emptying the cesspool next door to the clang of the old bells—we by our bedroom-fire heard the wholesome sounds in a dream. At the very turn of old year into new we embraced with the simple wish 'A happy new year'—I like all these forms in their purity" (1897, 4r, EC). What better sign of purity than a clean cesspool? What better way to start the new year than by contemplating one's neighbor's sewage challenges? The "wholesomeness" here is truly humorous, both for its irony and for its earnestness. Cooper engages the full spectrum of domestic activities far more honestly than Victorian writers do typically. The cesspool, the bells, the bedroom, the fire, the dream, the embrace, the purity: this is happiness in the new year, for Michael Field.

And it goes on. The year 1897 was in many respects a deeply happy year for the poets. Also on New Year's Day, "The morning is hot and wet, but we do not care—Best to begin obscured, drear even, than too bright" (1897, 4r, EC). The day continues with a bit of financial management, as it does every New Year's Day for Michael Field, and a bit of play:

> We meet dividends, bills—an Apollyon-fight with addition and subtraction and part extravagance. At Redhill we have a gay ten with Delia and Lygel, who have been won by blue china and blue Xmas cards. We tell them to make good resolutions on the last night of the old year to the voice of the bells, but to break ~~them~~ all the next day if they would prosper. However we go back to face my condemned allowance, and Michael proposes extreme pain as a heaven-sent punishment—that the £5 ^to be^ paid down for *Rosamond*, and ~~[illeg.]~~ dedicated already

> to ~~bringing~~ ^buying^ her my marriage-ring, should be devoted to the settlement of my finance. Woe!—and yet there is a cleanness in paying every bill, and we grieve in a kind of bliss. (1897, 4r, EC; emphasis in original)

This is not the last time we will see Cooper struggling with money, nor with simple arithmetic. Nor is it the last time Bradley will step in as the voice of financial prudence. What is more unusual here is the lightness of tone, the account of sociability, cards, and gaming one's New Year's resolutions. And also the underside of domestic management, the cleanness Cooper feels in paying her bills, the tantalizing plan—introduced here for the first time—for the purchase of marriage rings in the near future.

This narrative reflects the larger mood of January 1897. On a new year's visit to their publisher Elkin Matthews in London, Bradley makes "The Elk" blush and panic when she misremembers an awkward financial clause in their contract for Michael Field's most recent play *Attila, My Attila!* Bradley describes the terms of their quick holiday to Liphook, in Hampshire, continuing a passage we saw earlier: "We have fled from Reigate," she writes, "as from a land of abortions, drains and damp. And it is good in this still country, though we wake to the mournful hedgerow, and long sheep rack, and the tree that has no sense of style, but grows dowdily for the cow, we are content. [. . .] I feel as a bulb below in the manure, bulb-stuff, no feel or push of the flower in me as yet; but distinct consciousness. I am bulb-stuff, not manure" (1897, 5v, KB). The distance traveled from cesspools, drains, and damp to manure might not seem far, but the psychological distance is vast. If Reigate is home to abortions, Liphook is the place of quickening potential: Bradley is bulb-stuff, not manure, the flower pushing through soil toward light. The unstylish tree is not vulgar like Oscar Wilde; she is simply dowdy, bovine, content. And, back to the bedroom. "What games we have by our bed-room fire at night!" on this holiday, writes Bradley. "We lie in our bed, read proofs and poems, and stick roses in our ears" (1897, 7r, KB).

Frolicking and playing and writing in bed by the bedroom fire, and sticking roses in their ears. Dreaming the new year in together from their little blue bedroom in Durdans. Michael Field cooing "Master" when she hears her lover's footsteps in the hall, little imagining that she brings news of tragedy. The nature of their relationship in this year's volume of *Works and Days* is a bit giddy—not a term usually applied to Michael Field—and quite tender and intimate. We see this again and again. In the wagon-lit sleeping cabin, for example, on their first journey to Zermatt, Michael Field seem to be made slightly hysterical by the circumstances. Cooper writes,

> The little padded den makes us laugh—living, humorous laughter. We ask for our bed to be made up and ~~[illeg.]~~ ^one bed^ springs aloft while the other remains. We stifle outside ~~from~~ ^at^ the very look . . . we enter and the door shuts. Ha! Beds in all the space, rugs to our knees—the window, it has a modern scientific spring . . . cannot be opened by the mere human being! The door! It has a modern scien^ti^fic spring—cannot be opened! The mere human being must come to an end and beats in death-struggles against the door. At last rescue arrives; the bed above is wound down to the bed below, the ^mere human being's^ hand trained to the springs, and we sleep . . . we can get no coffee . . . and this is civilization, the roof and crown of it! (1897, 83v–84r, EC)

In the sleeping car, Michael Field face off with technology, and for a time anyway, technology wins. "Modern scientific springs" are eventually vanquished, but then Michael Field find no coffee to be had. The pinnacle of civilization itself does not well accommodate human poets.[21]

More hysteria in bed ensues in Zermatt itself. "Brightly-burnished last day!" Cooper writes. "The turmoil of having to leave Zermatt has surged through the night and sleep ~~[illeg.]~~ ^has^ made us laugh like demons with hysteria. In the ~~[illeg.]~~ ^dark,^ ~~[illeg.]~~ Michael gets out of bed and strikes a Lucifer on its box—there is a flare . . . Michael holds it ^the fiery box^ out, sawing the air with it, but so vague in mind that ~~there is~~ a long pause ^ensues^ before she ~~declares~~ ^says^ ~~[illeg.]~~ majesterially [*sic*] with—a slow and heavy emphasis ^on the word!^—Water! We laugh as if to crack the walls" (1897, 99r, EC). And on a visit to Oxford, Cooper awakens on a Monday morning and marks the diary "Monday—and as Michael says in bed, we may be thankful that God did not make it another Sunday" (1897, 113v, EC), for Sundays have long been difficult days for the blended Cooper-Bradley family.

Michael Field spend several occasions languishing and laughing in bed in 1897. It is worth speculating that they have done so frequently during a shared life over decades, which left no shortage of opportunities for physical intimacy. I hope for their sake that they enjoyed such intimacy. But we know only what they chose to write about, and how they chose to write it. And we know that in 1897, Cooper and Bradley peppered *Works and Days* with a number of these lovely, funny moments, as they do in no other volume of their diary.

Though Cooper and Bradley had no way of knowing that James Cooper would fall on a rock and die in June 1897, the strong thread of intimacy that they track through this period has to do with their shared identity apart from him. They construct a narrative of strong, shared female intimacy that exists in spaces untouchable by the father's law. The fact that James Cooper disappeared and was later found dead only accelerates the inevitable. The quiet assertion of the poet's coupledom within his house on New Year's Day, as they budget for the purchase of their rings, matches the giddier, sharply observed account of that evening on their diary's early pages. Alone in an inn in Hampshire, they frolic in bed, sticking roses in each other's ears, stretching their coupled identity in new ways outside the father's house. And they write about it. Even as that father lies unburied on a rock in a remote Swiss forest, they visit Oxford and, for the first time, the Bodleian Library, home today to their letters. From Oxford, Cooper acquires "reams of paper for tomorrow's work, and bits of blue English china [. . .] At Abrams we see the perfect Queen Anne Table in old red mahogany. We dine together and our triumph revels! To be free to do, enjoy, eat what we like and as we like it—Truly, Visiting is delicate imprisonment" (1897, 120v, EC).

"A delicate imprisonment" represents a condition most appealing to Michael Field, reflecting an important balance of autonomy and structure. Psychologically and artistically, Michael Field are creatures of convention who aspire to a frisson of experimentalism, however gentle; in this case, shopping and dining in Oxford. In the wake of the father, the poets have the chance to define a life on their own terms. First, a family of their own. In Cooper's narrative of the very day the poets exchanged rings on the Zmutt, she writes: "When we come in from our walk a letter from Amy tells that *the Basset* is coming! That beloved One of mine has asked Dan to get my chosen kind of dog to be at home to cheer the return. What a divine forethought of bounty, of tenderness. My 'Musico' and my diamond are insepabl inseparable joys—belonging to this one day forever" (1897, 97r–97v, EC; emphasis in original).

This is the next stage of Michael Fields' serious dog love, which will culminate not with poor Musico but in Whym Chow, who will arrive at Durdans in 1898; Whym Chow's death in 1906 will inspire the sequence of elegiac poems Michael Field published as *Whym Chow: Flame of Love*, bound in a suede russet cover like the coat of Chow himself.[22] (In the family pecking order of siblings, Musico is quickly relegated to the status of pedestrian Amy, in contrast with the glamorous Chow or Edith.) But with months to go before the unanticipated arrival of the Chow, Musico has his moment in the sun. He is greeted with joy. His mistress writes:

> A "dust to dust" day—all the word falling, it seems, to pieces from very grayness and futility . . . yet my basset hound comes to me in a big box, and we run him about the garden till we could weep with exhaustion. But what curtain-ears he has—folded and tan! His body is white with a gt black spot on each flank—a white river runs between his eyes to the end of his nose. He is a most dignified, sentimental beast: we quote at him
>
> "Sir Launcelot mused a little space,
> He said 'she has a lovely face
> God in his mercy grant her grace
> The Lady of Shalot [*sic*].'"
>
> Basset is a still dog and tho only 5 months old has scarcely a trace of puppyhood: yet we have not had a tranquil meal since he came, and the night is a space of dread to our forethought. (1897, 105v, EC)

The poets find Musico a rather prosaic creature, and though dignified as puppies go, he is still disruptive to the household of relatively staid adult humans. He is sentimental and not aesthetic at all. The pleasure Cooper and Bradley derive from him has nothing to do with beauty or sublimity. Musico has tan, floppy curtain ears and he is great fun to chase around the garden. He is a lovely diversion at a sad time.

That said, what is it about this pup that prompts "The Lady of Shalott" to enter Cooper's mind? Now, in August 1897, Tennyson's poem was a relic of a simpler time, the era of Bradley's childhood. The version Cooper cites was published in 1842, fifty-five years ago, when there were fewer modern springs to stymie traveling poets. Like Musico's face, the world of "The Lady of Shalott" is bisected by a river: "On either side the river lie / Long fields of barley and of rye, / That clothe the wold and meet the sky." In the romantic world of Camelot, these fields offer a rather prosaic take on nature: cultivated and orderly, not wild. The poem's vibrant energy inheres not in nature but in a woman in "delicate imprisonment," an artist weaving night and day and perceiving the world secondhand: "And moving thro' a mirror clear / That hangs before her all the year, / Shadows of the world appear." It seems obvious to suggest that Michael Field recognize common ground less with the "fields" than with the woman in the tower as she contemplates prospects for new freedoms outside the enclosure of confinement.

If we understand Cooper's citation of the poem as an act of identification from one captive woman artist to another, the lines she chooses to chant to the puppy are suggestive. Tennyson published two versions of "The Lady of Shalott," one in 1832 and the second in 1842. Cooper cites the final four lines of the 1842 version—lines that did not appear in 1832. In 1842, the poet gives the last word to Lancelot, gazing on the corpse: "She has a lovely face; / God in his mercy lend her grace, / The Lady of Shalott." The lady is dead and beautiful, and on those merits Lancelot and God combine to grace her face. In 1832, the lady is also dead, but her voice nonetheless concludes the poem; she has the last word. In the 1832 version, the "wellfed wits at Camelot" find a curious parchment on the breast of the corpse who floats up to their "planked wharfage." On the parchment is the lady's signature: "The web was woven curiously, / The charm is broken utterly, / Draw near and fear not,—this is I, / The Lady of Shalott."[23]

We might imagine that in August 1897, Cooper was contemplating whether she wants to be the Lady of Shalott—or to be the heroic Lancelot on his horse with the world ahead of him. Her father's death has offered this latter-day Antigone the ultimate chiastic opportunity to appropriate his potency. So Cooper has the last word on Lancelot's last word on the pages of *Works and Days*: with her pen, and in her voice, and to her puppy, she makes those words her own. As a male poet who has clearly thought of herselves alongside Tennyson, Browning, and other poetic titans of the age, Michael Field has as much or more cause to identify with the living poetic voice of "The Lady of Shalott" than with the Lady of Shalott herself; she is dead at the end no matter which version of the poem they read. Cooper, in the guise of Michael Field, often writes poems about women, beauty, creativity, and captivity. As two women writers and as one male poet, the question of who—and how—Michael Field identify with their female poetic subjects is complex.[24] But right here, in *Works and Days*, in 1897, with her puppy, and in the garden of the house of her probably dead father, Edith Cooper utters Lancelot's words, not the lady's. This recasts James Cooper as the Lady of Shalott. He is not dead in a boat on the river; unbeknown to his daughter, he is dead on a rock in the forest. And far from beautiful in death, his facial features have decomposed to the point of unrecognizability. "God in his mercy grant [him] grace." For Edith Cooper as Lancelot, there's both sadness and immanence about this moment. It only looks like playing with a puppy in a garden.

In fact, what if worldly possibility really did look like playing with a puppy in a garden? Just as 1897 is noteworthy for the poets' accounts of their giddiness in bed, I cannot recall another episode in *Works and Days* that shows them chasing around a garden, or anywhere for that matter. Domestic affect, forged through intimacies of house and home, is the bedrock of hope and possibility—and dare I say plot?—for Michael Field.

Musico also adds the excitement of a new third term to the Michael + Field equation. At a sad and uncertain moment, he taps the undercurrent of whimsy that characterizes this year. He gives the poets the kind of focal point in which they take pleasure, and through which they animate and secure their bond of two. He was not the only new man to cross their doorstep, however. In December, the famed explorer Edward Whymper visited the poets at Durdans. Whymper, by profession an engraver and illustrator, led the first successful ascent of the Matterhorn (in 1860) as well as other significant achievements in exploration.[25]

Whymper was a provocative "third" to the Michael Field couple, a figure directly out of Kipling. Whymper first crossed their paths in Zermatt, when he was helpful and solicitous toward the women as they navigated the complexities of multiple Swiss bureaucracies that were involved in investigating the disappearance and death of James Cooper. Bradley and Cooper do not yet know this, but in the months ahead, they will name their next dog, a gift from family friends, in Whymper's honor. Whymper is an appealing figure to Michael Field on his own merits, a chivalrous person who allows them to rely on his protection and expertise. He also becomes a father figure within the Michael Field mythology, as the "father" of his namesake, Whym Chow.

Now, however, Whymper seems every bit as prosaic as Musico; in keeping with the mood, Michael Field seem as bemused and delighted by him as they are by the puppy. "Like all people of fine strain who live much by themselves," writes Cooper, "his talk is often on the things he likes to eat and drink, and he has many 'fads.' His sugar must be sifted that he may have only a suspicion of the fattening sweet in his tea. He rolls on the couch, bows over Musico and kisses my little hound. When the hour comes for dressing he asks if we have a strong desire to see a black coat—'I don't think it a pretty thing to see, but if you wish it shall be put on.' We pray him to do as he likes, and he wears his gray suit at dinner" (1897, 159r–159v, EC). Clearly "the hero of the Matterhorn" marches to the beat of his own drum, faddish, demonstrative, and a bit simple.

All that and, like the basset puppy, Whymper is also fun—in a poetic life that does not admit much frivolity. Cooper continues:

> He likes his dinner I have paid 8 [shillings] for his golden grapes—the only other fruit, tangerine oranges! In the midst of dining he breaks out "Now don't you give me tea tomorrow morning." We are instructed in

> the kind of toast to offer—"And an egg"—Michael suggests—"*Two* eggs." Michael and he have their weed together, and a suggestion is made that he should get us, the infirm, to the top of Mt Blanc for a Contract—"dead or living." "And the dogs?"—"That, madam, wd add considerably to the contract." When Michael leaves the room, Whym asks if she ~~is a~~ has been married—at the negative answer he appears astonished and remarks "I don't know why I should think so, but she has the manner of a married lady." Michael and I make our bed shake with laughter at her stories of the young Mr Bradley who died in the Canary Islands—"You must have noticed that I could never bear the mention of a Canary" sobs wicked Michael as I attend to these disclosures of a hidden past! (1897, 159v, EC; emphasis in original)

Whymper and Michael Field seem equally matched. Smoking cigarettes with Bradley and imagining schlepping the aesthetic ladies and pets to the summit of Mt Blanc, Whymper is clueless about the aesthetic nature of the household whose company he enjoys. Miss Bradley does indeed have the manner of a married lady: she wears her new sapphire ring to prove it. Michael and Field are wicked hosts, making their little bed shake with laughter that night as they share the open secret of their marriage in the pages of the White Book. Like ladies in a tower, they weave a fiction of Michael's tragically deceased young husband, come to grief in the Canary Islands, a story reminiscent of Kipling or Haggard for the brave adventurer. Bereft Katharine never could hear the word "canary" again! But though the women wear rings and share a bed, they do not disabuse Whymper of his (accurate if misplaced) sense of Bradley's married manner. The house remains a closet; the marriage an open secret hiding in plain view.[26]

For all that, "the hero of the Matterhorn is not punctual at breakfast—the coffee grows cold, and the toast grow cold and the eggs grow cold." Whymper may be a hapless guest, but he helped the women immensely in the task of sorting bills and bureaucratic detritus from Zermatt. "Our discourse is simple and most friendly," Cooper writes as he departs, leaving the family to its Christmas. "When he goes after lunch we miss—the only guest who has given us the feeling of __________" (1897, 159v, EC). A long line completes Cooper's sentence, and begs the question: What is the feeling? Of simplicity and friendliness, perhaps? Perhaps of the ordinary, the helpful, the casual, the kind. Their brief friendship with Whymper offers the poets the kernel of something that they seek to preserve in their later life. And preserve it they do, in the form of Whymper's namesake, whose arrival at Durdans is only a few weeks ahead, in January 1898.

The 1897 volume of *Works and Days* is conventional, with a beginning on New Year's Day and an end on New Year's Eve. Typically for Michael Field, its unconventionality exists precisely within its model form (or dare I say cliché?). The way deaths happen, the ways in which love is expressed, and the sheer number of evenings spent in bed and writing about it later—Field are intent here on understanding a world at home. Yet, as affectively solid as that home is, there are many signs of its precarity: most obviously, the death of the father who owns it. But also cesspools that must be cleaned, and eggs and toast that grow cold. Powerful moments with new friends, who are frank and friendly and then leave. The poets' Christmas is intensely domestic in a way that is most secure when they squint and look to the past: "Nursery Rhymes, nonsense Rhymes, and living Animals alone give us consolatory amusement now-a-days. [. . .] We have drunk to our Beloved Ones together, and read childish Rhymes of immortal value—we have talked of far off Christmas Days and I have washed my basset white as new cream" (1897, 160v–161r, EC).

The future, though? It is fragile:

> [S]uddenly while we were all seated at lunch Eva, our housemaid, went entirely out of her mind. She began to talk utter nonsense. I answered her calmly, but as soon as she had left the room, we agreed her wits were gone. It was an awful moment—of Zermatt acuteness—to hear a sober, loving, faithful human creature, contradicting herself—the fearful way of madness. It makes one feel how all sin is negation, some no-ness to one's most inward, real self. And madness is of course sin without responsibility—Durdans seems to be gradually turning [from] the old, traditional Durdans—the cats, the Master, now it will be the servants—the novelties are Music, Rye—in the distance another Rye—new servants, lovers. (1897, 161r–161v, KB)

This year began with the contemplation of a cesspool, as Michael Field introduced the domestic apparatus of everyday life much more vividly than Victorian narrative (or aesthetic poetic) conventions would typically tolerate. The episode on Boxing Day of Eva's madness reminds us again of that domestic apparatus: we almost never see or hear of the servants that make Durdans run, much less hear from them as we do in Bradley's account of the family lunch.

We have not heard as much from Bradley during this year as we have from Cooper, and Bradley here at year's end is feeling the fragility of the household, and possibly of sanity itself. She recognizes that she is in a time of change with pets and patriarchs turning over, with new servants and possibly lovers to come. The diary realizes a powerful plot of emotional and physical intimacy among Michael Field during this year. But the material security that surrounds and supports the couple seems to be giving way: cesspools need to be emptied, eggs get cold, the housemaid loses her mind.

Cooper writes a conclusion to 1897 that emphasizes the bright side of her father: "[A]ll the trouble of a jealous, passionate ~~tep~~ temperament being removed, we can know how piercingly sweet his nature was in its faith and tenderness, in its *virtue*, in its appeal and its answer. He gave us love—lover's love . . . and when to the full ~~it~~ ^it^ could not be ~~his, he rejoiced~~ ^returned, he rejoiced^ to see how we loved each other, and in our love he wondrously gained some sort of fruition." James Cooper appears here as an instrument of the love between his daughter and sister-in-law, the would-be lover spurned but not jealous, gallantly embracing the lovers' love just down the hall. "It is beautiful to think he ever approved our love, and has sealed it by his death," his daughter writes. "The bond between us is a new thing in strength, in reach, in profundity, in vigilance—that bond of the rings by the Smutt, that bond of diamond and sapphire. And Michael is singing of him with an open wound of passion and sorrow . . . it is our new marriage hymn" (1897, 164r–164v, EC; emphasis in original). "An open wound of passion and sorrow" is Michael Field's would-be marriage hymn. Through his very mortality, the dead father seals the women in marriage new in strength, reach, profundity, vigilance—bound for all time by diamond, by sapphire. Imagine the counterfactual narrative: What if James Cooper had not tripped and fallen to his death? What if he had brought his irascible self back to Reigate and continued in his dyspeptic, violent ways?

As we know, novels of the British nineteenth century often conclude with a marriage as the summit of the quest known as courtship.[27] We know that Michael Field use and repurpose the forms and patterns of literature to make meaning of their experiences. In the case of 1897, the marriage comes in the middle, in July in a field along the banks of a river in Switzerland. Here the poets recur to the moment at year's end, linking the father's death, as in a martyrdom, to the consecration of their bonds. But being Michael Field, they choose to conclude the year's narrative on a very different note. Here is Cooper:

> The bells are ringing—
> and what of New Year?

> We begin as in a desert on a cleared space looking in each other's faces . . . the old home-life gone, Amy absorbed in a new love . . . there

> is almost something of terror in all this—but I am convinced that the dead in unison with the Spirit are working intensely and mean well. I think joy may have come to us ~~with~~ ^this time next-year on^ one of its spring-tides. [. . .] We shall have rising life as we watch our dogs, our garden, and our little home growing more beautiful. I think we shall have more friends and be less hard on them, if they only will *give*.
>
> And I shall see my little Dionysus of my youth—shall I see those eyes and lips again? I totteringly think I shall have to meet them and hear them. How when I think of Life in the image that expresses it to me, Bacchus—I must think of the mortal I love—now almost as impersonally as if he were a legend of imperishable charm of a fawnish sculpture. And in so many ways he resembled father, and so has his own new link with my being. (1897, 165r–165v, EC; emphasis in original)

Twelve months later, those bells sound quite different. The household is breaking up, "the old home-life gone," the poets gazing on each other's faces in the blank clear space of a desert.

Cooper has not yet decided if she is in an English novel or a French one. Newly married to Michael, her heart remains with Bernhard, the Fawn. She cannot stop herself from longing for the eyes and lips of her own personal Bacchus. And now she sees that he resembles her father, which makes his connection with her all the more powerful and intimate. Connecting Fawn and father, Field establishes a new triangular relationship: father-Fawn-Field is layered over Fawn-Michael-Field, which is adjunct to father-Michael-Field, which collapses into Fawn/father-Michael-Field. The moment the poets pause to celebrate their "rising life" and their new married bond, the question of what is—or who may be—available beyond reveals itself as the frame around the picture, the predicate of the narrative. This is what Michael Field knew all along. No wonder Katharine Bradley was feeling so apprehensive.

CHAPTER FOUR

"Lilies and Light and Liquor"

1899

I toddle forth with my two dogs Music and Whym on the towing-path, in the grey mist. [. . .] Suddenly, almost close to our door—a heap of gross human refuse.—I turn away in disgust and anger, and a little further on, along the same path, I find a dropt rose, fair, still delicately fair, and without soil.

And I linger: but modernism lingers to emphasize its disgust, and passes by the scarcely perceptible fairness.

One common towing-path for us all—but we may each determine what shall arrest us.

—KATHARINE BRADLEY, DECEMBER 7, 1899

ON THE TOWING-PATH of life, sometimes you encounter "gross human refuse." Sometimes you encounter a rose. Modernists would linger over the viscera of disgust, even as they leave fragile beauty unremarked.

Michael Field present 1899 as a year of desire—and a year of action, in anticipation of a new century. Though it begins in apprehension about the meaning and implications of their desires, volume 13 of *Works and Days* is a narrative of Michael Field's new possibilities. Here the women take the abstract, emotional concept of a "home" firmly into the domain of the material: the nitty-gritty stuff of the everyday, from paint colors and ventilation to sublime satinwood. In 1899, *Works and Days* takes the measure of the domestic ideal using the yardstick of the domestic real.

Their home is the anchor of the poets' identities, and their decision in late 1898 to leave their home at Durdans and seek a new one verges on the existential. But in an entirely stunning embrace of the pleasures of homemaking, Michael Field use their artistic powers to create a temple to their marriage. To Michael Field, acquisition by means of shopping, or the power of the purse, pays psychological dividends: it represents the power of having, of discernment and selection, and the execution of personal taste.[1] And theirs is no mere shopping for shopping's sake: the composition of their new home in 1899 represents the incorporation of their shared and explicitly married identity. The poets purchase beautiful items to furnish beautiful rooms. Those material things become the extrinsic expression of a deeply felt private truth: theirs is a marriage realized in poetry; the house beautiful is but one more expression of that poetry.[2]

In late 1898, Cooper notes in the diary that the year had been "a year of delicious expenditures—flowing income and satisfying outlay." She was grateful for the opportunity the year presented her, to shower her lover with "gifts, gifts to my marvellous givver" [*sic*]. The poets' agent, Mr. Daniell, "has teazed us on our 'riotous living.' When he saw the magnificent photographs of the dogs—'so many and so many and such glee'—the photographs of the father and of the rest of us, he shrugged his shoulders and with amusement in the reproof of his voice remarked 'very riotous living'" (1898, EC, 143v). "Riotous living" involves the deep pleasure they take in their material things, a pleasure that will come to represent the stuff and substance of their married life.

Though they are thrilled to embrace their first new married home together, the very prospect of a new, private home raises an important question that may be unique for Bradley and Cooper. Their identity as a couple was forged within the structure of a family system in which they were cast, however imperfectly, as daughters. The "open secret" of their marriage was sustained within a larger household that belonged to a different, powerful, and "official" married couple: James and Emma Bradley Cooper. Michael Field thrived in captivity, and exported this mode of relationality as they began to circulate in the world: triangulating through the mother or the father or Browning or Berenson, for example. Michael Field constitute the psychology of their intimate relationship through engagement with a third, formative, informative presence.

But now they will move into a home of their own. This begs the question of how their intimacy functions with nobody else watching. In their own married home, how will they conduct a marriage—alone? And if from the marriage of two minds flows their art, will the recalibration of their intimacy result in alterations to their identity as poets?

"Who does not know how terrible are those preparations for house-moving," writes Anthony Trollope in *The Small House at Allington* (1862), "how infinite in number are the articles which must be packed, how inexpressibly uncomfortable is the period of packing, and how poor and tawdry is the aspect of one's belongings while they are thus in a state of dislocation?"[3] On New Year's morning 1899, Edith Cooper awakens to confront just such a "harrowing" decision "to give up Durdans as a *sacrifice to Life* and to seek with courageous will for a new home among the strangers" (1899, 3r, EC; emphasis in original). Cooper recognizes the two elements to her psychological dilemma: sacrifice of Durdans, the patriarchal home, and the heroic quest for a new, married home.

Now orphans—and thus independent women—Michael Field understand that the moment has come to seize destiny. If they are to stay at Durdans, they will have to remake it in their image as poets; as Cooper writes, "If fate [. . .] gives us back Durdans, we shall alter it fearlessly, selling all those things that are not become vitally associated with us as poets; we shall lead a new life with our God and our dreams" (1899, 3v, EC). The poets understand that they are socially buried in the country, but even equipped with that understanding they remain apprehensive about where they might land: "Human fellowship we shall seek after in seeking for a new home, and more engaging country—we may find there is little hope of either, since we hate town life and are too apprehensive and sad for deep country life" (1899, 3v, EC).

The resolution to Michael Field's conundrum is the embrace of suburban life, and with help from "the Artists," Charles Ricketts and Charles Shannon, that is precisely where they will wind up. Vadillo describes suburbs as "utopian rural spaces predicated on the metropolis, and as such, places with a double special identity: both town and country. It was this dual identity that attracted Michael Field to suburbia. Poetically, socially and politically, suburbia represented for them the only modern space where authentic works of art could be produced. In other words, for Michael Field to live in the suburbs was to be modern."[4] On the way there, however, the poets embrace—and remake in their own way—one of the significant representational principles of the British nineteenth century: the concept of the domestic sphere. In the rough binary thinking that would divide the world into public and private spheres, the division of the genders follows, with men in principle "owning" the public, and women, in the cliché of the Angel of the House, ruling over the domain of the private. The private sphere of the home is endowed with all kinds of gendered, ideological meanings: it is the dwelling place of love and family, peace and repose, and deep interior emotion, all formed in the image of its ruler, the angelic and idealized mother. The public sphere in contrast represents the "masculine" world of power and dynamism, industry, money, and change.[5]

Most aspects of the gendered division of private and public spheres break down in the case of Michael Field. For one thing, the privacy of their intimate relationship—as lovers and as artists—was never constituted within a sphere that could be described as private, unless we view them as creating a private sphere of their own adjunct to and dependent on the dynamics of a larger family in which they have been embedded. We have seen that the poets are more than willing to embrace the cult of the Beloved Mother-One as a strategy for ordering and representing their psychological and emotional identities: Mother→Poets. And we have seen, too, that they have experienced the home as a powerfully, dispositively patriarchal space made uncomfortable for them by the rage and judgment of the Father. When they construct a private sphere within that private sphere, the women call it, variably and interchangeably, Art, Love, and Marriage.

For Michael Field, "Mother" is a portable concept, an icon that will travel along with them. But the dramatic death of the father offers the poets the opportunity to reclaim "home" less in his image than in their own. This is, of course, a variation on the standard marriage plot of Victorian fiction: the newly tested and proven adult protagonist, having departed the family of origin in favor of the family of destiny, constitutes a fresh, new domestic sphere. Marriage narratives are technologies of the reproduction of the Victorian bourgeoisie. Furnishing the married household offers Michael Field another means of fusing art and intimate pleasures in the name of marriage.

The trauma of contemplated departure emerges as a topic on which both poets are most eloquent. Every aspect of their domestic life, from the walls around them to the dirt in their garden, now screams loss. Cooper writes: "I am very much tired and sore on the brain and as I look at every clod with bulb under it, of the roses sappy and pierced by buds, at the well-compassed work of the garden, so satisfying at this season—I sulk" (1899, 5r, EC). For Bradley, it is now their "defaced home" in which they cannot stay, but which they cannot forsake: "I have not even Durdans to cling to. I have put away my dead in Durdans. It is unsanctified, and unclean, and cannot be renewed or blessed to us any more until we have proved our willingness to give it up" (1899, 6v, KB).

Both poets also recognize the fact that "home" has been for them an emotional prosthetic. On January 9, Bradley writes: "I wake to feel the firm earth gone from me. In all our sorrows we have been sustained by the firm thought of home[.] Now we have no home, no-one *who is ours* to return to. We must found a home" (1899, 11r, KB; emphasis in original). The firm earth of security has given way for Bradley; she equates "home" with the concept of someone "who is ours" to return to. In the absence of such assurance, the poets feel compelled toward creation, not by finding a home somewhere that already exists but by founding a home through the establishment of a household they can call their own, on their own terms.

The unknowns in this plan frighten Cooper badly. After detailing the various gifts presented to her on her birthday on January 12, she writes, "We plant too much faith in restlessness. We seek, with a fever in the seeking, and no solid goal. Where shall we be next Birthday, I and my Love and our Dogs? Life's solution of this mystery will be peace: the mystery is distraction and the desert. I long for Time to say to us 'Peace be still'" (1899, 13r, EC). Is restlessness an end in itself or the means to the end of peace?

Home is psychic freedom for Michael Field. But home as they have known it has now become inhospitable. Their new alienation from their safest space is overwhelming, even apocalyptic. Cooper describes a frightening precarity, still in January:

> Yesterday I was holding the ^whole^ *Times* in front of the fire in Michael's bedroom; there was a bright stab at it inside, and the whole mass was flame between my hands. The moment was perilous, for a smoke-screen blocks the opening of the chimney—there is scarcely a hearth-stone and a mere brass-rim of fender. With shovel and tongs and most deliberate movements at last I got the flashing heap on the top of the fire and breathed ^again.^ I even trembled for half-an-hour after. How near one is to death any common moment. Time, there is no need *we* should recognize this, Death should be out of sight behind a blood-red curtain, that life may dance and be healthy: but only a gray veil is between us and we always see the menace that should be thickly hidden—therefore we halt or falter ^trip^ in our steps measure and are languid. (1899, 19r, EC; emphasis in original)

Death and its reminders are indeed around every corner in the father's house. The property's caretaker, a man the poets call Old George or "Father's Man," has developed oral cancer, and the immanence of his loss is one more source of alienation from the family home. "Since Old George's calamity the last chain has broken that held me on to Durdans. The garden now ^frames^ holds two ghostly forms—the Master and his Man—both in their degree reverend, most human and pathetic forms. All the bulbs and roses are sepulchral—the air is memory's softness of mist. This must end—we should mop and mow at each other if we stayed wholly with death and the dead" (1899, 19r–19v, EC). Later, and with disregard for sentimentality, much less humanity, Cooper regards George's sadness at the women's departure with some bemusement: "It moves one so much that he should sorrow for us, ^for^ our very sakes: ~~for~~ we have promised him his wages just as ever ~~as long as~~ ^while^ he is spared to us—so he is only thinking ~~[illeg.]~~ as sadly of the farewell. Perhaps he will be spared it. Would he had died amid the 'lulling charities' of the opiate!" (1899, 29v, EC). Nonetheless, George will insist on living, not only with his cancer but with his unreciprocated sadness at the poets' departure.

The factors propelling the poets forth from Durdans multiply. They feel the burden of an awful choice between sepulchre and life. As Bradley writes, "Oh, that we might leave Durdans next week, and begin again: we cannot repair this chance of life. The Materials are worn out. They no longer can bear the strain of life. My Beloved is putting away the pride that so hinders and besets her, and consenting in humbleness to 'starve, feast, despair, be happy'" (1899, 18r, KB). Michael pushes and Henry resists, breaking down gradually until she accepts the inevitable move away from the father's house. Yet even as Michael Field prepare themselves to embrace all the risks of change, they confront the reality that house hunting in the fin de siècle was no easy prospect. From the first, their most promising leads came from their friends, Charles Ricketts and Charles Shannon, who played "the Artists" to Michael Fields' "the Poets." Ricketts and Shannon, both designers, painters, and craftsmen, lived in the London suburb of Richmond from 1894–1902.

From the first, the seduction of Michael Field to Richmond had to do with both substance and style: the substance of an actual prospective home for their careful consideration; the style the prospect of aesthetic assemblage that would enable the Poets to follow their Artists in the material composition of domestic identity.[6] When the Artists share with the Poets their aesthetic home, and their decorating philosophies, they open up a new world of artistic possibility for Michael Field: "One ought to have very beautiful furniture and objects that are dear, calling a chair 'Jennie,' for example.' [. . .] After lunch—coffee and sloe gin [. . .] I grow enthusiastic, and the [A]rtists describe how, with waving of hands. I shall tell my fellow there are ten bed-rooms and two bridges, ^etc.^ In a cab, we reach 1. Paragon—the straight, old, red-brick house, with its pretty white paint and old pillared doorway" (1899, 13v, EC). This was Michael Field's first introduction to the tall, skinny house on the Petersham Road called 1

Paragon.[7] Unprepossessing from the front, the house backs on to the Richmond towing-path that provides a pedestrian walkway along the banks of the Thames. Standing at the towing-path and looking back on the house, Bradley writes, "I look houseward. High up in the sky, I see a bay window.—'What is that'—'Oh, that is your bed-room.' *That*—with England's own river in smooth, country-stream flowing by! [. . .] I return, the news as a gift in my hand" (1899, 13v–14r, KB; emphasis in original).

"If in Durdans, the women had created an aesthetic interior that located the aesthetic and erotic in the world, at 1 Paragon they aimed to transform their life into Art," writes Vadillo.[8] From the first, in company with the Artists, their sloe gin, their male attention, and their aesthetic encouragement, the prospect of 1 Paragon is exciting for Michael. She responds to an air of specialness to the tall, awkward house, with "England's own river" flowing behind. Later, Cooper writes, Ricketts "gives a quaintly true description of Paragon—'a doll's house in front and the poop of a vessel behind'—he thinks the combination perfectly delightful" (1899, 44v, EC). The home's special significance is to Bradley as a gift for her love, held safe in her English haute bourgeois hand.

In addition to offering coffee, sloe gin, home-decorating advice, and repartee, the Artists are men who desire the company of Cooper and Bradley; as Vicinus reminds us, Michael Field have a long history of playing to an audience of "sympathetic but sexually unavailable men."[9] The Artists' irreverent, playful attentions have everything to do with the pleasure Michael Field take in homemaking as a creative enterprise in the name of their marriage. Shannon, for example, writes a floor-by-floor description of 1 Paragon for Cooper, ahead of her first visit to the house, concluding with an account of the garden:

> *Garden* Room for three rose bushes wh: dog can destroy in 14 minutes—7 minutes if helped by another. Little wooden summerhouse overlooking tow-path. Three roses still in bloom today. Wall taller than a man matted with minute Ivy (not observed by the Poet). The garden is at such an incline that the Basset sitting at the top of the garden would at once stride into the river if it was not for the door. Unprecedented opportunity for pushing relatives through doorway at high tide. You are on the Petersham Road, in a nest of beautiful old houses, minutes' walk from the precipitous town garden full of rooks and sparrows who feed from your hands—they spit out currants—so ask for seed-cake—5 minutes to 10 minutes['] walk from [the] station. Petersham Park in sight, Hampton Court near—Kew a good walk—charming walks by the river.

> The house must not next week be judged by its furniture only by its possibilities. Neither must Richmond be judged by its winter aspect. (1899, 14v–15r, EC transcription of letter from Charles Shannon)

Shannon gives the poets the chance to reimagine themselves through his eyes, as people whose naughty dogs might tumble down the steeply pitched garden, as hardy souls who might stride briskly to destinations that are both local and aspirational, and who might give uncooperative relations a well-deserved shove out the back door into the Thames. The Paragon animates possibilities for a new, deeply appealing, lively way of being for Michael Field.

Shannon was right to warn Cooper away from judging the house based on its appearance. Cooper's experience was more mixed feelings than love at first sight.

> Alas, the walls are yellow brick with only red bricks round the windows, and the garden is asphalte [*sic*] and a few ferns under ivy-mould-soil. The lovely white door is an unsupported piece of loveliness. It opens—a delicious little hall and staircase—a sunny room, and through long windows the sweet Thames flowing softly. This room would be the study. The dark cool room behind the Sheraton Drawing room. The bedrooms are large and low and beautiful to dwell in—even the attics are not common attics—tho' we shall be sorry if we have to banish guests there. The parlour and sulking room are *home*, with all the attractiveness of the word. The kitchen is bright—but pantries and scullery dark and, we fear, smelling ill—expert necessary.
>
> The garden-bed would hold 150 roses—and many bulbs—the rim of soil under the ivy-hung wall would hold lilies and herbs, pansies, daylilies and auriculas. An arbour watches the river-door on one side, an acacia tree ^on^ the other. Without the danger of Musico's presence we could make this miniature garden a symbol of Eden. (1899, 16v–17r, EC; emphasis in original)

The front is disappointing; the back is promising, and Cooper finds more happy prospects in the small garden than others do. She makes a list of pros and cons:

> *Advantages*
> Lovely little rooms and passages . . .
> Nearness to the Artists
> Nearness to the Gardens, Terrace, Park, Petersham, and the Thames.
> Outlook on to white river air, and its tidal currant.

A gravel subsoil.
Something brisk and joyous about the genius of the place.

Disadvantages
Nearness of place of Embarkation, with loafers and holiday-makers.
Extreme ugliness and humble^ness^ of approach.
The dirt, viciousness and degradation of lower Richmond on the way to the station.
[The drainage, with light thrown on it, will not always be deterrent, I believe. And the fact of being at the edge of the river will not, I fancy, prove unhealthy—the subsoil being gravel and the current of breeze frequent.]
No place of freedom for the dogs.
A basement.
A woman next door who plays and sometimes sings. (1899, 17r, EC)

Cooper considers issues of drainage both a plus and a minus for the house, but ultimately comes down on the plus side: the gravel subsoil and good breezes off the river seem like a workable combination. The neighbors, too, have pros and cons: the Artists are a positive, as are features such as gardens and parks. The list of negatives includes the prospect of contact with the hoi polloi of Richmond and the musical lady next door. Ultimately, the most important factor in favor of 1 Paragon comes at the end of Cooper's list of advantages: "Something brisk and joyous about the genius of the place."

"Brisk and joyous" are appealing new ways of being for Bradley and Cooper, and in this house they can see themselves as people who employ such a style of life. That the home has its own genius, to be animated in combination with their own—of which they are entirely secure—offers Michael Field a new partner in triangulation.

Thus the decision is made: the poets charge their lawyer to inquire about the particulars of a lease. They dub the Paragon "Mon Abri," or "my shelter"—a nickname for the new home that did not stick for long. Cooper and Bradley are accustomed to understanding themselves as beleaguered, in need of refuge and respite, of shelter from the storm. But the animating spirit of this dwelling is different: Brisk. Joyous. Soon enough, they drop the pretense of refuge and embrace the name the house had when they met it: the Paragon. Perfect for the Greek women, the house derives its name from *parakonen*, "to sharpen"—a whetstone or touchstone, an exemplar, an idea, an ideal. And 1 Paragon, as well: the first, the best, the paragon of paragons. Cooper writes, "It seems as if there were some life for us yet" (1899, 23v, EC).[10]

Perhaps inauspiciously, though, elsewhere "Paragon" is a synecdoche for the disastrous newlywed housekeeping of David and Dora Copperfield; Dickens comments on the irony of the couple's servant's moniker: "Her name was Paragon. Her nature was represented to us, when we engaged her, as being feebly expressed in her name. She had a written character, as large as a proclamation; and, according to this document, could do everything of a domestic nature that ever I heard of, and a great many things I never did hear of."[11] Indeed, Bradley and Cooper run hard into the unyielding wall of the material world in all its squalor—in all its pleasures, too, but first, the challenges, a little bit of everything on the towing-paths of 1899. The pages of *Works and Days* in 1899 are surprisingly thin on updates about poetry and plays in progress, and unprecedented in their attentions to the writers' material choices as they furnish their home; as Vadillo has argued, their aesthetic life is their aesthetic practice in 1899.[12] On February 1, the Mother-One's birthday, Cooper writes, "Round the Mother we have placed dawn-bright anemones and catkins lit by a rose-coloured candle—they are keenly lovely and encouraging. To think what may be this time next year . . . we by our river, Amy by a husband's side, perhaps with new hopes at her bosom. Providence is very busy shaping our ends after years of keeping our sides banked" (1899, 26v–27r, EC).

The bad part of materiality involves leases and renovations. February 5 appears in the diary as "Lease Sunday": "It is here, the monstrous, crabbed, cancerous thing, eating into our very souls, devising evil for us, now and in the future. It is here" (1899, 27r, KB). Just a few days later, on February 9, Bradley describes the most varied of days:

> I sign my will, Dr Hewetson being witness. I toil extremely with doves, and dogs, and house-keeping ^and George's wife,^ and orders for the garden that is to me as a churchyard, round a disused church. The flower-man comes, bearing gayest daffodils and tulips of a rare rose satin over daintiest underlinen. I rush to the shops for stamps and change. As I reach the door of Durdans I am met by my Fellow. She embraces me with the greeting—"You are the mistress of 1, Paragon, Richmond." We kiss over a bunch of white, fragrant stocks I carry in my hand.—Then lunch, and the letters of reference that the trustees may be satisfied, and Chow I tell Cuddie—bearing to her at last a joyous telegram, and more walks in the moist garden where the snowdrops are bursting, and the hair-dresser to cut and wave;—never have I done, or been subject to, in one day, so many divergent things. (1899, 28r, KB)

Durdans is an onomatopoetic drag, dreary and defunct. Bradley does not belong there anymore: the new Michael rushes about, busy with stamps and change, telegrams, and a new hairstyle. The mistress of 1 Paragon, Richmond is a busy woman of the modern world. The poets quickly share the good news: "We send to the Artists 'an annunciation by the flower of all-spice' (2 blossoms—sole on our plant)—Michael Field, At Home, March 25th and all days following—1, Paragon, Richmond" (1899, 28r, KB). In its striking, mundane details (daintiest underlinen, stamps, a hairdresser), this is capsule narrative like no other I recall in *Works and Days*. Of course, Bradley knew she was on her way to the Paragon before she wrote that day's diary entry; she has already reinterpreted her daily activity through the lens of her new identity. She offers us a taste of the bustling life she envisions in her new future as the mistress of 1 Paragon, Richmond.

Cooper (who was dressed, Bradley noted, on this important day "exquisitely in garnet-necklace and bloom bodice" [1899, 28r, KB]) soon recounts the same events from her own perspective. Her account is more tempered, quieter, and more typical of the poets' worldview: "It was exhilarating to gather my Love out of the very wet rain and tell the news through a kiss that 1, Paragon is ours. I feel *renewing* as a process that is as yet a wild confusion in me—but the certain movements of the confusion tell me it will become a dance. 'Sweet Thames flow softly till I end my song.' Indeed the song in my heart is an Epithalamion—a marriage-song of absolutely joined lives: a dream that Eros returns to us after the years of a lifetime as a gift" (1899, 28v, EC; emphasis in original).

Cooper often filters challenging experiences through literary forms. An epithalamion is a poem in tribute to Hymen, the Greek god of marriage, celebrating a bride's passage to her bridal chamber. In 1594, Edmund Spenser's *Amoretti and Epithalamion* offered a series of lyrics in anticipation of Spenser's marriage and married life, initiating the English poetic tradition of epithalamia. Thinking about Spenser, Cooper borrows the refrain of his 1596 "Prothalamion" to link river and marriage in 1 Paragon: "Sweet Thames flow softly till I end my song."[13] Cooper was fully aware of the triunity of marriage, married sex, and home in the history of this poetic form. In her "marriage-song of absolutely joined lives," she finds "a dream that Eros returns to us after the years of a lifetime as a gift." The Paragon is a rebirth into new marriage for Michael Field, a marriage that is equal parts eros and domus—indeed, that is a perfect blend of eros and domus: the intimacy of household things.

The Artists receive Michael Fields' good news with characteristic idiosyncrasy. Shannon returns the poets' telegram: "We are glad to hear that you are glad. We are also glad for a gray blue ^Persian^ Kitten who is like a lamb, a bear, an elephant, a pig, a moth, a caterpillar, a mouse, your gloves and Ricketts' pocket handkerchief. When you come to Richmond it shall scratch the Chow. C.H.S." (1899, 29v, EC transcription of letter from Charles Shannon). Gladness abounds, with the possible exception of the Chow. Though Cooper and Bradley stayed up all night the night they were awarded their lease, making plans for their own new rooms, they must be ready to endure a tutorial at the hands of their aesthetic "twins." Ricketts writes, "pressing his pen with the instantaneousness of his own nature," his advice about color, decor, and life with clumsy visitors:

> In colouring a house see that the temper of each room is kept. When a room hides from the sun provide it with colours and hanging that love the shade: the green of green shadows in the heart of a wood, blue of that blue haunting a grot, the colours found under the sea; place also mirrors in it that listen to you, that look like pools. In these cool rooms various objects may be hung or placed—shadow is kind to ugly but useful books.
>
> In rooms that love the sun use colours that love the sun also: white, ivory, gold, yellow, fawn, some shades of rose even. In these rooms the objects should be well-chosen; the sun is angry with ugly thick shapes, but loves the corners of delicate frames and dainty furniture. Here the mirrors should be allowed to *talk*: provide them with subjects of conversation, carnations, roses, anemones, woodbine, rings on hands, fruit in a basket or on a silver dish—Chinese embroideries. In all these rooms strive to keep the furniture close to the walls as in Persia. The air and light will love you for this—a rare carpet may then brood in an open space, lady-friends will not overset snowdrops in slender glasses or bump against things and male friends or relations will not leave hot briars or smouldering cigarettes upon satinwood—or even galoches. We beg you to kiss the Chow behind the left ear for our dear little Cat. I think [. . .] basset paws on Perigord might induce him to leave Durdans—if not, there is still the river gate. We shall expect to see your roses in an ebony car drawn by zebras, you of course will arrive in a charriot of ivory drawn by pards. Please consider us in the matter of meals or other small matters of assistance. Your slaves on the date of your arrival. (1899, 35v–36r, EC transcription of letter from Charles Ricketts; emphasis in the original)

Ricketts's house beautiful takes its cues from the play of nature within the built environment of the home: individual rooms should respond to social invitations from sun or shade. Like the sun harmonizing with delicate edges, mirrors, too, need conversational partners. And the whole apparatus should be safeguarded against clumsy interlopers whose elbows, cigarettes, and galoches menace the room's delicate habitat. Ricketts envisions a full-on aesthetic arrival for the poets, in a leopard-drawn chariot of ivory. The women's move to an affluent suburb of London transforms domestic realism to epithalamion to epic.

That is, until Ricketts changes his mind the next day, sending the poets a "correcting card": "I have repented—warm colours shd pervade the house, warm blues, warm greens, warm whites, warm everything" (1899, 36v, EC transcription of note from Charles Ricketts). Both theoretically and in practice, the decoration of the house is the stuff of great collective enthusiasm between the Artists and the Poets. Bradley and Cooper wholeheartedly embrace the spirit of partnership the Artists offer; it cuts against the loneliness and isolation they feel as poets generally disdained by the modern world. The poets' married home is a perfect temple to their love and to what they hope to stand for as artists. The fact that it is a private space is immaterial to the continued pleasure of shared creativity: "We see our Paragon in fog—the river but a Whistler shadow across obscurity. [. . .] We talk about Paragon and its furnishing—the Artists will mix our paints. They want us to have the walls of our parlour covered with the gold of the Dial-Screen at Warwick Street—then to treat it in a Dutch manner and devote it to tulips" (1899, 43v–44r, EC).[14]

Ricketts plays midwife to this experience, and the poets hew closely to his guidance. In the midst of contemplating Paragon, Cooper writes, "What makes Ricketts so essentially an artist in conversation and in composition is the quality of strangeness by which Life becomes art. He has many weaknesses, many whims (that with him are not affectations, but tendrils out of the very stock of his nature)—but because he can make all that he touches unfamiliar he belongs to that Kingdom that must differ from the world if it is to exist. Personality is the Power of a will to impress the world; genius the power of a will to translate it into another world" (1899, 44v–45, EC).[15]

"How Ricketts fascinates!" Cooper writes as the poets contemplate the lease of Paragon. "He is just like his own *Psyche in the House*—soft, illusive, yet confiding the intimateness of his being, through having a body too fine to screen its secrets" (1899, 18r–18v, EC).[16] In his artistic genius, which makes the familiar unfamiliar, and in "the intimateness of his [bodily] being," Ricketts combines abstract and material qualities that are compelling to Michael Field. As they contemplate departing the patriarchal household and establishing their married home, they themselves struggle—hard—to balance bodily needs for shelter and repast against psychic needs for intentional beauty. The very combination of qualities they identify in Ricketts illustrates how they hope to be in the world.

That charge is not easy, particularly as it must be performed before the eyes of Ricketts himself: "We reach the Artists in time for ¾ of an hour's talk," Cooper writes. "Ricketts receives us depressingly—he is so afraid we may come and be ill—he is cautious as a savage. 'Really, Ricketts,' says the confident Shannon 'you are talking like a doctor.'" Ricketts's sensitivity manifests as social unpredictability, which keeps Cooper off her balance. Cooper keeps Ricketts off his as well. The poets attempt reassurance:

> We promise quiet thought and a lawyer if we ~~think~~ ^entertain^ ~~of~~ the beloved little hovel. Our butterflies are poised on old glasses. The "gee-gee" carpet has a ground^-colour^ of dead roses. "You must lie down on it" commands Ricketts. I fall like Whym Chow in a heap—then become conscious of my huge winter-coat, and see myself a black Russian Bear before the eyes that love bony grace and veils. I rise sensitive. The Artists always seem to regard me as a new exhibit in a deep-sea-water tank—I feel I ought to blink and expand my lips with spectral novelty in every movement. We are introduced to "Fatty," "Swallow" and "Bulfinch"—the three new Sheffield jugs—also to the "Jack-in-the-Box," named Dr Ibsen (and a perfect portrait) and to ~~Father~~ ^the^ Christmas ^God^ "just like God the Father seen by Blake" (He had the grey Capuchin and the wild, windy eyes) Ricketts forgets to hand us our bag when we enter our cab—we discover our loss too late. (1899, 17v, EC)

Clearly Cooper experiences as awkward the varied personae she is expected to adopt while keeping company with the Artists. Even from one sentence of this account to the next she struggles to shift appropriately: a lawyer. Butterflies. Oh, Edith, you must lie down on the Artists' rug. She feels large and burly and ursine in her outsize winter coat, the opposite of the Artists' wispy ideal of femininity. She feels like a fish in a tank, on display for observers: "I ought to blink and expand my lips" with every movement. Here are new Sheffield jugs that are named like pets—time to depart, only for the poets to realize they have forgotten their bag.

The "gee-gee" carpet becomes the symbol for Cooper's feelings of awkward ungainliness around the Artists. Later, she reflects:

> Now I must relate a strange thing—the spell of the "gee-gee" carpet over me. It simply makes me awkward and enormous. Three times I kicked ^it^ into rucks in the floor, with helpless imbecility of movement; and the strangest thing of all is that I felt where my feet ^soles^ touched it to grow elephantine—my knees were to me as bolsters, my dress was Esquimaux in bulk—my boots—well if I had vast turtles as feet, their shells could not have been heavier than my shoe-leather. And Michael knew all this by merely looking at me, saw I was amplitudinous. Curse the gee-gees! (1899, 45r–45v, EC)

The Artists have warned Cooper to beware clumsy guests with their giant feet and stray galoches, and to prepare for them by hiding fragile and valuable objets d'art. Cooper becomes aware that she herself is that clumsy guest in the Artists' home. She has no more to set eyes on the "gee-gee" than she's transformed into an "amplitudinous" clod, her feet elephantine, her knees bolsters, her dress the girth of Esquimaux, her boots the hard shells of vast turtles.[17]

Cooper is clearly not in harmony with this aesthetic home. She feels clumsy, makes dumb mistakes, and obviously feels more uncanny than at home within a space whose floor covering holds her in thrall.[18] Michael Field frame their 1899 transition as a struggle to balance the pragmatic demands of the material world against certain ideals of critical importance to their aesthetic marriage. Those ideals, including beauty, demand something awkward relative to the material limits of servants, stoves, and carpets. It is hard work to compose a married household, especially one where family castoffs are unwelcome, and the discerning eye of Ricketts rules all.

The work is also expensive, and that is a meaningful consideration. Again, Cooper:

> We love the lowly, bright Paragon—we shall soon make our tiny front gay—a very smart little front, with paint and latticing. And the river-arbour can be made a kennel for Musico. The Parlour! It is perfect! The "hovel" is sweet-smelling, sun-full, (except, alas, at the back)—a strong, comely, loveable strip of a home. [. . .] And there we lean on Richmond Bridge where the people will gather to see the Chow and Basset take their waterside airing. The tide swings down and overflows the path of the sunset across it. And then we buy flowers—and the man looks as if he were entertaining angels that would stay or at least return—four bunches of fresias, four of anemones, and a love-knot of Neapolitan

> violets—We have to return ^travel^ part of the way home third-class—and ^to^ know the separate existence of each penny in our purses. (1899, 23r–23v, EC)

The poets make their new local flower man's day with the magnitude of their purchase. Mrs. Dalloway did not worry about the expense of her flowers, and neither did Michael Field—but only Michael Field accidently overspent their guineas and had to travel home in third class. The poets sold books "to realise the price of Michael's wedding present to Amy 'An old silver Dutch tea-pot with one dove on the top'—'to exclude the other pigeon' smiles Ricketts finely and with joy" (1899, 44v, EC). It is costly for the poets to surround themselves with beauty.

In Paragon, the poets have committed to a major rehabilitation project, beginning at the most basic levels, even in advance of their aesthetic aspirations. In an entry from March 25 that is especially challenging to decipher—because she was agitated? Rushed? Both?—Bradley describes the simultaneous transfer of tenancy and responsibility: "On Friday night the key of Paragon front door was laid in Edith's hands. Saturday morn—Drain-new, furniture-new Gardeners—the Zermatt wreath, a contractor.—the lawyer" (1899, 47v, KB). Just a few days later, Cooper takes up the horror at what lies ahead: "To Richmond—after storm with Ellen the maid—We ring and ring, thinking Mr Bagaley, our Builder, is inside. . . . The bell rings into the great Void. At last Mr Bagaley and his son arrive ^from the station,^ and we enter to smells, piled filth, paper piled on dust [. . .] The people have only left a stained glass window and on the parlour mantel shelf, the husband's funeral card—a catafalque of an erection. The toil of reviewing the needs of each room wearies me to desolation" (1899, 48r, EC).

Yet, even in darkness, there is hope. Bradley visits the Paragon on her own one Friday, writing:

> Alone, for Henry is ill, and Amy removing her bride-things to Bristol, I knock at the knockerless Paragon. Blinds and gas-stoves are on the floors, and kennel doors; but no work that edifies is being done. No woman scrubs. I telegraph. Then I sit in my leads, and watch the afternoon gaiety begin—the launching of the pleasure-boat, the gilding of the trees. Suddenly the painter tells me of a robin's nest with six young.—It is in our ivy-sod. Four brilliant young beaks gape as the leaves are pressed back.—The sight of those craving young mouths so sheltered [. . .] quite frenzies me with happiness: And it is there in our garden they build! (1899, 66v, KB)

New life inspires Henry into a frenzy of happiness. She takes the mama robin's choice of the Paragon garden personally, proud of the hungry promise of "our garden" on a sparkling afternoon on the water. Notwithstanding the grim interior of the "knockerless Paragon," its garden is a place where desire and pleasure flourish on a beautiful spring afternoon.

Shopping is the great unexpected flourishing of Michael Fields' domestic transition. On Wednesday, March 20, they traveled to Guilford "to get table, chairs, sideboard—necessary things—*'Result'*—we sit in Williamson's shop and Michael buys for me my wedding present for Richmond . . . a small tea-casket (call it not caddy) of ivory and tortoiseshell—the loveliest object I have ever loved; 'nothing too much' dreamt into a shape. And we buy old cut-glass liqueur glasses and old silver egg-spoons, and three of the most perfect coffee-tables with seed-legs! There is in our behaviour a riot of luxurious contrariety" (1899, 49v, EC). This epithalamion is lyric to an ivory tea-casket, and all that is promising in Michael Fields' new life.

Recalling the guidance they sought from Berenson in Paris during the summer of 1893, the poets here seek the Artists' didactic example: "They smoke at the Paragon and turn over Morris papers, with puffs of *Whew! . . . My goodness . . . Crikey!* But their creativeness seems paralised and we only settle the guest-room with Morris 'Blackthorn' and blue ceiling; Michael's River-bedroom in the 'Larkspur and Rose'; grot with Old Woodbine-paper; sun-room with ivory paint; Dutch room with gold Japanese paper . . . in the Sulking-room we wanted Morris' Acanthus: it is described by the artists as 'liver and bacon'" (1899, 49r, EC). As this suggests, there is no shortage of aesthetic competition in Ricketts's masterminding of the Paragon. Later still, the Artists come to dine with the Poets in the new home: "Ricketts enjoyed^s^ the reeking old baize on our satinwood table that smells 'like stupid Pater'" (1899, 96v, EC).

Ricketts and Shannon will insist on leaving for a long-planned trip to Italy in the midst of all this planning, but before they depart, Michael Field corral Ricketts into a West End shopping trip. There, Ricketts annoys Cooper by insisting on chatting about the Vale edition of Keats instead of her decorating project. Finally, though: "At last we start to look at Spanish Rugs, with many conjurations that we will leave Ricketts to settle everything, breathe 'it is too long' if we very much want a carpet, and with such fuss of caution and self-importance as man so amusingly makes when he goes to a shop in woman's company. There are no gee-gee rugs to be had." Notwithstanding his self-appointed role of bargainer in chief, "Ricketts is very low-toned and submissive in manner and never a breath of bargaining does he draw after all his conjurations." Further, "He refuses to enter Liberty's to see a piece of old Venetian brocade specially chosen out, and we retire to St James's Tea-Rooms with nothing accomplished and an atmosphere of ineffectiveness round us" (1899, 58r–58v, EC).

Shopping with Ricketts is not a success. Soon enough, Ricketts dropped out of the day-to-day work of accumulation, unleashing Michael Field on London's shops on their own. "We are choosing that on which our eyes shall rest—haply for years.—This little homelandscape it is in our power to provide, what shall it be?" (1899, 55r, KB). To furnish the "homelandscape," Michael Field turn to Miss Toplady, an aesthetic shop established in 1898 by their friend Mary Costelloe and her brother, Logan Pearsall Smith.[19] Toplady served a few functions for Costelloe and Bernhard Berenson, including the cultivation of Berenson's reputation for connoisseurship, and as a channel to legitimize his business as an art dealer. For Michael Field, however, the shop served as a resource for all kinds of aesthetic odds and ends. Cooper writes of their first trip on a Wednesday. Michael Field emerge like Botticelli's Venus:

> Michael and I put on our scallop-shells and away to Toplady's. The things are well-chosen, with the restfulness of love. Ivory-coloured Wedgewoods, Sheffield egg-cups, Dutch sconces greet us, and inside an American accent, a pleasant face that reminds in black and white of Mary Costelloe's pastel effects, and a most serviceable pleasure-seeking kindness. [. . .] I buy a Demon's toasting-fork, two lovely sconces, and Michael a cut-glass silver-mounted mustard-pot, "a real Toplady article," for Amy. We really enjoy ourselves—these Americans set life capering—strange that all "*the set*" shd now be "fizzing" over furniture and we be contemporaneous! After lunch at Club, we buy at Morris' the Brussels carpet for Michael's River-Room. Ridiculous Miss Toplady! I am glad I have enjoyed her wares. (1899, 60r–60v, EC; emphasis in original)

Cooper is always cheered by success in the shops, and this excursion is no exception. She celebrates, as well, the rare chance to be "contemporaneous" with "the set": Michael Field find themselves fashionable for once; though none in London are eager to see them for their art, they find themselves enjoying good company in aesthetic consumerism. When she reenters Bernhard Berenson's space, Cooper captures the old elusive desire for the "contemporaneous," if even only for a moment.

It was such a success that Michael Field returned, just three days later on a Saturday:

> Saturday. Again to Miss Toplady's. We find French stuffs of exceeding value—a Triton-woven stuff such as waves are made of for the River-Room, and blues that never will forget the sea. I buy an iron knocker from my Siena, a Wedgewood sugar basin and coffee pot. A gentleman doubted the existence of Toplady—he was invited to meet her at afternoon tea—great tension due to hope. A telegram. "Ill—unable to come. Many regrets. Sell suite for £70—Toplady." Surely the telegram proved the real existence. (1899, 61r, EC)

Amid the Sapphic orts and fragments of these "Toplady articles," it seems entirely fitting that the shop itself is bedecked in an aura of mystery. Who is this Toplady, and what is the motive force of the enterprise? Surely the arrival of a telegram instead of a person increased the gentleman's degree of doubt about Toplady's existence (quite correctly), rather than "proving" anything at all.

If the "set" is now "fizzing" on the matter of furniture, Bradley and Cooper embrace once again their contemporaneity with this moment. Yet at Miss Toplady's their purchases are almost entirely accessories to the ordinary matter of everyday life: toasting forks, sconces, and a mustard pot for Amy; a knocker, a sugar bowl, and a coffee pot. The eggcups and the carpets, chosen for beauty, come together in an aesthetic combination that serves entirely pragmatic ends, especially on behalf of consumption, of eating and drinking. In the composition of their married home, the poets are intent upon making the everyday beautiful, and making beauty every day, right down to the spoons and eggcups. Jonathan Freedman reminds us of the quirky history of aesthetic accessories within the home, which originated in the concept of the "Bathroom Beautiful": "On the one hand, it suggested that the commodities one purchased were not so much objects for use as objects of art, to be acquired and appreciated the way a connoisseur purchases a fine oil; at the same time, the strategy was linked to the mass production of these commodities: only when sinks are being produced on a mass scale is it possible—or necessary—to suggest that sinks be differentiated on the basis of their relative beauty."[20]

Vadillo writes suggestively of the poets' "inhabited aestheticism": Michael Field "strove to create aesthetic interiors that expressed them, their own history, their own dreams and desires. As Bradley so eloquently noted: 'It is *we* who bring the harmonies not *time*. An uninhabited room would remain crude whatever happened to the colours.'"[21] The Paragon's interiors, in other words, are the manifest expression of Michael Field's interior selves: the lived expression of their aesthetic practice—what

Vadillo describes as the "expressive, living, aestheticism where the self is located in and expressed through the aesthetic interior." Vadillo demonstrates the influence of male aesthetes—Ruskin, Morris, Pater, Berenson, and Ricketts—on Michael Field. And just as importantly, that the poets aspire to create homes "embedded in history: the history of art, aesthetics, but most crucially their own. . . . [T]heir homes were not aesthetic just for art's sake but truly expressive of their identity as aesthetes."[22] I would add to this that Michael Fields' aesthetic identity in 1899, as they crafted the home space of 1 Paragon so carefully, was enmeshed intimately with their praxis of marriage.[23]

For having stuff, including a married home, can never be all—or only—about the beautiful. "Henry takes a pencil and writes down a long list of fixtures for the lease.—'Who shall deliver us from the body of this death?[']" (1899, 46r, KB), writes Michael. We have already seen Bradley write a new will this year, just as the Poets acquire the lease for the Paragon. The Artists, too, are thinking about their wills:

> As we drink tea Ricketts tells us how he and Shannon are making their wills. [. . .] They dare not go to Italy until they have given their Hokusai Col to the ~~Brist~~ British Museum, their bits of Antiquity to Oxford; and left all their work in the hands of Sturge Moore. So they have got Whittaker's Almanack and are their own la^w^yers. Without the lawful intervention of Sturge Moore Ricketts' sister, who has married a German doctor, wd claim his unpublished cartoons or Shannon's family in the depths of Lincolnshire wd wish "to have all dear Charlie's drawings." "If we make our wills we think the little railway accident will not occur." (1899, 58v–59v, EC)[24]

Though Ricketts and Shannon are convinced that making their wills will forestall a train crash, their concerns here highlight considerations that are also on Michael Fields' minds. Beautiful things are at least theoretically eternal; humans are not. What will become of one's works and beautiful possessions in the afterlife of their human owners? And in the case of "spinster" women, or of men who are "roommates," who are the logical beneficiaries of their well-curated matter of everyday life, or of their artworks? On Thursday, March 30, Bradley and Cooper pay a call on a Miss Combes and "buy from her her grandmother's small oval mirror and some old blue China. She likes to know where they will be.—'The things are my own—I have no one to leave them to'—what a comment on the severance from one's race that is the abnormality of the single life or the forlorn life—*The things are my own*" (1899, 50r, EC; emphasis in original).

"The things are my own," and Miss Combes likes to know where they will be after she is no more. The single life, or the forlorn life, or the life with family of choice supported by no legal mechanisms for inheritance, creates the need for intentional action on behalf of Miss Combes and her fellow travelers in the forlorn. Death is immanent in life, certainly for Michael Field. Except for Miss Combes's grandmother's mirror, Michael Field display no interest in the provenance of the beautiful odds and ends they purchase. Homemaking for Michael Field represents a curatorial practice: the careful selection of beautiful objects that both comprise and evoke their marital intimacy. Theirs is a fetishism akin to the imperial fetish for exotic objects, for things that signify and constitute dynamics well beyond their material function.[25]

Yet, in one sense, the poets were haunted by the specter of Miss Combes and the plight of those who live the single or forlorn life. The concern arises again when they turn to write their last wills about a decade from this point. To whom will they leave their blue china, their mirrors, their mustard pots? We know where some of the material tokens of Michael Fields' marriage ended up after the Paragon household broke up when Bradley died in 1914. Just as Miss Combes's grandmother's small oval mirror survived its owner, so Michael Fields' carefully chosen new possessions will survive them. By the end of their lives, the women had grown sufficiently isolated or "forlorn" that the dispensation of their things posed a challenge.

The immortality of things must raise the specter for Michael Field of their own mortality, of their human frailty; though they understand themselves to coexist with their dead, that coexistence depends on the spectral dematerialization of their deceased loved ones. Given their longer-term dedication to their objects than the poets have yet enjoyed, the Artists fancy a plan to address the place of human death in the midst of life's abundant material pleasures. "In a grovy field beyond," Cooper writes in the summer, "the [A]rtists want to build a house—a builder's house of 2 stories in which they are to live till they get a very old house in wh: death will come on them while they are still furnishing rooms. There must be so many rooms they will never know in which they will die" (1899, 82v–83r, EC). For the Artists to live is to furnish the house that will be as a casket to them. Death will sneak up on them in the midst of designing a new room in a house so vast, on a day so distant, they cannot envision it. As the poets prepare to depart Durdans, the house of the father, they struggle with the meaning of the space itself, as the container for the memories of experiences and losses they suffered in their life there. Durdans is already haunted: "There is a sense of ~~[illeg.]~~ the dead about the fragrance and entreaty of the air" Cooper says, describing a walk in the garden with Bradley. "I feel to lean on the father's arm and with him overlook the teeming ^bit^ of Earth that was his that will, we trust, continue to be ours! And it is a terrible joy to feel my own Love's arm where his used to support me" (1899, 49v, EC). The Oedipal triangle emerges again, the steady arm of Cooper's father morphing vertiginously into that of her lover. "Our new home is a void; our old home is doomed," writes Michael a scant month before the poets moved, "and has lost its living hold on us" (1899, 52v, KB).

As we know from how Michael Field narrate painful and difficult stories in other volumes of *Works and Days*, they tend to write and rewrite challenging narratives, incorporating subtle and important variations. The sad experience of departing Durdans is no exception to this narrative rule. "It is Saturday-Night, May 13th—The last in Durdans," writes Cooper. "I sit in a dismantled study, with only the ivory tulips of the south bed bowing over the newly acquired Leeds china and the ivory tea-caddy. Our steps are terribly loud on the stairs—we are weary and resigned" (1899, 68r, EC). The next night, Cooper casts the poets as vestal virgins: "The last real night in Durdans—Tomorrow everything but a bed or two will be gone. [. . .] We have packed—we have gathered treasures from our borders for the Thames-side, we have prepared for the future, and its claims, its rights, its difficulties. [. . .] Then Michael has lighted the altar and we have knelt together, naturally, simply—loving the lights and the lighted flowers in front of the great threefold Unity. These lights will be lit again at Paragon—so we carry our Sacred Fire" (1899, 68v–69r, EC). In yet a third last night, Bradley writes her heading in bold, huge letters: "May 15th LAST NIGHT AT DURDANS." And she continues:

> Between noon and one o'clock I looked out and a van was being thrust through the lime-tree leafiness—There was a second one behind—two coffins to receive all that remains of the home *he* made for our shelter; two brutal coffins. [. . .]
>
> Well, Father remains, and Durdans remains—they are both of my life-stream, of my self.
>
> The rooms are walls with papers on them, I know and floors of straw and lumber—so Durdans ends, to remain forever alive as on Jubilee Day with its banners and roses, or on Midsummer Day 1897 with its gray irises and the sprinkle of wild sweetbriar starlets beyond.
>
> I must sleep . . . (1899, 70v–71r, KB; emphasis in original)

The vans approaching Durdans are the caskets that will take away the remains of a dead home that the patriarch created for the shelter of his family. But, as Bradley puts it, "Father remains and Durdans remains—they are both of my life-stream, of my self." So in remembrance and in wallpapers and straw, Durdans the physical house remains, though Durdans the home for the Cooper family has died. It is retained only in memories of Jubilee Day celebrations, of Midsummer Day 1897 when, unbeknown to Durdans or to the two women in residence on that day, everything changed and something new began. Like Adam and Eve, the poets "go forth, we two, to found a home. I and my Love, we have chosen each other with all our strength, inspiration, and ~~tenderness~~ ^yearning^—may our home be a nest, a place that fosters, and makes warmth; may it be pleasant by its riverside and shelter joyousness!" (1899, 70r, EC).

Notwithstanding her embrace of the epithalamion, Cooper feels keenly the pain of departure from the nuclear family home. "Ricketts said, 'At Richmond you will forget Reigate,'" she writes. She disagrees: "No, the locked treasure is the unforgettable—but oh, it must be locked, this existance [*sic*] on our own bit of England, where we have borne dreaded sorrows" (1899, 70r, EC). Michael Field have not sold Durdans; they intend to rent the home to another family, and Cooper celebrates the fact that her "own bit of England" will remain her father's, through the vehicle of Henry and Michael. From here forward, Durdans will become for her the unforgettable "locked treasure," the past persisting forcefully—even more forcefully because it is memory, not material.

Michael Field reach for the idiom of empire to describe themselves as "founders" or "colonists" of their new home. On May 21, Cooper writes from Paragon:

> Our beautiful meadows are misty; the buttercups hide behind the river-mist; the full Thames has many boats along its mid-currant. The Chow is at my feet in the River-Room; Michael is at Petersham Church. I am thankful for my towering little home; and almost welcome the many trials it entails as a pledge it is not too perfect. The servants have behaved as only servants can, and brilliantly supported the arguments for slavery—no-one has done the work promised; we live among work-people, unfinished rooms, ladders, complaints, and gabble. But the tides swing up and down our river, and the light is full of the water, and the greenness of the meadows rejoices calmly in its own ~~plent~~ plenitude. Also our rooms grow toward sweetness. The carpet is down in

the River-Room, the solemn Queen Anne Room has its pictures, the Durdans study begins to re-incarnate itself in the Grot. (1899, 71v, EC)

Like any idealized version of reality, mistiness cloaks the machinery that props up the facade. In the case of Paragon, pulsing with the tides and the lights, the house grows toward sweetness despite the failings of servants who have misbehaved "and brilliantly supported the arguments for slavery."[26] Cooper knows she lives in a construction zone; she has pulled back the curtain and revealed the mechanics of aesthetic production. That those mechanics include actual human beings, workpeople among "unfinished rooms, ladders, complaints, and gabble," they find a nuisance. Indeed, keeping servants in Paragon, "a towering little home" with the business in the basement and multiple staircases between the workrooms and the living areas, will be a perennial challenge for Michael Field.[27]

Brigadoon on the Thames it is not. As Cooper's caustic allusion to slavery demonstrates, Michael Field struggle to keep their abject dependence on servants and other workers an open secret in the diary narrative during this time of "founding" a home—indeed, a home wholly subsidized by the Bradley fortune, derived from the transformation of a raw imperial product, tobacco, into a functional commodity. The Barretts' sugar was the Bradleys' tobacco, absent EBB's ethical stance concerning the commodity and the means of its production. As Emma Donoghue puts it memorably, "Like many other devotees of Art for Art's Sake, the Michael Fields came from solid bourgeois stock; they preferred not to remember that their exquisite reveries were funded by cigars."[28] The women are persistently frustrated in their effort to exercise crude power to force the mechanics of that founding because of an inconvenient truth: the practical elements of homemaking require the arms, legs, and intelligence of other human beings. The servants who had originally agreed to follow Michael Field from Durdans persist for only a few weeks: "Sarah and Ellen leave us—unregretted of is sad; but they have been so selfish and disobliging, so iron in their tyranny over mistresses of broken nerve that their departure is deliverance" (1899, 81v, EC). Absent Sarah and Ellen, Cooper and Bradley are forced to "climb up and down the stairs of Paradise till our limbs are on the rack" (1899, 82r, EC). If Sarah and Ellen left mistresses with broken nerves, their departure exacted a toll on their limbs as well. Michael Field's store of empathy seems to be long depleted.

Bradley and Cooper work hard to write the idyll of epithalamion in the midst of the grubby work of relocation; their seesawing back and forth between these two narrative modes verges on the slapstick. Bradley writes: "The kitchen grate has presented hollows as of an old woman's gums; work people have strewed arsenic in our path, and the bitter din of devils has been in our ears. Never shall I forget the enchantment of the first three wakings at Richmond.—everything blank of sorrow, the air light May with the Thames, my dearest on earth waking beside me to the rapture" (1899, 72r, KB). Both of their dogs are ill, but Bradley longs to claim consecration of their poetic spaces in the name of marriage. But how is this honeymoon to occur?

> —So, though I was as a creature half dead after carrying that Basset—bless him—down those many flights, and striving to dose the Chow, I have recovered slowly [. . .] But it was last night! Henry and I sat, first on the sofa, then on the settle together, consecrating with kisses this little room of re-opened memories and love.
>
> Henry, my beloved, head now of this my little home, God's gift to us, here may we live for a little while in blessedness, here die ~~[illeg.]~~ rapid and passionate as the tide in its swift pressure to the sea. (1899, 72v–73r, KB)

The language of power asymmetry emerges here once again, with Bradley careful to subordinate herself to Henry's will as the head of their married household. Bradley is the servant to the dog-children's needs. And like the Artists, she carves out the home space as the container not only for life but also for death, rapid and passionate as the tides that throb in the Thames just outside.

The home thus consecrated, Field begin to figure out how to live in this new, married life framed by axial ideals and material challenges. Cooper writes, "I came home to find a strange letter that had not come through the post laid on the study table for me—£100 from my dear Love, tenderly given at sacrifice to herself, that the weight of my heavy expenses might be lightened. I had wings—clean, sweeping joy. Our little home wd not have a corner's weight of debt on it—Beloved!" (1899, 76v, EC). The domestic differential flips again. Though the women shared a close family relationship as well as a primary relationship of choice, Bradley had personal wealth that Cooper did not. Bradley's family inheritance from her parents was shared with her sister Emma (Beloved Mother-One to Edith). Emma Bradley Cooper in turn kept a full household with her husband James at Durdans; and her daughter Edith divided the family inheritance left by Emma and James with her sister Amy. The expenditures Michael Field undertook to acquire and furnish Paragon would have hit Cooper's purse much harder than Bradley's; this gives us a rare glimpse of the financial asymmetry between Michael and Field.

"After gardening, we lie down in the study," Cooper writes, "—Music and Whym sharing the Morris Couch with me. We have not changed for the evening; we have worked ourselves into callousness—the cotton blouse is thus as the satin bodice. We yawn and sleep—the dogs yawn and sleep; the Room is a cave of sleep. Suddenly the Artists! The dogs wake—their mistresses only seem to wake" (1899, 76v–77r, EC). How to be alone? Or perhaps the harder question: How to produce narrative about being alone?[29] The narrative incitement this afternoon comes courtesy of the Artists, whose visit makes narrative-worthy an afternoon otherwise fit for a cotton blouse. The poets have significantly less control over spontaneous visitors in Paragon, even as they have more cause to labor on behalf of a home over which they hold primary responsibility. "We are driven from our bedrooms by varnish and can scarcely eat in our parlour for varnish. It is rare to get one ideal moment" (1899, 78r, EC). The Paragon does indeed seem to be fulfilling its pledge not to be too perfect: the domestic real still surpasses the ideal.

Fittingly, one of the first events in the epithalamial house is a marriage. Amy Cooper, who had been engaged to a man named James Ryan for some time, accepted "with a thrill of joy [her sister's] offer that the marriage should take place from Paragon, Richmond, with father Thames to give the bride away" (1899, 36v, EC). The poets were by turns put out by and gracious about hosting Amy's wedding. Ryan, who compounded the sin of his Irishness with Catholicism, and Amy had repeatedly deferred their wedding, preferring (sensibly?) to wait until Ryan had stable employment. Meantime, however, responsibility for Amy—how to accommodate her within the married home of Paragon, how to manage the expansion of the home's canine community to accommodate her dog too—weighs grumpily on the poets. Tellingly, Amy's wedding is an episode the poets narrated repeatedly and fragmentedly in the diary—a sure sign that Michael Field are conflicted.

The poets are consistently grudging about Amy's needs during this period, at least in the pages of their (ostensibly private) diary. Shortly after their move to Paragon, "We determine that if Amy's marriage does not come to pass before the winter, we will bear the terrible inconvenience of 3 dogs and no guest-chamber, as if the delay made no difference to us that Amy may not lose for the least while in her life the sureness of a home" (1899, 90r, EC). Despite her need for a home—a need of their own that distresses the poets beyond description—Amy's aunt and sister privately regret the potential extended occupancy of their guest room. It is hard for them to see how Amy, who is prosaic like Musico the basset hound, fits in to the silver, gold, and satinwood "homelandscape" of Paragon. "Amy's little room looks hard—I don't think she will ever be able to make a room breathe—for Venus must come and touch the walls with the stroke of her finger, if they are to live, and Amy is afraid of Venus" (1899, 50v, EC). Clearly Amy lacks the pagan inspiration that has touched her nearest relations. Her ostensible fear of Venus, however, also casts subtle shade on Amy's forthcoming marriage. After all, the poets' married love, like their home-decorating strategies, is the product of inspiration from the goddess of love and prosperity. Later Bradley is entirely candid about the chance that Amy might someday read the entries about her in *Works and Days*. In the course of suggesting the publication of a new Michael Field play was more interesting than Amy's wedding, Bradley cringes in anticipation of Amy's discovery of her candor: "How much more of life this is to us than the wedding-day—O pardon, little Amy, if you ever read this" (1899, 105r, KB). Later still, a passage that Edith wrote after rehoming Amy's old dog, and then imperfectly crosshatched, is clearly a dissection of the "~~old Amy~~" (1899, 128r, EC).

Yet, as eager as the poets clearly are to get rid of Amy, they also need her. Though they have been quick to claim dominion over their married home at the time they moved into Paragon, it is true that coresidence with Amy for a few months maintains for them the familiar, safe structure of an audience to witness their married life. The importance of this fact becomes clear when the poets take still more victory laps, declaring anew the commencement of their married life, after Amy's wedding. In fact, their deepest reflections on the meaning of their new life together occur only after Amy departs. The conventionality of Amy's wedding and marriage—perhaps as epitomized in her use of the Coopers' castoff furniture and photos—suggests pridefulness on the poets' behalf. I do not believe that Michael Field condescend toward Amy's conventionality in favor of their own unusual profile; after all, Michael Field claim marriage, married home, and married love over and over again in the 1899 volume. Rather, I think the poets contrast themselves favorably with Amy on a host of measures, including their connection to beauty, eros, love—the whole package of being "dear, Greek women." According to Michael Field, Amy fears Venus. Amy's aunt and Amy's sister do not.

Amy's wedding appears in glimpses throughout the autumn's diary entries: the event is far more important and much more conflicted than the poets would suggest directly. Edith's perspective on the wedding occurs entirely through glimpses. "On the day itself I was toiling like the

Marchoness [*sic*]—in pantry and panelled Room. I only saw the Bride drink tea in her violet Fisher coat and skirt and hat with gold and white jasmine in white chiffon—a ~~coil~~ ^end^ of the chiffon curling half-round her neck, ~~half~~ like a ^half-^veil" (1899, 106v–107r, EC). Cooper had hardly changed her clothing when news came that the deed was done:

> I scarcely got into my old brocade blouse and violet skirt before news came "it is all over—Miss Amy is Mrs Ryan." No waiter had arrived; Lizzie, our third maid, had bleeding at the nose—Sarah was in bed, Crofts was pale as egg-shell china. I slashed at the Fowls and only left them when the arrival of the ^bridegroom's^ parents and the rest of the party was announced. They came in ~~—the unwelcome strangers~~ by our little river-gate round which Michael had lavishly gathered palms, bamboos, late roses ~~and~~, clear-blue plumbago and white bavardias. Michael and I so entirely lived where these people were ^not^ and so entirely left the sacred kingdoms where they were not, that the entertainment was a success and all shoals were avoided. [. . .] Our rooms endured the company very well—they ceased to be intimate, and schooled themselves to be receptive with dignity—and the light from the Thames silvered them. (1899, 107r–107v, EC)

It is amusing to see Cooper in light of the grudging martyrdom of her role as hostess. Typical of Paragon luck, the waiter and the servants were failures, leaving Cooper herself to "slash . . . at the Fowls," an image that alarms. She and Bradley gave it their all and created a successful party. Even their rooms rose to the occasion, swapping married intimacy for sociability with an anthropomorphic flair.

And so the newly married couple depart, taking the party with them:

> Our quiet little bride and ~~the [illeg.]~~ ^her^ bridegroom left us by the river-gate, passing by the palms, bamboos, late roses, clear-blue plumbagos and white bavardias, while rice beat them and old shoes were slung after them. Outside the door was the river, the beautiful old bridge, the tide of wave and light and wind^—an angler who looks once and angles thereafter.^ The pair walked away along the towing-path and waved from under Richmond Bridge. So it ended. We bade farewell to the strangers—and returned to the strange house full of broken meats, piled fruits, champagne glasses, and the sweetness of tuberose and of stephanotis clutching one's sense intolerably. (1899, 107v, EC)

"The wedding over, and the bride people gone": this is the very moment when story begins for Jane Austen's Emma Woodhouse.[30] For Michael

Field, this is also the moment story begins, or begins again. The bride people have departed, along with the bride and bridegroom, and they set to the task of making their strange house familiar again. On October 1, 1899, Bradley announces:

> It is Sunday—the first Sunday of our married life. The river is deep and flowing; there is a river too in our hearts flowing deep.
>
> She is above me, or below me, in the house, she only—gladness in her steps.
>
> We are intensely desolate, yet so snug and warm, a squirrel in its winter nest.
>
> The wind and rain have been wild and sweeping—the west edged with gold. The dead are gone, the little bride is gone; but the dead remain.
>
> The dead have bidden farewell, the bride has bidden farewell; but the dead return.
>
> In the autumn, in the spring they come to us, but the little bride will come no more for ever.
>
> For death binds; it is Life that severs.
>
> We have the ^her^ old terrier abandoned in the house. She is gone, the little bride is gone *for evermore*. (1899, 104r, KB; emphasis in original)

"She only." Married life in Bradley's vision is a measure of the poets' coupled solitude, the privacy that they have always craved and so rarely found. But even in the wake of the "little bride" and the bride people, Bradley and Cooper find themselves surrounded by their dead: "For death binds; it is Life that severs." Whether the company of the dead is comforting or yet another sign that the poets remain frustrated in achieving married solitude remains to be seen.

Bradley has announced again and again that the poets' married life has begun. Indeed, there have been sufficient celebrations of its commencement that one begins to wonder if it really has begun at all—or, perhaps, if the poets are reaching for ideas about what "it" is, after all these years. Cooper continues the inquiry, deeply felt:

> The remnant Bride-Cake has been despatched in a Dog-Biscuit Tin (Spratt) to Clifton. A huge packing-case waits in the hall to be removed—full of the trousseau—Michael and I begin to live—We begin to write [. . .]—we have long breakfasts, reading our letters in fire-light—we have long sitting-still while the mists cradle the sunset—How we have suffered! People write how we must feel the blank of Amy's departure. Ah, we feel it as *Rest*—as that that builds the morning, as

> ^like^ a good night. We have suffered too much not to enjoy peace as the most vital and promising experience we can have. Our chief ~~rest~~ feeling is of deep rest and ~~the~~ a thankful turning to those things that make for our life. (1899, 108v–109r, EC; emphasis in original)

What, then, is this "living," this married life? After Amy's departure, Michael Field return to their work, revising *The Race of Leaves*, a play they will eventually publish in 1901. They linger over breakfast, read their letters, sit and watch the sunset. They make up for suffering by enjoying the peace of their surroundings. Far from mourning her sister's absence, Cooper feels that absence as the "Root" and source of future promise. She writes, "Our chief feeling is of deep rest and a thankful turning to those things that make for our life." Again, though—aside from rest and a good breakfast, now that they have found their home, decorated it, moved in, and seen Amy off to Ireland, what are "those things that make for our life"?

Michael Field embrace this moment of peace and quiet as a mindful start to a new chapter. But equally, Bradley and Cooper—who searched time and again for a "plot" that would signal more engagement with the world, who crave critical regard, who were so energized by the staging of *A Question of Memory* and by the aesthetic composition of a beautiful home—flirt with anticlimax when they have finally achieved their desire to begin "married life." In 1901, Cooper writes: "as I write the Thames runs by ~~[illeg.]~~ cloudy and energetic with the South Wind—the River that binds our days together with its influence of light and tide. [. . .] We are poets now, with nothing really dramatic about us for the nonce" (1901, 46v–47r, EC). Bradley and Cooper respond to the quiet by entering a thoughtful period, taking stock of who they have become and why, and also what kind of artist they are. Realizing with astonishment that August marks a full decade since "the Mother-One rose up to God—no chariot—the beating upward of the soul's own wings to God," Bradley situates the present moment as new growth: "Storm after storm has burst over us—fever, and love-fever, disillusion and loss,—then, 'mid the lies and deceit of human lips, ~~our~~ ^the^ simple, true-hearted old Father disappeared into the unknown—we have left Durdans: we are colonists—and tho' we pile round us satin-wood tables sky-high—our new life must be here young, and other, and new. We must plant and water afresh; but on the old traditions" (1899, 94r, KB). The image of Michael Field as colonists surrounded by satinwood tables piled high suggests that they have fortified themselves within an aesthetic bunker, and perhaps they have. But Bradley also acknowledges that the novelty of this colonial moment resides not in satinwood tables alone but in making a new life beyond the old traditions.[31] In 1901, Cooper acknowledges the metaphysics of the process, while listening to firefighters respond to a local blaze: "One thing I must mention that I felt grief but no tumult, no passion at the thought that all the beloved of objects, my satinwood, pictures, vases—wd be burnt if our fear were realized. I am glad of this peace, because some of the secret of impermanency must be mine—the power of joy and the power of facing its loss" (1901, 9v, EC).

Marking the anniversary not of the Mother-One but of Father, Cooper also measures the new against the yardstick of loss. As she notes the passage of another Midsummer Day, Cooper writes: "This is such a strange anniversary—spent in the home Michael and I so longed for, our first married home. Everything is so much sharper than last year at Durdans. [. . .] I long to tend [Father's grave] with my own hands and to make that bit of foreign land a portion of my country. To think he died and is buried *a stranger*, he who always hugged home and was never for trusting himself to the unfamiliar" (1899, 79r, EC; emphasis in original). Bradley and Cooper both reach for metaphors of nation and colony to express their claim to space in their married home and, in Cooper's words, to annex a cemetery-plot-sized rectangle of Switzerland to call her own. That her father, a creature of the home, rests in unfamiliar soil is intolerable for the daughter who shares the homebody trait. Cooper continues:

> How little anyone knows about us! They think we have lost an old man, who hindered the expansion of our lives, who often rendered us rebellious, who was good and limited. They little know we have lost our profoundest lover, our Curse laid on us by the Mighty Love, the fashioner of my genius, of Michael's Inspiration, the form that rules our lives, the pulse of our Fate—the tenderness that is an abiding grace to those who have once known it. His power is inconceivably terrible. It has nothing to do with an end—it is in force whether he lives or dies. Yes, here it is, as it was it will be—^He^ encompass~~es~~ing those he loves with his unsurpassable love, his utter influence—~~his [illeg.]~~, his darkness. (1899, 80r–80v, EC)

This is a strange reframing of Cooper's ambivalence toward her father, whose "good and limited" qualities were fully on display both before and during the dramatic circumstances of his death. Here Cooper focuses on her father's dark power, which holds her in thrall as strongly, or more strongly, in death than it did in life; he provided form to Michael Field's lives, honeycombs to their honey. Though their friends consider Michael

Field liberated by the death of the old man who so hindered them in life, Michael Field themselves have internalized his "inconceivably terrible" power and find themselves still shaped by it.

Cooper has recast her frightening, angry father as a combination of lover and muse, responsible for the capacities both she and Michael bring to their art. Now that the poets have departed the father's home, Cooper is quick to attribute to him "the form that rules our lives": she has left the container of his home behind but credits him with the habits and patterns that govern who Michael Field are, and who they will be in the future. While there is something metaphysical in Bradley's sense that the poets live still in the company of their dead—something ethereal about the dearly departed drifting nearby, perhaps available for the occasional invocation—her dead father remains for Cooper entirely present: "His power is inconceivably terrible." Contrary to what "anyone" might think about Michael Fields' new liberation in the wake of the father's death, it is very important for Cooper to assert much more directly than she has before that she remains, firmly, her father's daughter.

Even at the very end of the year, Bradley writes of Cooper's ambivalence, and owns a touch of her own: "My Sweet looks around him a profound pleasure in his eyes; but he touches nothing he has been wont to touch;—my home-loving one is not quite at home, even her fellow feels the strangeness of 'the little patch of sky' above Paragon" (1899, 138v, KB). Though the colonists are in charge, they are misplaced; though the environs are pleasing, the sky above is different. Someone has changed the water in Cooper's fishbowl, and she feels more apprehensive than honeymoonish. In August, between the anniversaries of her father's and mother's deaths, Cooper attempts to gain perspective on her home and her life. In the case of Paragon, this means literal perspective: coming upon the house from the outside, during a walk.

> We see our new home in perspective as we walk—it is good to see it—its simplicity, its harmony, its river-lit charm. And we are grateful for these gifts in spite of our clear sight of its disadvantages—its steepness, its unpopularity with servants, its age and infirmity. We find its little garden is like a rich ^bit of^ carpet in our hearts. This home of ourselves—not of our past—is close and extraordinarily precious to us. We see our new lives in perspective—the temptation to think too much of the freedom so desperately longed for. (1899, 89v–90r, EC)

It is still not ideal. Notwithstanding the satinwood tables and the carpets, the best carpet remains outside in the little garden. This is the poets' home, the "home of ourselves—not of our past," yet they struggle to understand the nature of the present and future even as they attempt to move forward from the past. The freedom they had so desperately craved is tempting to overvalue, thinks Henry, but must be kept in perspective.

"This last week I have chanced to take up and read, while drinking coffee in Amy's little room, some of the *Sonnets from the Portuguese*," wrote Cooper in the early summer.

> They have the ~~ugliness~~ ^hideousness^ of ~~movement you see in~~ new-born animals. It is the recent and callow love that is so painful to me in them . . . Love should not come as a *new experience* to any woman—she should belong to Aphrodite the first time she looks at her face in the mirror—she ~~should generously~~ should feel behind her the inheritance of Eve, Cleopatra, Queen Mary, Juliet. Womanhood should be the Evocation of Love—and the ancient sovereignties of the god be hers by right. In the love-letters of the two poets there is triteness because no divinity ~~with a divine universe~~ receives their love into a divine universe—neither God, nor Nature; ^there is no^ light beyond sun-light, nor radiance from sunny days; no shade of mythes [*sic*], nor darkness from ~~above~~ ^higher than^ ^beyond^ the stars. (1899, 55v, EC; emphasis in original)

At this moment when Cooper herself is attempting to fathom who she is and who she will be in the future—the conundrum of the married poet—she recurs to another married poet, Elizabeth Barrett Browning, to strike a negative comparison. EBB loves wrong, like a wet, hairless puppy in her passion for the formidable Robert Browning. "Womanhood," in contrast, should, says Cooper, be ennobled by the female heritage of Love, "the ancient sovereignties of the god be hers by right." In contrast to the "closer married" Michael Field, the other pair of poet-lovers share a love that is "trite" because characterized by mortality and not the divine.

Love should never be new or callow or hideous, by this account, but what does noble, mellow love resemble? Well, it resembles the quotidian, for one thing. Bradley, entirely more inclined to be merry than her fellow during this period, writes:

> Sunday, October 8th
>
> A most happy day, though outside it begins in winter mist and winter. [. . .] we watch the sun drop red behind the elm-branches, and are much with our dogs (perhaps the last Sunday of the 3) moved by the extreme devotion that constrains them to forsake the warm

> study-carpet, and lie down on the Indian-matting in the sun-room at our feet.
>
> Henry dresses our altar there with sloe-gin in the old Murano bottle: we sing
>
> "Lilies and light and liquor: liquor, lilies and light"
> 'Tis thus the sweet hours flicker
> 'Tis thus we claim delight.
>
> We both are busy with *The Race of Leaves*. In the depths of the home is Sally—who sends up dishes browned and heated as by the Prince of Coals. She has the touch of an artist, the simple contributions of a statesman. Boiled mutton and a carrot—yes; but both in one, and the broth that sings them. Or beef—assertive, spreading itself as we should spread ourselves across the transvaal, trickling from its red heart, and moated with gravy. (1899, 109r–109v, KB)

Michael Field are now singing drinking songs in their sunroom, sloe gin that is theirs instead of the Artists' decanted into a bottle of Murano glass. And the artist—and statesman—of the home dwells belowdecks in the kitchen, sending forth sublimity in the form of mutton, beef, and gravy, warming the drinkers, body and soul, and allowing them to expand across the empire. The Michael Field of old would have claimed lilies and light for themselves. Liquor, assertive beef, and gravy moats are new.

As artists, though, this time remains lonely. For Bradley it is more sepulchre than lilies and light: "The larger world now is totally indifferent to anything I may say or sing. Deeper and deeper may I plunge with my beloved into dream-laurel—away from all noise—where the fruits drop silent from the trees, and one watches only that which, yet disappears, will recur" (1899, 63r, KB). How to go forward? "[W]e confess to a sense of pause in our creative work," Cooper confided to Ricketts in the fall (1899, 135r, EC). Ricketts has been devastating in the candor of his criticisms in the past: "He reproaches us—there is no humour in our work for it lacks tenderness and swiftness!" (1899, 106v, EC). And an ad feminam commentary: "Ricketts confides to us that when we are each by ourselves we are *sane*—but when we are together we are *impossible* and *insane*. We asked him to define the madness—his reply was that Michael is the worse than I—but something makes us mad when we are in Company" (1899, 103r, EC; emphasis in original).

Impossible and insane—perhaps, but at the point of realization of their marriage plot, Michael Field are lost and wandering, unsure of how to go forward. It is as if they have claimed their married life only to discover that someone removed the windmill they had been tilting at all these years. "Virgil, in the midst of his labour, allows a pleasing personality to appear. Spenser made the English language; Shakespeare used it; Milton shut the cupboard—that was not opened again till the poets of our age began their work. Keats, who might have gone up under with drawing-room prettiness, or archaic rubbish borrowed from Spenser was saved by Milton: but we want to be saved from restraining influences and be as wild and free as we could be. Our gold chain is English, not French, about 1730" (1899, 106r, EC). If the poets dream of becoming "wild and free," of breaking the bonds of their restraining influences, they are also conscious of the bit in the mouth: the "gold chain" of their attraction to forms and idioms of 1730. As Cooper's valediction for her father makes clear, freedom from restraining influences, and the wildness to be gained from such a liberation, is not available to her. The poets critiqued for their use of language from times long ago must still yearn for their wild freedom from constraint.

And they are right on the cusp of a future that they do not understand. It is 1899, and when they close the current volume of *Works and Days* and open next year's to a fresh new page, they will do so in a new century. Cooper marks the century to come in terms of desire realized:

> *The last morning of the Old Year*
>
> Amy has been with us and gone—she came the day after Christmas, and we lived the old life together seamlessly for four days. Now she is gone and Michael and I watch each other in a little round mirror of Ricketts' design that hangs on our gold wall and reflects our life in its circle—this new life of our deepest desire realised for us. (1899, 141r, EC)

Amy has departed, leaving the married couple alone in their home for the beginning of the new year. Absent Amy, the poets triangulate their love through Ricketts's little round mirror: they watch each other and interpret the life reflected back to them in its glass, "this new life of our deepest desire." Never have the mechanics of triangulation been more explicit, nor more needed, for Michael Field.

Cooper continues to interpret the moment:

> After lunch we lie on our condemned Chesterfield couch and look round our white sun-room aglow with spring warmth. The river is a stream greater and greater by virtue of its own expansion toward its banks and the meadows. We lie "warm in the wraps of love" and realize in a calm like that of old Age that we cannot ever have such an afternoon again—cannot wait the birth of a new Century Together. [. . .] I

> find Michael has lighted her Altar Candles and set our 14 Volumes on the altar, rededicating them to the new Century in wh: they trust to live, praising the God of Life for the joy we have had of their creation: Our Passion this year is gratitude—wh: is the looking round on all that has influenced us and beholding it is very Good. (1899, 141v–142r, EC)

This moment will never happen again: the passage from one century to another. The rededication of fourteen volumes of their poems and plays, consecrated anew to the century in which they will outlive their authors. Yet again Michael Field find themselves moving from the known toward the unknown—from the past toward an uncertain future.

Though 1 Paragon represented for Michael Field the material realization of their poetic vision, it was a curated vision that remained suspended in time. Gordon Bottomley writes,

> Their rooms were not less flawless than their poems. . . . [A]lways there was the same feeling of choice and unity everywhere: in a jeweled pendant that lay on a satin-wood table, in the opal bowl of pot-pourri near by on which an opal shell lay lightly—a shell chosen for its supreme beauty of form, and taken from its rose-leaf bed by Miss Cooper to be shown to a visitor in the same was as she took a flower from a vase, saying, "This is Iris Susiana," as if she were saying "This is one of the greatest treasures in the world," and held it in her hand as if it were a part of her hand.[32]

Having created a "flawless" temple to their marriage, Michael Field still found themselves challenged by a world that kept moving forward, in time and in space.

"It is terribly moving," Cooper reflects, "to leave our great and beloved Dead in their Century."

> [I]t seems as if Time laid over them another coffin-lid. I feel a mourning and lamentation that can take no voice. But how I bless the era that has given me the love of Father, Mother and a noble Poet. How I shall always bless the last year of that era, for without any impiety, my own Love and I have been able to dwell in our own home by the great river of England, to dwell there in unity, in devoted happiness.
>
> The year has been just what was foretold to me—a year of the rebuilding of life—full of the dusty trials of the mason, made small by the details that build up a whole. We have scarcely worked at all. [. . .] yet much has been accomplished. We have founded our beautiful little home after the wrench from Durdans. We have made each room

beautiful at great cost and by great economy, and as we were able. We have established a great friendship on gold foundations. Amy has been married from our home, and gone to make a new home. She is happy in the state of marriage—her husband has a fixed appointment.

Finally our domestic arrangements are not defaming and impossible as they have been for many months, and, as harass withdraws, our minds lie open and fallow to the Spring. Surely looking round we have reason to behold this year has been very good. (1899, 142r–143r, EC)

In Cooper's characteristic accounting of the year's end, 1899 was a year of losses: of Durdans and Amy, of companionship in the century contemporaneous with their dead elders' lives and deaths. The poets have not worked, but they have created—in this case, a beautiful home. And the prospect of creating twentieth-century poetry stands ahead of them, now that domestic harass has begun to withdraw.

Like our Country we shall face the difficulties of Empire-building when circumstances are stubborn. I believe both England and Michael Field will win. We have to conquer the pressure of detail on our lives, of constrictions on our power of travelling—we have to be plastic as we have never been. We have to conquer the pain of Bernhard's probable marriage with Mary, to hold ourselves strong against their old fatal influence. This year built our circumstances—the century will find us building ourselves. I do not feel 1900 will be a peaceful year—but the strain to us and England will be athletic not weakening.

My love lights the altar-flames—O to worship more constantly, to obtain the tri-une blessing of creativeness. (1899, 144v, EC)

Cooper clearly sees the road ahead as hard but bracing. As householders themselves now, the poets' capacity to afford ambitious travel is severely limited. They will have to be "plastic" as never before to adapt challenges not to circumstance but to self. Cooper aligns Michael Field with England, and anticipates muscles strengthened through challenging exercise. The hope and prayer: "to obtain the tri-une blessing of creativeness"—to get their work back.

Motor-cars clatter by—the amusement 1899 ends with. Ah me! . . .

It was ^will^ soon be midnight when 1900 draws breath—1900—the Father and Mother were not to see, that we see. And the road of our desires is in front of us as far as we may look! [. . .]

All hail 1900. Welcome through the silence. (1899, 144r, 145r, 145v, EC; fig. 9)

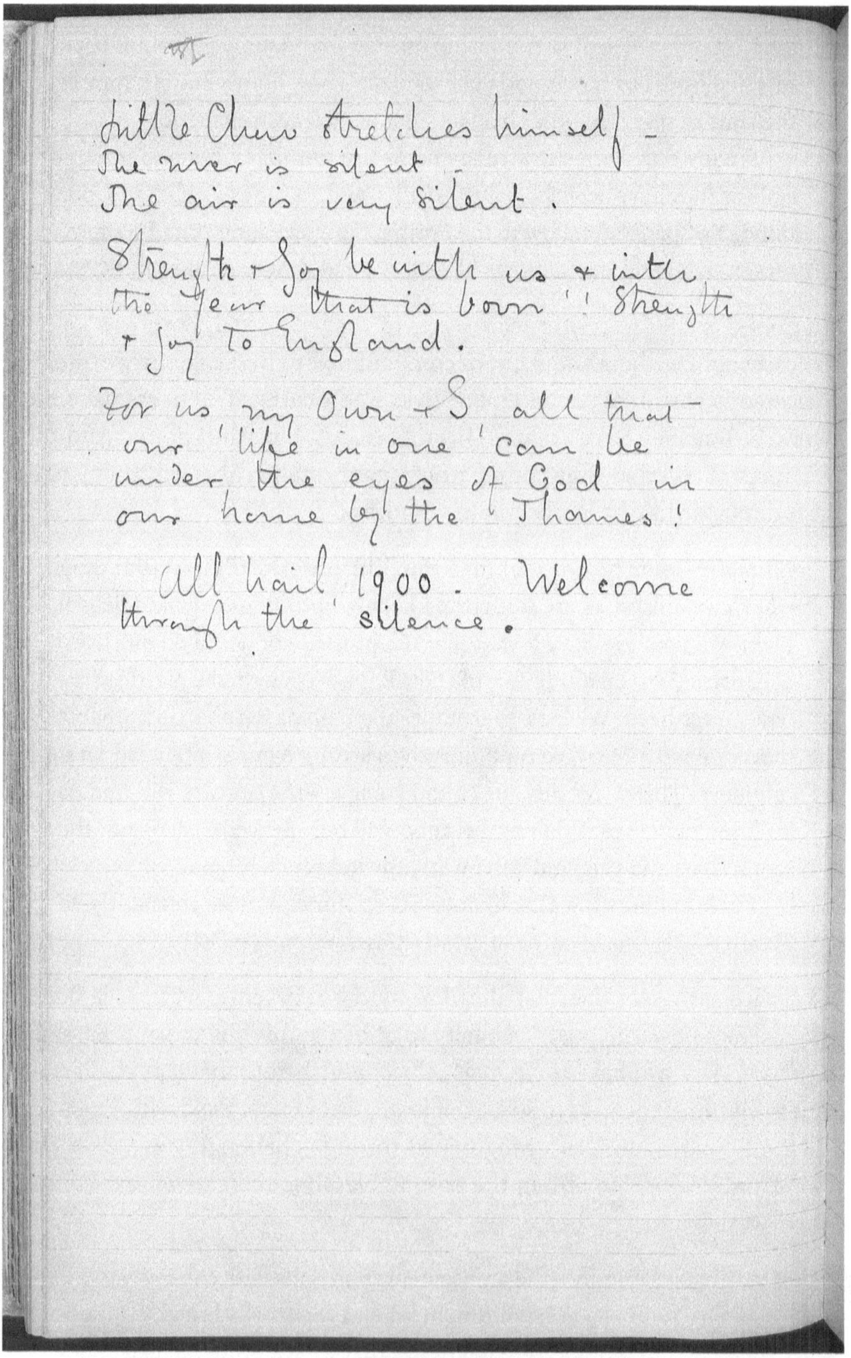

Little Chum stretches himself –
The river is silent –
The air is very silent.

Strength & Joy be with us & with the Year that is born! Strength & Joy to England.

For us, my Own & S, all that our 'life in one' can be under the eyes of God in our home by the Thames!

All hail 1900. Welcome through the silence.

FIGURE 9. The silent demise of the nineteenth century; the arrival of the twentieth.

CHAPTER FIVE

"Venite Adoremus"

1906–7

The Adeste *wraps me*
into star-lit, angel-lit adoration.

—EDITH COOPER, DECEMBER 31, 1909

She gave to me Adeste Fidelis.

—KATHARINE BRADLEY, DECEMBER 24, 1913

IN MANY VOLUMES of *Works and Days* in the British Library, you will find one or more sheets of thin typing paper attached inside the front cover. These are the notes that Thomas Sturge Moore used to produce his 1933 collection of excerpts from *Works and Days*, fulfilling one of his responsibilities as Michael Field's literary executor. Though Sturge Moore's notes are more typically indexes than commentaries, the 1906 volume offers an exception. Inside that front cover, Sturge Moore left this observation for himself and those that followed: "the wyole [*sic*] of the first half of this volume is permeated with Chow" (1906, iii).[1]

And so it is. Sturge Moore was aware that the period leading up to and following events of 1906 was anomalous in the narrative of Michael Field. I would go one step beyond anomaly to suggest that "permeated with Chow" represents the moment the entire structure supporting both Michael Field, the women, and Michael Field, the author, came crashing down. The period "permeated with Chow," and events that followed subsequently through 1906 and 1907, mark the end of the great narrative experiment of *Works and Days*. Not its chronological end; that will come in 1914, when Bradley died nine months after Cooper, silencing the White Book's voice(s) once and for all. The poets kept writing after the explosive events surrounding the Chow, but the structure they put in place is a hollow form for Michael Field's story and for their intimacy.

To understand the narrative of 1906, with its complex, overlapping meanings, we must reach back to 1898, when the story of Chow began. When James Cooper died in Switzerland in 1897, his daughter Edith was comforted by the gift of her basset hound, Musico, who in his own prosaic way lightened the emotional tone during a painful period. In the evening of Friday, January 28, 1898, Katharine Bradley received her gift: "Whym-Chow arrived—a dusky, sable—a wolf with civilization's softness, an oriental with musky passion—white rolling eyeballs, and the power of inward frenzy—velvet mariners and the savages of eastern armies behind" (1898, 11r, KB). Named for Edward Whymper, the explorer and mountaineer who assisted in the search for James Cooper's body, Whym Chow in all his wildness and eastern passion immediately lodges himself at the heart of the poets' household. He is the adored child, the master at whose every "whym" the household turns—the ultimate third term that pulls the poets together. With the advent of Chow, Michael Field become parents to a truculent, occasionally violent canine son. Born in October 1897, the month James Cooper's body was discovered and the month of Bradley's birthday, the poets assign Chow a position of patriarchal potency, as well as a vaguely star-sign congruence with Michael; from the first, the dog was overdetermined with meaning. Writing on the evening of Whym's arrival, Bradley speaks of the women's need for companionship in an increasingly lonely world: "I suppose our new love of animals is a desire to get into another kingdom—we reach after the kingdom of the dead—we can penetrate into the kingdom of animals. Mortals all round us defeat or mislead for the most part, we seek a companionship we can determine" (1898, 11r, KB).

Bradley here hopes that dog love, unlike human companionship, will offer a relationship the poets can control.[2] From the first, Bradley portrays the Chow as exotic in his Orientalism, and as powerful in his capacities to shape her reality through his actions. In short, he was a little tyrant: "February 1st. [. . .] We rise from wrecked We couches. We have no flowers ready. . . . We have the chow. I rush to him at 6.30. His fury of greeting floods my heart with joy. Is one little passionate heart so thrilled at my waking? Heaven bless the chow" (1898, 11r, KB). The dog is glad to see his mistress in the morning. In turn she vests him with powers both phallic and mystical:

> When first we lifted him up, he turned on us the whites of his eyes, oriental white—with the sprung lustre of a sword from its scabbard, and yelled. He has 2 notes—like his mistress!—the first passionate personal protest and revolt, the second a long moan, full of impersonal tears that such wrong should be done in the world, and such cruel hearts allowed by Providence to beat. As for his religion, it is *me*. I can be a good god to any one who loves me—so responsive, so utter. (1898, 12r, KB; emphasis in the original)

The puppy worships the god of Michael, who in turn rises to the occasion, constituted in the image of his passion. The Chow is the ideal lover, with the voice of a poet and a sword unsheathed.

This lover is passionate and judgmental, and he validates and also expands Bradley's view of the uncaring world:

> He greets me when I go to him in a morning, as mortals greet the sun—brushing away the milk, and scattering spray to the winds. He is infinitely beautiful, with every beauty, except the beauty of holiness.—It is almost painful to see how his little brows are chafed by temper—sheer shock at the atrocity of men and things—the Swiss—one has only to mention them—and he rolls his eyes to the sword glare. I will never make him a Christian dog. I will civilise the seven devils.
>
> Oh, I love him!
> Hennie loves him.
> He is Michael's own little brimstone soul.
> Hennie loves him!
> Amen. (1898, 12r–12v, KB)

The Chow is to Bradley as Berenson was to Cooper: a bad boy who tests the limits of the poets' tolerance, and who leaves them rapt with admiration. And just as it did with Berenson earlier in the decade, the idea of such passion commands the poets' attention and secures the bond they share.[3]

But in this case, unlike the case of Berenson, the realized love of Chow is a bond the poets can enter together. And join they do. At year's end, it is Cooper who writes of future possibilities offered by the events of 1898:

> "No new friends" so I say—Why, we have learnt the whole precious nature, we have adored the love and faith and passion of our Whym-Chow. We bless him, our dark-red beam of a happiness from the depths of the heavenly clouds—ripe, ripe, dark rapture. God bless our Chow. [. . .]

> I have just put out the lights, and bade farewell to the parlour where [Father] used to sit, where the soft gray hair attracted with such comeliness in sunshine or lamplight. The bells are ringing out the Old Year—Chow is at my feet, my own Love in little night-gown and socks reading the Zermatt sonnets. I have kissed the carbuncle-ring on her finger—my loyalty to the deathless Old that can never be left for the New.
>
> I feel we shall *found* during this year—it will be a colonists' year—wh: means hard conditions, suffering, endeavors to be overcome by patience, hope, house-founding. We shall have to toil for our joy, my life's Joy and I—but heart to heart we shall have strength, and heart to heart we shall be blessed. We shall receive a home as a crown to our day—a home for our marriage. (1898, 142r–142v, EC; emphasis in original)

Chow lives in the heart of the poets' intimacy. Just as Flush served a constitutive function for Elizabeth Barrett Browning (or, more precisely, perhaps, for Virginia Woolf's constitution of EBB), Whym Chow is the engine of Michael Field's social confidence at a low ebb of their reputation.[4] Propelled by Chow, Michael Field can stride forth and conquer obstacles that stand in the way of their own married home. Not even an infestation can stand in his way: "Whym Chow [. . .] is all over minute sores; the fleas had found a nest for themselves [. . .] and were bringing forth thousands and ten thousands in our streets" (1899, 101, EC). Their "dark-red beam of . . . happiness" gives Michael Field an entirely—amazingly ("a nest for themselves")—unambivalent object for the projection of their positive emotions and their apprehensions. Unlike Berenson, Chow triangulates Michael Field in a way that brings the poets powerfully together; as Kathryn Bond Stockton writes in her study of queer childhood in the twentieth century, "The family dog . . . is not just a pet. It is a metaphor for all that is loyal, familiar, familial, and family-photogenic." If the dog is the signifier of family, Vanita argues for the species' pride of place in signaling queer family: "Since an animal cannot speak, it is a perfect symbol for 'the love that dare not speak its name.' As a trope, it is multifariously suggestive: of domesticated yet natural instinctive life, as that which is despised as beastly and fleshly but may also be read as peculiarly innocent, of the oppressed victim who cannot protest, and of sexuality outside of social law."[5]

Unlike the Beloved Mother-One and the Father, Whym Chow enables Michael Field's fusion as a married couple rather than as daughter figures ancillary to someone else's nuclear family. As Lee Edelman writes, "A pantomime of erotic tension resolved in the figure of the Child (who gives such tension in the meaning that relieves it of all taint), by reading the constitutive friction—the determining aggression—inherent in eros as the agency that generates meaning and the child in a single blow, breeding thereby a happy heterosexual economy in which the Child means 'meaning' for adults, who can only attain it by virtue of participating in the labor of giving (it) birth" (126–27). In his role as Child, and Michael Field's role as parents, Whym Chow grows to "mean 'meaning'" for the two poets. The dog's death in turn introduces Michael Field to the death of meaning itself, draining poetry and Paragon and life of the capacity to signify. In 1906, Edith Cooper has begun to use a different kind of pen (modernity approaches) to write in the White Book, which seems to lend her words a different tone. In this new hand, she writes of "Paragon—a faded fairyland. The golden Prince whose home it was—gone! We realise it was *his* house, we are but relicts" (1906, 52r, EC; emphasis in original).

Given the Chow's outwardly unpleasant personality and appeal to vermin, it is reasonable to wonder about the poets' seemingly unambivalent attachment to him. To some degree, it seems willful. Perhaps in his phallic mastery, the Chow offers the poets a vehicle for a form of agency that would otherwise elude them. He is an aggressive, scowling dog, and of this Cooper and Bradley are very proud. To recur to the infamous example, while on a holiday near Brighton, Michael Field call on Rudyard Kipling and his family. Bradley reports on this memorable visit:

> I walk round the great weedy garden of nasturtiums, and leave Chow in the garden, ^the rabbit in his hole.^ I come in: I look forth—Chow and the rabbit are one—Chow pecks, the rabbit rolls, and Chow pecks again. I run forth, I shriek, and chase. He locks and closes again, and again—Finally Edith extracts and exalts the rabbit apparently lifeless—I return to Henry. Slowly my boiled blood cools; we set set the rabbit up under shelter of shavings, we leave him munching a cabbage-leaf, and I find Henry, quietly stretched on his couch at the Alfonso Murder scene, adding certain little cries and flutterings and follies of collapse. But the Chow! The incident has made a man of him. I shall never forget the air with which he dashed in, and drank water, like a young hero who flings aside his casque and refreshes himself. (1902, 156r–156v, KB).

Whym Chow was the heroic appendage that Michael Field never realized they had been missing all these years, the young hero returning from battle, and leaving on the field (or, in the garden) the bloodied form of . . . Rudyard Kipling's bunny. Cooper writes this in the White Book as a triumphant literary-world announcement: "Rudyard Kipling's rabbit died on Monday—slain by Michael Field's Chow. He was but a white lump by our flaming little Minister Whym—but I am sorry death came so leisurely" (1902, 158r, EC). The white lump taken down by Michael Field's flaming phallic weapon. Cooper does not seem too terribly sorry that it took Kipling's pet a while to die.

Chow was the living vehicle for the poets' most passionate and heroic fantasies of their agency in the world. And he was the heart and soul of their marriage, with the privileged standing Edelman describes. Cooper, admiring the Chows at a dog show in 1908, writes of the breed's "majesty that rejects domesticity for passion in every recorded impulse of limbs the little royalties!" (1908, 98v, EC). Chow is the animating force within domestic quietude for two bored, lonely poets. That is what makes the narrative of 1906 so catastrophic for Michael Field, for when Chow died in January of that year, he revealed that the poets' bond was now hollow at the core.

Early in 1906, Cooper could still celebrate nature's glory in the company of Chow. On January 13: "Such a river to walk by . . . the most beautiful fabric in the world! . . . Is it sun I am feeling as if I were being turned into gold? Are my eyes really seeing red when I close them? No wonder Whym Chow, fighting eczema, grins and is a-glow. Spring! Ah, and Spring-tides!" (1906, 5r, EC). Too soon, though, that glow turns ice cold. Just a week later, witnessing the dog's stiffness and confusion, Cooper writes, "The Vet says Chow will probably be well by Monday . . . 'He will not—he is seriously ill' Michael comments. I try to assure my self she is overanxious. [. . .] I say yes to zealous eyes, but as we go out of the Sun-Room instead of turning down stairs he walks into the wall—It freezes me" (1906, 9v, 10v, EC).

On the diary's fourteenth page, in ink blotted with tears, Cooper writes: "Sunday—how terrible Sundays are! Milestones of doom to us as a family. Today I have had the worst loss of my life—yes, worse than that of beloved Mother or the tragic father—my Whym Chow, my little Chow—Chow, my Flame of Love is dead and has died—O cruel God!—by our will!" (1906, 14v, EC; see fig. 9). Whym Chow is dead, and he has died. His loss is the worst for Cooper, even worse than the deaths that orphaned her.

As they do around events of traumatic loss, Michael Field narrate circumstances of Chow's death repeatedly. A veterinary specialist named Sewell has said, "'I am sorry, it is a [illeg.] bad case—I cannot say he will recover.' Yet if Chow were his dog, he would 'give him a month'—there is chance, though it is [a] vague chance, for life" (1906, 14v, KB). Sewell's words return as the refrain:

> Next day Specialist—Sewell—called in—sickening suspense till he comes, and grips the situation with eyes, lips and nostrils like grappling

> irons. Chow's beauty admired—his strength and condition as well as his glorious coat. "He has a great deal of strength—the case is a very bad one but there is a vague hope. If he were my dog I should give him three weeks or a month." We determine to do this; and we set about arranging ~~for~~ to nurs~~ing~~^e,^ removing all the broad ruby head might knock against in its soft and cautious butts. Mostly Whym visited the corners of the room with "distrait" nose; standing humbly on his proud feet, or else he whirled round like a stately were-wolf with such terrible rhythm as drew the imagination into its circles. (1906, 15v, EC).

The dog is blind and pitiful, running into walls and standing in corners, his poet's voice arrhythmic and his heroic gait halting. Writing after the fact and interpellated across pages, Henry describes a night of exquisite torture. With morning comes clarity. She writes:

> I see it in dream: it scares me; I wake with ~~ends~~ nerve-ends like scalding water and with a great passion at the heart ^that^ little Chow should be set free from all his misery. My poor Love comes to me dazed with sleep—Whymmie has dropped [here the narrative skips two pages, and picks up again] asleep ^under a draught.^ . . . O beating of the manifest wings of Pain! Under the pulsing cold that is within me I tell her I am sure that this unbearable torture must end for our Adored—inexorably during the Night I have seen *it has been coming on for long*; there is only the chance of one to a hundred he could ever get over a disease that every day strengthens. (1906, 16r, 17r, EC; emphasis in original)

Cooper tells Bradley that the pain must end; the lovers must relieve the beloved of his suffering. They send for the doctor at dawn, but the Chow vomits his first dose of morphine, and the poets are left to care for him till the vet's return hours later. Cooper writes,

> But there is something to do! Out of blindness and perpetual motion of the lovely feet and perpetual bumping of the brow (save when it stayed against Michael's knee, arrested by the soft patting and then with gentle insistence passed on to reach the opposite wall) out of all this, Whym Chow snuffed the morning air with his ~~Bacchic~~ ^free-^joyance. I saw him in the midst of the ivy leaves in the front Garden a happy Bacchic cub, the ivy doubly-alive against his flaming fur. Earth, air—how he snuffed and my agony knew he was going to leave them. *How I loved him, how I printed him on my mind—^Little Chow, God bless thee; Little Chow, God bless thee!^ The crease of ruby down his brow,

> the soft almost blue-shaded ears, the roughness round the neck, the tender swirl of silk where cheek and ~~"rough"~~ ruff were at one [. . .]— Such energy and singleness! O my Whym Chow, my little Chow. Chow! (1906, 17r–17v, EC)

The asterisk in Cooper's writing refers back to a space on page 16v that she has filled with this: "*Our Bacchic Cub, passionate and enjoying and fervid, even with clouded eyes and sweet, little, undirected head" (1906, 16v, EC). Though the Chow was blind and agitated, to Cooper he remained entirely beautiful, against the measure of nature itself and to her personally. He brings the world doubly alive for her. Her love for him is visceral, as she imprints on her own mind the look and feel of his brow, his ears, his neck, his cheeks. He is the beloved as lover, as child, and also as aesthetic ideal: offering the power of beauty to evoke and realize surpassing human emotion.

Chow's death was botched horrendously, from the first dose of morphine that did not stay down to the fact that once he was eventually sedated, the poets were told that the dog could not be euthanized with a bullet within the confines of Richmond: "[The fair little body has to be taken to Twickenham,]" across the bridge to a municipality with more flexible ordinances. Ultimately it took the better part of a day to euthanize Whym Chow. Michael accompanied him to Twickenham, and afterward she returned to "our desolated Paragon, home no more forever" and announced his death: "My little dog is at rest—at rest, you hear ^it—he is^ at rest." Cooper writes: "It is like hearing the sound of icebergs ^that^ gnaw and laugh and then break up. It is hideously and greatly tragic. Our grief is blind, is potent . . . we scarcely touch food, but bring back to order the Rooms, now grown so hateful that we realise we must go. 'Yes,' I say to Michael, [']We must let Paragon and get a ^little^ flat in town'" (1906, 18r, EC). Michael Fields' attachment to their beloved Paragon was extinguished along with the life of Chow, muse of their marriage. "The sense as we approach Paragon of the nothingness of it—the entrance into a silent hall, where has been a whirl-storm of the most golden welcome—a dance as if the sun had come down carrying love instead of his light. [. . .] Oh, the bitter tears for that silent hall the symbol of a silent World where for us there is no welcome. Whym Chow, Whym Chow—O my little love!" (1906, 19v, EC).

In the structure they frequently employ in times of acute grief, Michael Field exchange narrative positions during the tale of the Chow's martyrdom. In the middle of Cooper's account, Bradley breaks in with her own retrospective narrative. This time, she visits an entirely different sort of morgue:

> I go down to order Chow's coffin and grave—I see him—not curled up dead and dripping in his basket as I saw him yesterday—tho then he was quite sweet—the face still scowling a little at death—He lies rigid, and very beautiful—quite glad now to be still—holding as in a casket his royal love for me—not the flowing gold now—but there, there the treasury for me of the dead heart—the glorious little frame is a tomb to his passion. Hamlet—over Yorick's skull is not like that—"there hung these lips that I have kissed so oft." But every throb of that heart—and all these dances of joy round me—are hardened [. . .]
>
> Such a manly little chap he looks! I am so proud of his love—
> What he would have been to me in age!
> My Dear, My Dear!
> Oh it is the great strain, and stretching out of this love to me that has brought him to his death. (1906, 16v, KB)

As we have seen the poets do in the Paris Morgue, Bradley seeks to make meaning of the Chow's outstretched, rigid corpse. Unlike the Paris corpses, however, Whym Chow is not marked by the drapery of unworn clothing. Rather, the Chow body itself is the tomb that will memorialize the great love of Bradley once and forever. For Bradley herself, that love is now a sarcophagus, hardened and inanimate and "a tomb to his passion"—warm and throbbing no more. Chow is a heroic martyr to Bradley; his very love for her has brought him to his death. Though she still has Cooper, Bradley has lost the companion of her old age.

In the early hours of Chow's prolonged euthanasia, Cooper wrote: "Michael, who needs must kill the thing she loves, determines he shall have full joy of the Earth. The little frenzied one is led round by the Towing path . . . I see him enter the River-door for the last time. [. . .] Then the vet. . . . Chow is left in the garden, pacing and breathing. I hear the Vet and Michael go down. I bow in prayer—I lie, where he used to sleep, in an agony of submission" (1906, 17v, EC). Michael sees the painful euthanasia process through, while Henry prostrates herself in submission in the house, on the dog's bed.

When Cooper writes of her spouse, "Michael, who needs must kill the thing she loves," she invites Oscar Wilde into this death scene. Wilde was Michael Field's contemporary and (usually) ally; Michael Field encountered his often charming, occasionally obnoxious, and always elephantine form frequently in London in the 1890s. Wilde was in the audience during the one-night run of Michael Field's *A Question of Memory* in 1893, and he showed loyalty to the poet during the play's traumatic aftermath. Cooper's introduction of Wilde to the Chow's deathbed overwrites a queer event with the queerest of idioms. In 1895, Wilde was tried and imprisoned for "gross indecency." He was sentenced to hard labor and imprisoned in Reading Gaol until 1897, and died in 1900 in Paris, reportedly in the midst of converting to Catholicism. For Michael Field as for the Artists, even posthumous discussions of Wilde feel unsafe; while discussing Wilde's death, Ricketts resisted Michael Field's probing questions about Wilde's relationships, saying, "[I]t is much too serious to speak of" (1900, 165v–166r, EC).[6]

Wilde published "The Ballad of Reading Gaol" in 1897, shortly after his release from prison. The poem takes as its prompt the execution of a man convicted of cutting his wife's throat, which Wilde witnessed in prison. It takes as its meditation the relationship between love and murder:

> Yet each man kills the thing he loves
>   By each let this be heard.
> Some do it with a bitter look,
>   Some with a flattering word.
> The coward does it with a kiss,
>   The brave man with a sword!

Regenia Gagnier writes, "'The Ballad of Reading Gaol' was the triumph of the forces of law," offering a "subjective vision of prison as a place where lovers go when they have killed the thing they love."[7] Here, Bradley is the man who "kills the thing he loves," and she does it, not with a look nor a word nor a kiss but with a sword, or in this case, more properly, a bullet—the great kindness, the great cruelty, the great sacrifice to her and of her lover. When Wilde wrote this poem, he was a prisoner observing another prisoner executed for murdering his wife. Wilde, too, had caused his wife great pain: exposed as a "somdomite," shamed by the reading in open court details of his encounters with rent boys, imprisoned for "gross indecency."[8] Wilde destroyed love and was destroyed by love. In his poem, "word" and "sword" are rhymed slant. Both are lethal.

The moment crystallizes several linked concepts: the pain of wives and the vulnerability and punishment of same-sex love in the British fin de siècle—something Michael Field can identify with, despite speaking their love's name quite regularly in poetry and in *Works and Days*. Wilde's name is one that the poets hesitate to speak throughout this period. For example, they had been bound in close friendship with Ricketts and Shannon for a very long time before they dared to introduce Wilde's name. This, in late 1899:

> Then we leave the Gold Room and in their well-loved White Room for the first time in our Friendship we speak of Oscar. Ricketts, his hand laid back over his brow painfully, tells of the prison of how Oscar said to him that everyone was kind and the warders ~~mang~~ managed to give him, as an extra, buns—"As they throw Bibles to bears." R. with great tact and shrewdness advised a retreat of 6 weeks in a Benedictine Monastery after prison and an immediate quiet entering of English society.—But with rare perversity, Oscar went to Dieppe, was very foolish and reckless and left debts behind, choosing to live in Paris and drink hard. The Artists promise to lend us *The Importance of Being Earnest*. (1899, 116r, EC)

The very act of "speaking of Oscar"—he needs no last name—is a risk for the two queer couples whose lives and safety depend on not speaking the truth of their love in public, and on the tacit, unquestioning acceptance of their domestic and social arrangements in a world that could easily do them great shame and punitive harm. For Ricketts and Shannon in particular, the example of Wilde would have struck very close to home following the criminalization of "gross indecency"—namely, even the suggestion of male sodomy, even the appearance of effeminacy—in the 1885 Labouchère Amendment to the Criminal Law Amendment Act.[9]

What, then, does Oscar Wilde have to do with Chow? For one thing, killing the one you love represents epic relationship disaster—to say the least. And this, Bradley has now undertaken. But has she also killed her wife? Or exposed this marriage as already, silently dead? Are the poets nothing but puppets to the whyms of a scowling orange dog?

Both Oscar Wilde and "The Ballad of Reading Gaol" have haunted Michael Field's relationship with Whym Chow from the moment of the dog's arrival in January 1898. In the midst of puppy joy, Cooper undertook a critique of Wilde's then new poem. She writes:

> Oscar's Ballad of Reading Gaol [*sic*] is not literature. To experience experience won't make art—it must be imagined ^as well as suffered.^ I see this so clearly when I look from the beautiful photograph of our little Chow in front of our bed to the ~~[illeg.]~~ photographs of Mantegna and Timoteo della Vito on the same wall. Robinson has presented all he could see of the body and soul of ~~the~~ ^our^ chow in the best light, at a vital moment—but the subject of a work of art must be transmuted

> from the centre—and it is only the superficies that the photograph from life can reach. So with Oscar; the real part of his work is ^mostly^ arranged experienced, not imaginatively translated experience; and much of his work is special pleading—rhetoric the cold-hearted with hot voice; and some is deliberate appeal to the weaknesses of the English public, and [therefore] is an attempt to commit hypocrasy [*sic*]. The book contains an immortal outrageous Paradox—a very Colossus of the kind. "We needs must kill the thing we love." Oscar was sent into the world to generate this stimulating monster. (1898, 18r, EC)

What does Whym Chow have to do with killing the one you love? With a "stimulating monster"? As it does at the end of the dog's life, here at its beginning Cooper's engagement with the poem takes her mind directly to the dog—directly to what the dog constitutes and enables: the awareness that married love is in some meaningful sense deathly.[10] For Michael Field, that has always come most powerfully in the form of a triangle, with the two women convening their passion in view of, and in relation to, a third.

In the case of Chow, however, this a very different form of triangle, and one that kills the women's dyad in a way that parental love and threatened infidelity could not: the dog was lethal to Michael Field. Whym Chow was the axis upon which their married home and their married love came to turn. The women invested domestic love in great quantities, but they directed it toward Chow rather than toward one another. When the dog died, the triangle broke down. Each poet killed one she loved; in the case of Michael, Whym Chow; in the case of Henry, her marriage to Michael. "Our desolated Paragon, home no more forever."

Cooper's critique of Wilde in 1898 centers on his treatment of experience. She reads "The Ballad of Reading Gaol" as documentary description, and on that basis, dismisses the poem's intervention as a failed work of art. To make art requires imagination, she says, not simply experience. Cooper's assertion that it is not enough to experience experience and simply write it down is suggestive, among other things, of the literary significance of Fields' three-decade experiment with their shared diary: *Works and Days* itself, as a literary work, represents an extended exploration of the translation upward from experience to art. Art depends on a leap to abstraction that takes a poem, for example, or a photograph, or a diary entry, from the realm of the material to a higher realm, that of the idea. Cooper is tough on Wilde: she sees his work as rhetorical, the curating of experience rather than its translation. To her he is no more than a provocateur, his paradoxes not poetry but hypocrisy.

What a difference seven years makes. What in 1899 is an "immortal outrageous paradox," a "stimulating monster," is in 1906 this: "Michael, who needs must kill the thing she loves, determines [Chow] shall have full joy of the Earth." Michael must kill the love of her life. And she does. While Cooper watches and waits, prostrate in submission, lying in a dog bed.

Just as Wilde does, Bradley strives to make meaning of her actions, and of the life lost, after the fact, not through simple documentary reporting but by means of translation. Cooper, far from dismissing Wilde's powerful equation of love and destruction, has finally opened the door, admitting the immortal outrageous paradox right into the heart of Paragon. Killing a wife, destroying a life and a lover. The punitive destruction of same-sex desire, its silencing and its relegation to the interstices of language, where the love dare not speak. The punitive destruction by same-sex desire of lives molded into contortion by brutal silencing.[11]

Edith Cooper finds herself right back in the familiar stew of isolation and loneliness. She writes:

> We cannot reach our Flame of Love; we cannot reach Nature, or a happy garden; no friend crosses the doorstep, and the relaxing air is doubly pernicious now we have no form of gaiety, no shape of hope, to raise us up from depression. [. . .] And time! Oscar speaks of the leaden-footed hours in prison—our hours have no feet at all. [. . .] I feel that no-one can even be expected to understand our earthly loss—No-one knows how lonely we are, without human successors, and in the world rejected from among our contemporaries as if accursed. We had but one devoted lover, spirit to spirit, our Whym Chow; between us and him there was "the first secret of the world" as Oscar says of love. (1906, 54v–55r, EC)

Again, it falls to Wilde to provide the idiom appropriate for this mix of love, loss, and secrecy: what Cooper had with Chow, and what Bradley had with Chow, was "the first secret of the world." A bigger secret even than the love that dare not speak its name.

Michael Field are done. They have both experienced a primal loss of the third that makes them whole, leaving them with just one another. The dog's death results in (or makes possible) a fundamental, structural reorganization of Michael Fields' relationship with one another. They do find another "third," the Catholic Church. The Church, however, externalizes Michael Fields' passion rather than consolidating it; it channels love outside married intimacy in favor of individual intimacies on behalf of two women, each with her own Savior.[12]

Cooper's critique of Wilde's "failed" art contains the seeds of a way forward for Michael Field: in their emergent devotion to the Church, they translate their relationship from the material into the realm of ideas. Their love transcends matter and translates from experience to the imaginary; in the process it becomes something akin to art. This is glorious in theory. But just as it is painful to kill the one you love, it is painful to abandon the matter, substance, and flesh of a lifelong love.

The poets turn Paragon itself into a morgue for their love: they bring the Chow—their "brazier of love, the flames and the incence [*sic*], the motion and thrill" (1906, 20r, EC)—home to rest. On January 30, Cooper writes:

> Tender preparation from my Love—tenderest and unforgettable. I am in the Panelled Room—there is the full-furred head I adore—[. . .] Over the eyes the bullet-mark—the loved ears as pliable, as dearly soft as ever—the fur with all its gentle silk, its harsh threads; its fleece of the distaff, its ripples and its shag . . . all its gold, umber, roan and palest amber—yet no warmth at the base of the fur, no spring of light, the day-spring, on the surface of colour. And as one looked out the familiar attitude one trembled with terror at it because it would never change . . . the impatient, vivid Chow would never change . . . what rigour! Sculpture ^and yet^ nor apart from actuality—Terror! yet the dear man looked beautiful—flowering daphne—like wine-drenched sprays—against his muddy brow; under his dark little chin a nest of wine-columned Christmas roses, a few of our snow drops among them; the Bacchic ivy in strands around him. (1906, 22r–22v, EC)

There is an uncanniness to the Chow still, rather than his usual motile self. Is he sculpture or is he real? As he becomes one with Michael Fields' floral funeral tributes, what is the matter here, and what is the spirit? For Michael Field, the passion of the Chow is the gateway to the sublime; Cooper writes, "But, well, well, we mortals gave him back to sight and the sweet ways of his genius—for among dogs his mind had genius. He could feel and provoke the most wonderful emotion" (1906, 38r, EC). The genius of Whym Chow unlocked transcendent emotion for Michael Field, and in his return to sculpture we can witness the emergence of the function he will serve for Michael Field in the years ahead: in death even more powerfully than life, the Chow serves as a conduit, a focal point, for the powerful emotions that inspire devotion.

The souvenirs Michael Field send to the grave with Chow are far more personal than those they provided the Beloved Mother-One in 1889.

Cooper's offerings include hair drawn from the roots of her head. Bradley's, a precious fire-opal, birthstone of October, their shared natal month:

> I gave him the best lock of my hair from its roots, and a one of my precious blue shells, and his Mistress dropped between his paws her fire-opal (he the fire, she the opal—both born in October)
>
> And we gave him her Sonnet to him and words from her to him and the inscription
>
> Whym Chow
> Flame of Love
> Born October 29th 1897
> At Rest January 28th 1906.
> (1906, 22v, EC)

Like the Beloved Mother-One, Chow was buried with poetry. But unlike the Mother-One, his was poetry written specifically for him, to him, and about him. Michael Field kept writing about Whym Chow for a very long time, and in 1914, after Cooper's death, Bradley published, famously or perhaps notoriously, a book of elegiac poems written by Cooper. The book takes its inspiration from its muse: *Whym Chow: Flame of Love.* The volume has velvety russet covers, like the dog himself (fig. 10). From matter to idea: that is art.

The Chow was conveniently buried in Paragon's back garden, an event that occasioned yet another failure by Michael Field's servants: "I see [the coffin] lowered and the 4 men with uncovered heads; but old Forbes, who has led our Whym for months, stands covered and unmoved before Death. His fate is sealed" (1906, 24r, EC). Forbes, instantly added by Cooper to her list of enemies even in the throes of her grief, is only the first of the humans around Michael Field who fail to comprehend the magnitude of their loss. The world quickly splits into the good and the bad, the good including Marie Sturge Moore and the household serving boy: "You have understood" (1906, 20r, EC). Those whose compassion failed the moment include the Artists, Bernhard Berenson, and Mary Costelloe Berenson (until she rapidly backpedaled once she realized her gaffe). The perceived eccentricity of Michael Field's profound sorrow following Chow's death played to Michael Field's reputation as cast by Logan Pearsall Smith: dotty spinsters, divorced from the realities of the world. Though I would be the first to credit Michael Field with eccentricity, I believe their typecasting as crazy dog ladies misses an important point about them—and about the literary experiment they have undertaken in writing *Works and Days*, producing nearly three decades of "private" writing into which they

FIGURE 10. Michael Field designed the cover of *Whym Chow, Flame of Love*, the volume of elegiac poetry Cooper wrote while mourning their dog, to resemble the dog's body in color and texture. Mark Samuels Lasner Collection, University of Delaware Library, Museums, and Press.

intended to invite the world. The work offers us insight at this point to the evolutionary cycles that shaped Michael Field's lifelong bond: here they enter their last cycle, coda to a vibrant history. As we read the narrative of Chow's death and its aftermath, the intensity of Michael Field's emotion is our first clue. The dog's death provided the women a way to speak directly of their love, and to admit tacitly what that love lacked. And it provided the poets a way forward as artists. Again, "The Ballad of Reading Gaol":

> Some love too little, some too long,
>   Some sell, and others buy;
> Some do the deed with many tears,
>   And some without a sigh:
> For each man kills the thing he loves,
>   Yet each man does not die.

"Yet each man does not die." What will happen after Michael Field kills the one he loves?

Writing to Marie Sturge Moore, who was compassionate toward the women in their loss, Cooper begins to express these big, hard questions of love and loss. Yes, Cooper actually realized that Whym Chow was a dog: "Chow was too noble to be demonstrative, so only those who lived along with us or who were very penetrative realise that this loss is heavier than any we have had, in a certain way. That we are human beings and he our animal makes no difference: there is one coinage for love throughout the Universe and he gave us divine measure" (1906, 20r–20v, EC). Cooper describes the difference between the public and private Chow: people who did not know him did not have the chance to understand the nature of his charismatic appeal, nor the nature of the loss that the poets have experienced. Love is what it is, and animal though he was, Whym Chow gave his in "divine measure."

The poets write the story of the death of a family and the death of romantic love, along with the death of the dog. For the first time, they do not immediately transfer death into immanence and omnipresence; the searing pain of loss is close to incapacitating. The narrative of pain tells as much about the shared experience and shared grief of Michael and Henry as it does the dog himself. In response to an insensitive letter of condolence from Ricketts, Cooper writes, "Well may he be jealous—Michael and I love Chow as we have loved no human being—for central and to us was is his Love—our Flame of Love" (1906, 25v, EC). Now that Michael Field's Flame of Love has been extinguished, the women are left alone to recalibrate their bond. Bradley, too, responded to Ricketts, and Cooper transcribed her response into the diary:

> Try to learn a little of what we suffer. I could have been happy in age with Whymmie—alone quite alone. Whymmie is my eternal attribute. I am St Katharine now without her Wheel—my power, my grace are gone. I must see Paragon no more. My little Gold Room is where I parted with Chuckles—the Grot is where he paced and paced in frenzy; my comfort, that he snuffed the fresh morning air there from open windows, that my voice almost to the last was recognized. And all this Henry feel [*sic*], only sharper, because Henry loved me in Chow. (1906, 26r, EC transcription of KB letter to Ricketts)

Again, Bradley emphasizes her vision for a dotage *coupled with the Chow*. She also makes entirely clear what Cooper has been saying, that the Paragon, their married home, is now dead to Michael Field: it is a tomb to the lost beloved. And finally, though the Chow belonged to Bradley, the pain of his loss is as acute for Cooper because in the Chow, Cooper has situated her love for Bradley. And that is now extinguished.

Not everybody loves as Bradley and Cooper do; of this Michael Field are keenly aware. For example, when Mary Berenson finally awoke to the scale of Michael Field's grief and expressed her empathy for them, Bradley is skeptical: "A letter from Mary—She is near me in Chow's worship—'she understands too well how I loved him'—Poor Mary and if either she or Doctrine lost each other they would go to Japan, and seek new acquaintance" (1906, 41v, KB). For the Berensons, easy come, easy go: loss for them would offer an opportunity to move along, and evidently to date in Japan. For Michael Field, however, quite the opposite is true. There will be no moving forward. Notice that Bradley strikes a telling equivalence between Berenson's loss of her husband and Bradley's own loss of Chow. Cooper is nowhere to be seen in this measure of the magnitude of love and loss: the loss of Whym Chow is for Bradley the loss of her spouse.

Responding to the urgent need to leave Paragon, the poets departed for a few weeks' respite at Rottingdean, in Brighton, where the Chow had previously distinguished himself among the Kipling family and the rabbit population. From Rottingdean, the poets make urgent efforts to find tenants to rent Paragon for a few years, imagining that they will set up household in a modest rental in turn, perhaps in Oxford. Throughout this period, Cooper finds her love too caught up in the world of matter. From Rottingdean, on Ash Wednesday, Bradley writes, "Henry finds I live too much in flux—not rising to Being—I dare say he will put it better—I cannot understand. My great sin is *Mortality*—especially as it exists in Memory—the mental moments must not photograph—I must break the negatives—too much I ever grieved over the vile exposure of the loved Father's body by photograph—These things are of the transitory—Memory—Mother of the Muses—is incorruptible" (1906, 42r, KB; emphasis in original). As she struggles to understand Cooper's point, Bradley takes herself back to the tragedy that resulted in Whym Chow in the first place: James Cooper's accidental death by falling in Switzerland in 1897. Now, Cooper is telling her that "the mental moments must not photograph"—that Bradley must break the "infamous cliché" in her own mind, just as she did in Switzerland, because matter does not matter. Only Memory, "Mother of the Muses," is incorruptible.

Cooper explains: "We have passed through our mortal anguish ^of loss^ to the realisation of that word of St Paul—'as having nothing, and possessing all things.' All our little Whym Chow is ours—Michael and I are closer in spirit; for we love in unity with the little Spirit of Flame our interchange" (1906, 46v, EC). In this Pauline vision, matter does not matter: to have nothing is to possess all things. The death of Chow constitutes the "Spirit of Flame" that burns Michael Field into unity. Now, they are "closer in spirit, for [they] love in unity." Cooper is intent upon displacing the material and the bodily into the spiritual.

Michael Field asked Lucien Pissarro to produce the Chow's death notices, a request the artist obliged without charge.[13] They further celebrated a beautiful drawing made from a photograph of Michael holding Chow. The photographer was Florence, Amy Bell's maid: "Florence was in a highly wrought condition of second-sight when she snap-shotted this moment—hence its almost un-endurable such sensitiveness of expression—almost barely radiant from so new a little soul" (1906, 47r, EC). Recalling the poets' critique of Wilde for his "documentary" style of art, detached from the transcendence into the realm of ideas, Florence's photo achieves the aspirational style. An artist—even a lowly photographer—with the gift of the second sight can see beyond the material world. No doubt this powerful aesthetic underpinned Michael Field's dismay at the "infamous clichés" produced by rogue photographers at the scene of James Cooper's death.

"[W]e have to go back to Paragon, home no more—," Cooper realizes:

> [T]o go with no golden burthen in our arms, no more bearing with us our one perfect love—save as our deathless joy and light, but denied us in his sweet, sweet earthly life. We have to go back—face memory;

> constant suggestion of mortality, and be true to the holy mystery we have had strength to enter among these infinite curves of Dawn and under the tonic airs. I have been able to resolve to have my dead, not in memory, but in being. Others are faithful to their dead by remembrance—I by essence. I am sure a very sensitive film would be able to show the form of Chow by us—actually there. He is of every hour, of every moment rather—with us of the grasp I had of him and by virtue of the soul he won through his mistress. (1906, 50r–50v, EC)

This is the point that Bradley was struggling to understand. Cooper is not vesting memory with the power of the dead's presence. She is vesting material life with the power of the dead's presence. As she did years before at the time of her mother's death, Cooper has resolved to introject Chow: to take him within herself, to deny his absence through claim to his immanent "hereness." The fact of Chow's death alone does not alter his presence, her love, or his function as muse and inspiration. Chow may not be visible to the naked eye, but a "very sensitive film" would prove the material fact of the Chow's presence. Technological progress in the film industry might just be on Cooper's side.[14]

The dead might be omnipresent for Cooper, but in the absence of the dog, home is empty: again, "*Paragon*—a faded fairyland.—The golden Prince whose home it was—gone! We realise it was *his* house, we are but relicts. [. . .] Every lovely room is meaningless" (1906, 52r, EC; emphasis in original). He is gone, but he is here. Cooper catches glimpses of Chow in the glitter of light on the water, and on the color of double tulips. "The satinwood is radiant fire as Chow's coat—the Sun-Room one flicker and splash of brilliance . . . O my last little home—the first I ever had with Michael!" (1906, 52v, EC). Homeless in their hearts, Michael Field struggle with how to move forward to live in a world that still seems rejecting of them: "We go forward simply for our souls' health," Cooper puts it, clearly struggling between the theory of transcendent presence and the call of the physical world (1906, 59v, EC). Shopping helps, as it often does for Cooper. They travel to Oxford and repeat the spending spree they undertook in the summer of 1897, while James Cooper's corpse lay undiscovered in an Alpine forest:

> Then at Abrams, where we bought our first things after Zermatt, Michael buys me an old, very fine satinwood tray. How in a dark furniture shop a bit of satinwood glows and heartens like Chow! All satinwood now is to me as a tablet of gold to his fur. [. . .] I buy Michael a silver ware Bowl, a lovely little Sheffield cruet and two excelling iron

trays. There is relief in this buying—it seems a pledge to some kind of life. (1906, 61v, EC)

And to what kind of life is this shopping a pledge? The poets have by this time decided to remain at Paragon, not least because Chow resides there still. And they still respond to the aesthetic beauty of the rooms they so painstakingly decorated in the image of their marriage—even if those same rooms are bereft of their animating spirit, the dog. Cooper polishes her furniture to invoke the radiant passion of Chow: "Many tears of bitterness I have eased by bringing Whym's own glow out of the ancient, dulled satinwood chair we bought at Brighton" (1906, 84r, EC). Cooper works hard to transform Chow's painful absence into a ubiquitous and beautiful, so inspiring, presence, even in the furniture.

The death of Chow is the story of the collapse of the married union of Michael Field—not of their companionship, nor of their cohabitation. It is the end of the poets' intimacy. And it is the end of the line for the marriage plot Michael Field have written and rewritten throughout the years of *Works and Days*. Love triangles have provided Michael Field a familiar and workable structure to advance that marriage plot for many years. But the love triangle with Whym Chow is the first and only mode of intimacy that has infiltrated within, and permanently altered, the dyad of Michael and Field. If, in Michael Field math, three has always helped two to become one, the case of the Chow demonstrates a new equation: when two become three and then become two again, they remain two. There is no more union: the two are no longer one. Indeed, the only hope for one is in three; as Bradley writes in December about the role of the dead Chow, "To part with one another will not have that bitterness or strangeness—we three are for ever one." "The New Year Book is purchased," Bradley writes, referring to the notebook in which the poets will document 1907 (unaware at this point that the year to come will take up two books). "One thing—it cannot contain—I thanked God, as I touched it—not the parting with Chow" (1906, 218v, KB). The worst has come and gone. No future volume of *Works and Days* will be asked to record a loss of this magnitude.

The scale and grandeur of the grief the poets experience at the time of Chow's death is not primarily about the Chow, or not *only* about the Chow. Rather than understanding the death of the dog as the cause of the loss of intimacy for Michael Field, perhaps the demise of that intimacy was well on its way—and the painful loss of a beloved pet gave them a vehicle for the expression of grief and mourning. Perhaps instead of surprise at how over the top Michael Fields' grief seems, we would be wise to notice that this is the very moment that the central structure of their shared life narrative collapsed. Bradley killed Chow after Cooper insisted it was morally imperative. Cooper's are the bloody hands though: she was the actor who moved on both fronts to euthanize the Chow, to euthanize the poets' intimacy. After decades of seeking outside the tight bonds of Michael Field for other plots, Cooper finally pulled the trigger she had held for nearly thirty years.

Regardless of where we attribute the act of killing, or its object, someone has murdered love. Love is dead, and it has died. The dog's death was not only important on its own terms; it was important as a figure for the end of Michael Field as he had existed for decades. The poets' acknowledgment of this fact creeps into the pages of *Works and Days* as 1906 carries on. "[M]y love for Whym-Chow is the very core and living of my whole heart," writes Cooper. "Even Michael in herself alone is not quite at that origin of all that is profoundest in my love—her dog just reaches it first and waits for her impatiently to come into her mightier possession than his" (1906, 126r, EC). Here Cooper expresses as plainly as she ever does the fact that she loves the dog first—that he, not Bradley, is at the "origin of all that is profoundest in my love." Here is the first visible wedge between Michael and Field—or, the first wedge as expressed in the shared pages of the women's diary, for in the pages of *Works and Days*, each of the two authors is her lover's confessor. Even here, when Cooper describes Michael's love as a "mightier possession," she presents no possibility of love between the women absent the presence of the dog.[15]

After midnight on Saturday, September 15, 1906, while traveling with Cooper on what she described—and drew—as the "great triangle [of] Edinburgh-Dublin-London," Bradley records this poem in the pages of *Works and Days*:

> But, if our love is dying, let it die
>   As the rose shedding secretly,
> Or, as a noble music's pause:
> Let it move rhythmic as the laws
> Of the sea's ebb, or the sun's ritual,
>   When sovereignly he dies;—
> Then let a mourner rise, and three times call
> Upon our love, and the long echoes fall.[16]
> (1906, 169v, 168v, KB)

Bradley's poem presents the organic death of "our love."[17] In dramatic distinction to Whym Chow's arrhythmic agitation when he faced death, this poem offers the possibility of taking death in stride—in the poetic stride, that is, of meter. Let love die as the rose sheds petals, as music pauses, as the sea ebbs or the sun sets. And let a mourner call the banns on the lost love, which will echo long. Bradley's poem is peaceful and calm. Death is a process of nature, a process of art, a process of belief. The death of love is no exception to what is organic and orderly.

For Wilde, too, the death of love is an occasion to recognize human injustice—and the compassion of Christ. Again, "The Ballad of Reading Gaol":

So never will wine-red rose or white,
    Petal by petal, fall
On that stretch of mud and sand that lies
    By the hideous prison-wall,
To tell the men who tramp the yard
    That God's Son died for all.

Outside the walls of the hideous prison, even rose petals cannot fall secretly. Or perhaps those petals are destined to remain a metaphor: the world of men is harsh and unforgiving. The worlds of nature, of beauty, of the Son of God know a peace that is not to be found on this ugly stretch of mud and sand. Bradley invokes those worlds to hold the death of her love.

What, then, for Michael Field, and for *Works and Days*? The poets' breach concerns the interior of their intimacy; viewed from outside, little has changed except for their newly Chowless state. It is no accident that the words "die" and "secretly" offer us the first, uncomfortable-because-slant rhyme of Bradley's poem. The poets feel the world is too much with them: "We have suffered less from the traffic of Hell this autumn has brought to our quiet Petersham Rd—the motor buses that rush past every three minutes to turn at the Petersham Inn. What an age this is! The crash of speed the only delight of the inhabitants thereof. People will tolerate anything—mournfully the houses quake—the air fills with sickening oil, the brain registers avalanches of steel" (1906, 202r, EC). Paragon feels urban to Cooper; on the last day of 1906 she rues the possibility of a Channel Tunnel, complains again about the dreadful motor buses, and expresses horror at the prospect of "other motor-buses in the sky!" (1906, 234v, EC). The allure has diminished since 1893. The Petersham Road is not unlike Reading Gaol in its harsh filth.

"Michael Field's persistent search for their affinities in the past led them through various changes in worldview," writes Ruth Vanita. "In 1887 they saw themselves as rationalists, but in 1897 they declared themselves pagans and their poetry of this time is saturated with Greek mythological imagery. In April 1907, Edith converted to Catholicism."[18] Catholicism offers Cooper a familiar idiom to frame and navigate her moment of crisis: the language of a trinity. Cooper is clearly aware of the important role the concept of a trinity has always played for her—and, differently, Bradley. "For years I have worshipped the Holy Trinity, ever since I prayed, and Michael used to pray for the little Earthly Trinity Whym Chow, and Hennie and Michael to the ineffable Divine Trinity—that symbol all creators must adore who attain to its fastness of Life" (1906, 230v–231r, EC). Trinities holy, earthly, and divine have always organized Michael Fields' faith, and will going forward. The death of Chow has offered Cooper a new understanding of the sacrifice of "Love unto Death": she declares her desire for a faith that includes "an altar with its present Deity" (1906, 231r, EC).

Just as Cooper's mother and father were easier for her to manage once they had ascended to the afterlife, and just as Berenson remains appealing as long as he remains inaccessible to her, the absent presence of a deity resolves into psychological satisfaction for Cooper: Whym Chow, sacrificed on the altar of Love, is the organizing principle for Cooper's passion. She writes at the year's end:

> And—Oh, Truth—*Vera Veritas*! My Love and I and Chow are together and garner what this year 1906 has brought of marvel and of immediacy of life. Though our Whym was taken at once from our mortal sight and touch and the dear habit of being in the flesh—let me say rather in his golden fleece—at our side, we are closer to him now, more instant to the marvellous love of his heart and soul than when he lay on our couch. And ever is he living by our hearts and thoughts and conception are with us ^both^ and with each, prayed for, dwelt on, adored forever and in the might of the Divine Majesty—*Sancta Trinitas*. (1906, 233v, EC)

The triangle holds its form not in spite of Chow's death but because of Chow's death. "The dear's habit of being in the . . . golden fleece" is but a habit; the passion that he convened through his death gives the poets the kind of "immediacy of life" they so crave. Not rattling, smelly motor buses but the peace that translates essence from the stuff of the material world. Chow has transubstantiated from mortal beloved to deity. Sancta Trinitas: the holy trinity.

At 11:30 p.m. on New Year's Eve 1906, Cooper writes:

> I feel my Love and I are only beginning to love as we shall—thoughts in thoughts—hearts drawn along together into far depths of attraction

> and peace. Glad are the Dead tonight—they have lived and will live so far-reachingly with us. The Holy Trinity bless my Love and bless our Chow—I kiss the dear little nose and bless the ruddy head of my deliverance! O Chow, O little Love! The Trinity bless me and make me worthy of my great Love and my Little Love—And the Trinity inspire and enlarge our Art to the true Exaltation of Religion as the Fastener not Destroyer of splendid things! (1906, 237v–238r, EC)

Cooper marks the moment as a beginning, when she and Bradley will love as they mean to continue. This precise moment marks a sea change in the women's bond; again, subtle from the outside but profound on the inside of the relationship. There are several ways of thinking about Cooper's embrace of the Holy Trinity: clearly, Cooper, Bradley, and Chow comprise a trinity; clearly also she has begun to engage the prospect of the Holy Trinity as understood by the Catholic Church, Father, Son, and Holy Spirit. The concept of the Trinity allows Cooper the flexibility to retain Chow in her relationship with Bradley, even after his death—even because of his death—and thus for Michael Field to remain, in essence, a triune formation rather than the sum of his two component women.

Because Michael Field remains a trinity, his functional form remains intact. This enables Cooper to leave Bradley without actually leaving her. And she does, for the Catholic Church: "And I go out," she writes in 1907, "for the first time for so many years, to face a strange experience without Michael." She opens the door to greet the priest, and Cooper begins: "Now tell me how I can enter the Church. I know nothing" (1907, v. 1, 58v, EC).

Just as she admitted Chow into her heart ahead of Bradley, Cooper welcomes an intimacy with the Church that leaves Bradley surprised and uncertain, feeling left out or left behind. The year 1907 was such a challenging year for Michael Field that they filled two volumes of *Works and Days*, one for the period of January to September, and the second a different kind of notebook altogether (which seems indicative, given the changes all around), from September through December. Welcoming the Church into the intimate center of their relationship adds fresh complexities to Michael Fields' life in this period. Though Bradley follows Cooper and converts herself, she never does quite get past the surprise of Cooper's conversion announcement, presented as a fait accompli. As Vanita writes, "According to Ricketts, when Katherine was told of Edith's conversion she 'helplessly exclaimed . . . "but this is terrible, it means that I too shall have to become Catholic!"'"[19]

The intimacy that the Church requires of its parishioners reorders the structure of Michael Fields' intimacy. It creates new secrets between them, and also between the women and their confessors. The confessional becomes a closet for Bradley and especially for Cooper: for the first time, they are forced to explain and normalize their domestic relationship in the patriarchal eyes of the Church. The women's blood relationship is a convenient fig leaf: "Michael feels that [the priest] must be puzzled and startled by my first interview with him—and comes up from her garden to speak with him first—to tell him we are old inhabitants, that she has 'maternal' care for me, is delighted I should join the Church" (1907, v. 1, 63r, EC). The strategy seems to have been effective; the priest, whom Michael Field nicknames Father Goscannon or "Goss" in *Works and Days*, was entirely softened and convinced by Michael's motherly account.[20]

The prospect of confession is terrifying to Cooper. Until this moment in Cooper's adult life, *Works and Days* has served some functions of the confessional for both poets. Though they intended the diary for publication in the decades following their deaths, in life the diary is a forum for narratives by a readership of just two. Early in 1906, Cooper records a telling anecdote from a conversation with Mary Berenson: "Husbands and wives shd never read each other's letters—she reads B.B.'s—and tells him what to say to Ladies . . . but there are many people who will not allow 2 pair of eyes to rest on what was meant for one pair of eyes . . . In a flash my eyes convey to hers the reason of my profound silence toward 'Doctrine.' She now knows" (1906, 4v, EC). If husbands and wives should not read each other's letters, it would seem to follow that they should not read each other's diaries either. But *Works and Days* is a diary of two writing as one: its pages are always meant for "2 pairs of eyes," and in those pages Michael Field has confessed all of her unrequited passion for the "Doctrine." She has not written of her love to Berenson himself, and only at this late moment does she tell the story to Berenson's wife, her eyes flashing the whole story wordlessly: "She now knows."

The Catholic Church requires Cooper to keep intimate secrets from Bradley and vice versa, imposing new boundaries among Michael and Field and *Works and Days*. Further, Cooper is deeply frightened at the prospect that she might have to confess the secret she shares with Bradley to a punitive Church; we know, because *Works and Days* tells us, that the relationship between Michael and Field has not been maternal for a long time. In volume 21 of *Works and Days*, for the first time, Michael Field find themselves burdened by the unspeakable, in the words of Wilde's lover Lord Alfred Douglas, "the love that dare not speak its name."[21]

Cooper creates a closet of the confessional, as a means of both maintaining and adapting her marriage to Bradley.

In August 1907, Cooper confesses to *Works and Days* her fear of confession to the Church: "Long, long I have been hoping to find in a strange church a Confessor in his Confessional or at call to whom I could confess a secret sin, I hoped was included ~~under~~ safely under my General Confession—but the hope was an hypocrasy [*sic*] ^of fear^ and, I had discovered, a complete delusion too" (1907, v. 1, 182r, EC). Cooper hates the dentist's chair, but she hates the confessional more: harboring what she later calls a "terrible sin," Cooper feels inhibited from describing it in confession, hoping that her general confession had done the job and made her as one, as lovers, with God (1907, v. 2, 2r, EC). She knows, though, that to speak of the unspeakable love will require a penance that she fears will dismantle Michael Field altogether—rather than allowing the poet to live platonically together in their faith, in appearance only suggesting no change from their previous state.

On a badly tearstained page, Cooper considers a letter Father Gray sent to Bradley: "The soul's life he rightly holds is between the Soul and its Lover. He wd make Michael feel this—Henry must not be mixed in the matter. 'There is no communication in this between Michael and Henry'—I begin to fear he will tamper with our bond . . . We have ^a^ panic he may impose a penance of 3 years' silence [. . .] This life of revolt, of panic, and of fascinated love in an eternal mode for what we dread!" (1907, v. 1, 76r–76v, EC). The poets' admission to the Catholic faith was predicated on a lie of commission—Bradley's voluntary declaration that she has "maternal care" for Cooper—and many lies of omission: that the poets' relationship of decades was emotionally and physically intimate, their dwelling a married home.[22]

In this new life, that married home is converted into a temple to Whym Chow and the Spirit: "Now for our Paragon—our Home Whymmie has made Catholic, our Bacchant, our Flame of Love! Now for the Vineyard Church we have reached through him!" (1907, v. 1, 152r, EC). Her new life becomes for Cooper her art practice, itself a form of spirituality. She comes out—as Catholic—to Berenson:

> It is not only that I apprehend the Symbols now, but humbly and with *Askesis* I have begun the Practice of the gt. Art of Life. You always admired the rigorous way we lived to the idea of Beauty, putting by all that was inexpressive, crowded, unbecoming to its Kingdom. Well, so it is now with Life—so every hour is under ideal claim and what is

> simple, what is axial in the spin of life I am training to set my hours to; and this effort is sustained by the communication of my ~~soul~~ spirit with the Divine through a will and heart broken in to these living symbols my mind alone had adored. The Catholic Faith is to me the only organic canon of the Art of Life, the one Initiation, the one Discipline. (1907, v. 2, 57r–57v, EC)

The idiom in which Michael Field used to speak of their love—as the passionate basis for their art—Cooper now uses to speak of her life independently: ascesis is the rigorous discipline practiced by the devoted in their effort to achieve communion with a divine spirit. Perhaps that spirit is Whym Chow, or perhaps that spirit is God. Perhaps there's no meaningful difference? The absence of Bradley from the axial spin of Cooper's devotion represents a departure. The secret of the poets' intimate and primary love has become a thing of the past, replaced for Cooper by a different mode of artistic life.

For Cooper, her artistic life as a Catholic has everything to do with the peculiar predicament of her gender. She is not a nun. Where then does she fit? Watching a line of Catholic women pass, she writes, "Then the nuns file out, ~~with~~ ^holding^ candles, moving on draped feet—their faces crucified in mouth and eyes, but in their restless womanhood peace and permanence and stability and aim that reach one as a rich taste to one's thirst" (1907, v. 1, 118r–118v, EC). In their unique form of womanhood, these nuns are appealing to Cooper, offering "a rich taste" to her thirst. Orderly like the domesticated fields of "The Lady of Shalott," their faces martyred, in their "restless womanhood" the nuns share a form of peace and purpose that calls to Cooper. But she recognizes that her own role is different, and she views it as far more difficult from the role suggested by the nuns' placid faces: "How much easier to take the absolute vow to Idealism than to vow yourself to create Beauty for God! The Artist is always in the middle Region; he can make no ^absolute^ vow to Heaven or Earth—only the conditional vow of temperate and lovely poise between the eternal and the transient, the symbols and the senses, the spirit and the flesh . . . O, God, we are Thy Creators of beauty, *miserere nobis*!" (1907, v. 1, 118r, EC; emphasis in original). Have mercy on the creators of beauty, Cooper beckons her God. As she has expressed in secular form within her critique of Wilde, the Artist's role is translational. Resident in neither heaven nor earth, the Artist is the synthesizer of elements that would seem to be opposites: the eternal and the transient, the symbols and the senses, the spirit and the flesh. In this translational or synthetic work, Artists create beauty. Cooper the Artist must dwell in the paradox of synthesis.[23] Holding neither spirit nor flesh, she holds both spirit and flesh.

"A word on the Artist and his soul," Cooper writes. "Remember he has the Word given to him, and all incarnation demands in the Instrument a certain loss and dereliction: women cannot utter the generations in child-bearing without giving their virginity up to desire: artists cannot utter the word of Beauty in poetry, painting, sculpture, architecture, music without tolerant and vivid acceptance of the sensuous, the material" (1907, v. 1, 139v, EC). We have seen in Cooper's writing the clear, even hedonistic pleasure she takes in shopping; recall in the emotional turmoil of 1906: "There is relief in this buying—it seems a pledge to some kind of life" (1906, 61v, EC). Material accumulation, sensuality, and pleasure play a role in the work of the artist who then translates the stuff of the real to the media of Beauty: poetry, painting, sculpture, architecture, and music. Cooper gives that artist and his soul the male pronoun, perhaps generically or "universally" signifying both genders—or either. But one version of the rich mix of "loss + dereliction" pertains to women in particular: "Women cannot utter the generations in child-bearing without giving their virginity up to desire." Women are different from artists, but women "utter" generations just as artists utter Beauty in what they bring forth.[24]

But where are Michael Field in this equation? A male artist, deeply committed to sumptuous materiality and to its translation. Two female humans who have given themselves to desire and to art and not to generations of children. They have given themselves to passion but without sacrifice to their "virginity" in the sense that Cooper uses the term. Cooper claims a distinctly Marian quality: Female. Virginal. Bringing forth "utterances." Sacrificial. Notwithstanding her "terrifying secret," Cooper readily identifies a place for herself—a married lesbian male artist—within the Catholic Church *because of* the Church's call to dwell in paradox, not in spite of it. This is the novel logic of Michael Field.

Predictably, given the context, Christmas was difficult:

> Christmas Eve.
>
> And beloved Michael is suffering terribly from a "thorn in the flesh"—a not dangerous but distractingly painful one. Oh, the sharp-edged Christmas! And we are fasting—And the Dead we love so profoundly press round this altered Christmas Eve; old scenes, old motives of joy; radiant faces full of feast not fast—the strangeness almost made one *déroutée* in one's humanity. We have a quick drive into Richmond for fruit and flowers and last gifts—I could laugh with a mouth like a

> cave at the shops gutted with turkeys and blood-covered sheep, and boxes of fatted sugar-plums and lustreless greens, and mistletoe of tortured agonizing little wings and pearls withering into age. I pile Eucalyptus and trumpet-lilies on the Sun-Room Table, and golden-berried holly from the ~~of~~ only golden-berried tree in the Park, on the bowl of Leeds Ware: mistletoe and lilies of the valley on each mantelpiece, and the "bough" in the grot—*voilà tout.* (1907, v. 2, 63v–64r, EC)

Unlike their diary personae in 1893, 1897, or 1899, Bradley and Cooper no longer hunger—they are no longer hungry. Cooper's cave-like maw laughs—it does not eat. It does not kiss.

Instead, Bradley was grouchy because she was in pain. Both poets were cranky from their fast; fasting was always a particular challenge for Cooper. The press of memories from their very merry Christmas feasts of old leaves the women with feelings of desolation—but the Richmond shops glutted with gross, bloody, wasteful foods only disgust them. For Michael Field, flowers: *voilà tout.* But how different is that, really, from what has always been? Flowers heaped on the mantel, heaped next to and inside the Beloved Mother-One's coffin. Perhaps the meaning and intention behind these flowers is different: "O flower of the Martyrs, O our Rose, our Whym Chow, our Victim by whom we have been saved to life!" (1907, v. 2, 68r, EC). Whym Chow is Jesus, sacrificed for the salvation of the unredeemed and mortal sinners: he is both flower as flesh and flower as symbol. It is in the convergence of flesh (or fur?) and symbol that Cooper finds meaning. The servants of Paragon find their meaning in other festivities, and for their sake Michael Field mimic the holidays of old, though the rituals are hollow: "The Maids receive presents and show theirs and we talk vociferously about our Cards to make belief that old Father-Wenceslaus Christmas is not dead. But he is, for all our noise, and we are but keeping his wake—and we know it and go to bed (Compline read first!)" (1907, v. 2, 66v, EC). Christmas merriment is a sham performed for the Maids; Christmas 1907 in Paragon saw the wake and funeral for Father Wenceslaus.

What a year of "infinite joy and of infinite suffering!" writes Cooper on New Year's Eve. "A year of strife, and over the flesh of triumph through the dedication of my will to be a sanctuary lamp before the Real Presence of the God who dies for me" (1907, v. 2, 70v, EC). Here Cooper describes the discipline of her will over her flesh. Notice that Cooper's pronouns are singular. The great art of life exists in relation between "The Soul and its Lover"—and the Lover is not Michael. Is not even mortal.

Cooper characterizes 1907 as a struggle: "Then the awful struggle with mortal pride before the Life-confession could be made, the doubts, the distrust of the Instruments of the Church—these strange-half inhuman priests. Then the plunge into the River of the Water of Life that was to sever one from all one had been . . . The jar between Michael and me at the broken confidence, the ragged unity at first exalted by the conditions of initiation—the demon-strife against change in oneself and another and in all one's days!" (1907, v. 2, 69v–70r, EC). The year 1907 was one of severance (from her past) and breakage (of the confidence between Bradley and Cooper) and strife (against change, both individual and collective). What then does the future hold?

Michael Field might hope for a different marriage: "God make us one in a new tenderness of love, in a compact joy in each other as Catholics—May we have confidence in each other as poets—word by word, poets that we are poets in God, the Eternal Word incarnate" (1907, v. 2, 72v, EC). A new bond made by God between the poets as Catholics—poets who are "poets in God, the Eternal Word incarnate" rather than poets in and for each other. And Cooper closes with an invocation: "O Whymmie, golden in rest by us—always near, and now on the couch for my kisses. O little saviour on Earth—your work, your work! We are Catholics; we know the Real Presence—it is with us—and you Angele faciei of us!" (1907, v. 2, 72v, EC). Chow is now guardian angel to the poets, their hardworking, ever-present savior. Chow, even in death the Real Presence of sacrifice and forgiveness—Chow, even in death curled up on the couch in the temple of marriage, receiving imaginary kisses. "O Beata Trinitas!" (1907, v. 2, 73r, EC). The Trinity, once and always, makes Michael Field Michael Field. Yet Cooper and Bradley were always aware of what kind of story they are telling. During this transitional period in their narrative, they are careful to craft an arc of vocative passion, summoning the spirits of those who have gone before—the Chow, the Mother, the Christ—to presence on behalf of Art.

CHAPTER SIX

The Ends

1913, 1914, AND BEYOND

Custom "cruel as frost and deep almost as life" has shut the lips of most women—[. . .]

Why what would these ballads be if one took from them the story of woman's unsurpassed love?

—EDITH COOPER, *WORKS AND DAYS*, 1895

IN THE END, Katharine Bradley had the last word.

This is a simple statement of truth: Michael outlived Henry by just over nine months.

Edith Emma Cooper died of cancer of the bowel in 1 Paragon on December 13, 1913. Katharine Harris Bradley died of breast cancer near Hawksyard Priory in Staffordshire, in a place she nicknamed "Paragon Cottage." She died while dressing for Mass on September 26, 1914.

Cooper's death came after months of suffering. She contributed less frequently to *Works and Days* than she had in her prime; in fact, her final entry, days before her death, begins, "To think how long it is since I wrote a word in the White Book!" (1913, 94v, EC). Even as she lay dying, Cooper uses her diary voice to recall the love language of Michael Field. This is her last word on her love for Bradley, and their lifelong bond:

> Oct. 27th· It is the early morning of my own Love's birthday. How dear she is to me—how the sweetness and clench of love grow pain and joy as I look at her, touch her, and receive her little wreath of kisses in my withered hair.

> We have had the bond of our Art, precious, precious: we have had the Bond of Race, with the delicious adventure of the stranger co nature introduced by the beloved father: we have had the bond of Life, deep-set in the years.—and now we have the Bond of the Faith and the Bond—different from any other Bond—of threatened Death. (1913, 93v, EC)

Sweetness and the clench of love have given way to pain and joy. Bradley places a wreath of kisses on withered hair. And though the love Cooper describes is long and true, it is also distant: "How dear she is to me," writes the dying poet. Michael Field have had the bonds of Art, of Race, of Life, and more recently, of Faith and threatened Death. Their bond of "Race" is distinguished by "the delicious adventure of the stranger co nature introduced by the beloved father." The "race difference" of the father insinuates estrangement between women who have trafficked in sameness for decades.

"My love and I are growing closer and closer in spirit," Cooper wrote on November 25 (1913, 95r, EC). Bradley reads her Wordsworth and Keats, and Thomas Hardy's story "A Changed Man." In Cooper's final entry, she writes: "Again, we pray we may love God with all our heart and *mind*. Sometimes we have to give that mind wholly to Him—as we give ^it in^ the heart to do what He likes with. We must remember we don't give to dictatate but to delight. The only Sacrament of Thanksgiving precedes in His precious death the blood-drenched weaknesses and merely mortal strength of dereliction that God Himself endured when dying" (1913, 97r–97v, EC; emphasis in original). Thus Cooper departs the stage of *Works and Days*. Her last words in the diary return to the need for rigorous discipline of the self in relationship to the transubstantiated Christ.

Bradley knew that she herself was dying of cancer at the time of Cooper's death, and she chose to keep this fact a secret from Cooper and from *Works and Days*. She revealed her secret in her first entry after Cooper's death. Taking up on the very page of Cooper's final written words, Bradley writes directly to her absent love, recapitulating the narrative structure of "first readers" that Michael Field have used in the diary since April 1888. In elegiac language that is more formal and archaic than Bradley's typical style in the diary, she writes: "Christmas Eve 1913. O Hennie, Hennie, but a little blue nun has been with me in the river-room dressing a wound in my breast-cancer. [. . .] I have been a bad nurse—this little extra offering I have been able to make clean for thee. Two days after thou wert gone—bleeding came—God's quiet sign that I must open my secret" (1913, 97v, KB). "Hennie" has become Bradley's confessor; the pages of *Works and Days* her confessional as she "open[s] her secret."

An important rhetorical function of *Works and Days* remains constant following Cooper's death. Michael Field's shared pages have always served the implicit purpose of enabling the poets to write not only with each other but to each other. Now that one of its voices is silent, the other must find a way to reconstitute the conversation. Bradley does so through invocation, by summoning her lost love through direct address. Her technique extends the dialogic narrative of *Works and Days*: Michael Field resolve in weft and woof. Bradley writes apostrophically to and of Cooper within days of Cooper's death, on Christmas Eve 1913: "O Hennie, Hennie." She reaches for invocation repeatedly in the months remaining to her: "My Beloved—." And then, "My beloved, my beloved!" "Hennie My Beloved." "O little Hennie, my most loved—I give myself in service to thee—to grow sweeter to thee every day." "O little Henry." "Henry, my Beloved." "And in secret Henry and Michael are one. Sing with me, through me, O My Beloved." "Be again my lithe, sweet, fine Henry—be my Ariel." "Lovely, make me Loveable!" "Pray for me, my Beloved. Draw very nigh me; so soon we shall both be dead." "Henry, how my heart cries after thee—but in this book, I retrospect." "Beloved, come back, sing over me, sing with me." And, heartbreakingly, in the last entry of 1913, the single word: "Beloved." And the signature, "End of 1913" (1913, 97v, 98r, 98r, 98v, 98v, 99v, 100r, 100r, 100r, 100r, 100r, 101r, 101r, 101r, KB).

The pattern continues through the months of 1914 that Bradley had left to her, before her own death in September. To summon her lost love through prosopopeia or apostrophe offers Bradley a powerful, expressive strategy eerily suited to *Works and Days*. As Paul de Man writes:

> The figure of prosopopeia, the fiction of an apostrophe to an absent, deceased, or voiceless entity . . . posits the possibility of the latter's reply and confers upon it the power of speech. Voice assumes mouth, eye, and finally face, a chain that is manifest in the etymology of the trope's name, *prosopon poien*, to confer a mask or a face (*prosopon*). Prosopopeia is the trope of autobiography, by which one's name . . . is made as intelligible and memorable as a face.[1]

By summoning Cooper just as Cooper has summoned other departed loved ones, Bradley presents one more useful quality to the "Michael Field" masquerade. As Garrett Stewart writes, "Implicated by apostrophe or by proxy, by address or by dramatized scenes of reading, you are deliberately drafted by the text, written *with*."[2] The poets' shared identity again offers them a vehicle to surpass time and space and the constraints of lived experience to remain, however melancholically, among the narrative's woven strands. Through the vehicle of the Michael Field mask, Bradley makes Cooper's absence and silence into a presence. Such a practice is entirely familiar to Michael Field: voice is the technology that conjures copresence, that makes one poet from two women. To a degree their poetic practice simply amplifies what fin de siècle technology also offers Michael Field; in 1905, Cooper wrote, "We have again talked through the telephone—oh, we need nothing but the voice to be to each other. All my loved is in her generous laugh, with its little pricklets of amusement. Nothing delights us so much as chattering to each other. And Michael says she understands why the Dead talk such nonsense—what logic would any lovers utter?" (1905, 32v, EC). Because the poets need only voice to conjure Michael Field, the telephone too can serve poetry's function of transmitting sweet nothings between distant lovers. Bradley would wish to retain access to her telephone to the afterlife.

Bradley alone wrote the first volumes of *Works and Days* in the 1860s. In 1888, Bradley joined with Cooper in writing the annual volume of the White Book together, a practice that they continued until the end of 1913. *Works and Days* comes full circle in 1914, when Bradley opens volume 29 alone. Here is her beginning, on New Year's morning:

> But the charge, since I write from my rapture
> "Queen Dawn shall find us on one bed."
> Henry! To work for thee, to defend thee, my one Love! To write with
> thee. O Verbum Dei. (1914, 3r, KB)

Michael invokes Henry, and her desire to work for her, to defend her, to write with her, and with an erotic passion that was absent from Cooper's more transactional dying words on their bond. Bradley turns to Michael Field himself to express this end, citing the last stanza of the poem "Atthis, my darling, thou did'st stray," published in 1889 in *Long Ago*, the book buried with the Beloved Mother-One:

> My darling! Nay, our very breath
> Nor light nor darkness shall divide;
> Queen Dawn shall find us on one bed,
> Nor must thou flutter from my side
> An instant, lest I feel the dread,
> At this, the immanence of death.[3]

Where Cooper insisted on the "stranger co nature," Bradley insists on the indivisibility of the speaker and her darling, together on one bed, breathing as one and as one in light or darkness. Free of the boundaries of light and dark, of this body and that, two are one on this bed, on this morning, in this poet.

But the speaker knows that she and her beloved exist in the fragile bubble of dawn. Even the idea of her lover's departure recalls "the immanence of death," the separation that ends all separations. Or does it? "Queen Dawn shall find us on one bed." Stay in bed, lover, and we shall be indivisible, together forever.

That did not happen for the poet Michael Field, nor for Katharine Bradley and Edith Cooper. For a long time, the two were as one, but always through the transformative vehicle of three: filtering their relationship through their connection to a third figure enables them to define their sense of coupledom. The events of 1906 and 1907—the death of the Chow and Cooper's conversion to Catholicism—called the question on the triangular dynamic the poets maintained for a very long time. With Cooper's death, the structure collapsed. In 1914, Bradley was alone, grieving on Cooper's birthday eve, longing for reunion: "O little Hennie pray that to-morrow thou mayest give sign that we are together, longing, praying for, loving one another. Little Hennie, to whom I have been so loveless—O Hennie that we had loved one another more!" (1914, 4v, KB). Their bond had failed. And Bradley is candid about how it was damaged following Whym Chow's death in 1906:

> How we loved one another then—[. . .] the year before we entered the Catholic Church. Out with thy tablets, truth: we have never loved each other since, as then—As she was dying she spoke to Fr Barret of meeting him in Heaven, and I hear she spoke to Jane wondrously—as Jennie deserved—of her gratitude to her Nurse . . . O little Hennie, how I have borne the uttermost of pain! The Priests, the Church's set words, the rocking-infinitudes at Life and Death—Might we not have rocked awhile on them together? How you loved me little Hennie, in Chow! Break up the crusts! Show me how you love me now.—We have loved so that all men have marveled, and yet—the Church severed us. (1914, 7r–7v, KB)

Queen Dawn has not found the poets on one bed. Bradley was abandoned: she has witnessed her lover's good-byes to her priest and her nurse. But not to her. Michael yearns for a sign from Henry that their love of old, their love realized through Chow and through poetry, lives on. But Henry is silent. She is gone.

Michael does not know where Field is, nor how to find her. On her last Easter Monday, Bradley, in the roughest of handwriting that is difficult to read at the best of times, reports her conversation with Father John Gray:

> I open up my grief at the Church's action—first speaking of the Loved as among the Angels; then after a few weeks, in Purgatory. I tell him how this has checked me—and use the simile of Henry landing in Australia—and engaging the kangaroos, and Henry still tossing on an unknown sea. Michael, he says, you must accept this ~~miracle~~ paradox. He always thinks of a dead friend as with God. The awful thing is for it to become possible to God to have His desire, and be able to admit man into his presence. Father Gray makes me feel how awful God's task is. Yes: what I feel about Henry's being gone—is *aridity*: it happens. (1914, 29r, KB; emphasis in original)

Frederick Roden understands Michael Field's embrace of Catholic "paradox" as a mechanism for sustaining Michael Field: "Thus we are left with a paradox. Bradley and Cooper: two women, one Field; Victorian and Modern; religious women writers as lesbian Catholics; trinitarian theologians in a lesbian-canine trinity. . . . At the end of their lives, at their new-millennium, end-of-life conversion, Bradley and Cooper claimed the Christian paradox of life through death for its promise that Field might remain a unity in eternity."[4] But Bradley now is not quite certain how to think about Michael Field's copresence. Has Henry arrived somewhere? Is she with God and kangaroos? Or is she still tossing—alone—on the unknown sea? For Father Gray, Cooper is with God, whether that is a miracle or a paradox. For Bradley: "aridity: it happens." Though the poet is thirsty, life is dry.

Through pain and abandonment, and apocalyptic world change, Bradley falters, and tries to write on. "I begin again—when, how? August 25th. Incredible! I begin again, writing in a Park Farm parlour, and my beloved Father Vincent is Prior of Hawkesyard, and the Pope is dead, and Europe seething in blood. On August 5th England declared war. That night I returned from Liphook there's a little book Chow bound that fills in some details between now and the operation. It is my duty now to write in the big year book of the big events" (1914, 34r, KB). The arrival of "a little book Chow bound" intercedes in the line of apocalyptic "big events" that Bradley has recorded dutifully. The book is *Whym Chow: Flame of Love*, Cooper's sequence of elegiac sonnets written in the period of intensest grieving after the dog's death. The book's body is wrapped in soft russet like the Chow himself, and signed "Michael

Field." Sarah Kersh interprets the Chow's appearance here as a surrogate for "details of [Michael Field's] lives that cannot be composed in the diaries; the volume's metonymy 'fills in some details.' It is the stand-in for both love and mourning on a personal as well as continental scale."[5] The "stand-in" fuses the body of Chow and the voice of Cooper, and once again converts loss into abundance, absence into presence, and death into life. Michael Field's was a marriage of poetry, and in 1914, their offspring arrived. It was clothed as a book.

Bradley died on September 26, 1914, a month and a day following the arrival of "the little book Chow bound," Europe seething in blood, just six days after her last words on the pages of *Works and Days*, a writing experiment of almost half a century: "God take my offering" (1914, 37v, KB).

"God take my offering." Clearly, at the end of their time, both Cooper and Bradley were thinking about the meaning of *Works and Days*. Their massive text is no documentary record of late-Victorian and Edwardian history, except perhaps incidentally. It is a vast, complex, and often dazzling document of two women writing to and about each other, negotiating challenges of art and life against the backdrop of massive changes to their world. There are many towing-paths running throughout *Works and Days* for future readers to discover; textual and conceptual maps to energize new ways of thinking about Michael Field as deft writers of narrative prose, as keen interpreters of past, present, and future, as indispensable thought partners about matters of beauty, desire, and identity. This, I think, is the crux of their experiment: in *Works and Days*, Michael Field stake claim to agency realized through a poetic voice that conjures the future into presence, and their presence into the future. Kate Thomas writes of a "glitch" that features in Michael Field's writing: "[T]hat recognition that they are not and will not be famous in their lifetimes . . . It shows that they feel historical and that this feeling derives from their embrace of a specifically broken, interrupted teleology. Michael Field theorized a queer futurity: they lived their afterlives as simultaneous to their lives; they saw themselves as coming after themselves."[6]

On Ash Wednesday 1914, Bradley prepared for death by writing her final will, a first last offering: "And now to the great task of giving up my will—giving the jewels to Painter [Ricketts], with him determining their last-resting place. This costs—And trying to reconcile myself to Works and Days being with Tommy. To the Verbum Dei, I commend it. Faith, faith, faith!" (1914, 15r, KB). "Tommy" is Thomas Sturge Moore, who served as a literary executor for Bradley, who retained the shared intellectual property of Michael Field when Cooper died. Bradley wrote:

> [A]s regards the unpublished manuscript entitled "Works and Days" . . . [Sturge Moore] shall comply with the directions hereinafter contained for the custody of the said manuscript for the period of fifteen years from the date of my death and after the expiration of the said period and as soon thereafter as shall be conveniently possible shall publish under the name "Michael Field" such parts thereof as shall form a connected biography of the years covered by the said Diary but subject thereto as he shall in his uncontrolled discretion think fit and no more. (Bradley, Last Will and Testament, 1)

Sturge Moore followed these directions, publishing a selection of excerpts from *Works and Days* in 1933. Afterward, also following Bradley's instructions, Sturge Moore deposited Michael Field's papers in the British and Bodleian Libraries, where they remain today.

"A connected biography." Emphasis on "connected." In death, if not in life, Michael Field—the name of the author, the story of this unique writer—will remain connected. Queen Dawn shall find us on one bed?

Cooper's will focused on various financial settlements: Bradley was her principal heir and inherited most of their household goods as well as copyrights and manuscripts. In contrast, Bradley's will accomplished the melancholy unwriting of the material accumulation that had given Michael Field such pleasure in 1899, as they created their aesthetic married home in 1 Paragon. A choice sample:

> To Marie Appia wife of the said Thomas Sturge Moore the two gilt mirrors in the said north and south sitting rooms and all my rugs wheresoever [. . .] to Charles Ricketts of Lansdowne House Holland Park in the said country of London all my satinwood furniture except two small satinwood boxes and except such articles as are hereby otherwise specifically disposed of together with all my lithographs and prints except such as are hereby otherwise specifically disposed of and together with the coral rosary formerly belonging to his mother the Waterford glass bottle on the mantel piece of the said South sitting room the silver bowl in the same room and the tortoiseshell mirrors in the said dining room. (Bradley, Last Will, 3)

The stuff came in. And the stuff went back out. It goes to live another life, the mirrors to witness the activities of other lovers, perhaps, in other sunrooms.

Along with Michael Field's portable property went Placidia, the satinwood chest that "enwombed" *Works and Days*. But because Michael

Field ensured an afterlife for *Works and Days*, we see them once again take matter and level it up to the conceptual—take life and make it art. "We cannot possess what we experience," Bradley wrote in 1889. "To the Verbum Dei, I commend it," she wrote in 1914. Placidia, transubstantiated, morphs from a voluptuous satinwood bookcase into the metaphysical carrier of *Works and Days*, the holder of the idea of this text more than a cabinet holding the text itself. Even now, even after the lifetimes of Michael Field, wherever we hold *Works and Days*, and however we hold space for the text, here, or in future incarnations, we take on a share of Placidia's enwombing work.[7]

The signature that Bradley requested for the "connected biography" known as *Works and Days* was not her own, nor Cooper's: it was "Michael Field." Bradley left the question of how to translate the difference between the author's name and the (auto)biographical subjects of the text itself to Sturge Moore's discretion. Bradley also left it to Sturge Moore's discretion to edit *Works and Days* according to his own preferences. So, when Sturge Moore went to publication in 1933, he presented "Michael Field" simply as the nom de plume of two women who shared a life and a poetic voice. As we know, he presented the poets as a bit simple and naive, and he focused the excerpts less on their ideas, emotions, or craft than on their encounters with the moment's most famous thinkers; as Sharon Bickle writes, Michael Field "were effectively reduced to little more than celebrity groupies."[8]

Sturge Moore's most powerful action on behalf of Michael Field's legacy was his devotion to the second part of his charge, the more obviously "Placidian" part: making homes for art. As Emma Donoghue writes in what is the first fully candid "connected biography" of Michael Field, "To his great credit, Sturge Moore destroyed nothing, and left the Michael Field papers neatly indexed in the British Library for a less shockable generation. And a century after their small peak of fame in the 1890s, the Michael Fields are beginning to be rediscovered by critics and readers. As the speaker urges in a 1908 poem called 'A Palimpsest,' 'Let us write it over, / O my lover, / For the far Time to discover.'"[9]

Here is the entire poem from which Donoghue quotes, published by Michael Field in *Wild Honey from Various Thyme* (1908):

. . . The rest
Of our life must be a palimpsest—
The old writing written there the best.

In the parchment hoary
Lies a golden story,
As 'mid secret feather of a dove,
As 'mid moonbeams shifted through a cloud:

Let us write it over,
O my lover,
For the far Time to discover,
As 'mid secret feathers of a dove,
As 'mid moonbeams shifted through a cloud!

Just a few years later, in 1925, Freud followed Michael Field in expressing interest in the palimpsest as a technology that enables past, present, and future writing to coexist—a technology that thwarts both temporal and spatial concepts of difference. In an essay called "The 'Mystic Writing Pad,'" Freud wrote: "[I]t is easy to discover that the permanent trace of what was written is retained upon the wax slab itself and is legible in suitable lights. Thus the Pad provides not only a receptive surface that can be used over and over again, like a slate, but also permanent traces of what has been written, like an ordinary paper pad: it solves the problem of combining two functions *by dividing them between two separate but interrelated component parts or systems*."[10] On the mystic writing pad, the old writing and the "golden story" remain, waiting only "For the far Time to discover." Michael Field, too, "solve . . . the problem of combining two": their diary is the palimpsest, *Works and Days* their mystic writing pad. It tells a "golden story," hidden among feathers and moonbeams, for the future's readers to discover.

NOTES

Introduction: "Axial in the Spin of Life"

1. Michael Field, *Works and Days*, London, British Library, Michael Field papers, Add.MS.46776: vol. 1 (October 1868–January 1869), written by Bradley alone. Add. MS.46777–Add.MS.46804A: vols. 2–29 (1888–1914), written by both Bradley and Cooper. Add. MS 64796: vol. 21 (ff. iii+225). Jan.–Sept. 1907, 57r, EC. Further citations from *Works and Days* will appear parenthetically in the text, including the year and page of the relevant volume and a notation of the author, using KB to indicate Katharine Bradley and EC to indicate Edith Cooper.

2. As Ana Parejo Vadillo writes in "Passengers of Modernity," the introduction to her book *Women Poets and Urban Aestheticism*, "This emphasis on transportation is not incidental" (2). Nor is my use of metaphors of transport incidental; I am indebted to Vadillo for her work on Michael Field, on aesthetic women in the public sphere, and on transport both literally and figuratively as a sign for modernity as gendered experience.

3. George Eliot, *Middlemarch*.

4. See Angela Leighton, *Victorian Women Poets*, 202–4. Michael Field's pseudonymous identity was one of the worst-kept secrets of the fin de siècle. Lionel Johnson, in his headnote to selections from Michael Field's work published in 1907, wrote: "It is no longer a secret that the *nom-de-plume* 'Michael Field' for years concealed the identity of two ladies writing in collaboration—Miss Bradley and Miss Cooper" ("Michael Field," in *The Poets and the Poetry of the Nineteenth Century*, 298). On the joint pseudonym, see Yopie Prins, *Victorian Sappho*, 82; Virginia Blain, "Michael Field, the 'Two-Headed Nightingale,'" 239–57; Holly Laird, "The Coauthored Pseudonym," in *The Faces of Anonymity*, 193–211; and Katharine (JJ) Pionke, "Michael Field: Gender Knot," in *Michael Field and Their World*, 23–28. On the poets' various efforts to maintain the "Michael Field" identity, see María DeGuzmán, "Attributing the Substance of Collaboration as Michael Field," 71–82 in the same volume, especially 75–76. On the prehistory of "Michael Field," see Matthew Mitton, "Before Michael Field: Katharine Bradley as 'Arran Leigh.'"

Emily Harrington argues that Michael Field work to distance themselves formally from the lineage of Victorian women poets (*Second-Person Singular*, 5–6). Given Michael Field's preference to be read as a single male authorial voice, it is intriguing to consider their standing in light of Wayne Koestenbaum's *Double Talk*. Koestenbaum suggests that Michael Field gained an important degree of freedom from their pseudonym, allowing them their "natures set a little way apart" (173).

5. For a splendid account of the important literary work performed by notebooks and other text fragments, see Simon Reader, *Notework: Victorian Literature and Nonlinear Style*. My account of Michael Field is sympathetic to the aims Melanie Micir expressed in her moving study *The Passion Projects: Modernist Women, Intimate Archives, Unfinished Lives*. Micir writes about "the years after the height of

Anglo-American literary modernism, when women began to feel themselves being marginalized and excluded from emergent accounts of the period," and addresses "the ways that queer women, in particular, wrote themselves . . . into a literary and cultural history that refused to accommodate them" (3).

6. Marion Thain, *"Michael Field": Poetry, Aestheticism and the* Fin de Siècle, 3. Thain has led the effort to digitize the open-source version of *Works and Days*, and she also provided the editor's note to the Adam Matthew microfilm publication of *Works and Days: Michael Field and Fin-de-Siècle Culture and Society*. On the digital diary project, see Thain's "Perspective: Digitizing the Diary," 226–41. Thain and Vadillo were editors of the volume *Michael Field: The Poet*, which excerpts passages of *Works and Days*.

Though the full literary biography of Michael Field remains to be written, important biographical efforts on the poets' behalf have included Mary Sturgeon's *Michael Field* and Emma Donoghue's remarkably perceptive short work, *We Are Michael Field*. The poets' close friend Charles Ricketts provided a pamphlet on Michael Field for the Sturgeon biography; it is on deposit at the Bodleian Library (Misc. b. 46308-11), as is Ursula Bridge's unpublished typescript *Diary of Michael Field: A Biographical Study of a Forgotten Poet* (Misc c. 655). Ivor Treby collected and published several volumes of Michael Field–related work, including *The Michael Field Catalog*, *Uncertain Rain*, and *Binary Star: Leaves from the Journal and Letters of Michael Field, 1846–1914*.

From a biographical standpoint, different "Michael Fields" emerge from different archives. Emma Donoghue, for example, like Mary Sturgeon, relies on the *Works and Days* archive in the British Library as a primary source. Sharon Bickle importantly reminds us of the Field archive held in the Bodleian Library, which includes a trove of letters and other miscellaneous, and tantalizing, work that shows Michael Field in different lights ("Rethinking Michael Field," in *Michael Field and Their World*, 39–48). Like Bickle's, Angela Leighton's archive draws primarily from the Bodleian. Martha Vicinus makes important use of the Field letters to Bernhard Berenson and Mary Smith Costelloe Berenson, held in Villa I Tatti; see "'Sister Souls': Bernard Berenson and Michael Field," 326–54. On the history of the Bradley family, see Jackie E. M. Latham, "The Bradleys of Birmingham: The Unorthodox Family of 'Michael Field,'" 189–91.

7. Since Cooper and Bradley use the earlier spelling of Berenson's first name—Bernhard—I have used it throughout for consistency's sake.

8. Although we do not have information from Michael Field about when or why they named the diary *Works and Days*, it is likely that they borrowed the title from Hesiod. Hesiod's *Works and Days*, a poem written around 700 BC in dactylic hexameter, describes Hesiod's instructions to his brother on the principles of successful agriculture and the virtues of hard work. I find a number of suggestive links between the two versions, ancient and modern, of *Works and Days*, including the narrative introjection of dialogue within pairs of close relatives, important elements of formal experimentation, and the "innovative didactic enterprise" of both works. See especially Lisa Grace Canevaro, *Hesiod's "Works and Days,"* 219.

9. Katharine Harris Bradley, Last Will and Testament. Sturge Moore published his edition of *Works and Days* in 1933, with a focus on the literary and artistic luminaries who appear in Michael Field's narrative, with the effect of shining the spotlight away from Michael Field themselves. The volume was published absent an index

and citation information for each entry. See Thomas Sturge Moore and D. C. Sturge Moore, eds., *Works and Days: From the Journal of Michael Field.*

Laird writes, "[T]he 'White Book' should probably be understood as itself a work composed for the public. As Marion Thain points out, it contains too many signs of artistry and self-dramatization to be taken as sheer jottings of private moments of their lives. We can guess that Field would have chosen to keep some things private or at least unpublished, if they had directly overseen publication of the journal.... Nonetheless, that they willingly gave the manuscripts to another person without considerable instruction as to what to select, despite knowing in advance of their coming deaths—the fact that they were willing for all their journals to survive them—suggests that there was less division than with some other writers of their time between what they deemed private in their authorship of this journal and what could foreseeably become public. In this, as in so many other respects, they can seem prescient; they must have harbored hope that precisely who they had tried to be, as well as what they had written together, would one day attract our interest and respect." ("Michael Field as 'the Author of *Borgia*,'" in *Michael Field and Their World*, 31). Christine White has made the case that at some point in the 1890s, Michael Field developed the intention of publishing *Works and Days*. See "'Poets and Lovers Evermore,'" 197–212. White describes the diary as "a remarkable resource, but it is [not] assimilable to a linear narrative" (197). Elizabeth Meadows characterizes Michael Field as using "their journal to record the process of shaping their lives into aesthetic form" ("Morbid Strains in Victorian Literature from 1850 to the *fin de siècle*," PhD diss. [2010], 152). As Devin Griffiths convincingly demonstrates, the cataloging and indexing processes of the British Library have both a history and a politics that merits consideration. See "The Radical's Catalogue," 134–65.

10. T. Sturge Moore and D. C. Sturge Moore, *Works and Days*, xxi.

11. Leighton, *Victorian Women Poets*, 211; Thain, *"Michael Field,"* 9.

12. I concur with Marion Thain's assertion relative to the practices of literary aestheticism, for example: "If Bradley and Cooper are an odd couple, I would suggest it is because they embody to such an extreme the paradigms of aestheticism, not because they work outside of them" (Thain, *"Michael Field,"* 12). "The Fields adapted themselves to conventions they seemed to defy," writes Laird in her discussion of Michael Field's collaborative writing practices (*Women Coauthors*, 86).

13. Cooper names the diary's bookcase after the character Placidia in Michael Field's 1896 play, *Attila, My Attila!* In the play, Placidia is mother to Honoria, whom Michael Field describe as "the *New Woman* of the fifth century" (vi). Placidia, presumably the "old woman" to her daughter's fifth-century modern self, constrains the younger woman's sexual autonomy, producing a breach that ultimately results in Honoria falling in love with Attila the Hun, though she has never met him. To name the "womb" of *Works and Days*, "Placidia" recasts the poets as New Women in turn, perhaps: their modern lives "enwombed" by the chunky bookcase. For a compelling reading of *Attila, My Attila!*, see Joseph Bristow, "Michael Field's 'Unwomanly Audacities,'" in *Michael Field: Decadent Moderns*, 125–50.

14. Thain and Vadillo, *Michael Field: The Poet*, 45.

15. Talia Schaffer, *The Forgotten Female Aesthetes*, 5. Krista Lysack writes that Michael Field, "who lived together as lovers in aesthetically decorated homes in

Reigate and Richmond, came to reconstitute literary aestheticism as a same-sex enterprise for women, a space where both writing and pleasure could be exchanged and circulated between themselves" (*Come Buy, Come Buy*, 112). For a foundational discussion of aestheticism and gender, see Kathy Alexis Psomiades, *Beauty's Body*, especially the introduction, as well as Jonathan Freedman, *Professions of Taste*; Richard Dellamora, *Masculine Desire*; and Talia Schaffer and Kathy Alexis Psomiades, eds., *Women and British Aestheticism*.

16. The Berenson text was quoted in Ana Parejo Vadillo, "Outmoded Dramas," 243. The same quotation, and the subsequent convincing argument about it, appears in Murray and Parker's *Michael Field, "For That Moment Only" and Other Prose Works*. Donoghue lists among Michael Field's planned, unfinished, or unpublished works a contemporary prose play by Edith Cooper called *Old Wine in New Bottles* (1892), and notes that the manuscript is most unfortunately lost (148). My understanding of forms as hardworking shapers of meaning owes a debt to Caroline Levine, whose book *Forms: Whole, Rhythm, Hierarchy, Network* borrows the concept of "affordances" from design theory: "Affordance is a term used to describe the potential uses or actions latent in materials and designs," she writes (6). "Affordances point us both to what all forms are capable of—to the range of uses each could be put to, even if no one has yet taken advantage of those possibilities—and also to their limits, the restrictions intrinsic to particular materials and organizing principles" (10–11). When Michael Field think about pouring old wine into new bottles, they propose to shape well-known stories in formally different—and thus differently useful—ways.

17. In her will, Katharine Bradley wrote: "I direct my trustee to destroy all letters written to me or to my niece the late Edith Emma Cooper except those contained in my green shagreen box and in one or more tin box or boxes addressed to my trustee" (Last Will and Testament, probated November 20, 1914, 2).

18. Michael Field, Notebook containing prose piece by Miss Cooper entitled "New end to the house of the seven gables," c. 1882. MS. Eng. misc. e. 941.

19. Alex Murray and Sarah Parker have edited a volume of Michael Field's collected short stories and other prose works; see Michael Field, *For that Moment Only and Other Prose Works*. On Michael Field's letters, see Sharon Bickle, "Rethinking Michael Field." Bickle's extraordinary edition of Michael Field's love letters has been published as *The Fowl and the Pussycat: Love Letters of Michael Field, 1876–1909*.

20. In *Between Women*, Sharon Marcus writes, "Just as the 'homosexual' is a recent invention, so too is the opposition between marriage and homosexuality" (194); for an important discussion of sexual modalities emerging from the incest taboo, see 194–96. See also Joseph A. Boone and Deborah Epstein Nord, "Brother and Sister," 164–88; Claudia Nelson, *Family Ties in Victorian England*; Mary Jean Corbett, *Family Likeness*; Leonore Davidoff, *Thicker than Water*; Denis Flannery, *On Sibling Love, Queer Attachment, and American Writing*; Holly Furneaux, *Queer Dickens*; Leila Silvana May, *Disorderly Sisters*; Helena Michie, *Sororophobia*; and Valerie Sanders, *The Brother-Sister Culture in Nineteenth-Century Literature*.

21. Katharine Bradley, May 16, 1886, quoted in Donoghue, *We Are Michael Field*, 43.

22. Laird, "Contradictory Legacies," 126.

23. In the introduction to their edited volume, Margaret D. Stetz and Cheryl A. Wilson recount the unusual challenges that face those writing about the poets. See

Michael Field and Their World, 7. See also Elizabeth Primamore, "Michael Field as Dandy Poet," 137–46 in the same volume, and Elaine Showalter, *Sexual Anarchy*.

24. Charles Ricketts, letter to Michael Field, February 14, 1903, quoted in Delaney, *Letters from Charles Ricketts to "Michael Field" (1903–1913)*, 9.

25. In a pathbreaking reading of Michael Field's early volume of Sapphic poetry, *Long Ago* (1889), Yopie Prins layers the meaning of the "Michael Field" signature in all its complexities with the lyric signature "Sappho": Are Michael Field, is Sappho, a split subject, a doubled subject, or an exploration of both? Prins advances the argument that the poets were writing, and writing about, "Michael Field" as two-in-one, as male and females, as lesbian, in every work: "Bradley and Cooper therefore manipulate the conventions of authorship in ways that cross-couple gender and genre, and it is significant that this cross-coupling happens through Greek" (*Victorian Sappho*, 76).

Vicinus makes a forceful case for decoupling Michael and Field, building from the effects of Berenson's relationship to the poets: "Berenson pried apart their private persona as a devoted couple and forced each woman to reconsider what 'Michael Field' meant. I separate the couple and their writing in order to examine the mutually constitutive relation between their lives and their writing. I also question the recent critical construction of these two writers as one, and argue for their divergent aesthetic goals and separate writing careers" ("'Sister Souls,'" 328).

26. As noted earlier, Bradley and Cooper introduced dozens of nicknames for each other across the long arc of *Works and Days*; see Donoghue, *We Are Michael Field*, 37. Particularly in the later volumes of *Works and Days*, Bradley and Cooper often used male pronouns to refer to themselves and each other.

27. Laird, "Contradictory Legacies," 115. Laird makes an important point about Michael Field's protectiveness of their pseudonym over the decades following its adoption. As she reports, they wrote to Havelock Ellis: "As to our work, let no man think he can put asunder what God has joined." And to Robert Browning: "Spinoza with his fine grasp of unity says: 'If two individuals of exactly the same nature are joined together, they make up a single individual, doubly stronger than each alone,' i.e., Edith and I make a veritable Michael" (Laird, "Contradictory Legacies," 116, as quoted in Sturgeon, *Michael Field*, 47, and Field, *Works and Days*, 6). See also Blain, "'Michael Field, the Two-Headed Nightingale,'" 244, and Vanita, *Sappho and the Virgin Mary*, 119. The politics of pseudonymous publication by women writers is a perennial topic of interest in the media; see, for example, Holly Williams, "Why Do Women Write under Men's Names?," which considers Michael Field in company ranging from Anne Radcliffe to J. K. Rowling.

28. As Thain and Vadillo rightly contend, the diary is an outlier in the Field canon in its relative transparency about Michael Field's method of composition; the handwriting alone tells this story. See Thain and Vadillo, *Michael Field: The Poet*, 46, as well as Parker and Vadillo, *Michael Field: Decadent Moderns*, 2. Gallagher offers a provocative discussion of the "proper name" in "The Rise of Fictionality," esp. 360–61.

29. In an important article on Michael Field's 1892 volume *Sight and Song*, Vadillo argues for the book as "a manifesto for a sexualized observer" (16) that uses Michael Field's male mask to resituate agency in the object rather than the subject of aesthetic experience.

30. Blain, "'Michael Field, the Two-Headed Nightingale,'" 242.

31. Laird, *Women Coauthors*, 112. My thinking about how Michael Field use their pseudonymous mask has been influenced by Hilary Fraser's work on the poets' 1892 volume *Sight and Song*. Concerning how Field see and translate the paintings at the heart of their volume, Fraser writes, "But what if the gaze is not the unified monocular gaze of the heterosexual male, as it is often constructed, but the binocular look of two women, enacting lesbian desire but writing as a man? To what extent may the persona of Michael Field be said to constitute a space, a field indeed, of cultural encounter, enabling creative translations between art forms and the juxtaposition of subjectivities (Bradley and Cooper described their collaborative writing to Robert Browning as 'like mosaic work—the mingled, various product of our two brains')?" ("A Visual Field," 554). Fraser's broader argument about the lesbian gaze in nineteenth-century art history appears in *Women Writing Art History in the Nineteenth Century*.

"What was the nature of [Michael Fields'] personal relationship, if even for a moment it can be separated from their professional relationship?" asks Lillian Faderman in *Surpassing the Love of Men*, 210. Faderman answers her own question by suggesting that Michael Field were vague about Sappho's "lesbianism" "because they saw it in terms of their own love for each other, which was not as clear-cut as we would see it today" (211). Christine White was among the first to challenge Faderman's orthodoxy, and to claim Michael Field for lesbian history; see White's "'Poets and Lovers Evermore.'" In *Intimate Friends*, Martha Vicinus presents the poets in the context of a dynamic interchange of love and art: "Their names flaunted their male identification, even as their dress displayed ostentatious femininity. Seemingly self-sufficient in their love, they never ceased to seek the right audience for their writing and their lives. This was almost always sympathetic but sexually unavailable men—father-figures, older writers, homosexual men, and finally, Roman Catholic priests. These men, along with James Cooper and their male dog, all served to create fictive triangles, blessing their female unity" (100). Vicinus departs from Treby and Faderman but aligns with Donoghue in claiming that Bradley and Cooper "enjoyed an active sexual life for many years, based on evidence found in their early letters, numerous oblique comments in their diaries, and of course, their poetry" (104). See also Yopie Prins, *Victorian Sappho*, and Rachel Morley, "Talking Collaboratively," 13–21. Sarah Parker's *The Lesbian Muse and Poetic Identity* addresses how Michael Field and other lesbian poets appropriate the dynamics of the muse to establish poetic voice.

32. Kate Thomas also takes note of the odd occlusion of Michael Field's incestuous relationship from critical discourse: "Michael Field is understudied, to be sure, but this fact of the relationship has been so politely avoided that it is something of an elephant in the maiden-auntly parlor. Much work on Field thus far either adheres Field to a model of desexualized romantic friendship or identifies Field as lesbian. In both cases, incest hides in plain view" ("'What Time We Kiss,'" 328). Corbett's *Family Likeness* offers a historically rich recontextualization of Victorian views of "marrying in" and "marrying out," and the implications of endogamy for race and class especially. See also Ann Cvetkovich, "Does Incest Make You Queer?," in *An Archive of Feelings*; Laird, "Contradictory Legacies," 120; and Blain, "'Thinking Back through Our Aunts,'" 223–39. In *Thicker than Water*, Leonore Davidoff provides a helpful review of kinship theories. See especially her "Forgotten Figures: Aunts,

Uncles, Nieces, Nephews, and Cousins" (165–94), and Thiel on aunt narratives in *The Fantasy of Family*, 101–28.

33. Each of these metaphors pops up occasionally in critical discourses about Michael Field's poetry, as well as their personal relationship. Thain, for example, reaches for physics in her analysis of Michael Field's posthumously published play, *In the Name of Time*: as the protagonist Carloman struggles to reconcile personal experience against the backdrop of history, Thain writes: "These alternating phases of the centripetal and the centrifugal do not bring satisfaction" (*"Michael Field,"* 38–40). Thomas pursues the metaphor of exogamy for Michael Field as well; in a reading of Michael Field reading *A Winter's Tale*, Thomas suggests that Michael Field overwhelm "the law of exogamy" ("'What Time We Kiss,'" 346).

My reading of the marriage plot from an anthropological perspective is indebted to Kathy Alexis Psomiades's article, "The Marriage Plot in Theory," 53–59. Vicinus elaborates on Michael Field's use of triangulation to express masculine identification, arguing that Bradley and Cooper "could use, enjoy, and even possess the masculine without embracing the patriarchal as long as they constructed masculinity as part of a divine trinity in which they were equal participants" (*Intimate Friends*, 101). See also Terry Castle, "Sylvia Townsend Warner and the Counterplot of Lesbian Fiction," 132–33.

34. Blain, as well as Thain and Vadillo, link Michael Field's affective investment in sameness to the poets' reading of Spinoza, whom they cited in a letter to Robert Browning describing the writing practice that created them as "a veritable Michael." Thain and Vadillo write, "the idea there is one basic substance whose attribute is thought, as the philosophical foundation of their being. . . . On the basis of their decision to create a world of poetry, they began privately to close the gap between the real Katharine Bradley and Edith Cooper and their ideal 'Michael Field' with the writing of a journal, aptly entitled *Works and Days*, which the women began in 1888 and continued to write until the end of their lives" (*Michael Field: The Poet*, 23–24).

In the introduction to *Sexual Sameness*, Joseph Bristow situates an analytics of "sameness" at the heart of lesbian and gay studies: "By emphasizing sameness, lesbian and gay criticism works from an understanding that the notion of difference is not an infinitely elastic term. Its emphasis on sameness seeks to redress—if not reverse—such a notion of difference, drawing attention back to the particular interests—the same-sex desires—that theorizations of difference may occlude or disperse. There again, once the particularity of our concerns with sameness is accepted as a material fact—women with women; men with men—then the specific differences that inhabit the 'and' that brings us politically and critically together can be comprehended" (8). See also Vanita, *Sappho and the Virgin Mary*, 118–20.

Jill R. Ehnenn offers an important counterargument to the case for sameness in "'Our Brains Struck Fire Each from Each,'" in *Economies of Desire at the Victorian Fin de Siècle*, 180–204. Ehnenn argues that Michael Field's complexities and differences "manifest many of the contradictions now associated with aestheticism" (181). For a compelling discussion of the concept of "likeness" as the bedrock of companionate marriage, see Marcus, *Between Women*, 211–13.

35. Corbett, *Family Likeness*, 22.

36. Perry, *Novel Relations*, 141.

37. Nancy Armstrong, *Desire and Domestic Fiction.*

38. See Cynthia A. Huff, "Textual Boundaries," in *Inscribing the Daily: Critical Essays on Women's Diaries*, 123–38, for a thoughtful discussion of "extratextual" material in diaries of the period.

39. Michael Field, *Sight and Song*, preface.

40. As for the translation of the two German phrases transcribed here, it seems important to recognize that neither Bradley nor Cooper was especially conversant with the German language. I read the first, "die ganze Edith" as a statement akin to "Edith, you are everything to me." The second, "die hello Augen," is harder to parse, but I speculate that it's a mistranscription of "die hellen Augen," the bright eyes.

41. Vicinus, "The Adolescent Boy," in *Victorian Sexual Dissidence*, 91. "Of indeterminate character," Vicinus writes, "this handsome liminal creature could absorb and reflect a variety of sexual desires and emotional needs. The boy personified a fleeting moment of liberty and of dangerously attractive innocence, making possible fantasies of total contingency and total annihilation" (91).

42. Sigmund Freud, "Beyond the Pleasure Principle," esp. 13–17.

43. See Colleen Glenney Boggs for a provocative expansion of the concept of "queer" to species difference, embodied for Michael Field in Whym Chow: "Love Triangle with Dog," in *Animalities: Literary and Cultural Studies Beyond the Human*, 190–210.

44. Amy Kahrmann Huseby describes Michael Field as undertaking a "subtle social math": "How, the poets ask, can we be united when we are two people? How can we consider ourselves individuals when the two of us are the halves of an intimate whole? . . . Speaking mathematically, one might say that the poets understood their intimate relationship like rational numbers: as fractions capable of repeating infinitely. I am not suggesting that Bradley and Cooper were familiar with the mathematics of rational numbers, but their poetry employs numerical thinking that can be conceptualized in that way. I term such numerical thinking 'queer social counting,' and it appears in their work in the form of transitional states between unity and division" ("Queer Social Counting and the Generational Transitions of Michael Field," 201–2).

In their navigation of their complex "two-in-one" relationship, Michael Field play out a version of what Regenia Gagnier describes as the great mysterious compatibility of the 1890s: where socialism and individualism come together to challenge the relationship between the social whole and its component parts. See "Introduction: Individuals in Relation" and "The Ironies of Western Individualism" in Gagnier's *Individualism, Decadence, and Globalization*, 1–60.

Margaret Stetz argues for a different geometrical formulation for Michael Field and Mary Costelloe: two intersecting triangles, or a polygon. See Stetz, "'As She Feels a God Within,'" 47–66. See also in the same volume Parker, "Sister Arts," 100–122.

45. Claude Lévi-Strauss, *The Elementary Structures of Kinship*, 43. Theories of triangular desire emerging from Lévi-Strauss's include Gayle Rubin, "The Traffic in Women: Notes on the Political Economy of Sex," in *Toward an Anthropology of Women*, 157–210, and one of the foundational texts of queer theory, emerging from her study of Victorian novels, Eve Kosofsky Sedgwick's *Between Men.*

46. Hillary Fraser, "A Visual Field," 556; emphasis in original.

47. Quoted in Delaney, *Letters from Charles Ricketts to "Michael Field,"* 6.

48. Logan Pearsall Smith, "Michael Field," in *Reperusals and Re-Collections*, 92–93. Smith's description of the poets verges on the overwrought. For example: "Gradually, while Miss Bradley talked of words and chanted fine phrases, the silent and sibylline Miss Cooper would be roused from her dreamy lethargy; and as their voices rose and mingled in a kind of chant, the two quietly attired ladies would seem to undergo the most extraordinary transformations; would resume the aspect and airs of the disinherited princesses, the tragic Muses, the priestesses of Apollo, the Pythonesses upon their tripods, the Bacchic Maenads, they really were, and even—for there were no limits to their imagination, and they were by no means all compact of kindness—of the Sorceresses they sometimes seemed, Weird Sisters, who were about to mount their broomsticks with shrieks of malevolent laughter, and fly up the chimney or out of the window on some unimaginable errand" (91–92).

49. Smith, "Michael Field," 93.

50. See Fraser, *Women Writing Art History*, 94–95.

51. I empathize with Donoghue's description of her own relationship to Michael Field as a subject: "They were demanding Muses, and some days they drove me mad. (Even their devoted friends sometimes found the Michaels unbearable.) The millions of words Edith and Katherine [*sic*] produced, the excess of their emotions, the energy they poured into every opinion, every encounter, every detail of everyday life—all this can be exhausting. Yet it is that same energy that lights up their work, that makes parts of their diaries sound as if they were written yesterday, that gives this particular pair of ghosts their lasting power to haunt" (*We Are Michael Field*, 10).

52. *Noteworks*, 5. For work on "bibliodiversity," see Deidre Lynch, "Paper Slips: Album, Archiving, Accident," 87–119.

53. On Michael Field's odd relationship to temporality, see Joseph Bristow in Parker and Vadillo: "double temporality . . . at once antiquated and avant garde" (145). On theories of queer temporality, see Kate Thomas, "'What Time We Kiss,'" esp. 327–28.

54. The Michael Field archive at the Bodleian Library includes several tiny notebooks that the poets brought along on trips, making notes for full entries in *Works and Days* when they returned. See Ms. Eng. misc. g.16–17 and MS. Eng. misc. e. 341.

55. Micir, *The Passion Projects*, 55.

56. Barnes, *Ladies Almanack*.

57. In their editors' introduction to the volume *Michael Field: Decadent Moderns*, Parker and Vadillo contend convincingly that neither Cooper nor Bradley identified as a Victorian poet, emphasizing that "Cooper felt at one with modernity, embracing its possibilities and its perils" (2).

58. Henry James, preface to *The Tragic Muse*, 21.

59. My interest in Victorian novels and models of cognition is indebted to the work of Nicholas Dames, especially *The Physiology of the Novel*.

60. Marcus, *Between Women*, 8.

61. My experiment in thinking about *Works and Days* as a novel owes a debt to examples of Catherine Gallagher's brave and original thinking, both in "The Rise of Fictionality" and *Telling It Like It Wasn't*.

62. In contrast, Thain situates the diary's formal context in spiritual autobiography. Linda H. Peterson has written importantly about Victorian women writers'

struggles with spiritual autobiography in *Traditions of Victorian Women's Autobiography*. See also Oliver S. Buckton, *Secret Selves*, and Valerie Sanders, *The Private Lives of Victorian Women*.

63. J. A. Boone, *Libidinal Currents*, 419. Fin de siècle narratives, writes Elaine Showalter, "question . . . beliefs in endings and closures, as well as in marriage and inheritance. As endings opened up, the genre of the fantastic also introduced the theme of split personality at the same time that psychoanalysis was beginning to question the stable and linear Victorian ego. . . . Rather than being told by the omniscient narrator of Victorian realism, [fin de siècle stories] are told by multiple narrators, or by characters who reveal their own feelings towards the hero or heroine in the course of telling the tale" (*Sexual Anarchy*, 18).

64. Linda H. Peterson builds on Herbert F. Tucker's interpretation of *Aurora Leigh* as "a veiled autobiography, a reluctant novel, and an aspiring epic" in her analysis of the poem's standing among Victorian women's autobiographies. See *Traditions of Victorian Women's Autobiography*, 109. The quotation from Tucker is from his "*Aurora Leigh*: Epic Solutions to Novel Ends," in *Famous Last Words*, 62. Diana Souhami argues that lesbians in Paris, including Stein, Djuna Barnes, Sylvia Beach, and Natalie Barney, created the conditions that supported the emergence of modernism (*No Modernism Without Lesbians*).

65. I am grateful to Kate Thomas for this insight.

66. For a thoughtful discussion of Michael Fields' ideas of marriage and freedom, see Ehnenn, "'Our Brains Struck Fire Each from Each,'" esp. 184–90.

67. Elizabeth Freeman, *The Wedding Complex*, xi. See also Armstrong, *Desire and Domestic Fiction*; J. A. Boone, *Tradition Counter Tradition*; Lois E. Bueler, *The Tested Woman Plot*; Kelly Hager, *Dickens and the Rise of Divorce*; Maia McAleavey, *The Bigamy Plot*; Helena Michie, *Victorian Honeymoons*; Mary Lyndon Shanley, *Feminism, Marriage and the Law in Victorian England, 1850–1895*; and Elizabeth Thiel, *The Fantasy of Family*. Lawrence Stone's *The Family, Sex, and Marriage in England, 1500–1800* provides scholarly context for much of this work. Ruth Perry's *Novel Relations* represents a significant intervention into this discourse. As Schaffer writes, Perry "takes the myth of the romantic couple and turns it on its head, reading it not as the acquisition of a partner but as the loss of a family and a world. By restoring that older point of view, Perry enables us to see how stressful, upsetting, and dangerous the rise of romantic marriage felt for women" (*Romance's Rival*, 24).

68. Shaffer, *Romance's Rival*, 23; ibid., 7.

69. Shaffer, *Romance's Rival*, 8.

70. Peterson, *Becoming a Woman of Letters*, 123.

71. Marcus, *Between Women*, 21.

72. The collection *Replotting Marriage in Nineteenth-Century British Literature*, edited by Jill Galvan and Elsie Michie, helps to dismantle Victorian fictional conventions of marriage. See also Claire Jarvis, *Exquisite Masochism*. On the "un-marriage plot," see my "Gross Vulgarity and the Domestic Ideal," in *Victorian Vulgarity*, ed. Susan David Bernstein and Elsie Michie.

73. "Women and Natural Selection," interview with Dr. Alfred Russel Wallace, 3.

74. Rita Felski, *The Gender of Modernity*, 155. In *The Bigamy Plot*, McAleavey provides an excellent account of the historical concept of "plot"; see esp. 12–15. See also Amanpal Garcha's compelling theory of novelistic plotlessness in *From Sketch to Novel*.

75. Mary C. Sturgeon, ed., *A Selection of the Poems of Michael Field*, 242.

76. For an important discussion of the tensions between endogamy and exogamy, and the function of "cousin-marriage" to create a middle ground of "social reproduction" that at once protected class standing and provided generational diversity, see Schaffer, "Cousin Marriage," in *Romance's Rivals*, 123–58, esp. 130–34. See also Lévi-Strauss, "Endogamy and Exogamy," 42–51.

77. Sharon Bickle's collection of Michael Field's amorous correspondence between 1876 and 1909 includes some tantalizing hints about Michael Field's engagement with Victorian fiction. See, for example, the letter from Bradley to Cooper (September 1881) with an urgent request to purchase the Henry James story *Hawthorne* (1876), 47 and 48n7. Bickle also speculates that new nicknames Michael Field developed for each other in 1897—Master and Merle—might, in combination, "indicate a private joke regarding Henry James's sinister Madame Merle in *The Portrait of a Lady* (1881)" (206n3). See also Vadillo, "Living Art," in *Crafting the Woman Professional in the Long Nineteenth Century*, 246–47.

Bickle's work offers glimpses of other engagements as well. On August 5, 1882, Bradley wrote to Cooper about a visit to Ruskin's home: "In the bookcase I Saw—amazement! Harriet Martineau's autobiography in 3. Vols, Hood's poems, lots of Scott of course, and, Mary [Louisa Hall] says, Dickens, Darwin's Origin of Species, Heroditus etc. Quantities of dictionaries, and in the study side by side in old motley covers Chapman's Homer and Douglass's Virgil" (58 and 59-60n13). In an acerbic swipe at tourist mentality in a letter from Cooper to Bradley (September 1882), Bickle detects a reference to Trollope's Lady Glencora, from *Can You Forgive Her?* (80 and 82n6). In 1885, Bradley wrote to Cooper that she was avidly reading *David Copperfield* while in Yarmouth (153 and 154n6). In 1885, Cooper wrote to Bradley about Lewes family legends concerning George Henry Lewes's emotions about the late George Elliot [*sic*] (123), and in 1886 Bradley wrote to Cooper that she was "rich in books," including George Meredith's *Diana of the Crossways*. See Bickle, *The Fowl and the Pussycat*.

78. Lee Edelman, *No Future*, 35; emphasis in original. On "Sinthomosexuality" as the queer threat to the promise of reproductive futurity, see 33–66. Regenia Gagnier views Oscar Wilde's aestheticism as a queer opposition to heterosexualized politics of reproduction/reproducibility. See "Art for Love's Sake," in *Idylls of the Marketplace*, 139–76, esp. 158–60. Elizabeth Freeman argues for the importance of "queer temporalities" as "points of resistance to this temporal order that . . . propose other possibilities for living in relation to indeterminately past, present, and future others: that is, of living historically" (*Time Binds: Queer Temporalities, Queer Histories*, xxii). See also José Esteban Muñoz, *Cruising Utopia*, and Jack Halberstam, *In a Queer Time and Place.*

79. Dustin Friedman, *Before Queer Theory*, 2.

80. Marcus, *Between Women*, 203. As Yopie Prins has written, "the generation of unmarried middle-class women that came of age in the 1879s and 1880s played an important role in the transition from mid-Victorian Old Maid to fin-de-siecle New Woman; during the last three decades of the century, single women were beginning to redefine familial relations and conventional female domesticity" ("Greek Maenads, Victorian Spinsters," in *Victorian Sexual Dissidence*, ed. Richard Dellamora, 46).

81. Roland Barthes, *Camera Lucida*, trans. Richard Howard, 15.

82. Barthes, *Camera Lucida*, 27.

83. Barthes, *Camera Lucida*, 57; emphases in original.

84. Notwithstanding their diminished reputation later in life, Michael Field wrote on, undaunted: "When their poetry was spurned by their contemporaries, they retreated behind eccentric old-maidism but continued to write Dionysiac poems addressed to Bacchus, Pan, and Apollo," writes Martha Vicinus ("The Adolescent Boy," 46).

85. Thomas Wentworth Higginson, "Women and Men: Women Laureates," *Harper's Bazaar*, June 17, 1893, 482. See also Linda K. Hughes, "Reluctant Lions: Michael Field and the Transatlantic Literary Salon of Louise Chandler Moulton," in *Michael Field and their World*, 117–25.

86. "Michael Field," in *The Poets and the Poetry of the Nineteenth Century*, ed. Alfred H. Miles, 294.

87. Sturgeon, *A Selection of the Poems of Michael Field*, 59.

88. Smith, "Michael Field," 94.

89. Elizabeth Freeman, *Beside You in Time*, 20–21. See also Wolfgang Schivelbusch, *The Railway Journey*.

90. Freeman, *Time Binds*, 3.

91. Freeman, *Time Binds*, 172.

92. Martin Hägglund, *Dying for Time: Proust, Woolf, Nabokov*, 31–32 and 144; emphasis in original.

93. Muñoz, *Cruising Utopia*, 64.

94. Ezra Pound, *Make It New: Essays by Ezra Pound*.

95. See Fredric Jameson, "The Experiments of Time: Providence and Realism," in *The Novel, Vol. 2: Forms and Themes*, 95–127.

96. Terry Eagleton, "Buried in the Life: Thomas Hardy and the Limits of Biography," 89. See also Micir, *The Passion Projects*, 114. As Jameson suggests, novelistic endings work differently than those in life writing; for a useful overview, see U. D. Knoepflmacher, "Endings as Beginnings," in *Famous Last Words*, 347–68.

97. Marjorie Garber, *Dog Love*, 136–38.

98. Vicinus, *Intimate Friends*, 105.

99. Paul Ricoeur, "Narrative Time," 183.

100. Ricoeur, "Narrative Time," 181.

101. Abigail Joseph, *Exquisite Materials*, 243. On the portability of Victorian things, see John Plotz, *Portable Property*. In *The Ideas in Things*, Elaine Freedgood considers the metonymic and fetishistic power of things in Victorian novels.

102. Deborah Cohen, *Household Gods*, xvii.

103. Heather Love's case for the "spinster aesthetic" is germane here, signaling the sleight of hand Bradley uses to reclassify Michael Field's intimate relationship at this vulnerable moment. See Heather Love, "Gyn/Apology: Sarah Orne Jewett's Spinster Aesthetics," 305–34.

104. Micir, *The Passion Projects*, 18–19.

Chapter 1. "A Rebellious Hand," 1867–68 and 1888–89

1. Thomas Sturge Moore, Michael Field's literary executor, negotiated the deposit of *Works and Days*, as well as some letters and miscellaneous papers, in the British Museum in the 1930s, as requested of him in Katharine Bradley's will (Bradley, Last Will and Testament).

2. Katharine Bradley's diary from 1867–68 was acquired by the Bodleian Library in 1942, along with other Michael Field papers, primarily working papers. The Bodleian (New) Summary Catalog describes the acquisition of the Michael Field papers in this way: 46116–316 "Michael Field" was the joint pseudonym of Katharine Harris Bradley (1846–1914) and her niece Edith Emma Cooper (1862–1913). They instructed their literary executor, Thomas Sturge Moore, to offer their papers to the British Museum and the Bodleian Library. Sturge Moore succeeded in depositing the diary, miscellaneous documents, and some correspondence in the British Library (Add. MSS. 45851–56, 46776–804, 46866–67). The bulk of Michael Field's working papers was given to the Bodleian in 1942, except SC 46116–39, 46143, 46150, 46152, 46158–61, 46180, 46184, 46186, 46196, 46202, 46213, 46221, 46226, 46232, 46251–52, 46258, 46280–81, 46292, 46294, and 46299, which were bought from D. C. and Riette Sturge Moore in 1974. Papers of Thomas Sturge Moore and Ursula Bridge relating to "Michael Field" (46300–16) were given by Riette Sturge Moore and Quintin Bridge in 1974. The collection is arranged in five groups: 46116–45, correspondence of "Michael Field"; 46146–233, drafts, manuscripts and proofs of their plays, a few in prose (which are unpublished), the majority in verse (arranged in chronological order of publication); 46234–77, drafts and manuscripts of their verse; 46278–99, miscellaneous papers, mainly of personal and biographical interest; 46300–16 later papers relating to "Michael Field."

3. Emma Donoghue, *We Are Michael Field*, 20.

4. Katharine Bradley, Diary of Miss Bradley, 1867–68. Oxford, Bodleian Libraries, Michael Field papers, MS. Eng. Misc. e. 355, 46279, 20. Further citations of Katharine Bradley's 1867–68 diary will appear parenthetically in the text.

5. Charles Dickens and Wilkie Collins, *No Thoroughfare*, 1.

6. Oscar Wilde, *The Importance of Being Earnest*, 177. Charles Ricketts and Charles Shannon promised to loan Michael Field their copy of *The Importance of Being Earnest* in 1899 (1899, 116r, EC).

7. In *Jane Eyre*, Charlotte Brontë describes the final resting place of Helen Burns: "Her grave is in Brocklebridge churchyard: for fifteen year after her death it was only covered by a grassy mound; but now a grey marble tablet marks the spot, inscribed with her name, and the word 'Resurgam'" (77). In her history of the Bradley family, Latham presents the burial of Emma Bradley as another deliberate claim to conventionality on the part of a family with several generations of religious nonconformists in their past: "On Emma Bradley's death in 1868 her children Emma Cooper and Katharine Harris Bradley raised a plaque for her in the Ashbourne parish church, returning her to her family's respectable orthodoxy" (191).

8. Christina Rossetti, "Goblin Market," in *Nineteenth-Century Women Poets*, 126–29. Arnold borrowed the phrase "sweetness and light" from Jonathan Swift, and used it to represent the apex or perfect realization of culture, pursued through intellectual and moral development. Matthew Arnold, "Sweetness and Light," in *Culture and Anarchy*, 29–48. Marion Thain analyzes Michael Field's use of bee imagery, "a distinctively fin-de-siècle aesthetic worked out through the image of the bee which holds pagan and Catholic, aesthetic and economic, in fine balance, reflecting a fetishistic desire to have it all" (132). See her "Apian Aestheticism and the Lyric Book Collection," in *"Michael Field" and Their World*, 130–67.

9. On Dora and Agnes, the two wives of Dickens's David Copperfield, see McAleavey, "*David Copperfield*'s Angelic Bigamy," 71–93.

10. Even so, this is not a typical volume of *Works and Days*. Not until 1890 did Michael Field formalize the full range of conventions they pursued until death. For example, the familiar tall, white book Michael Field will use for each annual diary makes its first appearance in the 1890 volume, which begins on January 1 and honors the familiar stations of the calendar Field will observe for the duration of their narrative experiment. In contrast, the 1888–89 notebook is smaller, in black boards with an oxblood leather spine. Like the 1868 volume, the 1888 volume of *Works and Days* started off as Bradley's alone. While writing alone, Bradley refers to Cooper not as her lover, nor her love, nor her poet, nor Henry nor Hennie, nor Field, nor any of her myriad intimate nicknames, but rather simply as "Edith."

11. I have made the case elsewhere that maternal loss is the formative trope, the predicate, to all forms of Victorian life writing: "To write a life, in the Victorian period, is to write the story of the loss of the mother. In fiction and biography, autobiography and poetry, the organizational logic of lived experience extends, not from the moment of birth, but from the instance of that primal loss." See my *Death and the Mother from Dickens to Freud*, 1.

12. On Michael Field and flowers and scent, see Catherine Maxwell, *Scents and Sensibility*.

13. Martha Vicinus has written about Michael Field's lifelong interest in male approval, their triangulation through strong male figures, and their identification more with men than with women. On these questions relating to Bernhard Berenson, see Vicinus's "'Sister Souls'"; on boyishness, see her "The Adolescent Boy."

14. Anna Swanwick (1813–99) was a translator of important works from German and Ancient Greek into English. She published a well-regarded and widely reprinted English version of Goethe's *Faust* in 1878. She also published a number of scholarly works, including *Books, Our Best Friends and Deadliest Foes*; *An Utopian Dream and How It May Be Realized*; *Poets, the Interpreters of Their Age*; and *Evolution and the Religion of the Future*. Swanwick signed John Stuart Mill's petition for women's suffrage in 1861 and advocated for coeducation for women.

15. Quoted in Donoghue, *We Are Michael Field*, 39.

16. Ana Parejo Vadillo, private communication, April 1, 2021.

17. Cooper refers to Whitman's "When Lilacs Last in the Dooryard Bloom'd," which he published in 1865. Michael Field admired Walt Whitman. Bradley makes note of Whitman's death on March 26, 1892: "Some of the holiest hours of our life have been spent with him.—*Nevertheless he is gone*: he too is a phase, a period. The trials of life succeed one another too sharply; but this too must be faced. The things that thrilled us thrill us no more. It costs much to find Turner slipped away from one's mind as quietly as the dead slip from life. And then the poets . . . But the true courage is to face this. They will return into one's life no more for ever. She comes forth naked from the womb. Then one begins to accumulate: then one begins to drop by the way" (1892, 66r, KB; emphasis in original).

18. Oscar Wilde, letter to Ada Leverson, in *Letters to the Sphinx from Oscar Wilde*, 48–49. Marcia Muelder Eaton uses Wilde's quip to anchor a discussion of the relationship between aesthetic and ethical thinking. See her "Laughing at the Death of Little Nell," 269–82.

19. On Michael Field's prospective temporality, see Thomas, "'What Time We Kiss,'" 327–51. In "Morbid Strains in Victorian Literature from 1850 to the *fin de*

siècle," Meadows presents an important discussion of the layers within Cooper's representation of her mother's death (157–68). She concurs with Thomas's assertion that Michael Field claim poetic immortality over the corpse; however, she parts ways with Thomas—correctly, I think—by suggesting that Michael Field sought mortal as well as immortal notoriety (178–79).

20. George Meredith (1828–1909) was a novelist and poet who used experimental forms, including shifting and unreliable narrative perspectives, to develop psychological depth in his characters, and to draw attention to social issues. He is considered one of the earliest psychological novelists and a forerunner of the modernist movement.

21. Elizabeth Meadows, "Morbid Strains," 158.

22. The Ilkley couch is a late-Victorian invention that used hinged frames, pins, and castors to aid invalids in finding a comfortable reclining position: "All sick persons and those who cannot help themselves, ought to be grateful to the Ilkley workmen who first made this article" (*The Practical Cabinet-Maker*, 156).

23. Virginia Woolf, *To the Lighthouse*, 285–86. Meadows reads Cooper's treatment of Sissie's death as an adaptation of the elegiac form that works through the aestheticization of death, and of the artist: "Cooper becomes the immortal artist by making her mother into immortal art" ("Morbid Strains,"159). On gendered modes of elegy, see Meadows, ibid., 161. Though not relating directly to Michael Field, Vadillo writes about *To the Lighthouse* as Woolf's negotiation of generational differences between Victorian and modernist women; see her "Generational Difference in *To the Lighthouse*," in *The Cambridge Companion to "To the Lighthouse,"* 122–35.

24. Meadows reads this moment as a triumph of pre-Oedipal agency on Cooper's part; see her "Morbid Strains," 163–65.

25. Meadows, "Morbid Strains," 153.

26. See especially Maria Torok, "The Illness of Mourning and the Fantasy of the Exquisite Corpse," in *The Shell and the Kernel*, 107–24. I have written extensively elsewhere on this point; see "Psychoanalytic Cannibalism," in *Death and the Mother*, 39–80.

27. Hägglund, *Dying for Time*, 70.

28. Woolf, *To the Lighthouse*, 271.

Chapter 2. "The Hot Hands of the Modern," 1892–93

1. The poem by Bradley in the epigraph beginning this chapter was later published by Michael Field in *Underneath the Bough*. On the importance of the train journey to the poem, and to the concept of "transport" within the poem, see Ana ParejoVadillo, *Women Poets*, 177–78.

2. Martha Vicinus writes, "For Cooper, Berenson's delicate perceptions and finely tuned sensibility mirrored her own; she fell in love with a masculine version of herself" ("'Sister Souls,'" 331).

3. Alfred de Musset (1810–57) had good reason to be concerned about his heart at age thirty. His biographer and brother Paul de Musset reported that occasionally Alfred's head would nod with the beat of his heart. This is now known as the "de Musset sign," an affliction caused by aortic valve regurgitation; it cost de Musset his life at forty-seven. A Romantic French poet, novelist, and playwright, de Musset refused to stage his plays after an early failure, and instead wrote them for publication, like

Michael Field. De Musset wrote several of his most important poems, including "La Nuit d'octobre" (1837), during his romance with novelist George Sand.

4. Kathy Psomiades, *Beauty's Body*, 202.

5. For a discussion of Michael Field's program of art study and the origins of the preface to *Sight and Song*, see Julia F. Saville, "The Poetic Imaging of Michael Field," in *The Fin-de-Siècle Poem*, 189.

6. Sturgeon, *Michael Field*, 46.

7. On the book's design, see Nicholas Frankel, "The Concrete Poetics of Michael Field's *Sight and Song*," in *"Michael Field" and Their World*, 211–21, as well as Krista Lysack, *Come Buy, Come Buy*. Vadillo writes: "Keen readers of D. G. Rossetti, Michael Field believed, just like Rossetti, William Morris, and Wilde, that art, literature, and design could not be disassociated from each other. All of Michael Field's books were conceived as art objects, where form and content, design and poetry created together the aesthetics of the volume" ("Living Art," 243).

8. Mary Pearsall Smith Costelloe Berenson (1864–1945) is a fascinating figure, an American Quaker who left her two young daughters with their father, Frank Costelloe, in London to pursue her relationship with Berenson. She married Berenson in 1899, after Frank Costelloe's death. Fraser has written about Berenson's contributions as an art historian; see "A Visual Field." Also see Meaghan Clarke, *Critical Voices*, and Sarah Parker, "Sister Arts." On "Miss Toplady," the aesthetic curiosity shop Mary Berenson founded in London in the late 1890s with important ties to Isabella Stewart Gardner, see my chapter 4, "'Lilies and Light and Liquor': 1899," and Machtelt Brüggen Israëls, "Mrs. Berenson, Mrs. Gardner and Miss Toplady," 158–81.

Mary Berenson provides the most direct link between Michael Field and the Bloomsbury Group. Her elder daughter, Ray Strachey (née Rachel Pearsall Conn Costelloe, 1887–1940), was a suffragist, mathematician, would-be engineer, and founder of the Society of Women Welders. Ray Strachey married Oliver Strachey, older brother to Bloomsbury biographer Lytton Strachey; one of her children, Christopher Strachey, was a pioneer in computer science. Berenson's younger daughter, Karin Stephen (née Catherine Elizabeth Costelloe, 1889–1953), was a psychoanalyst who offered the first lecture course on psychoanalysis at Cambridge. Married to Adrian Stephen, brother of Virginia Woolf, Karin Stephen died by suicide in 1953. Berenson's brother, Logan Pearsall Smith (1865–1946), was a prominent essayist and critic whose biographical portraits included Michael Field in his 1936 volume *Reperusals and Re-Collections*.

9. Louisa "Louie" Ellis was the sister of Henry Havelock Ellis and a friend of Michael Field. Michael Field admired her aesthetic dressmaking, for which she was well known. Louie Ellis made the costumes designed by Cooper and Bradley for their play *A Question of Memory*. Vadillo reminds us that Louie Ellis often made dresses for Michael Field, in intense aesthetic collaboration with the poets. Louie Ellis was clearly also a third term for Michael Field, in aesthetic engagement. See Vadillo, "Living Art," 255–66.

Henry Havelock Ellis (1859–1939) was a sexologist and physician. His seven-volume *Studies in the Psychology of Sex*, written over the course of thirty-one years and published in 1928, was considered a scandal due to its public discussion of sexual matters. Only physicians could purchase the book until it became available to the public in 1935. Margaret Stetz has written about both Havelock and Louie Ellis as muses for Michael Field in "'As She Feels a God Within.'"

Edith Lees Ellis (1861–1916) was a writer, a women's rights activist, and the wife of Havelock Ellis. Their marriage was not sexual in nature, and Edith Lees had many love affairs with women; Havelock Ellis told Edith Lees that she was a congenital invert. Lees wrote regularly for the *Freewoman*, a feminist journal that supported sexual liberty and included discourse on topics about women and sexuality, including female purity, monogamy, and homosexuality.

10. Regenia Gagnier recalls that Ellis and his "lesbian wife were living in what [Edith Lees] described as a 'semi-detached' marriage, in which the partners were financially and sexually independent but emotionally connected, what [Gagnier calls] 'symmetric mutuality'" (*Individualism, Decadence, and Globalization*, 3). On Edith Lees's feminist socialism, and in particular her efforts to strike the conceptual balance between individual (and individual sexual) freedom and the needs of the polity, see 82–86.

11. Prins, *Victorian Sappho*, 94.

12. See especially Armstrong, *Desire and Domestic Fiction*; J. A. Boone, *Tradition Counter Tradition*; Freedman, *The Wedding Complex*; and Schaffer, *Romance's Rival.*

13. Vadillo presents a fascinating argument for the interdependence of late-Victorian art connoisseurship and the sciences of transportation and photography. See *Women Poets*, 157–62. Alex Murray reminds us that Michael Fields' 1892 arrival in Paris, vexed though it was, improved on their 1893 arrival, when their coach from Calais to Paris struck, dragged, and killed a worker in the street; "'Profane Travelers': Michael Field, Cornwall, and Modern Tourism," in *Michael Field: Decadent Moderns*, 167–87; Murray also notes the differences between the fully elaborated account of the accident written for the 1893 volume of *Works and Days*, and the quick notes recorded in the tiny travel notebooks Cooper kept in real time during the poets' trip. Murray points to these parallel accounts as an example of the differences between Michael Field's touristic and the aesthetic modes of writing (170). Cooper's travel notebooks are housed with the Michael Field archive at the Bodleian Library (Ms. Eng. Misc.g.16–17).

14. In "A Visual Field," Fraser writes Mary Costelloe back into the Berenson-Field relationship in important ways, by thinking about the couples as matched pairs of collaborators. See esp. 559–63.

15. See Sarah Parker, "Sister Arts," 116–18 in Parker and Vadillo, *Michael Field*, and Sharon Marcus, "Comparative Sapphism," in *The Literary Channel*, 251–85.

16. Martha Vicinus argues that "The relationship with Berenson affected not only Bradley and Cooper, but also Michael Field" ("'Sister Souls,'" 332), shaking each poet individually but also in relation to each other. Sarah Parker writes, "My point here is not to suggest that Berenson took advantage of either Costelloe or Bradley and Cooper but rather to emphasize that Bradley and Cooper's collaborative dynamic as Michael Field mirrored Berenson and Costelloe's working relationship," in "Sister Arts," 105. Michael Field's *Sight and Song* has produced a great deal of strong, significant critical analysis; see especially Fraser, "A Visual Field," 553–71; Vadillo on the "masculine" gaze and feminized object of Michael Field in "*Sight and Song*: Transparent Translations," 15–34; and Brooke Cameron, "'Where Twilight Touches Ripeness Amorously,'" 147–52.

17. W. B. Yeats wrote a famously harsh review of *Sight and Song*: "They have the poetic feeling and imagination in abundance, and yet they have preferred to work with the studious and interpretive side of the mind and write a guide-book to the picture galleries of Europe, instead of giving us a book full of the emotions and fancies which must be crowding in upon their minds perpetually" (*Bookman* 2, 116–17).

18. The Paris Morgue was a frequent destination for British writers of the Victorian period. Bianca Tredennick has documented Charles Dickens's many trips to the morgue, and his extensive writing about it ("Some Collections of Mortality: Dickens, the Paris Morgue, and the Material Corpse," 72–88). Britta Martens has written about how the morgue required Victorians, including Dickens and Browning, to walk the line between sensationalism and vulgarity: "Death as Spectacle," 223–48. See also Ashby Bland Crowder, "Bringing Out the Dead," 18–31, 85. Dickens writes the morgue into *The Old Curiosity Shop*, and the morgue transforms Count Fosco's corpse into a spectacle that helps resolve Wilkie Collins's *The Woman in White*. On visits by Cooper and Bradley to the Paris Morgue in 1890, see Meadows, "Morbid Strains," 168–87.

19. Charles Bernheimer has written about Olympia, and the contrast of her nakedness with artistic conventions of the female nude: "Manet's Olympia: The Figuration of Scandal," 255–77.

20. It is tempting to think, too, about beeswax as an ancient material in candle making, and the associations here with illumination that Michael Field are claiming for themselves. Wax cylinders emerged in 1885 as the basis of audio-recording technology. Marion Thain's "The Beehive" reviews Victorian thought about beehives (23–27), and her "Apian Aestheticism" creates an argument about Michael Field's use of bees for erotic, religious, and literary figuration (130–67 in *"Michael Field"*).

21. See Sarah Parker, "Fashioning Michael Field," 313. Parker also makes note of Michael Field's tendency toward the candid assessment ("usually rather unflattering") of the dress sense of their new acquaintances (318). Vadillo argues that "for Michael Field dress was a living form of aesthetic expression, an art, just as their writing" ("Living Art," 244).

22. Vadillo discusses this painful episode in "Living Art," noting that Berenson's "critique was particularly damaging because it was directed toward their mode of aestheticism. He saw the poets as an ekphrastic representation of their poetry and thus his critique was as personal as it was aesthetical" (258).

23. Vicinus, "'Sister Souls,'" 349.

24. Vadillo uses Michael Field's source of an underground news placard to open her book *Women Poets and Urban Aestheticism*, 1. Vadillo argues that late-Victorian women poets, including Michael Field, created a distinctive urban aestheticism by traversing a London made newly available to them by modern systems of transport.

25. On the aesthetic significance of this particular redecorating scheme, see Vadillo, "Aestheticism and Decoration," 17.

26. On the household display of photographic reproductions of artworks, see Psomiades's account of the relationship between aestheticism and commodification in *Beauty's Body*, 94–96.

27. On Bradley's socialism, see Diana Maltz, "Katharine Bradley and Ethical Socialism," 191–201.

28. The courtship of Robert and Elizabeth Barrett Browning, and the fierce opposition of EBB's father to their marriage, was famously memorialized by Rudolf Besier in the 1930 play (later a musical and a film adaptation), *The Barretts of Wimpole Street.*

29. Jan Macdonald has provided an engaging account of the protracted negotiations between Grein and Michael Field over the play's production ("'Disillusioned Bards and Despised Bohemians,'" 18–29). See also Joseph Bristow on the "conceptual and emotional ambition of *A Question of Memory*," as well as the challenges of realizing these particular ambitions onstage ("'Unwomanly Audacities': *Attila, My Attila!*," 132–34).

30. Archer (1856–1924) was a Scottish drama critic who helped bring Ibsen to fame by translating Ibsen's work and sponsoring productions of Ibsen's plays in London; he was also a supporter of Grein's Independent Theatre Society. Archer's play *The Green Goddess* (1921) became successful in its own right. Vadillo provides an especially useful consideration on the concept of "history" in the work of Michael Field, and particularly in the plays: on one hand, their response to Pater's historical criticism, and on the other, the production of "art that was not subjected to the conditions of late-nineteenth-century capitalism" ("Outmoded Dramas," in *"Michael Field" and Their World*, 238).

31. William Archer, review reprinted in his *The Theatrical "World" for 1893–[97]*, 252, 253.

32. Archer, *The Theatrical "World,"* 253–54; emphasis in original.

33. David J. Moriarty, "'Michael Field' (Edith Cooper and Katherine Bradley [*sic*]) and Their Male Critics," 127.

34. Bickle, *The Fowl and the Pussycat*, 149.

35. Tolstoy and Ibsen both introduce a mode of documentary realism approaching modernism, which holds particular appeal for Cooper in 1893. See William Archer's 1905 essay, "Henrik Ibsen: Philosopher or Poet," 1, and Toril Moi, *Henrik Ibsen and the Birth of Modernism.*

Chapter 3. "The Infamous Cliché," 1897

1. Victor Erlich illustrates the distinction between *fabula* and *sujet* through Tolstoy's *Anna Karenina*, a novel very much on Edith Cooper's mind in the late 1890s. He writes: "the 'fable' stood for the basic story stuff, the sum-total of events to be related in the work of fiction, in a word, the 'material for narrative construction'. Conversely, 'plot meant the story as actually told or the way in which the events are linked together. In order to become part of esthetic structure the raw materials of the 'fable' have to be built into the 'plot'. . . . The theme alone, apart from, or prior to, its artistic embodiment, can never account for the esthetic efficacy of a novel or a short story. The 'fable' of Anna Karenina, for example, can be stated in one brief sentence: this paraphrase, however, would not even hint at the richness and complexity of the novel. Art in general, and art of fiction in particular, stands or falls with organization" (*Russian Formalism: History-Doctrine*, 240).

2. Among Michael Field's private nicknames in circulation in 1897 were "Master" (Bradley) and "Merle" (Cooper). Sharon Bickle suggests that "The new names may indicate a private joke based on Henry James's *Portrait of a Lady*, but the letters

provide no explanation," 206n3. Bickle cites four letters that use these names, all dated during February 1897. See *The Fowl and the Pussycat*, xxiv, 205, 206n3, 209, 210, and 211.

3. Thomas Hardy and his wife visited Zermatt during the summer of 1897. By coincidence, they came into contact with the edges of the Cooper family drama: "By the end of the month the weather had turned uncomfortably hot. At Zermatt on the 29th Emma [Hardy] had a frightening ride on a mule to the Riffel-Alp Hotel and its view of the Matterhorn while Hardy laboured up on foot. Learning on his arrival that an Englishman—later identified as James Robert Cooper, father of one of the two authors known collectively as 'Michael Field'—had mysteriously disappeared while following that same route a few days earlier, Hardy retraced his own steps but could find nothing suspicious—and reported as much in a letter to The Times. This odd piece of officiousness on so hot a day made Hardy physically exhausted and when they moved on to Geneva he was obliged to rest in the hotel while Emma went exploring on her own and succeeded in locating the tomb of Sir Humphry Davy, the natural philosopher, whom she was able to claim as a distant relative" (Michael Millgate, *Thomas Hardy: A Biography Revisited*, 358).

4. Judith Butler, *Antigone's Claim: Kinship between Life and Death*, 10.

5. Butler, *Antigone's Claim*, 11.

6. James Strachey, introduction to *The Standard Edition of the Complete Psychological Works of Sigmund Freud*, vol. 4, *The Interpretation of Dreams (First Part)*, xviii–xix.

7. Freud, *Standard Edition*, 4:262.

8. In her discussion of Michael Field's play *Attila, My Attila!*, which was published in 1896, months before the Riffel-Alp episode, Mary Sturgeon similarly suggests that Michael Field are in a psychoanalytic frame of mind. She explains: "It may even be that we have had to wait for the teaching of Freud to make plain all that is implied in this play. Of him the poets knew nothing; and could they have known, would have disliked intensely, as most healthy minds do, his obsession with the idea of sex. Yet they have done the poet's work so well—which is to say, they have observed so carefully, thought so fearlessly, and so vividly imagined—that they have presented—without in the least intending to do so an almost pathological study of suppressed instinct: one which illumines and is in its turn illuminated by the residuum of truth which does underlie the fantastic theories of the psycho-analyst" (*Michael Field*, 195–96).

9. That said, Michael Field's connection to Freud's translation and dissemination in English involved at most one degree of separation: recall that Mary Costelloe's elder daughter, Ray Strachey, was married to Oliver Strachey, brother to Freud's translator James Strachey. Costelloe's younger daughter, Karin Stephen, trained and practiced as an analyst, and introduced coursework on psychoanalysis at Cambridge. Karin Stephen was married to Adrian Stephen, brother to Virginia Woolf, who founded Hogarth Press with Leonard Woolf in 1917. The "Woolves" named the press for their house in Richmond (1915–24); it stands on the path Michael Field would have walked from 1 Paragon, their home from 1899–1914, to the home of their dear friends Charles Ricketts and Charles Shannon. The Hogarth Press published James Strachey's English translation of Freud's *Standard Edition*.

10. Kate Thomas writes, "Butler has recently explicated how the figure of Antigone stands against heterosexual exogamy as the founding rule of culture. The daughter of an incestuous bond, she lives and dies for the incestuous love of her brother. She defies patriarchal and monarchical law in order to honor her brother with the ritual of burial (twice) and—by hanging herself in the family tomb with her bridal veil—turns a plurality of dead family members into her bridegroom" ("'What Time We Kiss,'" 346). Freeman writes, "Butler shows that Antigone disrupts the status of exogamy itself as the founding rule of culture" (*The Wedding Complex*, 37).

11. Catherine Maxwell, "Sappho, Mary Wakefield, and Vernon Lee's 'A Wicked Voice,'" 960–61. The 1897 sapphire ring was the first of two in Bradley's life. The second came to Bradley in 1904, when Charles Ricketts designed the "Sabbatai Ring" as a gift for her; as Maxwell describes it, the ring's "substantial bezel took the form of a gold mosque with pierced doors and windows and a blue dome made of a large cabochon star-sapphire" (*Scents and Sensibility*, 218). Bradley wrote a sonnet for Ricketts, "On beholding a ring set with a star-sapphire," as a gesture of thanks. The poem, signed "M.F.," appears on loose pages in the Bodleian's Michael Field collection, and in the 1904 volume of *Works and Days* (22r and 28r). Maxwell makes the case that Bradley's feelings for Ricketts paralleled Cooper's for Berenson. Particularly in the context of that argument, I find the sapphire poem, transcribed below from the Bodleian version, intriguingly suggestive of both sapphire rings, with its framing in the terms of "What is it? Not . . ."

> What is it? Not the fetter of troth-plight,
> What is it? Not the signet of a king
> Or ceremonial, or prodigious ring
> With alleys for the venoms that requite,
> Nor wrought for any separate delight;
> It is a dream, a mighty compiling;
> A flame from many windows flickering,
> *A domed heaven with one deep star in sight.
> It is a shrine and from the four-fold tier
> Of solemn towers that bind its cupola,
> From the high windows and the golden doors
> Glimpses there are that fade and disappear,
> The clinging of frailed spices, and the stir
> Of a god moving secret 'mid the floors.
> M.F.
> * A dome of heaven

12. Sharon Bickle interprets Michael Field's Zermatt wedding, as well as related expressions of independence from the father, as an extended exploration of "willfulness" on the poets' part. See "Living 'Willfully': The Same-Sex Marriage Ceremony of 'Michael Field,'" 116–28.

13. Prins, *Victorian Sappho*, 94.

14. Leighton similarly observes the free-floating erotic energy in the sonnets Cooper wrote after her father's death: "Edith invokes the ghost of her dead father almost as she might invite a lover to sport in the shade" (*Victorian Women Poets*, 220). As Ehnenn notes, Bradley and Cooper pursue another "nuptial" occasion: "In

February 1911, motivated by the realities of Cooper's illness, Bradley and Cooper decide to take vows to become Dominican Sisters of the Penance, to 'have new nuptials of love within the Church.' This act brings new weight to their devotional writings' standard trope of Christ as Bridegroom. On December 31, 1911, Cooper writes, 'We are here together, hoping together to take the Vow that gives us wholly to our Bridegroom Christ, hoping to love each other in Him . . . and beloved Michael, growing so patient, showing me such loveable fruits out of the pain, bitterer than mine she has to bear.' Looking forward to the rings that will join them—and in language that recalls the Trinity that she and Bradley formed with Whym Chow—Cooper writes, 'We shall be in Thee together and not alone—forever Thine and Thy Twain.' In this queer marriage, Christ as Bridegroom, like Whym Chow, becomes another erotic proxy for Michael Field" ("'Thy Body Maketh a Solemn Song,'" 205).

15. Butler, *Antigone's Claim*, 22. On the queer psychic and epistemic implications of anti-generationality, see Edelman, *No Future.*

16. Lévi-Strauss, *The Elementary Structures of Kinship*, 18, 12; see further "The Problem of Incest," in *Elementary Structures*, 12–25. See also Butler, *Antigone's Claim*, 19.

17. Bradley, *Commonplace Book of Charles Bradley*, MS. Eng. Misc.e.335, 46279, 40r, Bodleian Weston Library special collections. The diary records the next marriage as well, between Bradley's sister Mary Lou Bradley and Roger Holinsworth. For a discussion of the Bradley family's radical religious past, see Latham, "The Bradleys of Birmingham," 189–91.

18. Freeman, *The Wedding Complex*, 11, 15; emphasis added. Sharon Bickle interprets Michael Field's marriage ceremony as part of a pattern of willfulness that the poets use to establish their new life and home together. See "Living 'Willfully.'"

19. Butler, *Antigone's Claim*, 23. See Freeman, *The Wedding Complex*, 43.

20. Butler, *Antigone's Claim*, 24.

21. Michael Field's experience might merit an addendum to Schivelbusch's chapter on "The Compartment" (as ambivalent space) in *The Railway Journey*, 70–88.

22. As Donoghue reports, Bradley's breach with Ruskin in 1877 came about because Bradley declared two new forms of devotion: to atheism, and to her Skye terrier. Ruskin eventually expelled Bradley from the Guild of St. George, but not before declaring that "he loved dogs fifty times better than she did" (*We Are Michael Field*, 24).

23. See Joyce Green, "Tennyson's Development During the 'Ten Years' Silence' (1832–1842)," 662–97.

24. See especially Vicinus, *Intimate Friends* and "'Sister Souls,'" and Pionke, "'Michael Field': Gender Knot," 23–28.

25. Edward Whymper (1840–1911) was a wood engraver and a mountaineer. Whymper was a wood-engraving apprentice for his father's business at the age of fourteen, and in 1860, he went to the Swiss Alps to sketch and illustrate a book for Longman's. While he was there, he was inspired to become a mountaineer. After seven failed attempts, he was the first person to summit the Matterhorn on July 14, 1865. On the descent, one member of the party slipped and dragged three other climbers to their deaths. A snapped rope saved Whymper and two guides. Afterward, Whymper maintained his father's engraving business while traveling and climbing around the world. He wrote and illustrated many accounts of his travels, including *Ascent of the Matterhorn* and *Travels Amongst the Great Andes of the Equator*.

26. This theory of eroticism as "hiding in plain sight" is indebted in two directions: to Eve Kosofsky Sedgwick's *Epistemology of the Closet*, and to Barbara Johnson's "The Frame of Reference: Poe, Lacan, Derrida," 457–505.

27. See the introduction to this book, as well as Freedman, *The Wedding Complex*, and Schaffer, *Romance's Rival*.

Chapter 4. "Lilies and Light and Liquor," 1899

1. Regenia Gagnier, *The Insatiability of Human Wants*. On shopping, see Rachel Bowlby, *Carried Away: The Invention of Modern Shopping*; Erika Diane Rappaport, *Shopping for Pleasure*; and Thomas Richards, *The Commodity Culture of Victorian Britain*.

2. Ana Parejo Vadillo, "Aestheticism and Decoration." In "Living Art," Vadillo extends this argument to Michael Field's sense of aesthetic fashion (243–71). Sharon Marcus has written about domesticity as a class formation distinct from heterosexuality; see "At Home with the Other Victorians," 119–45. On the post-1850 explosion of artistic interior decoration, see Deborah Cohen, "Art at Home: How the House Became Artistic," in *Household Gods*, 62–88.

3. Anthony Trollope, *The Small House at Allington*. On the burdensome matter of portable property, see my "Gross Vulgarity and the Domestic Ideal: Anthony Trollope's *Small House at Allington*."

4. Vadillo, *Women Poets*, 154 and 162–63. On the importance of London to emergent lesbian identification, see also Kate Flint, "The 'hour of pink twilight': Lesbian Poetics and Queer Encounters on the Fin-de-siècle Street," 687–712. On suburbia and home decor, see Deborah Cohen, *Household Gods*, 101–4.

5. On the simultaneous fragility and durability of separate-spheres ideology, see Mary Poovey, *Uneven Developments*. The introduction to Vadillo's *Women Poets* provides an invaluable case for the public sphere and the formation of Aesthetic women poets (1–37).

6. For specifics about the Artists' residences, including addresses, see Van Capelleveen, "25. Contact Addresses," *Charles Ricketts & Charles Shannon* (blog), January 11, 2012, http://charlesricketts.blogspot.com/2012/01/25-contact-addresses.html. For an account of the cult of domesticity in the Artists' relationship, see Matt Cook, "Domestic Passions," 618–40, and Stephen Calloway, "'Tout pour l'art,'" 19–28. For an excellent account of aestheticism and home decorating in Michael Field, see Vadillo, "Aestheticism and Decoration," 17–36. Maxwell provides a sustained analysis of Michael Field's relationship with "the Artists," Ricketts and Shannon, focused especially on Bradley's expression of love for Ricketts through the discourse of flowers and scents. See *Scents and Sensibility*, esp. 216–31.

7. The residence at 1 Paragon and its adjacent buildings have been converted to an expensive boutique hotel, restaurant, and events venue called the Bingham Riverhouse. Judging from online reviews, it seems that the proprietors have had to face challenges similar to Michael Field's in managing the building's many staircases and small rooms. The building features no blue plaque marking Michael Field's years in residence, but the hotel's website acknowledges the poets in a brief section about its history: "From 1899–1914, tenants Katherine [*sic*] Bradley and Edith Cooper wrote love poetry under the pseudonym Michael Field. Katherine [*sic*] and Edith were aunt and niece and were discovered to be lovers. They entertained many literary visitors

at the Bingham including W. B. Yeats. All the Bingham's fifteen bedrooms are named after their collection of poetry." Perhaps the website is in need of an update; the bedrooms, many of which evidently feature large copper bathtubs near the bedside, have names such as William, Charon, and Sappho.

8. Vadillo, "Aestheticism and Decoration," 20.

9. Vicinus, *Intimate Friends*, 100.

10. "This I call building a home in the Heavens," Bradley writes, "—or as Nietche [*sic*] recommends, on the Open Sea!" (1899, 11r, KB). She is paraphrasing Nietzsche in *The Gay Science*: "I would not build myself a house (it is an element of my happiness not to be a house owner!). If I had to do so, however, I should build it, like many of the Romans, right into the sea. I should like to have some secrets in common with that beautiful monster" (32).

11. Charles Dickens, *David Copperfield*, 641.

12. In Vadillo, "Aestheticism and Decoration," as well as *Women Poets*.

13. On Michael Field and epithalamia, see Prins, *Victorian Sappho*, 90–93. Spenser published his "Prothalamion" in 1596, on the occasion of the wedding of the twin daughters of the Earl of Worcester. Though the Earl's daughters were marrying men and not each other, doubtless the circumstance of two women and a wedding did not escape Cooper. In 1922, T. S. Eliot will cite the "Sweet Thames" line in "The Waste-Land." For a thoughtful discussion of Edith Cooper's appropriation of lyric forms, see Meadows, "Morbid Strains," 160–67.

14. Parker, "Fashioning Michael Field," 323. Ricketts and Shannon were well acquainted with Whistler; they had taken over his house, "The Vale," in Chelsea in 1888. Ricketts named the Vale Press after this house, where the Artists lived until 1892. See J.G.P. Delaney, "The aesthetes of the Vale, Chelsea," in *Charles Ricketts: A Biography*, 38–93.

15. I find something peculiar and compelling about Ricketts's power of defamiliarization as an instrument of Michael Field's homemaking, something important to the psychological space Michael Field create in 1 Paragon. In his essay on "The 'Uncanny,'" Freud exposes the gripping power of the *unheimlich*—literally, the "unhomelike"—in the heart of the *Heimlich* (*The Standard Edition of the Complete Psychological Works of Sigmund Freud*, 17:217–52). What is unfamiliar is familiar, what is scariest is what is best known. As he stretches Michael Field's perspective on their own rooms, Ricketts invites the poets to make their spaces uniquely their own by creating a formal intention behind each room and behind the house as a whole. Like stanzas in a poem that invoke and revise a familiar form—perhaps a poem that is, and is not, an epithalamion as poetic tradition would have it.

16. Ricketts's "Psyche in the House" originated as a drawing reproduced in *The Pageant 1896*, and published later in the Vale Press edition of *De Cupidinis et Psyches Amoribus* in 1901. See Van Capellaveen, "401. Exhibition at the Heath Robinson Museum," *Charles Ricketts & Charles Shannon* (blog).

17. In "Aestheticism and Decoration," Vadillo details Michael Field's dedication to Ricketts and Shannon in their high-aesthetic vision for Paragon; see esp. 20–23.

18. According to physical descriptions of Bradley and Cooper, Cooper was the smaller and slighter of the pair, while friends tended to characterize Bradley with terms such as "sturdy." See, for example, Donoghue, *We Are Michael Field*, 33–34.

19. Machtelt Brüggen Israëls, "Mrs. Berenson, Mrs. Gardner and Miss Toplady," 158–81. I suspect that Mary Costelloe Berenson borrowed the name "Toplady," in irony, from the eighteenth-century Calvinist cleric Augustus Toplady (1740–78).

20. Freedman, *Professions of Taste*, 110.

21. Vadillo, "Aestheticism and Decoration."

22. Vadillo, "Aestheticism and Decoration," 19.

23. In *Materializing Queer Desire*, Elisa Glick helpfully considers the navigation of materiality and immateriality in fin de siècle lesbianism, though not specifically the case of Michael Field. On connoisseurship and queer sexuality, see especially Friedman, *Before Queer Theory*; Felski, *The Gender of Modernity*; Gagnier, "Production, Reproduction, and Pleasure in Victorian Aesthetics and Economics," in *Victorian Sexual Dissidence*, 127–46; James Eli Adams, *Dandies and Desert Saints*; Len Gutkin, *Dandyism: Forming Fiction from Modernism to the Present*; Jesse Matz, *Literary Impressionism and Modernist Aesthetics*; and Douglas Mao, *Solid Objects: Modernism and the Test of Production.*

24. The Artists both had years to live—indeed, more than the Poets. Ricketts died in 1931 and Shannon in 1937; unlike the Poets, both survived the Great War. They did eventually leave their Hokusai collection, as well as other objects, to the British Museum (Hokusai, *Kanagawa-oki nami-ura*, 1831, Colour woodblock oban print, 25.9 cm × 37.2 cm), British Museum, London, UK, https://www.britishmuseum.org/collection/object/A_2008-3008-1-JA, and to other museums, including the Fitzwilliam in Cambridge.

25. See, for example, McClintock, *Imperial Leather*. On the "lonely" as a form of spinster aesthetic, see Love, "Gyn/Apology."

26. Kate Thomas writes about Michael Field's relationship with blackness, both aesthetically and politically; see "Vegetable Love," 32–35.

27. As her imperious relationship to her servants suggests, Bradley has certainly come a long way from her youthful exploration of ethical socialism in Ruskin's Guild of St. George in the 1870s and Fellowship for New Life in the 1880s. Diana Maltz provides a particularly helpful analysis of this thread in Bradley's development in "Katharine Bradley and Ethical Socialism," 191–201. On fetishism, gender, class, and race, see McClintock, *Imperial Leather*.

28. Donoghue, *We Are Michael Field*, 13.

29. Deborah Cohen pursues just this question of what comes next, after decorating, in reading the 1912 H. G. Wells novel, *Marriage* (*Household Gods*, 119–21).

30. Jane Austen, *Emma*, 4.

31. I am interested in the belatedness of Michael Field's 1899 embrace of the "House Beautiful" movement. Elizabeth Aslin cites a vogue for satinwood in 1880, nearly twenty years before Michael Field furnished 1 Paragon (*The Aesthetic Movement*, 62). Gilbert and Sullivan's *Patience*, a notorious satire of aestheticism's pretensions, premiered at the Opera Comique in 1881, before moving to the Savoy later that year. Vadillo offers a careful contrast of the two models of aesthetic decoration Michael Field pursued in their homes at Durdans and at Paragon: the Dionysian mode at Durdans, indebted to Morris and Ruskin; and at Paragon, a high-aesthetic mode that borrowed from the eighteenth century, from Japanese design, and from Whistler.

32. Quoted in Sturgeon, *Michael Field*, 52–53.

Chapter 5. "Venite Adoremus," 1906–7

1. For details about Katharine Bradley's will and her charge to Michael Field's literary executor, Thomas Sturge Moore, see chapter 1, notes 1 and 2.

2. On Michael Field and Whym Chow, see Vanita, *Sappho and the Virgin Mary*; Boggs, "Love Triangle with Dog"; and Kersh, "'Betwixt Us Two,'" 256–77; as well as Kristin Mahoney, "Michael Field's Eric Gill," 230–55 in the same volume; Ehnenn, "'Drag(ging) at Memory's Fetter,'"; Frederick S. Roden, *Same-Sex Desire in Victorian Religious Culture*; Holly Laird, "Contradictory Legacies," 111–28. Marjorie Garber writes about Freud's strongly "parental" relationship with his Chow, Jofi, and successive Chows that followed; see *Dog Love*, 136–38.

3. As Vicinus has demonstrated in "'Sister Souls,'" the form of attention Michael Field sought from male admirers, and especially from Berenson, was formidable for the women. Their projection of these powerful qualities onto the dog recreates the intensity and excitement of the past drama.

4. Ruth Vanita, "'Love Unspeakable,'" 248–57.

5. Kathryn Bond Stockton, *The Queer Child, or Growing Sideways in the Twentieth Century*, 90. Vanita, *Sappho and the Virgin Mary*, 215–16.

6. See especially Ellis Hanson, "The Temptation of Saint Oscar," in *Decadence and Catholicism*, 229–96.

7. Gagnier, *Idylls of the Marketplace*, 171. See also Vanita, *Sappho and the Virgin Mary*, 130.

8. "Somdomite" was a misspelling of "sodomite," written on a calling card by Lord Alfred Douglas's father (the 9th Marquess of Queensberry) to Wilde. See Richard Ellman, *Oscar Wilde*; Ed Cohen, *Talk on the Wilde Side*; and Leslie J. Moran, "Transcripts and Truth: Writing the Trials of Oscar Wilde," 224–42.

9. As Judith Walkowitz and others have vividly demonstrated, the histories of male and female (homo)sexualities were divergent in the late nineteenth century; see especially *The City of Dreadful Delight*, and Richard Dellamora's introduction to the collection *Sexual Dissidence*. The Labouchère Amendment, for example, addressed only sexual behaviors and appearances between men, creating a climate of crisis and secrecy following what was dubbed the "Blackmailer's Charter." See, for example, Joseph Bristow, *Effeminate England*. On female homosexuality, see Vicinus, *Intimate Friends*, and Marcus, *Between Women*.

10. The concept of "deathliness" is central to Meadows's argument about female eroticism and authorship in "Morbid Strains," particularly for Elizabeth Gaskell's representation of Charlotte Brontë, and for Michael Field.

11. Michael Field's fascination with Wilde, and their association of Wilde and Whym Chow, continues. For example, in their elegiac 1913 volume *Whym Chow, Flame of Love*, they repurpose Wilde's *De Profundis* for a poem of the same name: "He lies / All love across a shadow's knee, his eyes / Beneath her gaze as if he were a child" ("De Profundis," in Thain and Vadillo, *Michael Field: The Poet*, 202).

12. Parker and Vadillo remind us that Bradley had linked her dog and her faith years earlier: "Bradley had angered her early mentor John Ruskin in December 1877 by declaring that the acquisition of a terrier had converted her from Christianity to paganism. An enraged Ruskin responded, '[T]hat you should be such a fool as coolly to write to me that you had ceased to believe in God—and had found some comfort

in a dog—*this* is *deadly*'" (Parker and Vadillo, *Michael Field*, 5; emphasis in original). See also Leighton, *Victorian Women Poets*, 207–8.

13. Lucien Pissarro (1863–1944) was a Neo-Impressionist painter, son of Impressionist Camille Pissarro and father of painter Orovida Camille Pissarro. Lucien Pissarro worked as an illustrator, woodcutter, and landscape painter. He moved to England permanently in 1890, drawn by the Arts and Crafts movement, and by his courtship of Esther Levi Bensusan, who became his wife in 1892. Pissarro and Esther founded the Eragny Press (named for Éragny-sur-Ept, the small French town where Pissarro's father lived from 1884 until his death in 1903, in a house he purchased with money borrowed from Claude Monet). Eragny Press was the publisher of the very limited edition of Michael Field's *Whym Chow, Flame of Love*, which was posthumous to Edith Cooper.

14. Kate Thomas discusses Michael Field's immortal quests, mediated through spirit photography and other technologies, in "Lesbian Postmortem at the Fin de Siècle," 122–35. On Victorian photography and its effects on literature and the visual arts, see Nancy Armstrong, *Fiction in the Age of Photography*. On spirit photography, see Clément Chéroux, *The Perfect Medium*. Walter Benjamin famously writes: "[W]hat withers in the age of the technological reproducibility of the work of art is the latter's aura," a point that for Michael Field concerned the fraught relationship between painting and photography, and presumably film, as well as the alignment of poetry and telephonic technology. Walter Benjamin, *The Work of Art in the Age of Technological Reproducibility and Other Writings on Media*, 22.

15. Sarah Kersh writes, "The sequence, printed in a limited edition through Eragny Press, was bound in soft, russet suede reminiscent of the beloved chow's own coat and acted as a relic for the lost companion. Even from the opening line—'I call along the Halls of Suffering'—the book grieves for Whym Chow; however, its publication also served as an elegy for Edith Cooper herself" ("'Betwixt Us Two,'" 256).

16. Michael Field published the poem as "If this love be dying let it die," in *Wild Honey from Various Thyme*, 24.

17. Huseby, "Queer Social Counting," 207.

18. Vanita, *Sappho and the Virgin Mary*, 132.

19. Vanita, *Sappho and the Virgin Mary*, 132–33.

20. On the effect of their conversion to Catholicism on Michael Field's intimate relations, see Vicinus, *Intimate Friends*, 103–8. On Michael Field and Catholicism, see Frederick S. Roden, *Same-Sex Desire in Victorian Religious Culture*; Roden, "Michael Field and the Challenges of Writing a Lesbian Catholicism," 155–62; Camille Cauti, "Michael Field's Pagan Catholicism," 181–89 in the same volume; and Vanita, *Sappho and the Virgin Mary*. See also Ehnenn, "'Thy Body Maketh a Solemn Song': Desire and Disability in Michael Field's 'Catholic Poems,'" 188–209. On decadence and male homoeroticism, see Hanson, *Decadence and Catholicism*.

21. Lord Alfred Douglas, "Two Loves," 1894.

22. Father John Gray emerges as a significant figure in the context of Michael Field's conversion, linking their religious transition to important aesthetic and queer communities. Gray (1866–1934), often identified as a source for Dorian Gray, was an accomplished aesthetic poet (and author of one novel) who converted to Catholicism in 1890. Gray was ordained as a priest in 1901. Along with his lover, the French poet Marc-André Raffalovich, Gray founded St. Peter's Church in Morningside,

Edinburgh. Gray and Raffalovich both wrote about the links between Catholicism and homosexuality. See Roden, "Queer Hagiography," 157–89, and Hanson, "Priests and Acolytes," 297–64. Roden ties Michael Field to Gray and Raffalovich in "Michael Field, John Gray, and Marc-Andre Raffalovich," 57–68.

23. Thain, *"Michael Field,"* 15–17. Both Sturgeon and Vanita argue that "there is no great difference between the pagan poems that precede and the Christian poems that follow this conversion" (Vanita, *Sappho and the Virgin Mary*, 133), with Vanita noting that the seamless transfer from Sapphic to Marian imagery leaves elements structural to Michael Field's poetry unchanged. See also Cauti, "Michael Field's Pagan Catholicism."

24. The site of the virginal Marian body as both source and prohibition recalls Julia Kristeva's analysis of maternal narcissism in "Stabat Mater," 133–52.

Chapter 6. The Ends: 1913, 1914, and Beyond

1. Paul de Man, "Autobiography as De-Facement," 75–76. See also Barbara Johnson, "Apostrophe, Animation, and Abortion." Meadows offers a compelling reading of Cooper's use of apostrophe to memorialize her mother into poetry; see "Morbid Strains," 164–66.

2. Garrett Stewart, *Dear Reader: The Conscripted Audience in Nineteenth-Century British Fiction*, 8. See also Thain and Vadillo, who write that Bradley's posthumous poems for Cooper seem "to be an attempt to commune with her ghost: to bring her back in whatever form is possible. And that form seems to have been a poetic one: it is as if by writing imaginatively with Cooper, and re-inscribing once again their joint authorship, Bradley can summon [Cooper's] presence to her again," *Michael Field: The Poet*, 218–19.

3. Thain and Vadillo, *Michael Field: The Poet*, 61–62. See also Linda K. Hughes, "Resisting Rhetoric: Art for Art's Sake," 251.

4. Roden, "Michael Field and the Challenges of Writing a Lesbian Catholicism," 161.

5. Kersh, "'Betwixt Us Two,'" 269.

6. Thomas, "'What Time We Kiss,'" 330–31.

7. Ana Parejo Vadillo writes movingly about ghostliness, aesthetic immateriality, and photography in the relationship between Michael Field and the poet A. Mary F. Robinson; see "Immaterial Poetics: A. Mary F. Robinson and the Fin-de-Siècle Poem," 231–60.

8. Sharon Bickle, "Finding Love in the Archives," 77.

9. Donoghue, *We Are Michael Field*, 126. On the praxis of archive formation, see Micir, *The Passion Projects*.

10. Freud, "The 'Mystic Writing-Pad,'" in *The Standard Edition of the Complete Psychological Works of Sigmund Freud*, 19:230; emphasis in original.

BIBLIOGRAPHY

Adams, James Eli. *Dandies and Desert Saints: Style of Victorian Masculinity*. Ithaca: Cornell University Press, 1995.

Archer, William. "Henrik Ibsen: Philosopher or Poet." 1905. Reprint in *Modernism: An Anthology of Sources and Documents*, ed. Vassiliki Kolocotroni, Jane Goldman, and Olga Taxidou. Edinburgh: Edinburgh University Press, 1998.

———. *The Theatrical "World" for 1893–[97]*. London: Walter Scott, 1893.

Armstrong, Nancy. *Desire and Domestic Fiction: A Political History of the Novel*. New York: Oxford University Press, 1987.

———. *Fiction in the Age of Photography: The Legacy of British Realism*. Cambridge, MA: Harvard University Press, 1999.

Arnold, Matthew. "Sweetness and Light." In *Culture and Anarchy*, ed. Samuel Lipman, 29–48. New Haven, CT: Yale University Press, 1994.

Aslin, Elizabeth. *The Aesthetic Movement: Prelude to Art Nouveau*. New York: Praeger, 1969.

Austen, Jane. *Emma*. Ed. James Kinsley and David Lodge. New York: Oxford University Press, 1987.

Bakhtin, Mikhail. *Problems of Dostoevsky's Poetics*. Ed. and trans. Caryl Emerson. Minneapolis: University of Minnesota Press, 1984.

Barnes, Djuna. *Ladies Almanack Showing Their Signs and Their Tides; Their Moons and their Changes; the Seasons As It Is With Them; Their Eclipses and Equinoxes; As Well As a Full Record of Diurnal and Nocturnal Distempers," Written and Illustrated by a Lady of Fashion*. New York: New York University Press, 1992.

Barnes, Julian. *The Sense of an Ending*. New York: Vintage Books, 2011.

Barthes, Roland. *Camera Lucida: Reflections on Photography*. Trans. Richard Howard. New York: Hill and Wang, 1981.

Beer, Gillian. *Darwin's Plots: Evolutionary Narrative in Darwin, George Eliot and Nineteenth-Century Fiction*. Cambridge: Cambridge University Press, 2000.

Benjamin, Walter. *The Work of Art in the Age of Technological Reproducibility and Other Writings on Media*. Ed. Michael W. Jennings, Bridgid Doherty, and Thomas Y. Levin; trans. Edmund Jephcott, Rodney Livingstone, and Howard Eiland. Cambridge, MA: Harvard University Press, 2008.

Bernheimer, Charles. "Manet's Olympia: The Figuration of Scandal." *Poetics Today* 10, no. 2 (1989): 255–77.

Bickle, Sharon. "Finding Love in the Archives: Editing the 'Lost' Love Letters of Michael Field." *Lifewriting Annual: Biographical and Autobiographical Studies* 2 (2008): 73–91.

———. *The Fowl and the Pussycat: Love Letters of Michael Field, 1876–1909*. Charlottesville: University of Virginia Press, 2008.

———. "Living 'Willfully': The Same-Sex Marriage Ceremony of 'Michael Field' by the Smutt River." *Hecate* 41, no. 1/2 (2015): 116–28.

——. "Rethinking Michael Field: The Case for the Bodleian Letters." In *Michael Field and Their World*, ed. Margaret D. Stetz and Cheryl A. Wilson, 39–47. High Wycombe, UK: Rivendale Press, 2007.

Blain, Virginia. "'Michael Field, the Two-Headed Nightingale': Lesbian Text as Palimpsest." *Women's History Review* 5, no. 2 (1996): 239–57.

——. "Thinking Back through Our Aunts: Harriet Martineau and Tradition in Women's Writing." *Women: A Cultural Review* 1, no. 3 (1990): 223–39.

Boggs, Colleen Glenney. "Love Triangle with Dog: Whym Chow, the 'Michael Fields,' and the Poetic Potential of Human-Animal Bonds." In *Animalities: Literary and Cultural Studies Beyond the Human*, ed. Michael Lunblad, 190–210. Edinburgh: Edinburgh University Press, 2017.

Boone, Joseph Allen. *Libidinal Currents: Sexuality and the Shaping of Modernism*. Chicago: University of Chicago Press, 1998.

——. *Tradition Counter Tradition: Love and the Form of Fiction*. Chicago: University of Chicago Press, 1987.

Boone, Joseph, and Deborah Epstein Nord. "Brother and Sister: The Seduction of Siblinghood in Dickens, Eliot and Brontë." *Western Humanities Review* 46, no. 2 (1992): 164–88.

Bowlby, Rachel. *Carried Away: The Invention of Modern Shopping*. New York: Columbia University Press, 2001.

Bradley, Charles. Diary entitled *Commonplace Book of Charles Bradley*. 1832–47. MS. Eng. Misc.e.335, 46279, 40r. Bodleian Weston Library, Oxford, UK.

Bradley, Katharine. Diary of Miss [Katharine] Bradley. MS. Eng. Misc. e. 336, 46279, 1867–68.

Bradley, Katharine Harris. Last Will and Testament. Probated November 20, 1914.

Bridge, Ursula. Unpublished typescript of *Diary of Michael Field: A Biographical Study of a Forgotten Poet*. N.d. MS. Eng. misc. c. 655. Bodleian Weston Library, Oxford, UK.

Briggs, Asa. *Victorian Things*. Chicago: University of Chicago Press, 1988.

Bristow, Joseph. *Effeminate England: Homoerotic Writing after 1885*. Buckingham, UK: Open University Press, 1995.

——. "Michael Field in Their Time and Ours." *Tulsa Studies in Women's Literature* 29, no. 1 (2010): 159–79.

——. "Michael Field's 'Unwomanly Audacities': *Attila, My Attila!*, Sexual Modernity, and the London Stage." In *Michael Field: Decadent Moderns*, ed. Sarah Parker and Ana Parejo Vadillo, 123–50. Athens: Ohio University Press, 2019.

——. *Sexual Sameness: Textual Differences in Lesbian and Gay Writing*. New York: Routledge, 1992.

Brontë, Charlotte. *Jane Eyre*. Ed. Deborah Lutz. Norton Critical Edition. New York: W. W. Norton, 2016.

Brooks, Peter. *Reading for the Plot: Design and Intention in Narrative*. New York: Alfred A. Knopf, 1984.

Brüggen Israëls, Machtelt. "Mrs. Berenson, Mrs. Gardner and Miss Toplady: Connoisseurship, Collection and Commerce in London (1898–1905)." *Visual Resources* 33, no. 1–2 (2017): 158–81. DOI: 10.1080/01973762.2017.1276721.

Buckton, Oliver S. *Secret Selves: Confession and Same-Sex Desire in Victorian Autobiography*. Chapel Hill: University of North Carolina Press, 1998.

Bueler, Lois E. *The Tested Woman Plot: Women's Choices, Men's Judgments, and the Shaping of Stories*. Columbus: Ohio State University Press, 2001.

Butler, Judith. *Antigone's Claim: Kinship between Life and Death*. New York: Columbia University Press, 2000.

Calloway, Stephen. "'Tout pour l'art': Charles Ricketts, Charles Shannon and the Arrangement of a Collection." *Journal of the Decorative Arts Society, 1890–1940*, no. 8 (1983): 19–28.

Cameron, Brooke. "'Where Twilight Touches Ripeness Amorously': The Gaze in Michael Field's *Sight and Song*." In *Michael Field and Their World*, ed. Margaret D. Stetz and Cheryl A. Wilson, 147–52. High Wycombe, UK: Rivendale Press, 2007.

Canevaro, Lisa Grace. *Hesiod's "Works and Days": How to Teach Self-Sufficiency*. New York: Oxford University Press, 2015.

Castle, Terry. "Sylvia Townsend Warner and the Counterplot of Lesbian Fiction." In *Sexual Sameness: Textual Differences in Lesbian and Gay Writing*, ed. Joseph Bristow, 128–47. New York: Routledge, 2013.

Cauti, Camille. "Michael Field's Pagan Catholicism." In *Michael Field and Their World*, ed. Margaret D. Stetz and Cheryl A. Wilson, 181–89. High Wycombe, UK: Rivendale Press, 2007.

Chéroux, Clément. *The Perfect Medium: Photography and the Occult*. New Haven, CT: Yale University Press, 2005.

Clarke, Meaghan. *Critical Voices: Women and Art Criticism in Britain, 1880–1905*. Aldershot: Ashgate, 2005.

Cohen, Deborah. *Household Gods: The British and Their Possessions*. New Haven, CT: Yale University Press, 2006.

Cohen, Ed. *Talk on the Wilde Side: Towards a Genealogy of a Discourse on Male Sexualities*. New York: Routledge, 1993.

Cook, Matt. "Domestic Passions: Unpacking the Homes of Charles Shannon and Charles Ricketts." *Journal of British Studies* 51, no. 3 (2012): 618–40.

Corbett, Mary Jean. *Family Likeness: Sex, Marriage, and Incest from Jane Austen to Virginia Woolf*. Ithaca: Cornell University Press, 1995.

Crowder, Ashby Bland. "Bringing Out the Dead: Dickens and Browning at the Paris Morgue." *Journal of Browning Studies* 2 (2011): 18–31.

Culler, Jonathan. *Structuralist Poetics: Structuralism, Linguistics and the Study of Literature*. New York: Cornell University Press, 1975.

Cvetkovich, Ann. *An Archive of Feelings*. Durham, NC: Duke University Press, 2003.

———. *Mixed Feelings: Feminism, Mass Culture, and Victorian Sensationalism*. New Brunswick, NJ: Rutgers University Press, 1992.

Dames, Nicholas. *Amnesiac Selves: Nostalgia, Forgetting, and British Fiction, 1810–1870*. Oxford: Oxford University Press, 2001.

———. *The Physiology of the Novel: Reading, Neural Science, and the Form of Victorian Fiction*. Oxford: Oxford University Press, 2007.

Davidoff, Leonore. *Thicker than Water: Siblings and Their Relations, 1780–1920*. New York: Oxford University Press, 2012.

Davies, M. K., and A. Hollman. "de Musset sign." *Heart* 82, no. 3 (1999): 262.

DeGuzmán, María. "Attributing the Substance of Collaboration as Michael Field." In *Michael Field and Their World*, ed. Margaret D. Stetz and Cheryl A. Wilson, 71–82. High Wycombe, UK: Rivendale Press, 2007.

Delaney, J.G.P. *Charles Ricketts: A Biography*. Oxford: Clarendon Press, 1990.

——, ed. *Letters from Charles Ricketts to "Michael Field" (1903–1913)*. Edinburgh: Tragara Press, 1981.

Dellamora, Richard. Introduction to *Victorian Sexual Dissidence*, ed. Richard Dellamora, 1–20. Chicago: Chicago University Press, 1999.

——. *Masculine Desire: The Sexual Politics of Victorian Aestheticism*. Chapel Hill: University of North Carolina Press, 1990.

de Man, Paul. *The Rhetoric of Romanticism*. New York: Columbia University Press, 1984.

Dever, Carolyn. *Death and the Mother from Dickens to Freud: Victorian Fiction and the Anxiety of Origins*. Cambridge: Cambridge University Press, 1998.

——. "Gross Vulgarity and the Domestic Ideal: Anthony Trollope's *Small House at Allington*." In *Victorian Vulgarity: Taste in Verbal and Visual Culture*, ed. Susan David Bernstein and Elsie Michie, 139–52. Farnham, UK: Ashgate Press, 2009.

"The Diary of Michael Field." Accessed via *The Diary of Michael Field Online Edition*. MichaelFieldDiary.dartmouth.edu.

Dickens, Charles. *David Copperfield*. Ed. Jeremy Tamblin. New York: Penguin Classics, 2004.

Dickens, Charles, and Wilkie Collins. *No Thoroughfare*. 1867. Reprint, Mineola: Dover Thrift Editions, 2020.

Donoghue, Emma. *We Are Michael Field*. Bath: Absolute Press, 1998.

Douglas, [Lord] Alfred. "Two Loves." *Chameleon* 1 (1894). London.

Eagleton, Terry. "Buried in the Life: Thomas Hardy and the Limits of Biography." *Harper's Magazine* 315, no. 1890 (2007): 89.

Eaton, Marcia Muelder. "Laughing at the Death of Little Nell: Sentimental Art and Sentimental People." *American Philosophical Quarterly* 25, no. 4 (October 1989): 269–82.

Edelman, Lee. *No Future: Queer Theory and the Death Drive*. Durham, NC: Duke University Press, 2005.

Ehnenn, Jill. "'Drag(ging) at Memory's Fetter': Michael Field's Personal Elegies, Victorian Mourning, and the Problem of Whym Chow." *Michaelian* 1 (2009): N.p.

——. "'Our Brains Struck Fire Each from Each': Disidentification, Difference, and Desire in the Collaborative Aesthetics of Michael Field." In *Economies of Desire at the Victorian* Fin de Siècle*: Libidinal Lives*, ed. Jane Ford, Kim Edwards Keates, and Patricia Pulham, 180–204. New York: Routledge, 2015.

——. "'Thy Body Maketh a Solemn Song': Desire and Disability in Michael Field's 'Catholic Poems.'" In *Michael Field: Decadent Moderns*, ed. Sarah Parker and Ana Parejo Vadillo, 188–209. Athens: Ohio University Press, 2019.

Eliot, George. *Middlemarch*. 1871–72. Ed. Rosemary Ashton. New York: Penguin Classics, 2003.

Ellmann, Richard. *Oscar Wilde*. New York: Vintage, 2013.

Erlich, Victor. *Russian Formalism: History-Doctrine*. 4th ed. The Hague: Mouton, 1980.

Faderman, Lillian. *Surpassing the Love of Men: Romantic Friendship and Love between Women from the Renaissance to the Present*. New York: Morrow, 1981.

Felski, Rita. *The Gender of Modernity*. Cambridge, MA: Harvard University Press, 1995.

Field, Michael. *Attila, My Attila!* London: Elkin Matthews, 1896.

———. Essays and short stories by Miss Bradley and Miss Cooper, with a (fols. 71–90) early draft of "A question of memory," published, London, 1918, and b (fols. 91–128) draft by Miss Cooper of "Quits." 1918. MS. Eng. misc. c. 303 46293. Bodleian Weston Library, Oxford, UK.

———. Notebook containing prose piece by Miss Cooper entitled "New End to the House of the Seven Gables." 1882. MS. Eng. misc. e. 941 46280. Bodleian Weston Library, Oxford, UK.

———. Prose sketches by Miss Bradley and Miss Cooper, entitled "For that Moment Only." N.d. MS. Eng. misc. D.976 46292. Bodleian Weston Library, Oxford, UK.

———. *A Selection from the Poems of Michael Field.* London: Poetry Bookshop, 1923.

———. *Wild Honey from Various Thyme.* London: T. Fisher Unwin, 1908.

———. *Works and Days.* British Library, London, UK. Add.MS.46776: vol. 1 (October 1868–January 1869), written by Bradley alone. Add.MS.46777–Add.MS.46804A: vols. 2–29 (1888–1914), written by both Bradley and Cooper.

Flannery, Denis. *On Sibling Love, Queer Attachment, and American Writing.* Aldershot, UK: Ashgate, 2007.

Flint, Kate. "The 'hour of pink twilight': Lesbian Poetics and Queer Encounters on the Fin-de-Siècle Street." *Victorian Studies* 51, no. 4 (Summer 2009): 687–712.

Foucault, Michel. *The History of Sexuality, Vol. 1: An Introduction.* Trans. Robert Hurley. New York: Vintage Books, 1990.

Frankel, Nicholas. "The Concrete Poetics of Michael Field's *Sight and Song*." In *Michael Field and Their World*, ed. Margaret D. Stetz and Cheryl A. Wilson, 211–21. High Wycombe, UK: Rivendale Press, 2007.

Fraser, Hilary. "A Visual Field: Michael Field and the Gaze." *Victorian Literature and Culture* 34, no. 2 (2006): 553–71.

———. *Women Writing Art History in the Nineteenth Century: Looking like a Woman.* Cambridge: Cambridge University Press, 2014.

Freedgood, Elaine. *The Ideas in Things: Fugitive Meaning in the Victorian Novel.* Chicago: University of Chicago Press, 2006.

Freedman, Jonathan. *Professions of Taste: Henry James, British Aestheticism, and Commodity Culture.* Stanford, CA: Stanford University Press, 1990.

Freeman, Elizabeth. *Beside You in Time: Sense Methods and Queer Sociabilities in the American 19th Century.* Durham, NC: Duke University Press, 2019.

———. *Time Binds: Queer Temporalities, Queer Histories.* Durham, NC: Duke University Press, 2010.

———. *The Wedding Complex: Forms of Belonging in Modern American Culture.* Durham, NC: Duke University Press, 2002.

Freud, Sigmund. *Beyond the Pleasure Principle.* 1920. In *The Standard Edition of the Complete Psychological Works of Sigmund Freud.* Vol. 18, trans. James Strachey, 227–32. London: Hogarth Press, 1961.

———. *Group Psychology and the Analysis of the Ego.* 1921. In *The Standard Edition of the Complete Psychological Works of Sigmund Freud.* Vol. 18, trans. James Strachey, 7–64. London: Hogarth Press, 1961.

———. *The Interpretation of Dreams.* 1900–1901. In *The Standard Edition of the Complete Psychological Works of Sigmund Freud.* Vols. 4–5, trans. James Strachey. London: Hogarth Press, 1961.

——. "The 'Mystic Writing-Pad.'" 1925. In *The Standard Edition of the Complete Psychological Works of Sigmund Freud*. Vol. 14, trans. James Strachey, 227–32. London: Hogarth Press, 1961.

——. *On Mourning, and Melancholia*. 1917. In *The Standard Edition of the Complete Psychological Works of Sigmund Freud*. Vol. 17, trans. James Strachey, 243–60. London: Hogarth Press, 1961.

——. "The 'Uncanny.'" 1919. In *The Standard Edition of the Complete Psychological Works of Sigmund Freud*. Vol. 17, 217–52. London: Hogarth Press, 1964.

Friedman, Dustin. *Before Queer Theory: Victorian Aestheticism and the Self.* Baltimore: Johns Hopkins University Press, 2019.

Furneaux, Holly. *Queer Dickens: Erotics, Families, Masculinities*. Oxford: Oxford University Press, 2009.

Gagnier, Regenia. *Idylls of the Marketplace: Oscar Wilde and the Victorian Public*. Palo Alto, CA: Stanford University Press, 1987.

——. *Individualism, Decadence and Globalization: On the Relationship of Part to Whole, 1859–1920*. London: Palgrave Macmillan, 2010.

——. *The Insatiability of Human Wants: Economics and Aesthetics in Market Society*. Chicago: University of Chicago Press, 2000.

——. "Production, Reproduction, and Pleasure in Victorian Aesthetics and Economics." In *Victorian Sexual Dissidence*, ed. Richard Dellamora, 127–46. Chicago: University of Chicago Press, 1999.

Gallagher, Catherine. "The Rise of Fictionality." In *The Novel, Vol. 1: History, Geography, and Culture*, ed. Franco Moretti, 336–63. Princeton, NJ: Princeton University Press, 2006.

——. *Telling It Like It Wasn't: The Counterfactual Imagination in History and Fiction*. Chicago: University of Chicago Press, 2018.

Galvan, Jill, and Elsie Michie, ed. *Replotting Marriage in Nineteenth-Century British Literature*. Columbus: Ohio State University Press, 2018.

Garber, Marjorie. *Dog Love*. New York: Simon & Schuster, 1996.

Garcha, Amanpal. *From Sketch to Novel: The Development of Victorian Fiction*. Cambridge: Cambridge University Press, 2009.

Girard, René. *Deceit, Desire, and the Novel: Self and the Other in Literary Structure*. Trans. Yvonne Freccero. Baltimore: Johns Hopkins University Press, 1965.

Glick, Elisa. *Materializing Queer Desire: Oscar Wilde to Andy Warhol*. New York: State University of New York Press, 2009.

Green, Joyce. "Tennyson's Development during the 'Ten Years' Silence' (1832–1842)." *PMLA* 66, no. 5 (1951): 662–97.

Griffiths, Devin. "The Radical's Catalogue: Antonio Panizzi, Virginia Woolf, and the British Museum Library's Catalogue of Printed Books." *Book History* 18 (2015): 134–65.

Gutkin, Len. *Dandyism: Forming Fiction from Modernism to the Present*. Charlottesville: University of Virginia Press, 2020.

Hadjiafxendi, Kyriaki, and Patricia Zakreski, eds. *Crafting the Woman Professional in the Long Nineteenth Century: Artistry and Industry in Britain*. London: Ashgate, 2013.

Hager, Kelly. *Dickens and the Rise of Divorce: The Failed Marriage Plot and the Novel Tradition*. Burlington, UK: Ashgate, 2010.

Hägglund, Martin. *Dying for Time: Proust, Woolf, Nabokov*. Cambridge, MA: President and Fellows of Harvard College, 2012.

Halberstam, Jack. *In a Queer Time and Place: Transgender Bodies, Subcultural Lives.* New York: New York University Press, 2005.

Hanson, Ellis. *Decadence and Catholicism*. Cambridge, MA: Harvard University Press, 1997.

Harrington, Emily. *Second-Person Singular: Late Victorian Women Poets and the Bonds of Verse*. Charlottesville: University of Virginia Press, 2014.

Higginson, T. W. "Women and Men: Women Laureates." *Harper's Bazaar*, June 17, 1893.

"The History of Bingham Riverhouse: Richmond, London." Bingham Riverhouse. https://www.thebingham.co.uk/history.html.

Hoffer, Lauren. "'She brings everything to a grindstone': Sympathy and the Paid Female Companion's Critical Work in *David Copperfield*." *Dickens Studies Annual* 41 (2010): 191–213. www.jstor.org/stable/44371447.

———. "'That Inevitable Woman': The Paid Female Companion and Sympathy in the Victorian Novel." PhD diss. Vanderbilt University, 2009.

Hokusai, Katsushika. *Kanagawa-oki nami-ura*. 1831. Colour woodblock oban print, 25.9 cm × 37.2 cm. British Museum, London, UK.

Huff, Cynthia A. "Textual Boundaries: Space in Nineteenth-Century Women's Manuscript Diaries." In *Inscribing the Daily: Critical Essays on Women's Diaries*, ed. Suzanne L. Bunkers and Cynthia A. Huff, 123–38. Amherst: University of Massachusetts Press, 1996.

Hughes, Linda K. *The Cambridge Introduction to Victorian Poetry*. Cambridge: Cambridge University Press, 2010.

———. "Reluctant Lions: Michael Field and the Transatlantic Literary Salon of Louise Chandler Moulton." In *Michael Field and Their World*, ed. Margaret D. Stetz and Cheryl A. Wilson, 117–25. High Wycombe, UK: Rivendale Press, 2007.

Huseby, Amy Kahrmann. "Queer Social Counting and the Generational Transitions of Michael Field." *Women's Writing* 26, no. 2 (2018): 199–213.

James, Henry. *The Tragic Muse*. New York: Harper Torchbooks, 1960.

Jameson, Fredric. "The Experiments of Time: Providence and Realism." In *The Novel, Vol 2: Forms and Themes*, ed. Franco Moretti, 95–127. Princeton, NJ: Princeton University Press.

Jarvis, Claire. *Exquisite Masochism: Marriage, Sex, and the Novel Form*. Baltimore: Johns Hopkins University Press, 2016.

Jenkins, David Fraser, and Helena Bonett. "Lucien Pissarro, 1863–1944." Ed. Helena Bonnett, Ysanne Holt, and Jennifer Mundy. *The Camden Town Group in Context*. Tate Research Publication, May 2012.

Johnson, Barbara. *The Critical Difference: Essays in the Contemporary Rhetoric of Reading*. Baltimore: Johns Hopkins University Press, 1981.

———. "The Frame of Reference: Poe, Lacan, Derrida." *Yale French Studies* 55 (1977): 457–505.

Johnson, Lionel. "Michael Field." In *The Poets and the Poetry of the Nineteenth Century: Christina G. Rossetti to Katharine Tynan*, ed. Alfred H. Miles, 281–98. London: Routledge, 1907.

Joseph, Abigail. *Exquisite Materials: Episodes in the Queer History of Victorian Style.* Newark: University of Delaware Press, 2019.

Kersh, Sarah. "'Betwixt Us Two': Whym Chow, Metonymy, and the Amatory Sonnet Tradition." In *Michael Field: Decadent Moderns*, ed. Sarah Parker and Ana Parejo Vadillo, 256–77. Athens: Ohio University Press, 2019.

———. "Naked Novels: Victorian Amatory Sonnet Sequences and the Problem of Marriage." PhD diss., Vanderbilt University, 2010.

Knoepflmacher, U. D. "Endings as Beginnings." In *Famous Last Words: Changes in Gender and Narrative Closure*, ed. Alison Booth, 347–68. Charlottesville: University of Virginia Press, 1993.

Koestenbaum, Wayne. *Double Talk: The Erotics of Male Literary Collaboration.* New York: Routledge, 1989.

Kristeva, Julia. *Powers of Horror: An Essay on Abjection.* New York: Columbia University Press, 1982.

———. "Stabat Mater." Trans. Arthur Goldhammer. *Poetics Today* 6, no. 1/2 (1985): 133–52.

Laird, Holly. "The Coauthored Pseudonym: Two Women Named Michael Field." In *The Faces of Anonymity: Anonymous and Pseudonymous Publication from the Sixteenth to the Twentieth Century*, ed. Robert J. Griffin, 193–209. New York: Palgrave Macmillan, 2003.

———. "Contradictory Legacies: Michael Field and Feminist Restoration." *Victorian Poetry* 33, no. 1 (Spring 1995): 111–28.

———. "Michael Field as 'the Author of *Borgia*.'" In *Michael Field and Their World*, ed. Margaret D. Stetz and Cheryl A. Wilson, 29–38. High Wycombe, UK: Rivendale Press, 2007.

———. *Women Coauthors.* Champaign: University of Illinois Press, 2000.

Latham, Jackie E. M. "The Bradleys of Birmingham: The Unorthodox Family of 'Michael Field.'" *History Workshop Journal* 55 (Spring 2003): 189–91.

Lee, Michelle. "Inventing Michael Field." *Poetry Foundation.* https://www.poetryfoundation.org/articles/69465/inventing-michael-field.

Leighton, Angela. *Victorian Women Poets: Writing Against the Heart.* Charlottesville: University Press of Virginia, 1992.

Leverson, Ada. *Letters to the Sphinx from Oscar Wilde.* London: Duckworth, 1930.

Levine, Caroline. *Forms: Whole, Rhythm, Hierarchy, Network.* Princeton, NJ: Princeton University Press, 2015.

Levine, George. *Darwin and the Novelists: Patterns of Science in Victorian Fiction.* Cambridge, MA: Harvard University Press, 1988.

Lévi-Strauss, Claude. *The Elementary Structures of Kinship.* Rev. ed. James Harle Bell and John Richard Von Sturmer; trans. Rodney Needham. Boston: Beacon Press, 1969.

Love, Heather. "Gyn/Apology: Sarah Orne Jewett's Spinster Aesthetics." *ESQ: A Journal of the American Renaissance* 55, no. 3–4 (2009): 305–34.

Lynch, Deidre. "Paper Slips: Album, Archiving, Accident." *Studies in Romanticism* 57 (2018): 87–119.

Lysack, Krista. *Come Buy, Come Buy: Shopping and the Culture of Consumption in Victorian Women's Writing.* Athens: Ohio University Press, 2008.

Macdonald, Jan. "'Disillusioned Bards and Despised Bohemians': Michael Field's *A Question of Memory* at the Independent Theatre Society." *Theatre Notebook* 31, no. 2 (1977): 18–29.

Madden, Ed. *Tiresian Poetics: Modernism, Sexuality, Voice, 1888–2001*. Madison, NJ: Fairleigh Dickinson University Press, 2008.

Mahoney, Kristin. "Michael Field and Queer Community at the *fin de siècle*." *Victorian Review* 41, no. 1 (Spring 2015): 35–40.

———. "Michael Field's Eric Gill: Radical Kinship, Cosmopolitanism, and Queer Catholicism." In *Michael Field: Decadent Moderns*, ed. Sarah Parker and Ana Parejo Vadillo, 230–55. Athens: Ohio University Press, 2019.

Malfait, Olivia. "'Against the World': Michael Field, Female Marriage, and the Aura of Amateurism." *English Studies* 96, no. 2 (2015): 157–72.

Maltz, Diana. "Katharine Bradley and Ethical Socialism." In *Michael Field and Their World*, ed. Margaret D. Stetz and Cheryl A. Wilson, 191–201. High Wycombe, UK: Rivendale Press, 2007.

Mao, Douglas. *Solid Objects: Modernism and the Test of Production*. Princeton, NJ: Princeton University Press, 1998.

Marcus, Sharon. "At Home with the Other Victorians." *South Atlantic Quarterly* 108, no. 1 (2009): 119–45.

———. *Between Women: Friendship, Desire, and Marriage in Victorian England*. Princeton, NJ: Princeton University Press, 2007.

———. "Comparative Sapphism." In *The Literary Channel: The Inter-National Invention of the Novel*, ed. Margaret Cohen and Carolyn Dever, 251–85. Princeton, NJ: Princeton University Press, 2002.

Martens, Britta. "Death as Spectacle: The Paris Morgue in Dickens and Browning." *Dickens Studies Annual* 39 (2008): 223–48.

Maxwell, Catherine. "Sappho, Mary Wakefield, and Vernon Lee's 'A Wicked Voice.'" *Modern Language Review* 102, no. 4 (October 2007): 960–74.

———. *Scents and Sensibility: Perfume in Victorian Literary Culture*. Oxford: Oxford University Press, 2017.

May, Leila Silvana. *Disorderly Sisters: Sibling Relations and Sororal Resistance in Nineteenth-Century British Literature*. Lewisburg, PA: Bucknell University Press, 2005.

McAleavey, Maia. *The Bigamy Plot: Sensation and Convention in the Victorian Novel*. New York: Cambridge University Press, 2015.

McClintock, Anne. *Imperial Leather: Race, Gender, and Sexuality in the Colonial Contest*. New York: Routledge, 1995.

Meadows, Elizabeth. "Morbid Strains in Victorian Literature from 1850 to the *fin de siècle*." PhD diss. Vanderbilt University, 2010.

Mermin, Dorothy. "Review [Untitled]." *Victorian Poetry* 39, no. 4 (Winter 2001): 621–26.

Michie, Helena. *Sororophobia: Differences among Women in Literature and Culture*. New York: Oxford University Press, 1992.

———. *Victorian Honeymoons: Journey to the Conjugal*. Cambridge: Cambridge University Press, 2007.

Micir, Melanie. *The Passion Projects: Modernist Women, Intimate Archives, Unfinished Lives*. Princeton, NJ: Princeton University Press, 2019.

Millgate, Michael. *Thomas Hardy: A Biography Revisited*. New York: Oxford University Press, 2004.

Mitton, Matthew. "Before Michael Field: Katharine Bradley as 'Arran Leigh.'" *Philological Quarterly* 89, no. 2–3 (2010): 311–35.

Moi, Toril. *Henrik Ibsen and the Birth of Modernism: Art, Theater, Philosophy*. Oxford: Oxford University Press, 2006.

Moran, Leslie J. "Transcripts and Truth: Writing the Trials of Oscar Wilde." In *Oscar Wilde and Modern Culture: The Making of a Legend*, ed. Joseph Bristow, 224–42. Athens: Ohio University Press, 2008.

Moriarty, David J. "'Michael Field' (Edith Cooper and Katherine Bradley [*sic*]) and Their Male Critics." In *Nineteenth-Century Women Writers of the English-Speaking World*, ed. Rhoda B. Nathan, 121–42. Westport, CT: Greenwood Press, 1986.

Morley, Rachel. "Talking Collaboratively: Conversations with Michael Field." In *Michael Field and Their World*, ed. Margaret D. Stetz and Cheryl A. Wilson, 13–21. High Wycombe, UK: Rivendale Press, 2007.

Muñoz, José Esteban. *Cruising Utopia: The Then and There of Queer Futurity*. New York: New York University Press, 2009.

Murray, Alex. "'Profane Travelers': Michael Field, Cornwall, and Modern Tourism." In *Michael Field: Decadent Moderns*, ed. Sarah Parker and Ana Parejo Vadillo, 167–87. Athens: Ohio University Press, 2019.

Murray, Alex, and Sarah Parker, ed. *Michael Field, "For That Moment Only" and Other Prose Works*. Critical Texts 72. Cambridge: MHRA, 2022.

Nelson, Claudia. *Family Ties in Victorian England*. London: Praeger, 2007.

Nietzsche, Friedrich. *The Gay Science*, ed. Janet Kopito. New York: Dover, 2020.

Nottingham, Chris. *The Pursuit of Serenity: Havelock Ellis and the New Politics*. Amsterdam: Amsterdam University Press, 1999.

Parker, Sarah. "Fashioning Michael Field: Michael Field and Late-Victorian Dress Culture." *Journal of Victorian Culture* 18, no. 3 (2013): 313–34.

——. *The Lesbian Muse and Poetic Identity, 1889–1930*. London: Pickering and Chatto, 2013.

——. "Sister Arts: Michael Field and Mary Costelloe." In *Michael Field: Decadent Moderns*, ed. Sarah Parker and Ana Parejo Vadillo, 100–122. Athens: Ohio University Press, 2019.

Parker, Sarah, and Ana Parejo Vadillo, eds. *Michael Field: Decadent Moderns*. Athens: Ohio University Press, 2019.

Perry, Ruth. *Novel Relations: The Transformation of Kinship in English Literature and Culture, 1748-1818*. Cambridge: Cambridge University Press, 2004.

Peterson, Linda H. *Becoming a Woman of Letters: Myths of Authorship and Facts of the Victorian Market*. Princeton, NJ: Princeton University Press, 2009.

——. *Traditions of Victorian Women's Autobiography: The Poetics and Politics of Life Writing*. Charlottesville: University Press of Virginia, 1999.

Pionke, Katharine (JJ). "Michael Field: Gender Knot." In *Michael Field and Their World*, ed. Margaret D. Stetz and Cheryl A. Wilson, 23–28. High Wycombe, UK: Rivendale Press, 2007.

Plotz, John. *Portable Property: Victorian Culture on the Move*. Princeton, NJ: Princeton University Press, 2008.

Poovey, Mary. *Uneven Developments: The Ideological Work of Gender in Mid-Victorian England.* Chicago: University of Chicago Press, 1988.

Pound, Ezra. *Make It New: Essays by Ezra Pound.* New Haven: Yale University Press, 1935.

The Practical Cabinet-Maker: A Collection of Working Drawings, With Explanatory Notes, By a Working Man. 7th ed. London: E. Menken, 1878.

Primamore, Elizabeth. "Michael Field as Dandy Poet." In *Michael Field and Their World,* ed. Margaret D. Stetz and Cheryl A. Wilson, 137–46. High Wycombe, UK: Rivendale Press, 2007.

Prins, Yopie. "Greek Maenads, Victorian Spinsters." In *Victorian Sexual Dissidence,* ed. Richard Dellamora, 43–81. Chicago: University of Chicago Press, 1999.

———. *Victorian Sappho.* Princeton, NJ: Princeton University Press, 1999.

Propp, Vladimir. *Morphology of the Folktale.* 1928. Austin: University of Texas Press, 1968.

Psomiades, Kathy Alexis. *Beauty's Body: Femininity and Representation in British Aestheticism.* Stanford, CA: Stanford University Press, 1997.

———. "The Marriage Plot in Theory." *Novel: A Forum on Fiction* 43, no. 1 (2010): 53–59.

Rappaport, Erika Diane. *Shopping for Pleasure: Women in the Making of London's West End.* Princeton, NJ: Princeton University Press, 2000.

Reader, Simon. *Notework: Victorian Literature and Nonlinear Style.* Stanford, CA: Stanford University Press, 2021.

Richards, Thomas. *The Commodity Culture of Victorian Britain: Advertising and Spectacle, 1851–1914.* Stanford, CA: Stanford University Press, 1991.

Ricketts, Charles. Typescript account of Michael Field prepared for Mary Sturgeon's biography of 1922. N.d. MS. Eng. misc. b. 46308–11. Bodleian Weston Library, Oxford, UK.

Ricoeur, Paul. "Narrative Time." *Critical Inquiry* 7, no. 1 (Fall 1980): 169–90.

Roden, Frederick Scott. "Michael Field and the Challenges of Writing a Lesbian Catholicism." In *Michael Field and Their World,* ed. Margaret D. Stetz and Cheryl A. Wilson, 155–62. High Wycombe, UK: Rivendale Press, 2007.

———."Michael Field, John Gray, and Marc-Andre Raffalovich: Reinventing Modern Friendship in Modernity." In *Catholic Figures, Queer Narratives,* ed. Lowell Gallagher, Frederick S. Roden, and Patricia Juliana Smith, 57–68. Basingstoke: Palgrave Macmillan, 2007.

———. *Same-Sex Desire in Victorian Religious Culture.* London: Palgrave Macmillan, 2002.

Rosenthal, Jesse. *Good Form: The Ethical Experience of the Victorian Novel.* Princeton, NJ: Princeton University Press, 2017.

Rossetti, Christina. "Goblin Market." In *Nineteenth-Century Women Poets: An Oxford Anthology,* ed. Isobel Armstrong, Joseph Bristow, and Cath Sharrock, 126–29. Oxford: Clarendon Press, 1998.

Rubin, Gayle. "Thinking Sex: Notes for a Radical Theory of the Politics of Sexuality." In *Deviations: A Gayle Rubin Reader,* 137–81. Durham, NC: Duke University Press, 2020.

———. "The Traffic in Women: Notes on the Political Economy of Sex." In *Toward an Anthropology of Women,* ed. Rayne R. Reiter, 157–210. New York: Monthly Review Press, 1975.

Sanders, Valerie. *The Brother-Sister Culture in Nineteenth-Century Literature: From Austen to Woolf.* Hampshire, UK: Palgrave, 2002.

———. *The Private Lives of Victorian Women: Autobiography in Nineteenth-Century England.* New York: St. Martin's Press, 1989.

Saville, Julia F. "The Poetic Imaging of Michael Field." In *The Fin-de-Siècle Poem: English Literary Culture and the 1890s*, ed. Joseph Bristow, 178–206. Athens: Ohio University Press, 2005.

Schaffer, Talia. *The Forgotten Female Aesthetes: Literary Culture in Late-Victorian England.* Charlottesville: University Press of Virginia, 2000.

———. *Novel Craft: Victorian Domestic Handicraft and Nineteenth-Century Fiction.* New York: Oxford University Press, 2011.

———. *Romance's Rival: Familiar Marriage in Victorian Fiction.* New York: Oxford University Press, 2016.

Schaffer, Talia, and Kathy Alexis Psomiades, eds. *Women and British Aestheticism.* Charlottesville: University Press of Virginia, 1999.

Schivelbusch, Wolfgang. *The Railway Journey: The Industrialization of Time and Space in the Nineteenth Century.* Oakland: University of California Press, 1977.

Schlovsky, Victor. *Energy of Delusion: A Book on Plot.* 1981. Champaign, IL: Dalkey Archive Press, 2007.

———. *Theory of Prose.* 1925. Elmwood Park, IL: Dalkey Archive Press, 1990.

Sedgwick, Eve Kosofsky. *Between Men: English Literature and Male Homosocial Desire.* 1985. Reprint, New York: Columbia University Press, 2016.

———. *Epistemology of the Closet.* 1990. Reprint, Berkeley: University of California Press, 2008.

Shanley, Mary Lyndon. *Feminism, Marriage and the Law in Victorian England, 1850–1895.* Princeton, NJ: Princeton University Press, 1989.

Showalter, Elaine. *Sexual Anarchy: Gender and Culture at the Fin de Siècle.* New York: Penguin, 1990.

Smith, Logan Pearsall. "Michael Field." In *Reperusals and Re-Collections.* London: Constable & Company, 1936.

Souhami, Diana. *No Modernism without Lesbians.* London: Head of Zeus, 2020.

Stetz, Margaret D. "'As She Feels a God Within': Michael Field and Inspiration." In *Michael Field: Decadent Moderns*, ed. Sarah Parker and Ana Parejo Vadillo, 47–66. Athens: Ohio University Press, 2019.

Stetz, Margaret D., and Cheryl A. Wilson, eds. *Michael Field and Their World.* High Wycombe, UK: Rivendale Press, 2007.

Stewart, Garrett. *Dear Reader: The Conscripted Audience in Nineteenth-Century British Fiction.* Baltimore: Johns Hopkins University Press, 1984.

Stockton, Kathryn Bond. *The Queer Child, or Growing Sideways in the Twentieth Century.* Durham, NC: Duke University Press, 2009.

Stone, Lawrence. *The Family, Sex, and Marriage in England, 1500–1800.* New York: Harper and Row, 1977.

Strachey, James. Introduction to *The Standard Edition of The Complete Psychological Works of Sigmund Freud* by Sigmund Freud. Vol. 4, *The Interpretation of Dreams (First Part)*, trans. and ed. James Strachey, xviii–xix. London: Hogarth Press, 1900.

Sturge Moore, Thomas, and D. C. Sturge Moore, eds. *Works and Days: From the Journal of Michael Field*. London: John Murray, 1933.

Sturgeon, Mary C., ed. *A Selection of the Poems of Michael Field*. London: Poetry Bookshop, 1923.

———. *Michael Field*. Exeter, UK: Sagwan Press, 2015.

Thain, Marion. "Apian Aestheticism: Michael Field and the Economics of the Aesthetic." In *Michael Field and Their World*, ed. Margaret D. Stetz and Cheryl A. Wilson, 130–67. High Wycombe, UK: Rivendale Press, 2007.

———. "The Beehive." *Victorian Review* 36, no. 2 (Fall 2010): 23–27.

———, ed. *Michael Field and Fin-de-Siècle Culture and Society: The Journals, 1868–1914, and Correspondence of Katharine Bradley and Edith Cooper from the British Library London*. Marlborough, UK: Adam Matthew Publications, 2003. [Thirteen reels of microfilm.]

———. *"Michael Field": Poetry, Aestheticism, and the* Fin de Siècle. Cambridge: Cambridge University Press, 2007.

———. "Perspective: Digitizing the Diary—Experiments in Queer Encoding (A Retrospective and a Prospective)." *Journal of Victorian Culture* 21, no. 2 (2016): 226–41.

Thain, Marion, and Ana Parejo Vadillo, eds. *Michael Field: The Poet*. Peterborough: Broadview Press, 2009.

Thiel, Elizabeth. *The Fantasy of Family: Nineteenth-Century Children's Literature and the Myth of the Domestic Ideal*. New York: Routledge, 2007.

Thomas, Kate. "Lesbian Postmortem at the Fin de Siècle." In *The Cambridge Companion to Lesbian Literature*, ed. Jodie Medd, 122–35. Cambridge: Cambridge University Press, 2015.

———. "Vegetable Love: Michael Field's Queer Ecology." In *Michael Field: Decadent Moderns*, ed. Sarah Parker and Ana Parejo Vadillo, 25–66. Athens: Ohio University Press, 2019.

———. "'What Time We Kiss': Michael Field's Queer Temporalities." *GLQ: A Journal of Lesbian and Gay Studies* 13, no. 2–3 (2007): 327–51.

Torok, Maria. "The Illness of Mourning and the Fantasy of the Exquisite Corpse." In *The Shell and the Kernel: Renewals of Psychoanalysis*. Vol. 1, ed. and trans. Nicholas T. Rand, 107–24. Chicago: University of Chicago Press, 1994.

Treby, Ivor. *Binary Star: Leaves from the Journal and Letters of Michael Field, 1846–1914*. Bury St. Edmunds: De Blackland Press, 2006.

———. *Michael Field Catalogue: A Book of Lists*. Bury St. Edmunds: De Blackland, 1998.

———. *Uncertain Rain: Sundry Spells of Michael Field*. Bury St. Edmunds: De Blackland, 2002.

Tredennick, Bianca. "Some Collections of Mortality: Dickens, the Paris Morgue, and the Material Corpse." *Victorian Review* 36, no. 2 (2010): 72–88.

Trollope, Anthony. *The Small House at Allington*. New York: Penguin Classics, 1991.

Tucker, Herbert F. "*Aurora Leigh*: Epic Solutions to Novel Ends." In *Famous Last Words: Changes in Gender and Narrative Closure*, ed. Alison Booth, 62–85. Charlottesville: University Press of Virginia, 1993.

Vadillo, Ana Parejo. "Aestheticism and Decoration: At Home with Michael Field." *Cahiers victoriens et édouardiens* 74 (Fall 2011): 17–36. https://journals.openedition.org/cve/1040.

——. "Generational Difference in *To the Lighthouse*." In *The Cambridge Companion to "To the Lighthouse,"* ed. Allison Pease, 122–35. Cambridge: Cambridge University Press, 2015.

——. "Immaterial Poetics: A. Mary F. Robinson and the Fin-de-Siècle Poem." In *The Fin-de-Siècle Poem: English Literary Culture and the 1890s*, ed. Joseph Bristow, 231–60. Athens: Ohio University Press, 2005.

——. "Living Art: Michael Field, Aestheticism and Dress." In *Crafting the Woman Professional in the Long Nineteenth Century: Art and Industry in Britain*, ed. Kyriaki Hadjiavxendi and Patricia Zakreski, 243–72. London: Taylor & Francis, 2013.

——. "Outmoded Dramas: History and Modernity in Michael Field's Aesthetic Plays." In *Michael Field and Their World*, ed. Margaret D. Stetz and Cheryl A. Wilson, 237–49. High Wycombe, UK: Rivendale Press, 2007.

——. "*Sight and Song*: Transparent Translations and a Manifesto for the Observer." *Victorian Poetry* 38, no. 1 (Spring 2000): 15–34.

——. *Women Poets and Urban Aestheticism: Passengers of Modernity*. New York: Palgrave Macmillan, 2005.

Van Capelleveen, Paul. "25. Contact Addresses." *Charles Ricketts & Charles Shannon* (blog). January 11, 2012. http://charlesricketts.blogspot.com/2012/01/25-contact-addresses.html.

——. "401. Exhibition at the Heath Robinson Museum." *Charles Ricketts & Charles Shannon* (blog). April 3, 2019. http://charlesricketts.blogspot.com/search?q=psyche+in+the+house.

Vanita, Ruth. "'Love Unspeakable': The Uses of Allusion in Flush." In *Virginia Woolf: Themes and Variations*, ed. Vara Neverow-Turk and Mark Hussey, 248–57. New York: Pace University Press, 1993.

——. *Sappho and the Virgin Mary: Same-Sex Love and the English Literary Imagination*. New York: Columbia University Press, 1996.

Vicinus, Martha. "The Adolescent Boy: Fin-de-Siècle Femme Fatale?" In *Victorian Sexual Dissidence*, ed. Richard Dellamora, 83–106. Chicago: Chicago University Press, 1999.

——. *Intimate Friends: Women Who Loved Women, 1778–1928*. 2004. Reprint, Chicago: University of Chicago Press, 2006.

——. "'Sister Souls': Bernard Berenson and Michael Field (Katharine Bradley and Edith Cooper)." *Nineteenth-Century Literature* 60, no. 3 (December 2005): 326–54.

Walkowitz, Judith R. *The City of Dreadful Delight: Narratives of Sexual Danger in Late-Victorian London*. Chicago: University of Chicago Press, 1996.

Warner, Michael. *The Trouble with Normal: Sex, Politics, and the Ethics of Queer Life*. New York: Free Press, 1999.

White, Christine. "'Poets and Lovers Evermore': Interpreting Female Love in the Poetry and Journals of Michael Field." *Textual Practice* 4, no. 2 (1990): 197–212.

Wilde, Oscar. *De Profundis and Other Prison Writings*. Ed. Tóibín Colm. New York: Penguin Books, 2013.

——. *The Importance of Being Earnest*. In *"The Importance of Being Earnest" and Other Plays*. New York: Signet, 1985.

Williams, Holly. "Why Do Women Write under Men's Names?" *BBC Culture*, Sept. 13, 2020. https://www.bbc.com/culture/article/20200911-why-do-women-write-under-mens-names.

"Woman and Natural Selection: Interview with Dr. Alfred Russel Wallace." *Daily Chronicle*, December 4, 1893.
Woolf, Virginia. *Mrs. Dalloway*. New York: Harcourt Brace Jovanovich, 1925.
———. *To the Lighthouse*. New York: Harcourt Brace Jovanovich, 1927.
Yeats, W. B. *The Bookman* 2, no. 10 (July 1892): 116–17.

INDEX

Note: Michael Field is abbreviated MF below.

GPSR Authorized Representative: Easy Access System Europe - Mustamäe tee 50, 10621 Tallinn, Estonia, gpsr.requests@easproject.com

www.ingramcontent.com/pod-product-compliance
Lightning Source LLC
Chambersburg PA
CBHW031053020726
47495CB00007B/1853
9780691264776